The Hard Sell
of Paradise

THE SUNY SERIES
HORIZONS OF CINEMA
MURRAY POMERANCE | EDITOR

The Hard Sell of Paradise

Hawai'i, Hollywood, Tourism

Jason Sperb

Published by State University of New York Press, Albany

© 2022 State University of New York

All rights reserved

Printed in the United States of America

No part of this book may be used or reproduced in any manner whatsoever without written permission. No part of this book may be stored in a retrieval system or transmitted in any form or by any means including electronic, electrostatic, magnetic tape, mechanical, photocopying, recording, or otherwise without the prior permission in writing of the publisher.

For information, contact State University of New York Press, Albany, NY
www.sunypress.edu

Library of Congress Cataloging-in-Publication Data

Names: Sperb, Jason, 1978– author.
Title: The hard sell of paradise : Hawai'i, Hollywood, tourism / Jason Sperb.
Description: Albany : State University of New York Press, [2022] | Series: SUNY series, horizons of cinema | Includes bibliographical references and index.
Identifiers: LCCN 2021054828 (print) | LCCN 2021054829 (ebook) | ISBN 9781438487731 (hardcover : alk. paper) | ISBN 9781438487748 (pbk. : alk. paper) | ISBN 9781438487755 (ebook)
Subjects: LCSH: Hawaii—In motion pictures. | Hawaii—On television. | Hawaii—In popular culture. | Motion pictures—United States—History—20th century. | Television programs—United States—History—20th century.
Classification: LCC PN1995.9.H38 S64 2022 (print) | LCC PN1995.9.H38 (ebook) | DDC 791.4309961—dc23/eng/20211130
LC record available at https://lccn.loc.gov/2021054828
LC ebook record available at https://lccn.loc.gov/2021054829

10 9 8 7 6 5 4 3 2 1

To Maggie

It really looked like Hawai'i

Contents

List of Illustrations ix

Acknowledgments xi

Introduction: Touristic Visions and Virtual Tourists 1

1 Save That Gag for the Tourists: The Hawaii Tourist Bureau and Post-tourism Narratives of 1930s Hollywood 37

2 Twilight of the Past, Island of Utopia: *December 7th* and the Contradictions of War Nostalgia 83

3 You're Still Talking about Class? Adapting for Statehood in *Diamond Head* (1963) 121

4 Founded on Truth but Not on Fact: Pastiche Narratives of Modernity in Adaptations of James Michener's *Hawaii* (1959) 151

5 Business or Pleasure: The Touristic Contradictions of the Elvis/Hawai'i Experience from *Blue Hawaii* (1961) to *Aloha from Hawaii* (1973) 189

6 Shoot All Winter, Show All Summer: Frontier Mythologies and the Hipster Tourism of Surf Documentaries 225

7 If You Can't Find It, Don't Write It: Genre and Competing Notions of Realism in *Hawaii Five-O* (1968) 251

Conclusion: Hawai'i Bound	275
Notes	285
Selected Bibliography	329
Index	333

Illustrations

I.1	*Honolulu* lobby card (1939)	5
I.2	Still from *The Story of Hawaii* (1934)	7
I.3	Still from *December 7th* (1943)	10
I.4	Photo of Kodak Hula Show (1992)	12
I.5	Tourist Bureau ad (1920s)	17
I.6	Still from *Diamond Head* (1963)	18
I.7	Still from *The Brady Bunch* (1971)	32
I.8	Still from *Blue Hawaii* (1961)	35
1.1	Still from *The Story of Oahu* (1934)	39
1.2	Still from *Waikiki Wedding* (1937)	41
1.3	Still from *The Black Camel* (1931)	43
1.4	Production image from *Bird of Paradise* (1932)	46
1.5	Still from *Waikiki Wedding* (1937)	56
1.6	Still from *Waikiki Wedding* (1937)	57
1.7	Still from *Waikiki Wedding* (1937)	58
1.8	Cover from *Hawaii USA* (1942)	61
1.9	Still from *The Island of Hawaii* (1930)	67
1.10	Still from *Honolulu* (1939)	75
1.11	Still from *Honolulu* (1939)	75

1.12	Still from *Waikiki Wedding* (1937)	77
2.1	Still from *December 7th* (1943)	86
2.2	Still from *December 7th* (1943)	90
2.3	Still from *December 7th* (1943)	95
2.4	Still from *December 7th* (1943)	95
2.5	Still from *In Harm's Way* (1965)	107
3.1	Ad for *Diamond Head* (1963)	125
3.2	Promotional material for *The 49th State*	132
3.3	Still from *Diamond Head* (1963)	149
4.1	Still from *Hawaii* (1966)	153
4.2	Still from *Hawaii* (1966)	157
4.3	Still from *The Hawaiians* (1970)	178
4.4	Still from *The Hawaiians* (1970)	184
5.1	Still from *Blue Hawaii* (1961)	193
5.2	Ad for Elvis charity concert (1960)	199
5.3	Still from *Blue Hawaii* (1961)	203
5.4	Cover from Elvis Album (1972)	221
6.1	Still from *Endless Summer* (1964)	227
6.2	Still from *Endless Summer* (1964)	230
6.3	Still from *Endless Summer* (1964)	234
6.4	Still from *Barefoot Adventures* (1960)	239
7.1	Still from *Hawaii Five-O* (1968)	253
7.2	United travel brochure (1962)	262
7.3	Still from *Hawaii Five-O* (1968)	268
C.1	Still from *The Brady Bunch* (1971)	277

Acknowledgments

The idea for a book on Hawai'i began in earnest in the early 2000s at a family gathering in Oregon, where my parents and grandfather collectively recalled their many fond memories of visiting Hawai'i, a side benefit of careers working in the aviation industry. During this conversation, my uncle spoke up at one point and mentioned in passing that the only time he'd ever been to the islands was on his way to Vietnam. It was a sobering moment—and it made me think both of the uncle who came back from Southeast Asia, and of the uncle who did not. This project would later begin, I think, with trying to reconcile such a contradiction—the tension between well-established, long-promoted touristic impressions of the Hawaiian islands, and all the cold truths often lurking quietly just behind those otherwise warm surfaces (of course, it was perhaps also encouraged by a childhood that intersected once too often with old Elvis movies and *Brady Bunch* episodes).

Several years later, the idea of developing this further came closer into focus during a steady diet of old *Hawaii Five-O* reruns that I would watch during lunch breaks from writing my dissertation on the reception history of Walt Disney's *Song of the South* a decade ago (I think a lot of what I was doing with the latter began to shape how I was thinking about the possibilities of the former). The original idea then involved exploring the industrial and cultural discourses around Hawai'i's post-statehood popularity in US film and television of the 1960s. And, as with the aforementioned Disney project—another one about the hidden twentieth-century histories of problematic US populist media—this one evolved significantly from its modest, unformed inspirations. In both projects, the research gradually led me further back in time to a much different framing than I originally envisioned, and to many more fascinating texts than I initially considered.

After years of having these ideas bounce around my head, the heart of this project's development began and ended across the span of five years, and at archives in two very different geographical locations. In the fall of 2014 and summer of 2015, I finally began preliminary research in the Center for Film and Theater Research at the University of Wisconsin in my hometown of Madison. This was complemented by a deep dive into the scholarship on the subject and followed by years of writing and rewriting. Then, in the summer of 2019, as a bookend, I finally made the journey to Honolulu to visit various archives on the island of Oʻahu. It seems apt that a project about the touristic visions of Hawaiʻi began in the rolling plains and valleys of snowy central Wisconsin and ended looking off to the wind-swept cliffs and beaches of Hawaiʻi.

Of course, a lot of work and invaluable assistance went into constructing such a gaze. At the UW archives, I benefited in particular from the helpful guidance of Mary K. Huelsbeck and Lee Grady. In Honolulu, meanwhile, I was aided by Alice Tran, Luella H. Kurkjian, Ju Sun Yi, and the very patient staff at the Hawaiʻi State Archives near Iolani Palace. Then, at the Hawaiian and Pacific Collections in the University of Hawaiʻi–Manoa Library, Dore Minatodani, Kapena Shim, and the staff proved equally indispensable. During my countless hours locked in reading rooms, poring over endless historical documents, I found these wonderful folks all to be especially helpful and patient during what would prove to be a stressful, but immensely productive, research trip to Honolulu. While I did manage on a couple of early mornings to wander down to the waters of Waikiki (chilled as they were by the dark, daunting shadows of skyscraper hotels and condo towers), the ironic imbalance here of labor versus leisure during the brief stay on Oʻahu was not lost on me.

In between those two trips, I presented earlier drafts of my research at the 2016 Film & History Conference in Milwaukee, and at the 2016 and 2017 annual international conferences for the Society for Cinema and Media Studies (SCMS), in Atlanta and Chicago, respectively. My rough ideas at the time benefited tremendously from conversations there with fellow panelists and colleagues in the field of film and media studies. These trips would also not have been possible back then without the support of Peter Seely and the Department of Communication Arts at Benedictine University in Lisle, Illinois. Finally, this research also was aided immeasurably from the many conversations I had with students on the general topics of media and tourism during classes at Indiana University, DePaul University, Northwestern University, and the University of Wisconsin–Milwaukee. On this note, too, my thanks to Michael Newman, Dave Tolchinsky, Mimi White, Greg Waller, and especially Barbara Klinger, who I am quite sure at one point thought I would never get around to writing this book.

In the final days of this project, I was assisted immeasurably by Murray Pomerance, Rafael Chaiken, James Peltz, and the rest of the staff at the State University of New York Press, who waited as I persevered through more and more revisions and unexpected research detours, and then worked with me through the long journey from proposal to publication. The final product reflects the fruit of their patience.

Finally, I'd like to thank Mom and Dad, who first introduced me to the topic—virtually and geographically—years ago, and who have supported me in countless ways large and small in the decades since.

Introduction

Touristic Visions and Virtual Tourists

> As desperate as my straits were [upon the cruise ship's arrival at Aloha Tower in Honolulu], my prayers were suddenly answered. Hal Bock and his lovely wife, Sybil, appeared at my elbow uttering cries of greeting in my own tongue. Astonishingly enough they were in native costume. I asked if the savages had committed any overt acts against them and Hal responded with heartiness, "Hell no! *We* are the savages. We have been living amongst them, peaceably, for three long years."
>
> "Are you missionaries?" I asked, confounded and amazed.
>
> "Quite the opposite," said Hal, "I'm in public relations."
>
> —H. Allen Smith, *Waikiki Beachnik* (1960)

IN THE EARLY 1960S, THE *New York Times* observed that "Hollywood has not ignored Hawaii in the past . . . but its current vogue overshadows all former interest."[1] Around that time, a writer for the *Washington Post* commented how "now that it's only five hours away from the Real World [with the postwar emergence of jet travel], Hawaii is becoming the new movieland—Hollywood with a hula. The stars, sometimes hard to find in the old Hollywood, are in ready view here, to the everlasting joy of the tourists."[2] Certainly, Hawai'i's admission as the fiftieth state into the union in 1959 was one key factor in the heightened focus. "The modern phase of tourism development" on the islands, wrote Luciano Minerbi, "can be said to have begun with the attainment of statehood . . . and the desire for economic development."[3] Hawai'i ranked third among Americans in 1959 only to Florida and California as preferred tourist destinations, while it "has ranked well above any other 'off-shore' or 'foreign' vacation area for many years."[4] Meanwhile, interest in California and Florida was in decline, while Hawai'i's appeal was growing.[5] Yet the mainland popularity of Hawai'i-themed film and television in the wake of statehood was a complicated proposition. As one character noted in 1931's *The Black Camel*—one of the earliest studio films shot in part on location in Honolulu—Hollywood always had a reputation as a "famous furnisher of mysteries," of fiction and fantasy (and was equally fond of reminding its audience of this fact at every turn).

Post-statehood, one writer for the industry trade paper *Variety* found himself looking back at the islands' heavily manufactured and long-promoted touristic appeal with a certain amount of skepticism, even a hint of exhaustion: "Hawaii's charm," wrote Walt Christie, "*has been on the hard sell for years.* Everybody ends up at Waikiki sooner or later."[6] A few years earlier, the NBC skit comedy show *Bob & Ray* (1951), known for its satire of popular TV commercials, used an advertisement parody for the fictional "Tourist Bureau of Hawaii" to poke fun at decades of oversaturation on radio and later television markets (the fake company's name was a thinly veiled swipe at the real-life Hawaii Tourist Bureau, which had spent the prior decades blitzing the mainland with print and radio marketing). In 1960, noted humorist H. Allen Smith—after being told by a friend that Hawai'i was really more a "Bing Crosby kind of place"—wrote that he knew what she meant: this version of "Hawai'i" that circulated in mass media "was actually a mythical land, a place invented and devised and dressed up for Crosby to sing about."[7] Across literature, radio, television, and film, the statehood-era ambivalence toward Hawai'i's touristic charms was understandable: for several decades prior, various business interests connected to the Hawaiian economy had been selling a very specific mass-mediated vision of the "Paradise of the Pacific" to mainland audiences.

As a 1939 economic report by the Honolulu Chamber of Commerce made clear, the revenue generated directly by tourism itself was an important but still minor economic consideration in a territory dominated by that continuing "mainstay of Hawaii's business": agriculture.[8] Before the postwar tourist boom, actual visitors to Hawai'i were a secondary consideration—especially given that expensive travel to and from the islands was still limited financially to the wealthy few (such as, not insignificantly, Hollywood elites on the nearby US West Coast) who could afford the time and money to voyage by ship to Honolulu. Rather, the origins of this long publicity campaign had more to do with two interrelated political goals. The first was winning a public relations fight locally in favor of the so-called "Big Five" group—the de facto oligarchy of businesses and banking interests that dominated all local industry and that was, in the era of the "New Deal," coming under heightened scrutiny from increasingly mobilized and organized labor groups (especially, in their case, workers in the fields of *agriculture and shipping*—two industries so often on display in Hawai'i-themed Hollywood films of the time). The other goal, meanwhile, involved winning support for statehood among skeptical Americans back on the mainland, a goal that had been present with various degrees of visibility since the illegal overthrow and eventual US annexation of the sovereign monarchy in the 1890s. Even before America's participation in WWII, at least one prominent local tourist organization in the early 1940s was already pushing the notion that "the next great coming event of Statehood is already looming."[9]

That Christie's point about "how everybody ends up at Waikiki sooner or later" had appeared in *Variety* (a publication largely involving Hollywood insiders discussing relevant news among themselves) highlights the close ties personally and professionally between the old studio system in Southern California and one of its closest getaway travel destinations. As a sometimes-willing accomplice, Hollywood had long been well aware of the same tired sales pitch to audiences of Hawai'i as a premodern tropical paradise. For decades, writes Delia Malia Caparoso Konzett, Hollywood has portrayed the islands through the "clichéd scenarios of tourism, romance, escape, or heroic military history, with only a few addressing the history of Hawaii's colonization by New England missionaries and its subsequent subordination to US interests."[10] Jeffrey Geiger, meanwhile, noted that the continued circulation in more recent years of the same "static image of Polynesia is remarkable, especially when one considers that it was already a long-standing cliché" by the 1920s.[11] As far back as a series of lightweight, mostly forgettable, often comedic studio films from the 1930s (*Waikiki Wedding, It's a Date, The Black Camel, Honolulu*), Hollywood even then foregrounded, and often poked fun at, the stereotypical touristic identity that the economic interests of the Hawaiian territory had aggressively constructed for themselves (even as those same hokey stories often embraced ultimately a similar lure of romance and adventure that fit their own tired genre formulas only too well). Meanwhile, later film and television shows such as *From Here to Eternity* (1953), *Diamond Head* (1963), *Hawaii* (1966), *Endless Summer* (1966), *Blue Hawaii* (1961), *The Brady Bunch* (1969), and the original *Hawaii Five-O* (1968–1980), reveal a much more historically specific glimpse into Hawaiʻi's popularity with mainland audiences, which in turn reflected uniquely timely cultural and economic concerns to those of the wartime and postwar generations.

In some ways, Hawaiʻi tourism was a victim of its own success by the statehood era—how to keep a very specific kind of tropical experience fresh and new, especially at a time when more visitors were finally seeing the islands *in person for the first time*. In his 1963 industry study for island tourism businesses, economist Paul Craig observed that "Hawaii probably received, free of charge, more promotion in all US news media during 1958–1960, than all paid advertising by all overseas tourist areas combined."[12] The newly minted fiftieth state's "place in literature, WWII and statehood, all gave Hawaii free publicity. But now that Hawaii is a modern developed state . . . now that the tour package masses are visiting Hawaii . . . *the free ride is over*."[13] To hear the aforementioned local bureau's own "hard sell" in 1961, the tourist sales pitch had never been easier (their audience in this context were travel agents). The reasoning behind this was obvious—in thinking about the future of the state's economic prospects at the time, Craig summarized it aptly: "All analysts of the Hawaiian economy agree on one thing—tourism is the most promising growth sector of the economy."[14] So, in the bureau's own forty-minute promotional film, entitled *Hawaii: Never Easier to Sell* (1961), narrator Webley Edwards (host of the hugely successful radio program *Hawaii Calls*, which also appeared in movie and television form) used the radio show's long-running staple of island music and hula girls to remind travel agents of the best ways to sell travelers on the still-enduring appeal of Hawaiʻi in a postwar age of air travel and expanding leisure culture that presented more domestic and international alternative options to mainland US travelers.

Of course, it had been organizations like the Hawaii Tourist Bureau (which changed its name to the more innocuous "*Visitors* Bureau" after WWII) in particular that had been selling Hawaiʻi most aggressively for decades—often employing in a range of aural and visual media, direct and indirect advertising, their own exotic fantasies of romance and adventure on which the studio system too had thrived. Both industries, tourism and Hollywood, were fundamentally about *mythmaking*, about selling intangible experiences as much as consumable goods. And, in both cases, the figurative and literal distances between reality and image, between physical

Figure I.1. Numerous films from Hollywood's classical studio system, such as 1939's *Honolulu*, often reinforced stereotypical touristic images of hula, palm trees, beaches, and pineapples. Yet some of them, such as this 1939 MGM film, were also often quite aware of the clichés of tropical romance and adventure they were selling the public.

feelings and distant spaces experienced as travelers and their mediated representations, which shape expectations and assumptions about those places, were never as clear as they first seemed. And it is perhaps those *distances* that speak to the industrial, historical, and cultural contradictions, ambivalences and frustrations involved in needing, or even wanting, to "sell" paradise (whether easy or hard). If an experience is so self-evidently sublime, why would it need to be so aggressively sold?

And yet that mediated *vision* of the dream Hawaiian vacation in the US imagination was a powerful one that would prove to be every bit as consequential for the islands and for Hollywood. "Hawaii increasingly lived off its own myth," write Beth Bailey and David Farber, "and therefore collaborated to a great extent in creating and perpetuating it. And the myths *did* have a kernel of truth. The beauty of the islands is real, and the Hollywood myth and its offspring, the tourist brochure, were attached—very securely—to scenes that actually existed."[15] These "scenes"—shaped through decades of touristic discourses—tend to gravitate toward simple images of swaying palm trees, sunny beaches, and warm breezes. Pushed further, one might conjure up images of hula girls and beachboys, with the seemingly omnipresent Diamond Head and Waikiki Beach always framed in the background. This, writes Native Hawaiian historian Haunani-Kay Trask, is the "Hollywood, tourist-poster image of our homeland as a racial paradise with happy Natives waiting to share their culture with everyone and anyone."[16] These images offer a limited, and at times entirely distorted, sense of life on the Hawaiian islands, instead reflecting a surprisingly resilient vision of middle-class leisure, postwar nostalgia, and racial utopia to which some tourists always strive to both visit and somehow hold on to. In this touristic fantasy, everyday concerns in the "real world," such as time and money, or class exploitation and racial tension, seem to have no consequence—despite long and ugly histories to the contrary.

Around the era of statehood, Daniel Boorstin described in his influential *The Image* (1962) what he called "pseudo-events"—moments in everyday life that were primarily, if not solely, constructed for media reproduction and dissemination, but which were intended to create the illusion to the casual viewer of being largely authentic and spontaneous. "Much of our curiosity" as tourists, he wrote, "comes from our curiosity about whether our impression resembles the images found in the newspapers, in the movies, and on television. . . . We go not to test the image by the reality, but to test reality by the image."[17] There are echoes here in one 1936 cruise ship passenger's description, while bound for Oʻahu during the long journey across the Pacific, of watching a travelogue film produced by the Hawaii Tourist Bureau: "It would do your heart good to see the effect the color movies of Hawaii exert upon the passengers. Never in my travels have I seen such gorgeous reproductions of nature. What grand publicity for our group of ocean gems."[18] Konzett notes that "this reversal of cause and effect in which cinematic reality would appear to have preceded reality also applies to the perception of modern Hawaii, which can be roughly dated to the end of its monarchy and the rise of cinema."[19] In a rapidly accelerating era of visual and aural mass media in the first half of the twentieth century, the construction of "Hawaiʻi" as an ideal tourist destination highlighted as much as any physical location the elusive boundary between image and reality.

Figure I.2. Cruise ship passengers in the 1930s would watch onboard promotional films of Hawai'i, such as the Hawaii Tourist Bureau's *The Story of Hawaii* (1934), while traveling to O'ahu. Even for actual visitors to the islands, their perceptions and expectations were heavily influenced by a touristic and cinematic point of view.

The islands prove to be a useful case study because they were, as Orvar Lofgren has noted, the first purely mass-mediated tourist destination—a location constructed throughout the twentieth century through the emergence of advertising, radio broadcasts, cinematic production, and later television: "a landscape not only to experience through colored postcards and illustrated magazine features but also a landscape set to music."[20] John Connell and Chris Gibson noted how original impressions of Hawai'i were derived in the late nineteenth century and early twentieth by the mainland audiences' ability to merge sound (recordings, sheet music) with image (paintings, postcards, album covers). This merging, they argued, constituted "the first forms of virtual tourism."[21] These stereotypical sounds and images of Hawai'i serve as a prominent example of what John Urry called the "touristic gaze"—this vision, he writes, "is constructed through signs.... When tourists see two people kissing in Paris [with Eiffel Tower in the background] what they capture in the gaze is 'timeless romantic Paris.' When a small village in England is seen, what they gaze upon is the 'real olde England.'"[22] Hawai'i's decisive *geographical* separation, its literal distance, from the US mainland is not inconsequential—the anticipation of traveling is "constructed and sustained through a variety of *non-tourist* practices, such as film, TV, literature, magazines, records and videos, which contrast and reinforce the gaze."[23] Though not wholly unique in this regard (as one example, a similar convergence of aggressive touristic branding, high-profile mass media, and distinctive geography occurred with the city of Las Vegas, Nevada), the perception of Hawai'i was—and to a degree still is—as much as any destination constructed and defined through its narrow visual and aural signification in popular culture. "From an economic point of view," writes Konzett, "one could argue that the selling of imperialist fantasies via cinematic illusions of Hawaii and the adjoining South Pacific proved just as lucrative as the actual economic exploitation of Hawaii."[24]

This is a book about the ways in which visual mass media solidified Hawai'i's function as an exemplary instance of *virtual* tourism, and how those mediated experiences assisted in the mainland United States' negotiation of postindustrial notions of national self, affective labor, and racial identity throughout a unique moment of profound political, economic, and cultural transition. In this respect, "tourist" refers not only to those physically traveling from one part of the globe to another, but also to media audiences figuratively touring the world via mediation. Mass media such as film, music, photography, literature, and television have long been surrogates for traveling. As Jeffrey Ruoff argues, "The cinema is a machine for constructing relations of space and time; the exploration of the world through images and sounds of travel has always been one of its principle features."[25] They can serve either as rich substitutes for the physical touristic experience, where the deferral can be as powerful as the actual journey, or as nostalgic mementoes of past travels—a medium's visual and aural "truth value" can evoke warm memories as strongly as a souvenir from the local gift shop. As something with both undeniable indexical power—and yet also contradictorily one whose framed content can be so easily selective, manipulated, and staged—the medium of film (both still photography and the moving image) presents the ultimate touristic souvenir. Indeed, part of media's power here was with the millions of working- and middle-class Americans of a wide range of economic, cultural, and racial backgrounds who could not afford to experience Hawai'i as anything other than fantasy.

These popular media representations of Hawai'i were situated within a postindustrial economy involving the complementary apparatuses of classical Hollywood and US mass tourism—both of which formed in the pre-WWII period and then exploded as part of a postwar economic boom that promoted an emerging middle-class leisure culture in which Hawai'i and commodified Hawaiian imagery were commonplace. Influenced by two seminal historical events (immersion into world war in 1941, and admission into the union in 1959), a uniquely *generational* arc developed, an audience of predominately working- and middle-class white Americans. This included both those who lived through the eras before and after WWII and their offspring, who enjoyed the postwar spoils of a new consumer culture driven by media synergy and directed at emergent teenager demographics. In this era, the appeal of the islands in the US collective imagination was roughly situated between four key contexts that were affirmed, contested, and elided in a range of films, television programs, and popular literary texts during this period: 1) Hawai'i's central role militarily as the hub of the US' immense naval presence in the Pacific, highlighted during conflicts with Japan, Korea, and Vietnam, and the ambivalent memories of said conflicts for both veterans and civilians; 2) the long held, and often contested, ideal of Hawai'i as a site of racial harmony, given its much more complex history of multiculturalism, a utopic fantasy that appealed in particular to mainlanders amid the overt racial tensions that marked the civil rights movement for African American equality; 3) the eventual development of a postwar leisure culture that focused in particular on the suburban family and baby boomer demographics, the increased affordability of airfare, and the general emergence of a new middle class with more disposable time and money on its hands; and, finally, 4) questions about understanding Hawai'i's long colonial history, while also defining its new identity, in the wake of statehood in 1959.

Given all these developments, it should be unsurprising that Hawai'i would have such a uniquely powerful presence in the American imagination of the mid-twentieth century, in particular dominating the 1960s pop culture landscape. So often these texts are directly or indirectly inflected by the logic of tourism, giving rise to what Paul Lyons terms "histouricism": "an imperial, developmental view of history, written from its imagined democratic result, that asserts a continuous historical

Figure I.3. *December 7th* (1943): For decades after World War II, all depictions of Hawai'i carried the specter of the Japanese military attack on US naval facilities at Pearl Harbor and the surrounding areas.

U.S. relation to Hawai'i, while employing romantic and distancing strategies, in which Hawaiian spirituality and socio-political forms are presented as atavism."[26] Such "histouricism" ranges from travel guide books to historical nonfiction by such writers as *Hawaii* (1959) author James Michener (who also wrote several introductions on the side to Hawaiian tourist guides, themed cookbooks, literary anthologies, and the like, throughout the postwar period). The rhetoric, narratives, and histories of tourism in representations of Hawai'i intersected with, and at times mystified, what Konzett described as Hollywood's "narration of nation. . . . The remote and highly imaginary South Pacific and Hawaii provide a convenient narrative that cements a nation internally torn and divided."[27] These narratives directly and indirectly reflected "Hollywood's expansionist, military, and Orientalist imagination"[28] as the center of the US' naval presence in the Pacific dating back to the nineteenth century. Meanwhile, US military personnel in the Pacific serve as both soldier and tourist, argues Vernadette Gonzalez, where their consumer status within the local economy masked their role in what she calls tourism's "softer" colonialism, which proved in the long run more resilient than older forms of conquest.[29]

"They Have Learned the Wisdom of Investing in Intangibles That Cannot Be Taken from Them"

Not incidentally, one prominent example that Boorstin highlighted in his book was the Kodak Hula Show, which was staged for audiences in Waikiki from 1937 up until 2002, the visual commodification of one of the tourism industry's most iconic performances. "Like the hula dances now staged for photographer-tourists in Hawaii (courtesy of the Eastman Kodak Company), the widely appealing tourist attractions are apt to be those specially made for tourist consumption," he wrote. "By the mirror-effect laws of pseudo-events, they tend to become bland and unsurprising reproductions of what the image-flooded tourist knew was there all the time."[30] In collaboration with Matson Navigation Company (the dominant cruise ship company in Hawai'i at the time), Kodak vice president Fritz Herman came up with the idea in the 1930s for an attraction that would encourage mutually beneficial consumption between the film camera industry and local tourism interests. A simple performance of what Rob Wilson has called "commercially transformed hula,"[31] or the "simulation of the local,"[32] the show was quite literally defined by its mediation, since the entire point of the show was to encourage tourists to take pictures and the occasional home movie that would then circulate back on the mainland, to an even wider audience of (virtual) tourists. Joyce Hammond notes that the show was "one of the oldest performance events created to accommodate and encourage tourist photography, and the only 'ethnic performance' to my knowledge that explicitly communicates the expectation of tourist photographic behavior in its very name."[33] In these respects, the show was a microcosm of the entire Hawaiian tourism industry during the mid-twentieth century—the commodified interpretation of contested Native Hawaiian culture whose immediate exhibition for island visitors masked how it was primarily intended for the rapidly proliferating culture of mass media in an unrelenting push by local business interests to shift Hawai'i from its stagnant agricultural-based economy to a more limitlessly lucrative tourist-based one.

Added to the artifice of that performative function was the show's tenuous link back to traces of an authentic Native Hawaiian culture (even as contemporary hula practices—within and outside the tourism

Figure I.4. The Kodak Hula Show (1937–2002) was an early marketing strategy designed not only to promote the consumption of camera equipment and film stock, but also to use visitors' own image production to spread specific touristic images of Hawai'i across the globe.

industry—can act also as potential sites of cultural reappropriation). "The Kodak Hula Show," adds Jane Desmond, "gave tourists a chance to photograph the hula dancers, a possibility unavailable during the dimly-lit night-time shows. . . . [Herman wanted] a natural background of palms, sun, and sand, a more iconic representation of the hula girl, a suitable souvenir."[34] The hula shows elided the modern value of the performer's labor by reframing it in a stage context as little more than a modern-day continuation of ancient leisure activities. The show was where several noted "hula girls," such as Clare Inter (better known as "Hilo Hattie"), got their start performing for the camera before moving on to roles in Hollywood films and television shows. Although she was never a regular, writes Milly Singletary, "her impact [at the show] was so great that a story of her life would be incomplete without a reference to the Kodak Hula Show—perhaps because several of her most publicized photographs were taken" there.[35] Many were also part of the hula circuits that toured the mainland to perform live hula shows in the first several decades of the twentieth century, and first helped create what Adria Imada has called "the *imagined intimacy* between the US and Hawaii, a potent fantasy that enabled Americans to possess their island colony physically and figuratively."[36]

In more recent echoes of Boorstin's argument about the simulacric nature of the Kodak Hula Show, Wilson argues that it "functions nicely as a postmodern art form, phasing out so-called real hula, or at least desacralizing it in the context of mass images, a trillion copies, flashbulbs popping."[37] Similarly, Hammond adds that "in the postmodern tourism industry, tourists may seem ironically to reverse the process of colonial predecessors by valuing that (or, more accurately, a representation of that) which was formerly destroyed and/or condemned by Western missionaries. . . . However, tourists continue the appropriation of Others . . . not the least of which is the photographic impulse to 'take' Others' images, 'shoot' them or 'capture' them on film."[38] Discussing the notion of "*legendary Hawai'i*" (how ancient local legends are adapted for a presumed touristic audience), Cristina Bacchilega has noted how the emergent technology of photography in the late nineteenth and early twentieth centuries was key to solidifying Hawai'i's appeal to outsiders. "Legendary Hawai'i" is "the antecedent and supplement of the 'hula girl,' the backdrop against which her performance is loosely placed and justified as 'culture' even when it is commodified 'entertainment for sale.' "[39] The wide circulation of these colonialist images, she adds, "and the excitement with which they were met in the West depended not only on their novelty, but on their [indexical] truth value. . . . Photographs of faraway places and people were thus seen to provide more powerful 'evidence' than words."[40]

The hula as modern commodified spectacle grew less out of local music traditions than agricultural economy—less the creation of Hollywood or the Tourist Bureau in the twentieth century than of the pineapple industry at the end of the nineteenth century. This mainland media blitz centered on the ubiquitous iconography of the hula girl—with the heavily manufactured connection to traces of Native Hawaiian heritage providing a cultural and historical "authenticity" at the core of this highly artificial fantasy. In the first part of the twentieth century, since most Americans could not afford to travel to the islands, the most common form of live hula performances were Hawaiian dancers and musicians who toured the mainland:

> From Seattle's Yukon Expo in 1906 to San Francisco's Panama-Pacific International Expo in 1913 and San Diego's lavish

1916 State Fair, Hawaiian entertainers such as Ernest Kaai and George E. K. Awai's Royal Hawaiian Quartet—many fresh from the supper club shows of Waikiki—sparked a craze that was to sweep the United States in the 1920s and 1930s.[41]

One such group were the "Aloha Maids"—Hawaiian woman who came to the continental US in the 1930s to perform across country. Other shows, such as Robert Bell's "Original Hawaiian Follies," featured native Hawaiian performers who offered a "clean" program of "Wicki-Wacki Wooing in Waikiki" but also clearly sexualized dancers who would perform "the secret love dances."[42] Short of seeing performers in person, however, the more common option for audiences was "commercial films with Hawaiian themes, travelogues, newsreels, mainland dance shows, radio broadcasts, and even fashion designs and canned food advertisements [that] reproduce variations on the 'hula girl' image at an unprecedented rate."[43] The pineapple industry's version of the hula girl was a particularly egregious act of cultural appropriation—using the performance of overt sexuality and distinctive regionalism, with little direct connection back to the local traditions from which the image was extracted, in order to sell fruit at those early twentieth-century World's Fairs throughout the US. "The Hawaii Pineapple Growers Association brought 'attractive' *hapa haole* (part-white, part-Hawaiian) women to serve pineapple to visitors at the official Hawaiian buildings," wrote Imada. "The icon of the 'hula girl' at first helped to sell commodities, but Hawaiian women would soon be marketed as commodities themselves, providing gendered labor for the territory in the form of hula."[44]

The evolution of hula girl from agricultural advertising model to primary symbol of Hawaiian tourism is an appropriate historical metaphor for Hawai'i's economic and cultural transition through the first decades of the twentieth century—symbolizing the transition from material commodity (fruit, coffee) to abstract experience (adventure, romance) as the islands' biggest selling point. Thus, economically speaking, the islands skipped the entire industrial age altogether—going straight from an agriculture-based plantation economy in the nineteenth century, to a postindustrial service model based primarily on the production and consumption of touristic experiences in the twentieth. The concept of experience is, as Dean MacCannell argued, "the ultimate postindustrial commodity"[45]—something that serves as a source of near limitless consumption, loaded with layers of affective investment, and yet requires relatively minimal use of material goods in its actual production (appropriately, the very real issue of Hawai'i's limited land supply as a plantation-based economy is in part what forced such an economic shift to begin with). In the midst of the Great Depression, the Hawaii Tourist Bureau's executive secretary predicted in 1932 that the country was on the verge of a new golden era of travel, arguing that "people who had denied themselves travel and other pleasures in order to accumulate fortunes, have seen their savings disappear . . . *they have learned the wisdom of investing in intangibles that cannot be taken from them*, such as the memories and rich experiences of world travel."[46] Desmond also observes that after the stock market crash of 1929, "the presumed equation of hard work with prosperity came under intense scrutiny, an emphasis on consumption challenged that on production, and the most popular self-improvement manuals [of the time proposed that Americans] needed to learn how to live, to stop deferring pleasure."[47] In the post-Depression era, the consumption of pleasure increasingly became a primary commodity in demand by those with the leisure time to afford it. Meanwhile, the emergence of a consumption-focused economy pushed the importance of labor and production to the margins as leisure, pleasure, fun, and the other attributes associated with the rhetoric of tourism took center stage in everyday life—and yet far from enabling people to recuperate from the stresses of work, coming back home "better rested," the seductions and deferred promises of leisure time ultimately can generate even more dissatisfaction with everyday life, and thus often driving them to continually seek out new sources of pleasurable and fun experiences elsewhere.

Selling Hawaiian Tourism

For decades, the Hawaii Tourist Bureau and its partners pushed for favorable press coverage aggressively. Although the bureau was responsible for helping coordinate positive experiences for tourists visiting the islands, the main goal in their early years was to harness various forms of mass media to shape outsider perceptions of Hawai'i. In 1962, the bureau listed as one of its primary activities "publicity and promotion through press releases, photos, cooperation with national television shows and major motion picture companies; and out-of-state presentation of Hawaiian displays, shows, and entertainments that help create the image of Hawaii."[48] An "autonomous affiliated committee"[49] of the Honolulu Chamber of Commerce, the Merchants Association, and the territorial government until 1959 (when it became its own incorporated company), the HTB was originally a public relations organization funded by, and responsible to, local economic groups with at least one hand in Hawai'i's burgeoning tourism economy (in its early decades, much of the money came from Matson Navigation[50]). The organization began as the "Hawaii Promotion Committee" in 1903, and initially was as interested in encouraging people to move permanently to the islands as in just visiting. "We cannot emphasize too strongly," wrote the bureau in one 1923 promotional pamphlet, "the fact that Hawaii is not only a wonderland to visit but far more important, an ideal country in which to establish a residence."[51] There was much debate in the early decades among Hawai'i business leaders over how much to invest in tourism directly. One of the leading proponents earlier of overthrow and annexation, editor and president of the *Honolulu Advertiser* Lorrin A. Thurston was also key to encouraging others to support the bureau both logistically and financially as much as possible. "In a very public feud in 1927," writes James Mak, "he argued with pineapple industry founder, James Dole, over legislative appropriations for tourism promotion."[52] In the days before the Great Depression, Dole believed that only cruise ship companies such as Matson and its smaller one-time rivals, such as the Los Angeles Steamship Company (LASSCO) and the Oceanic Steamship Company, benefited from such expenditures. However, Thurston was convinced instead that "tourism's economic benefits trickle down through the entire community"[53]—a prophetic vision that indeed would prove to define Hawai'i's economy for the next century.

In 1919, the organization changed their name to the Hawaii Tourist Bureau and played arguably the biggest role prior to 1942 in shaping mainland images of the islands. The December 7th attack on Pearl Harbor brought a pause to their tourism efforts, as they shifted their focus to supporting GIs stationed in Hawai'i during the war. After WWII, they reemerged as the "Visitors Bureau" (they later changed their name again in the 1990s to the "Hawaii Visitors and Convention Bureau," reflecting their increasing interest over the decades in supporting group travel and other forms of prepackaged group tourism). During their first aggressive push during the 1920s and 1930s, the HTB bought considerable amounts of advertising space to directly and indirectly affect print coverage and fostered close relationships with journalists, up to and including paid trips to the islands. Christine Skwiot notes that the HTB "proved quite successful in maintaining power over the production of discourses of Hawai'i. A cadre of town-and-gown experts was always on hand to guide reporters, travel writers, and others around the islands and through the archives. The [bureau] worked closely with reporters, travel writers, and editors."[54]

Figure I.5. In the prewar period, the most aggressive organization for the promotion of the islands' tourism interests was the Hawaii Tourist Bureau, which published its own literature, produced its own films and radio programs, and purchased a countless amount of advertising space in mainland periodicals.

Everything from magazine advertisements to radio broadcasts constructed the same ideal vacation in prospective tourist imaginations, experiences that companies such as one of the bureau's chief funding sources, Matson Navigation, was quick to provide with its synergistic monopoly on shipping lanes and majestic hotels. Matson began in the late nineteenth century primarily as a freight shipping company. "Capt. William Matson and his growing San Francisco concern," wrote Gordon Ghareeb and Martin Cox, "held a virtual monopoly on shipping between California and Hawaii, controlling over forty-five percent of all trade involving Honolulu."[55] Like other island-connected businesses, Matson then began to exploit, promote, and redefine the territory's emergent tourism industry as more people began to visit. In the late nineteenth and early twentieth centuries, Matson benefited heavily from protectionist maritime laws that restricted the travel of non-US ships within domestic shipping routes,[56] effectively meaning that between Hawai'i and the mainland, Matson had no international competition in the midst of otherwise international waters.

Figure I.6. Possessing a virtual monopoly on shipping lines and island hotels in the days before the dominance of affordable airfare to and from the mainland, Matson Navigation Company also helped fund the Hawaii Tourist Bureau, coordinated with Hollywood on film promotional campaigns, and frequently appeared in prominent studio films, such as *Diamond Head* (1963), seen here. While Matson was not the only cruise line that shuttled celebrities between California and Honolulu in the prewar days, it was by far the most powerful, in part because of its heavy direct influence over the larger tourist infrastructure of the islands.

In the 1920s, Matson's primary island rival for a time was the upstart LASSCO, a cruise ship company based out of Los Angeles. Given its close proximity to Hollywood, LASSCO also shuttled countless movie stars and studio executives to and from Hawai'i during this decade.[57] Much of its publicity in local and national print media came from celebrity sightings on its steamships.[58] Also unsurprising was that the Southern California–based LASSCO on several occasions loaned out part of its fleet to Hollywood productions looking to shoot cruise ship scenes onboard, such as the 1923 Harold Lloyd comedy *Why Worry*.[59] A few years later, another Lloyd star vehicle, *Feet First*, was shot on Matson's SS *Malolo* after original plans to use LASSCO's ship, the SS *City of Honolulu*, for production had to be cancelled when the steamer suffered severe fire damage while docked in Hawai'i.[60] Losing out on the filming of this 1930 comedy, Ghareeb and Cox argue, was a key part of what led to Matson to "usurping the LASSCO image as the 'Hollywood way to the islands.'"[61] Despite some success with Hawai'i routes, LASSCO never enjoyed the close synergy with, let alone control over, island tourist interests in the way that Matson had. Thus, they were forced to merge with its more powerful rival in 1930—part of a larger trend wherein Matson also acquired portions, and sometimes all, of four rival steamship companies operating in the Pacific between 1925 and 1931.[62] (As a way to further overwhelm any competition, Matson built several top-of-the line ships during this same window: the SS *Mariposa*, SS *Monterey*, SS *Lurline*, and SS *Malolo*.)

Once visitors had arrived in Honolulu, meanwhile, Matson retained its firm control on the tourist's experience. In 1927, the Territorial Hotel Corporation, in which the shipping giant had a primary financial interest, built the Royal Hawaiian Hotel to accommodate passengers. Then, five years later, they also acquired the biggest lodging rival in Waikiki: the Moana Hotel. The latter's construction back in 1901 had effectively announced the beginning of Waikiki's modern tourism industry. However, by the start of the 1930s, the Moana's financial fortunes were another of the Great Depression's countless victims, as the initial sharp drop in visitors forced the previous owners to sell. (The economic aftereffects of the 1929 stock market crash are also what forced the struggling LASSCO to merge their ships and routes with the one-time rival.[63]) By the end of the 1930s, Matson owned nearly 80 percent of all the hotel rooms located in Waikiki, and nearly half of all those on the island of O'ahu.[64] Matson's local dominance was not hard to spot—by the 1950s, their sixteen-story corporate office in Honolulu was "sometimes called 'Little Hawai'i' for the reason that many of the leading island commercial enterprises [had] their mainland offices in it."[65]

All these expansions and acquisitions in shipping and lodging solidified the Matson company's virtual monopoly on the primary opportunities available to those travelers who bought the HTB's idealized image of Hawai'i and chose to sail to Honolulu. "By the late 1920s," writes Desmond, Matson had become the centerpiece of tourism's "established industry in the islands. A formal system of tourist infrastructure—hotels, travel companies, a tourist service bureau, special tourist publications, new, vigorous advertising on the mainland, and so forth—had replaced the more haphazard services rendered to visitors during the nineteenth century."[66] Adds DeSoto Brown, the company went "after those with the time and money to travel in a tasteful and elegant manner. Their advertising featured the smart set at sea, in a way that made you wish you could join them."[67] Like the Tourist Bureau, Matson contributed to, and benefited from, Hollywood's depictions of the islands. From pre-WWII movies such as *Feet First* (1930), *Hawaii Calls* (1938), and *Honolulu* (1939) to postwar films such as *From Here to Eternity* and *Diamond Head*, Matson ships figured prominently in the background of Hollywood's Hawai'i, one that frequently featured cruise ships and extended maritime travel as a key component of the Hawai'i tourist experience. In 1938:

> Hollywood's army of press reviewers were cheated out of a cruise aboard the Matson liner Ansonia when the seamen's union refused to permit the ship to sail without its full trans-Pacific crew of 300 men. Principle [Pictures] had set the party, which was to feature a preview of "Hawaii Calls," featuring Bobby Breen, many of the scenes for which were shot on the Ansonia. Heavy nut in compliance with the union's demands caused Sol Lesser to call off the excursion.[68]

Matson also produced its own media, "broadcasting a weekly series of Beachcomber programs from KFRC, San Francisco."[69] In the postwar period, however, Matson struggled in its tourist-related businesses. It built two more Waikiki hotels in 1950 but had sold all of them to Sheraton Hotels by the end of that same decade. Ten years after that, Matson abandoned its cruise ships as well, and focused on its roots as a freight shipping company. Its struggles in the postwar era can be traced primarily to one development—the rise of commercial aviation, which quickly surpassed cruise ships in terms of cost, convenience, and popularity. While

Matson did briefly operate its own airplane service during this time, it failed to compete in the marketplace with larger and more established mainland-based airlines such as Pan Am and United.

"One of Those Great Twentieth-Century Paradoxes: The Leisure Industries"

The classic Hollywood studio era and the mass tourist boom that exploded in the Pacific and elsewhere throughout the twentieth century share at least one trait as markers of the postindustrial age—both promoted an information-based economy that deemphasized the value of physical goods in favor of the interrelated immaterial commodities of knowledge and experience. A postindustrial society increasingly marginalizes actual modes (and histories) of production—and the value of actual labor—in favor of simulated (but powerful) spectacles of production staged for the consumer. Tourism was a perfect manifestation of the postindustrial not because it emphasized consumption over production, but because it modeled the ideal consumer experience of a lifestyle that prioritizes leisure as the central goal of daily life. This was echoed by the bureau's renewed emphasis on the centrality of consumption and the value of experiences during the Great Depression, their belief that tourists who for too long had "denied themselves travel and other pleasures in order to accumulate" wealth through labor should instead be considering "the wisdom of investing in intangibles which cannot be taken from them."[70]

Hollywood, tourism, and other consumer-oriented industries operate within a self-theorizing triangle of production, knowledge, and experience. First, there is the *production* of knowledge and of experience—consumers want to see (others') work as spectacle, to go "behind the scenes" in order to appreciate the labor that goes into the construction of their leisure. This reflexivity becomes a key intermediary—grounding the desire for fun, pleasure, within a knowing wink to the production of experience that disavows actual modes of production. Such reflexive narratives turn history—the materialist histories of colonialist invasion, labor struggles, and capitalist exploitation—into entertainment. Everything—from the dancing hula girls at the luaus (whose labor is narrativized, and thus concealed, as an expression of leisure), to films about the emergence of a plantation economy in the islands, to television narratives explicitly about the touristic experience of Hawai'i—reinforces the notion of the "work displays" that transform labor into cultural productions attended by tourists and sightseers who are moved by the universality of work relations—not as this is represented through their own work (from which they are alienated) [and which, I would reinforce, they are trying to escape through literal and *virtual acts* of tourism], but as it is revealed to them at their leisure through the displayed works of others.[71]

One person's labor is less important for the physical product it provides than for its abstract commodity value as a performance, as an experience, to be consumed by the tourist's gaze. And the reflexive desire to see the work of others, meanwhile, gives the knowledge of production ironically an added perceived element of *authenticity*—as though seeing how things are produced gives them a genuine sense of depth, of origin. Hawai'i is most often situated through touristic discourse as being more real or "authentic" by virtue of the premodern opposition to modernity, to the grinding day-to-day hassles of the US mainland. "Just five hours away by plane from California," Trask writes, "Hawai'i is a thousand light years away in fantasy. Mostly a state of mind, Hawai'i is the image of escape from the rawness and violence of daily American life."[72] The problematic "quest for authenticity"[73] for the modern tourist, as MacCannell argues, was more an indictment of the perceived artifice and falseness of everyday life—more about the tourist's attempted escape from their own day-to-day routines—than a celebration of some clearly defined authentic experience or self located "out there" over the course of the touristic journey. "Authentic" is this regard is defined through a touristic lens as a simple, peaceful, even nostalgic, return to nature and the natural, matched with complementary visions of sand, water, volcanos, and palm trees. "The linked pleasures that South Pacific islands have, over centuries, afforded the consuming gaze of the west," writes Geiger, frequently center on images of "solitude, release from cares, and, more recently, *renewal from urbanized modern life.*"[74]

This touristic "quest for authenticity" further raises for MacCannell (expanding on the theories of Erving Goffman) the distinction between "front" and "back" regions of everyday life—from the public spaces where we are consciously performing for others in daily interaction, to the more private ones where we imagine letting our guard down and being truer to our authentic selves. This model becomes an effective way of describing touristic spaces—a continuum ranging from obvious tourist traps (front) to a space (back) perceived to be completely untainted by any touristic influence or function. It is the latter that the tourist desires to find, though its very impossibility is what motivates and sustains that endless quest. The appeal also, writes Rona Tamiko Halualani, "lies in the bold suggestion that modern tourism can enter and traverse an indigenous perspective, which makes the narratives circulating at Waimea Falls Park (the now gone native life) and Iolani Palace (the native monarchy that was never meant to exist) much more naturalized and disarming."[75] Luau shows, the Polynesian Cultural Center, Waikiki Beach—these are all examples of stage one tourist front regions—"the kind of social space tourists attempt to overcome or to get behind."[76] In contrast, touristic rhetoric about seeing the "real" Hawai'i, or getting "off the beaten path," and so on, appeals to the desire to find the parts of the islands that haven't been co-opted by that social space. Most back regions (such as beaches only accessible by helicopter, or the local gem restaurant that only the nearby residents reportedly frequent) are really just subtler variations on front regions made—to varying degrees by someone with a financial investment in the tourist industry—to *appear* to the traveler as though they were glimpsing behind the touristic curtain. This includes not only the actual physical locations of such destinations but also their mediation through highly reflexive literature, cinema, and television. Such depictions of a "real" Hawai'i in media both visualizes and romanticizes the elusive mystery of these established touristic spaces and serves as a front region simulating a back one (a Hollywood set, an advertising photo shoot, and so forth). Almost no place in Hawai'i is completely outside the influences of the tourism industry—perhaps most of all the tour guides (official or unofficial) who promise to take people to those "hidden" spaces on the islands.

Yet, the "work displays" also become sites of greater imagined authenticity because of their demystifying nature. They claim to take the tourists "behind the scenes" (pineapple plantation tours, "making of" features)—the idea that the visitor can get glimpses of the processes by which commodities (agricultural goods, experiences) are really produced is what gives it an illusion of added authenticity. This self-theorizing is the production of knowledge and the knowledge of production. Commodities are worth more when consumers see the work (real or imagined) that goes into producing them. Thus, tourists also want the *knowledge* of production and of experience—consumers want to *feel* informed, to not feel duped, in an era where education (and the performance of an educational discourse) is an important commodity unto itself. The key is not necessarily the creation of actual "new" knowledge so much as the reflexive recognition and appropriation of others' existing knowledge. For example, Urry has argued that earlier accounts of the tourist's desire for unique or authentic experiences fails to account for the ironic space of what he called "post-tourism," those attitudes toward traveling that embrace the artifices of tourism—or "tourist games"[77]—and the a priori impossibility of achieving the ideal "authentic" visitor experience to begin with. Connell and Gibson have argued that a distinctly "post-tourist" attitude toward Hawai'i did not emerge until later, after the postwar "golden age" period (1950s–1960s) of routinized mass travel and repetitious mass-produced music records.[78] Yet many classic Hollywood films suggest an awareness of this "post-tourist" irony decades earlier.

Just as the advertising industry was always savvy about how media messages are constructed, an information-based economy must by necessity theorize itself in order to maintain credibility and durability with a consumer who is always presented with the possibilities for more experiences and more knowledge. In the age of the "prepackaged" vacation experience, an awareness of the tourism industry's organized role in facilitating and coordinating one person's travels, as well as of the media's central role in reifying the ideals of that journey, is more or less unavoidable. The more effective way to sell that experience is to manage the knowledge in advance. Certainly, some hazy notion of a pure touristic experience—one untainted by mass-mediated expectations, industrial manipulation, and other economic influences—has long been met skeptically. While the tourism industry itself might traditionally sell the ideal unironically within the spatial limitations of print advertising, radio promos, and TV commercials, the wider narrative canvases of traditional cinema, television shows, and fictional literature require more dramatic action and tension to sustain that same ideal across a broader and more complex textual structure. MacCannell has noted that mass media (or what he calls the "modeling" of touristic experience) "must appear to be disinterested if it is to be influential, so that any influence that flows from the model can appear to be both spontaneous and based on genuine feelings."[79] In this respect, as part of the classical Hollywood three-act structure, the dramatic narrative disappointment of that touristic ideal is important to sustaining its longing. In other words, a certain post-touristic attitude was always embedded in Hollywood's conception of the Hawaiian vacation—but the goal was less often to subvert the larger romantic ideal of tropical paradise being sold than to celebrate the fantasy of its overcoming in an experience dominated by pseudo-events. Self-reflexive media narratives explicitly about touristic experiences feed the daydreaming, the need for release, but they also—as ostensibly "post-touristic" texts—agitate the simple irony or critical distance we might usually associate with the awareness of "pseudo-events." Post-tourism can be seen as a preemptive defensive mechanism against the inevitable disappointment that might greet many such actual experiences. Post-tourism does not so much negate the elusive quest for authenticity—by foregrounding instead the contrivances and clichés of the touristic experience, it acknowledges the tourist industry's role in facilitating, and commodifying, that quest.

Thus, consumers also want the genuine *experience* of knowledge and production—many don't want tangible goods so much as pleasurable feelings, visions, sounds, and other physical sensations, which provide their own genuine sense of authenticity—as in, the *real* experience of tourism—in spite of a certain knowing distance or irony (such as the notion of pseudo-events or post-tourism) that these artifices may also invite. These experiences are always already mediated in ways that create a constant dialectic between innocence (authenticity) and knowledge (irony), and between anticipation and fulfillment—a tension between the imaginary (how media, for instance, constructs a perpetual feeling of daydreaming, fantasizing, and anticipation) and reality (i.e., *actual* vacations, *actual* geographical locations, *actual* media representations). The interrelated commodification of production, knowledge, and experience in media and in tourism works to provide a powerfully *reflexive* relationship that constructs, sustains, and modifies the various pleasures underlining what Louis Turner and John Ash have called "one of those great twentieth-century paradoxes: the Leisure Industries."[80]

Aloha Multiculturalism

Hawai'i's distinctive touristic sign is also positioned by touristic rhetoric as uniquely American—a heavily manufactured loyalty that attempts to mask the US' militaristic presence and colonial history—and as distinctly multicultural in ways that affirm the mainland's collective desire to see the United States as always in a state of becoming a "colorblind" society. Betraying a sense of what Robert Stam and Louise Spence called the condescending or affectionate racism of the colonial gaze,[81] the notion of Hawai'i as a collection of diverse people who in some sense don't "see" race in the way other Americans do reflects the fantasy of mainland white tourists projecting onto the islands their own wish fulfillment. Certainly, this utopic impulse is not exclusive to one demographic. For instance,

Bailey and Farber have documented the appeal of Hawai'i during World War II to African American soldiers traveling for the first time to the islands, who discovered "a more welcoming environment than the one they had left behind. In letters home to family and friends, sweethearts and wives, they mused about its unfamiliar possibilities and explained how they were fighting to claim and to keep what new dignity and hopes Hawai'i's wartime racial fluidity offered."[82] Yet the particular vision of a post-racial Hawai'i that overtook the American imagination in the postwar period was deeply intertwined with notions of whiteness that seek to deny racial difference as they simultaneously reinforce older racial hierarchies and privileges. The desire to imagine equality across color lines is less an inherently progressive impulse among many white tourists than it is a reaction against contexts beyond their control. As Judy Rohrer has pointed out, "in Hawai'i, [white people] are made aware of our whiteness, whereas on the continent, for the most part, we are oblivious to it or took it for granted."[83] Indeed, films and TV shows about Hawai'i from the mid-twentieth century often used the contested term *haole* (with alternatingly positive and negative connotations depending on narrative context) to describe people of European descent in ways that the more common mainland term "white" is almost never used in media from the same time period (typically only in the rare classical Hollywood movie explicitly about race relations, such as the "social consciousness" films of the 1940s and 1950s, that directly acknowledge whiteness). Adds Rohrer:

> When many white Americans come to Hawai'i, they interpret the meaning of *haole* through a continental lens: white is not raced but the norm; race is Black, and talking about race is impolite at best, racist at worst. This tendency to overlay a continental race relations framework on the islands is possible because, for the most part, Hawai'i is considered unproblematically part of the United States.[84]

Haole was "originally a native Hawaiian word meaning 'foreign' that has come to mean white people and 'acting white' or acting *haole* in the islands."[85] The term's usage in mainstream US media varies from one of endearment (implying the white outsider has been welcomed and even embraced as part of the local community) to one of derision and contempt (where the white outsider is acknowledged *as outsider*, one whose presence is unwelcomed and even despised). In many mainstream Hawai'i-set films and television shows then and now, depictions of this white outsider followed what Christina Higgins and Gavin Furukawa have called formulaic journeys of self-discovery, wherein each narrative "privileges the perspective of a *haole* male character who sets off on a journey to find out various truths—about his career, romantic relationship, and more generally, his place in the world."[86]

The word *haole* and the racial diversity of Hawai'i generally forces white people to confront their own whiteness, in ways that both foreground and undercut their racial privilege. In this respect, the white desire for a colorblind society serves several distinct, sometimes overlapping, purposes. For one, it can be read historically as a white reaction against not only the explicit awareness of being a "racial" category but also the uncomfortable position as *haole* of being acknowledged as a *minority*. Additionally, this fantasy of racial utopia in the post-WWII era also sought to alleviate white anxieties over racial tensions in the mainland in the midst of the civil rights movement for African American empowerment in such matters as voting rights, housing practices, and educational access. Through this lens, the imagined racial harmony on the islands served as a model of hope for potential progress on the mainland. Seen in many Hollywood films of the classical era, this notion was no doubt a powerfully real one, even as it minimized the actual political struggles at hand, concealed the legal and economic power of whites living on the islands, and elided the cultural and political differences on both sides of the Pacific.

The desire to see the islands as a symbol of multicultural unity also had the effect of rewriting Hawai'i's history as being one not of cultural (and actual) genocide, economic exploitation, and a political coup d'état, but of an early experiment in some imagined coming age of racial enlightenment. The foregrounding of racial relations as a primary consideration—on both the islands and the mainland—also undercut the powerful struggles for economic and class equality that were deeply intertwined with the movements toward greater racial equality in Hawai'i. The Hawaiian tourism industry's socially progressive embrace of "aloha multiculturalism" also worked to erase issues of class. What united people in Hawai'i from a wide range of racial and ethnic origins in the first half of the twentieth century was the working-class fight for better employment conditions and higher wages within a deeply exploitative plantation economy, as well as a stronger political voice against the *haole* elites who were the de facto rulers of the islands (the move toward statehood began with these elites seeking greater representation in Washington, but later gained momentum from a working class also seeking greater political voice in Hawai'i itself). The complex struggles for collective political action regarding labor and class became somewhat undercut by individualist narratives of interpersonal harmony, as well as by appeals to national unity in the wake of the attack on Pearl Harbor.

The History of Labor as Leisure

As a metaphor for an ideal postindustrial lifestyle, the tourist pushes history and their labor to the margins in pursuit of a leisure-based life that somehow manages to merge effortlessly the competing tensions of labor and leisure—of work and play. The postindustrial fantasy is to pursue a form of leisure that still feels grounded in the value of labor, with as few of the actual physical and mental obligations of work as possible. In this regard, the hula girl (along with the beachboy) is one effective ideal—one whose very performance for the tourist collapses the distinction between leisure and labor. Wilson argued that the islands' reimagining as "some timeless primordial paradise" allowed "Hawai'i to be released from [the older] system of capitalist exploitation and teleology of modernity . . . and [become] a site of leisure and letting go."[87] Relatedly, this fantasy also often involves the leisurely pursuit of vaguely historical and cultural experiences without the actual weight of history. "History" refers not only to the legacy of colonialist exploitation, military expansion, and touristic commodification that heavily shapes the relationship between the islands of Hawai'i and the United States. It also refers to the material grounding of class consciousness—the dialectic between capital and labor, between leisure and work—within the profoundly immaterial fantasies of adventure, escape, and romance on which the twin postindustrial industries of tourism and Hollywood thrive.

Increasingly over the decades, Hollywood and touristic back regions attempted gradually to both acknowledge and also marginalize these histories—the documented colonial histories of Hawai'i masked and denatured by the tacky tourist clichés, or of the cultural origins of the hula dance within the spectacle of overblown luau shows. There are echoes here in what Barbara Kirshenblatt-Gimblett has called "heritage" tourism, an industry that adds value to assets that otherwise have ceased to be viable: "Heritage is not lost and found, stolen and reclaimed. Despite a discourse of conservation, preservation, restoration, reclamation, recovery, re-creation, recuperation, revitalization, and regeneration, heritage produces something new in the present that has recourse to the past."[88] In his 1963 economic report on the future of Hawaiian tourism, Craig wrote:

Hawaii is America's closest link with the stone-age. Few places in the world have made such a rapid transition from the stone-age to the missile-age. Within a few miles of each other we find the untended and unrestored remains of stone-age temples in active use less than 200 years ago and installations of the Pacific Missile Range. . . . We find nothing of Hawaiian village life, handicrafts or ancient customs. There should be an active public program to remedy this, *if not out of historical interest, then as an investment in tourism.*[89]

Craig suggested that embracing Hawaiian history and traditions was one key to sustaining a Hawai'i tourist economy that was quickly running out of momentum under the weight of its own clichés by the 1960s. (It was at this exact moment that Hollywood was in production on its epic adaptation of Michener's *Hawaii*—at one point even shooting scenes at Makua Beach within audible reach of a military firing range.) Within this history that Craig promoted of Hawai'i's "back region" was also one of labor's erasure—the work displays of "village life" represents not one's own labor but a tourist attraction for others; the belated reclamation of the islands' royal sovereign history at Iolani Palace not only minimizes the colonialist overthrow but also elides the exploitation of local and migrant labor over the centuries in between; the celebration of Hawai'i's multicultural identity erases the complicated history of collective labor and class tension that often united people of different racial and ethnic backgrounds around common economic interests against the ruling white oligarchy of the Big Five; and the hula shows deny the value of a performer's continuing labor by reframing it in the show context as nothing more than a continuation of ancient leisure activities. Instead, history for the tourist still remains here as the *experience of pastiche*—"in which the [commodified] history of aesthetic styles displaces 'real' history"[90]—perhaps nowhere more self-evidently than with an indigenous culture so thoroughly commodified, distorted, and even at times erased through a series of overdetermined stylistic clichés.

Often supplanting historical consciousness in touristic depictions of the islands are various personal and collective forms of nostalgia. While the concept itself is too often oversimplified as a purely reactionary desire, nostalgia nonetheless is an important framework for understanding how discussions of the past (personal memories, or historical questions in a broader sense) are less about the past than they are about history from the explicitly simplifying and sentimentalizing point of view of the present.

For example, Craig's poorly worded remark about Hawai'i's connection to the "stone age" reinforced what Houston Wood more recently noted as Hawai'i's distinctive brand of "echo tourism" (building on Spencer Lieneweber's concept), a "nostalgia for bygone days . . . [a modern-day] visitor's sense of experiencing an exotic past where being Hawaiian was once *but is no longer* important."[91] On a more individual level, the Kodak Hula Show was as much a nostalgia machine for the tourist as it was a public relations gimmick. Kodak was the first company of its kind, as Nancy Martha West documents, who "systematically urged its consumers to view photography—and the world it recorded—through the lens of nostalgia."[92] The indexical photographic powers of cinema always already contain the potential to evoke a nostalgic response—the physical presence of past images recorded for future consumption. Discourses implicitly or explicitly reflecting a nostalgic impulse are often most pronounced during periods of tremendous political, economic, and/or cultural change—for example, Hawai'i's nostalgic appeal by the 1960s should not be read only within the touristic context of its tropical evocation of a mythical "simpler time." Rather—as Craig implies in his discussion of Hawai'i's "rapid transition from the stone age to the missile age"—such intensely nostalgic urges were situated specifically within the pronounced divides between past and present in the wake of decades of combat in the Pacific, the explosion of postwar tourism, and the economic and political adjustments in being the US' fiftieth state.

Looking at media representations of Hawai'i during this time period reveals several different periods of the islands' history that intersect with what Wilson has called the United States' "nostalgia for master narratives"[93]—the need to see in the past reassuring visions of triumph, unity, and optimism. There are fairly direct forms of nostalgic appeal implied, as one example, in films and television shows that evoke images and/or memories of Pearl Harbor and the Second World War. But there is also the more indirect, affective nostalgia associated with classical Hollywood movies such as *Waikiki Wedding* made prior to December 7th—evoking for later audiences an imagined innocence to life on the islands before war. Such prewar nostalgia can also be seen as a companion to what Halualani has argued as Hawaiian tourism's recent *nostalgia for itself*—where contemporary tourist imagery and island attractions today play up "the golden age of travel" in its iconography: "Waikiki in the heyday of the 1920s and 1930s; postcards, luggage tags, advertisements, and Aloha shirts from the 1930s through the 1950s are emblazoned across tourist T-shirts and hotel displays as these become popular nostalgia kitsch and rare Hawaiiana collectibles."⁹⁴ Nostalgia in mass media today for such "golden age" tourism (both the elitism of the prewar era and the masses of the postwar era) can also be read partly as a disavowal of both memories of WWII and, later, the Korean and Vietnam conflicts. While these texts were not intended necessarily for such an interpretation, their significance evolves and shifts over time, and across different audiences. It is indeed hard to essentialize personal reactions to a range of implicitly or explicitly nostalgic texts that otherwise might evoke little more than tired touristic clichés about the islands and their history.

In short, nostalgia negotiates layers of affective investment for audiences—other *real* experiences—in these representations of Hawai'i that sometimes move beyond just the stylistic and narrative aesthetic choices of the text itself. As Urry argues, most accounts of nostalgia's relationship to tourism offer "no sense of the complexity by which different visitors can gaze upon the same set of objects and read them in a different way."⁹⁵ This can be broadened to include the ambivalence of nostalgia for a period more directly marked by war—the fond memories of positive events before and during WWII that explicitly and uncomfortably coexist with representations of tragedy, sacrifice, and loss—seen in films such as *From Here to Eternity* or *In Harm's Way* (1965). As Norman Douglas and Ngaire Douglas wrote on the appeal of touristic sites related to WWII combat: "War's waste would become tourism's treasures when the visitor traffic revived: *the more violent the conflict, the more 'attractions' it provided.* The Arizona Memorial at Pearl Harbor is the outstanding example of war disaster turned to peace-time profit."⁹⁶ Gonzalez, meanwhile, adds that "visitors to the Pearl Harbor complex consume a familiar and seductive story that begins with nostalgic innocence, gets interrupted by treachery and violence, and ends with sacrifice and triumph over adversity."⁹⁷ And, she goes on, "even though tourists experience grief and sadness during their visits [to war memorials], such emotions are crucially part of, and not contradictory to, tourist pleasure. Tourists identify with a beleaguered but eventually triumphant national masculinity and are rewarded with a satisfying (if emotionally wrenching) resolution."⁹⁸

Meanwhile, the increasing preoccupation with Native Hawaiian history suggests its own kind of collective, colonialist nostalgia—a desire to hold on to a past that had already effectively vanished. America's fascination with Hawaiian history in the twentieth century reveals one of the central paradoxes of modernity—an abstract desire for "progress" to preserve a past it was also complicit in destroying. Preservation is in some respects a deeply nostalgic act—the implicitly romantic desire to retrieve, recreate, and/or maintain a symbolic fragment of a time and a place that has been irretrievably lost to history. "If a colonial past, a past of missionaries and forced acculturation," writes Kirshenblatt-Gimblett, "threatened to produce 'de-culturation,' the heritage industry does not so much reverse that process . . . there is no turning back. . . . The process of protection, of 'adding value,' speaks in and to the present, even if it does so in terms of the past."[99] In historical epics such as *Hawaii*, the desire to preserve a threatened culture sought to alleviate liberal guilt over the legacy of US imperialism in the wake of first annexation and then later statehood by going back to the "ancient" culture of the local

Figure I.7. In this shot from an episode of *The Brady Bunch* (1971), the new Hawaiian State Capital dwarfs the nearby Iolani Palace, home to Hawai'i's sovereign monarchy prior to the United States' illegal and immoral annexation of the islands at the end of the nineteenth century. The image hints at not only the neoliberal tensions of acknowledging tradition while pushing for progress in post-statehood Hawai'i, but also the lingering ugly history of colonialism that films and television shows of the time often awkwardly recognize but generally fail to address in any meaningful way.

population and essentially attempting to erase the histories of conquest that happened in the intervening centuries.

Hawai'i Onscreen

Hawai'i has been a staple of cinema for as long as the medium itself has existed. Since the days in the late nineteenth century when Edison cameramen first arrived on the islands, Hawai'i benefited from early cinema's fascination with the genre of the travelogue—the ability for this new mass medium, with its unparalleled visual realism, to capture footage in one part of the world and return those images back to a distant audience who had never seen, and might never see, such visions for themselves. In 1898, Edison photographers shot footage both of Honolulu's street life and of local beachboys diving for coins—an early example of the literal connection between cinema, tourism, and class exploitation, given that throwing money at local children swimming in the harbor as cruise ships came in to dock was a common touristic activity. In 1906, one of Edison's employees, R. K. Bonine, came to Hawai'i to shoot the first such multi-reel-length film on location, *Hawaiian Islands*, a documentary about "downtown Honolulu, Waikiki, sugar plantations, railroads and street cars, and living and working throughout the Islands."[100]

Beyond early travelogues, movies either set, and/or shot, in Hawai'i tended to gravitate to the condescending artifices of the "South Seas Romance" subgenre, one of premodern tropical paradises filled with welcoming natives who worshipped volcanoes and shark gods. The "South Seas," as Geiger notes, "might correspond to a real sense of place, but it is also a mythical and textually constructed space, in a sense, outside place and history," one best defined as "a varied discourse of written and visual evocations of beaches, coral reefs, lagoons, coconut palms, and alluring native bodies, all holding the promise of sensual indulgence for western audiences."[101] Such film titles included *Hawaiian Love* (1913), *The Shark God* (1913), and *Aloha Oe* (1915). These sorts of stereotypes further abounded in the early narrative films about the islands (*The Bottle Imp* [1917], *The Shark Master* [1921], *Vengeance of the Deep* [1923], *Aloha Hawai'i* [1930], *Hawai'i* [1931]), though a few others also evinced a greater degree of self-awareness about Hawai'i as a more modernized plantation-driven economy, or as a destination shaped as much by promotional strategies as any inherent mythical and tropical qualities (*Passion Fruit* [1921], *The White Flower* [1923], *Publicity Madness* [1927]). These

Polynesian clichés, which run rampant in early cinematic perceptions of Hawai'i, can be traced back largely to the popularity of the 1912 stage play *Bird of Paradise*, which was later adapted into an epic pre-Code Hollywood film starring Joel McCrea and Dolores Del Rio and directed by King Vidor. The movie version was released in 1932 and later remade by Delmer Daves in 1951.

The timeline for this book picks up right around the time that the South Seas romance begins to lose Hollywood's interest in the 1930s. Just as common in these days of the classical studio system were depictions of Hawai'i well aware of its heavily manufactured status as a cruise ship tourist destination for the wealthy, including films like *Feet First*, *The Black Camel*, *Waikiki Wedding* (1937), *Hawaiian Nights* (1939), *Honolulu* (1939), *It's a Date* (1940), and *Moonlight in Hawaii* (1941). These films suggested a savvier understanding of the South Seas clichés within earlier Hollywood films than has usually been put forth. Certainly, the events of December 7th and the subsequent immersion of the United States into WWII brought the islands squarely into the mainland imagination in ways that partially obscured perceptions of Hawai'i prior to 1941. It also foregrounded a context that was often in the background of earlier movies about the islands—the US' significant military presence in O'ahu and throughout the Pacific, an occupation which began before (and led to) the overthrow of the sovereign Hawaiian monarchy in the nineteenth century and which built up exponentially after the start of WWII. During the war itself, movies that referenced Hawai'i tended to be documentary propaganda such as *December 7th* (1943) and *Why We Fight: War Comes to America* (1945), which focused on events leading up to, and including, the attack in Pearl Harbor. In addition to films being produced during the war, the ubiquitous presence of WWII's collective memory in films and later television shows of the postwar period proved equally revealing. The legacy of the attack (and its larger narrative of American sacrifice) dominated the mainland's collective memory for the next several decades in a range of texts, from WWII nostalgia films (*From Here to Eternity*, *In Harm's Way*), to decidedly un-nostalgic historical melodramas (*The Revolt of Mamie Stover* [1956]), to Cold War propaganda (*Big Jim McClain* [1952]), to film noir (*Hell's Half Acre* [1954]), to television time travel narratives (*The Time Element* [1959] and *The Time Tunnel* [1966]), and even to—in a particularly jarring example of tonal disconnect—one particular episode of *The Brady Bunch* (1972).

The popularity of Hawaiian content in US popular culture reached its still unsurpassed apex by the 1960s. Although there had been no shortage of interest for many years prior, movies—and, increasingly, television programs—about Hawai'i in particular reached "all-time highs" in the decades immediately preceding and following statehood, reflecting an unprecedented number of films not only about the islands but just as importantly increasingly filmed there and not on Hollywood soundstages and backlots.[102] The soundtrack to *Blue Hawaii* (1961) was the highest-selling album of singer Elvis Presley's lifetime, reflecting a popularity that also included not one, but three, generally successful films featuring the musical megastar and the islands. Amateur filmmaker Bruce Brown's *Endless Summer* (1964), a documentary about teen surfers who go in search of the "perfect wave" and who spend much of their time in Hawai'i, became one of the first mainstream commercial hits for an independent nonfiction film. With origins in nontheatrical cinema, the phenomenal success of *Endless Summer* was the culmination of several successful travelogue films Brown made about surfing on the islands (*Slippery When Wet*, *Barefoot Adventures*). Meanwhile, *Hawaii*, a historical epic about some of the first missionaries to visit the islands in the early nineteenth century, was 1966's top-grossing film at the domestic box office, while

Figure I.8. Popular movies and TV shows of the postwar era, such as *Blue Hawaii* (1961), not only depicted a new postwar leisure culture that appealed to younger demographics and newer markets such as soundtrack albums (featuring stars such as Elvis Presley) but also the ubiquity of air transportation provided by companies such as United Air Lines, which benefited from, and heavily promoted, a new, more affordable, age of mass tourism and prepackaged vacations in the era of jet travel.

the book on which it was based (Michener's novel of the same name) proved to be one of the decade's most popular reads. Finally, *Hawaii Five-O* debuted on CBS in 1968 and went on to be the longest-running nighttime drama in American television history, before being surpassed by *Law & Order* in 2003. Yet the roots of Hawai'i's immense post-statehood popularity in the 1960s can be found in the decades that preceded it. Movies and TV shows throughout the mid-twentieth century at least in part about Hawai'i had long since foregone the obvious clichés of South Seas romances and embraced the artifices, contradictions, and ironies, within tourism's "Paradise of the Pacific," while also at times carefully and not always successfully negotiating the very real and often painful memories of colonialism, racism, classism, and militarism. But first I return to that since mythologized decade before and after the events of December 7th—when Hollywood largely appeared to be anything but nostalgic or sentimental about Hawai'i's touristic reputation.

1

Save That Gag for the Tourists

The Hawaii Tourist Bureau and Post-tourism Narratives of 1930s Hollywood

"Paradise" was screened by layers of mediating Hollywood myth, and therefore hard to experience authentically and immediately. For men like [US sailor Samuel] Hynes, intelligent and acutely self-conscious, the mediating myths could yield any ironic—and uncomfortable—distance from their immediate experiences. For those of less reflective temperament, myth might validate experience, even shape reality.

—Beth Bailey and David Farber, *The First Strange Place*

IN A BOOK ON WORLD WAR II–era Hawaiʻi, Beth Bailey and David Farber recount the memory of a US soldier on the Pacific island of Majuro during a brief lull in combat. With beer in hand, Samuel Hynes wandered out to a moonlit beach and found himself overwhelmed: "It was a scene that demanded sentiment," he wrote, "and I knew I should have feelings about it, sad romantic yearnings for the far-off beloved, something like that. But how could I have any real response to a tropical island in the moonlight? It was too damn much, too like a movie with Dorothy Lamour; and I could only feel the way I did in movies like that—charmed but disbelieving."[1] This story highlights what was self-evident for many by the 1940s: mainland assumptions about the Pacific—and Hawai'i in particular—had been shaped by decades of advertising, radio, and movies that promoted the South Seas in general as a calm, tropical paradise for romance, filled with hula, moonlight, palm trees, and pineapples. "Invented images of love and paradise, created by appropriating the culture of indigenous island peoples and redrawing this culture to reflect the dreams and desires of, mainly, the West," writes George Lewis, "was what Hawaii became in the hearts and minds of the world audience."[2] Hynes's story also reflected how mainlanders had a more complicated, conflicted, even resistant, relationship to these utopic visions than previously assumed about Hawai'i and Hawaiian-themed films in the prewar period, and which were retrospectively situated postwar as a nostalgic space of innocence disrupted by the 1941 Japanese attack on US military forces in Pearl Harbor.

A year earlier, *Variety* noted Hollywood's "current Hawaiian vogue—still current after five years, which is something in itself."[3] Focused on music composer Harry Owens, the article credited his song "Sweet Leilani" (featured in *Waikiki Wedding* [1937], starring Bing Crosby) and the hugely popular radio program *Hawaii Calls* (1935–1975), which Owens and his band originally starred on, with being at the forefront of a trend that dominated a good deal of the decade before WWII. In 1937, fellow musician and regular collaborator Ray Kinney made a similar (admittedly self-serving) claim that while other forms of entertainment—such as the original *Bird of Paradise* stage play (1912) and the "South Seas Romance" imitators it spawned—had brought some attention to islands, the mainland's latest fascination with Hawai'i "lay more or less dormant until President Roosevelt and Bing Crosby (not together) visited the islands."[4] Crosby himself looked back nostalgically in 1970 with the observation that "surely no mainlander, and very few islanders, honestly have had such a lengthy love affair with the Hawaiian islands as Harry Owens."[5]

As part of a promotional campaign, Owens was brought to Honolulu in the early 1930s by Matson Navigation Company and Arthur Benaglia, managing director of the Royal Hawaiian Hotel (one of the first friends Owens made during the cruise to Honolulu was congressional delegate and future territorial governor Samuel Wilder King[6]). He was hired as bandleader for the orchestra at the Royal Hawaiian and subsequently performed extensively on *Hawaii Calls* (which was recorded on the beachfront patio of Matson's other Waikiki resort, the Moana). Owens's band was described by *Variety* as a "half-and-half band, Hawaiians to get the authentic flavor, Americans for swing."[7] Kinney insisted that "Hawaiian music has been modernized for dancing [in the nightclubs], yet kept its genuine flavor."[8] (Kinney had benefited financially from over four hundred new arrangements of public domain Hawaiian tunes.[9]) By the end of the decade, *Variety* declared—with no shortage of hyperbole—that Owens's efforts had managed to "salvage Hawaiian music from extinction."[10] In his own rags-to-riches autobiography, *Sweet Leilani: The Story Behind the Song* (1970), Owens later noted, with a bit more humility, that he was hired to "help perpetuate the music of the islands which had, to a degree, been passed along from generation to generation by word of mouth."[11] While Owens's version of the story suggested that originally he was brought out to Honolulu to play in front of hotel guests in the Royal Hawaiian ballroom, and then only gravitated to radio broadcasts after several months of success, *Variety* had previously reported as early as 1934 that Owens had been invited to Honolulu with the explicit

Figure 1.1. A key figure both in Hawai'i's post-Depression era tourism push of the 1930s and the attendant interest by Hollywood studios, Harry Owens is seen here leading the band of Waikiki's Royal Hawaiian Hotel in a scene from the Hawaii Tourist Bureau's promotional film *The Story of Oahu* (1934).

intention that his "orchestra from the hotel . . . be heard [across the Pacific] in several broadcasts during the summer."[12] By New Year's 1935, his band's performance was being broadcast to the mainland on NBC, CBS, and Mutual. "As a result of the tremendous publicity accompanying this radio-saturation," Owens claimed in *Sweet Leilani*, "NBC allotted us a half-hour slot weekly for four consecutive weeks"[13] (this program would become *Hawaii Calls*).

Produced in part by the Hawaii Tourist Bureau (responsible for several radio programs in the prewar period), *Hawaii Calls* was an immensely wide-reaching, long-running radio program "heard over hundreds of stations at the height of its success."[14] By 1953, the bureau claimed the show was broadcast every week on approximately six hundred stations throughout several countries.[15] Partially due to the radio program's success, Owens's band gained even more attention from Hollywood, first on movie soundtracks (and cameos in movies such as *It's a Date*) and then later with his own TV show in the 1950s, *Harry Owens and His Royal Hawaiians* (1949–1958). His "Sweet Leilani" won the Academy Award for Best Original Song after its appearance in *Waikiki Wedding*, reportedly due to Crosby's insistence after first hearing it performed in person by Owens and his band in Honolulu (Kinney himself claimed to have first called the singer's attention to the tune[16]). The circulation of his band's music—through radio, film, and sheet music, as well as subsequent live performance tours on the mainland—played a powerful role in building mainland buzz by creating the imagined impression of an "authentic" Hawaiian sound emerging from Oʻahu and traveling across the Pacific. Schmitt adds, however, that "many such efforts [at authenticity] were all but lost in the pervasive Hollywood glitz, savagely attacked by Island critics . . . for a wildly distorted view of Hawaiian dance and music."[17] Lewis notes the irony that, by 1937, "authentic" cinematic versions of Hawaiian music "had come to be defined as the difference between a song (and image) created by a non-Hawaiian band leader in a Waikiki tourist hotel, as opposed to a song cranked out in a Hollywood studio's back lot."[18] Within *Waikiki Wedding*, "Sweet Leilani" was implied to be a more "authentic" Hawaiian song than the others in part because, as Crosby recalled, it "was already a hit in Honolulu, and it didn't take any musical clairvoyant to discern that it would have similar success in the States."[19]

All this relentless media saturation by island tourism interests in the 1930s, meanwhile, gave the lie to the *Honolulu Advertiser*'s disingenuous insistence later during WWII that "Hawaii can't help the way Hollywood has pictured these islands. Hawaii just goes on being itself."[20] On the

Figure 1.2. Owens's Academy Award–winning song, "Sweet Leilani," was featured in the Bing Crosby romantic comedy *Waikiki Wedding* (1937), one of numerous Hawai'i-set films Hollywood produced in the 1930s, and one of the more interesting cinematic takes during this time on Hawai'i's heavily manufactured touristic identity as a location filled with romance and adventure.

contrary, the preceding anecdote about Owens, the Hawaii Tourist Bureau, "Sweet Leilani," and *Hawaii Calls* serves as a reminder that Hawai'i not only never experienced a moment of pre-WWII innocence untainted by aggressive self-promotion across a range of mass media, but also actively sought to intensify such attention from across the Pacific—however much that collective desire for such an imagined retrospective naïveté may have also intensified in the postwar period. In particular, a closer look at public relations, advertising, and other marketing efforts in US mass media of the 1930s reveals a very aggressive attempt on the part of the tourism industry itself to sell that romantic and adventurous vision of paradise to prospective tourists.

Just as fascinating, such a deeper look also reveals a prominent reaction against that same idealized image by a Hollywood studio system that even back then understood all too well (and sensed that savvy audiences, such as the Majuro sailor, also understood) the powerfully illusorily ways in which mass media could be used to deceive audiences, along with all the narrative contradictions and emotional ambivalence existing therein. Many films—aware of this particular touristic "myth" of Hawai'i, and perhaps also exhausted by the creative limitations of the "South Seas romance" genre—entered into a more complex negotiation with this mass manufacturing of paradise. Here, not only the experiences of "adventure" and "romance" but also the *knowledge* of their artifices became central to its resilience as commodity in the studio system. Hollywood's playful attitude toward the clichés of the Hawaiian vacation allowed it to disavow its own role in the manufacturing of similar romantic tales. The studios' narrative of traveler anticipation, disappointment, and finally affirmation both fit its own classic three-act structure and preempted audiences' own skepticism toward the authenticity of such touristic experiences. Some classical Hollywood filmmakers (perhaps drawing from the ambivalences of their own personal Hawaiian vacations offscreen) recognized this inevitability.

Many films explicitly foregrounded the touristic "construction" of Hawai'i in the (mainland) imagination: *Waikiki Wedding*, *The Black Camel* (1931), *Honolulu* (1939), *Honolulu Nights* (1939), and *Moonlight in Hawaii* (1941). "A remarkable number of pictures [over forty] made in or about Hawai'i" before statehood, writes Schmitt, "took place aboard aircraft, ships, boats, or submarines."[21] Repeatedly, the modern journey to Hawai'i was as important to the story as the destination itself—a touristic lens situating Hawai'i explicitly from the perspective of geographical distance, and of racial and cultural difference: *Honolulu*, *Hawaii Calls* (1938), *Feet First* (1931), *Charlie Chan Carries On* (1931), *One Way Passage* (1932), *Charlie Chan's Murder Cruise* (1935), *Trade Winds* (1939), *Charlie Chan in Honolulu* (1938), *It's a Date* (1940), and *'Til We Meet Again* (1940). Such seabound settings also often reinforced the common plots and subplots involving romance, since cruises reinforced "the widely held romantic notion of lovers meeting and getting married aboard ship."[22] Although most films of this era were still shot largely on studio soundstages and backlots, the traces of location footage from Hawai'i tended to be familiar tourist ones: "Favorite settings included Honolulu Harbor, the Royal Hawaiian Hotel, Waikahalulu Falls [a garden in the heart of Honolulu popular for 'jungle' shooting], Nuʻuanu Pali [the sight of King Kamehameha's victory over island rivals in May of 1795], and Pearl Harbor, all recognizable in numerous pictures."[23] Many also featured tourists and/or public relations

Figure 1.3. In *The Black Camel* (1931), one of several Hollywood films from the decade to foreground the superficial artifices of Hawai'i's touristic reputation, one character (Sally Eilers) initially flees the advances of a would-be suitor (Robert Young). A public relations man himself, he attempts to sell her the romantic allure of the Hawaiian islands, only to be rebuffed by a dismissive response: "*Save that gag for the tourists.*" The location of this shot is also distinctive as *The Black Camel* was one of the first studio productions actually filmed in part in Hawai'i itself. Note the young boys looking in the direction of the camera, not to mention the large cluster of folks in the distance watching the sequence with little apparent concern that they themselves were also being recorded. Intended or otherwise, these curious touristic onlookers effectively become background extras watching both the movie—and the movie within the movie—being filmed.

executives as central characters, which also reflected back to varying degrees on the process of constructing the vacation experience—*Feet First, Hawaii Calls, The Black Camel, Waikiki Wedding, Honolulu, Moonlight in Hawaii, Hawaiian Nights, It's a Date,* and *Song of the Islands*. "In 13, important roles were assigned to plantation and cannery owners," writes Robert C. Schmitt, "often described in these scripts as 'the *pineapple king of Hawai'i*.'"[24] Aside from reinforcing Hawai'i's brand as a prolific agricultural producer, the centrality of the pineapple industry in these narratives highlights the extent to which the collective mainland vision of the islands was more than a simple premodern paradise. Rather, it was one rooted in a specific type of economic modernity that supported the tourism industry. Most interesting in this regard are *Waikiki Wedding*, *Moonlight in Hawaii*, and *Honolulu*. Yet other high-profile films of the period, such as *White Heat* (its working title was *Cane Fire*), *Hawaiian Buckaroo* (1938), and *Song of the Islands*, also foreground the plantation as a centerpiece of the modern Hawaiian economy. Finally, many of these films—such as *The Black Camel*, *Honolulu*, *It's a Date*, and *In the Navy* (1941)—focused on celebrity trips to Hawai'i, emphasizing how the islands were a playground for the rich, "elite tourism"[25] in the pre-WWII days of cruise ships instead of more affordable postwar airfare. But more than just highlighting the luxury of a Hawaiian vacation, it reflected the reality of many real-life celebrity voyages, which "could also be a helpful publicity boost for Hawaii itself when photos of filmdom's well-known travelers were released all over the country."[26] (The Hawaii Tourist Bureau and its partners actively and aggressively circulated such publicity photos.[27])

Hollywood's "Current Hawaiian Vogue"

For decades prior, Hawaiian-themed films, known for their lack of historical and cultural authenticity, were mostly of the so-called "South Seas romance" variety—such as *The Shark God* (1913) or *Aloha Oe* (1915)—celluloid depictions of a romantic but dangerously premodern and unchartered tropical paradise, populated by sometimes benign, sometimes violent, primitive residents and natural elements (sea creatures, volcanoes) that contained supernatural powers. "Although semiotically complex," writes Jane Desmond, such South Seas romance narratives "render a simplistic image of Native Hawaiian culture—like Minnie Mouse's version of the hula in Disney's 1935 animated film, *Hawaiian Holiday*."[28] The short Disney cartoon was particularly egregious in this regard, depicting a virgin Hawaiian natural landscape completely devoid of any sign of local human population, let alone Honolulu's emerging urban modernity. This was typical, as DeSoto Brown writes, of how "films used Hawaii for all sorts of celluloid action, from tap dancing hula girls and angry volcanoes to murder mystery plots. . . . The fact that these movies were utterly unrealistic bolstered, instead of diminished, their selling abilities."[29]

"The early magazines' vision of a tropical paradise, with its gentle trade winds and nursery rhyme monarchs," writes Gary Y. Okihiro, in particular "laid the foundation for Hollywood's films of the 'South Seas,' in which the sea and land and their biotic communities were the sets and backdrops for featured white actors who moved across that dreamy stage."[30] The earliest Hollywood films shot on location in the islands, *The Shark God* and *Hawaiian Love*, Schmitt writes, "pretty much set the pattern: beaches, palm trees, native maidens, kahunas (priests, usually treated in these films as sorcerers), *haole* (Caucasian) interlopers, and interracial romance. . . . Frequently the butt of critical derision and audience merriment, the South Seas epics soon developed a set of favorite themes used with monotonous regularity."[31] Specifically, many of them were narrative variations on handsome young sailors discovering love with the native chieftain's daughter (usually played by female actors of white or Latina descent) on some remote mythic island in the South Pacific. This genre in particular revealed acutely and transparently the US' emergent obsession with what Delia Malia Caparoso Konzett labeled "the intertwined logic of colonial desire and domination"[32] that structured so many classical Hollywood exotic fantasies.

Released shortly before Owens's invitation to Honolulu was David O. Selznick and King Vidor's lavish production *Bird of Paradise* (1932), which Schmitt regards as the "archetypal South Seas romance."[33] By the early 1930s, *Bird of Paradise* was very much even then a nostalgic anachronism. Less an innovative cinematic novelty and more the big-budget, high-profile culmination of two decades' worth of a particular strand of Hawaiiana that held sway over the mainland, the film was an adaptation of a twenty-year-old hit Broadway play. *Bird of Paradise* is the story of a sailor (Joel McCrea) who visits a generic Polynesian island and falls in love with a local princess (Dolores Del Rio), whom he rescues from an arranged marriage with another native—an elaborate sequence involving all the implied musical spectacle of a luau show. After living out an idyllic romantic life on another island, the local girl returns to her people when the nearby volcano begins erupting. Only the princess's sacrifice to the Gods by throwing herself into the volcano, they believe, will prevent disaster. The sailor, meanwhile, is injured trying to take her back and subsequently captured. After they are both rescued by his fellow shipmates, the doomed lovers reluctantly agree to part—products of two very different worlds, he sails back to the States as she willingly sacrifices herself in order to save her people.

Bird of Paradise, Lewis observed, "was—with its Hawaiian theme and *hapa haole* music—a production that some mark as the critical introduction of Hawaii as a commercial theme into American popular culture."[34] Brown similarly argued that *Bird* "bears much of the responsibility for

Figure 1.4. The end of an era, King Vidor's *Bird of Paradise* (1932) was arguably the last high-profile traditional "South Seas" romantic adventure produced by the Hollywood studio system in the late silent and early sound film period. (The end of the decade would later see arguably more reflexive takes on the genre, such as John Ford's *The Hurricane* in 1937.) These narratives of colonialism, made at a time when the United States was expanding its military presence in the Pacific, depicted islands in the South Pacific as a seductive, premodern tropical paradise, where Western travelers encountered exotic natives who were alternatingly often both welcoming and threatening.

introducing Hawaii into American popular culture. . . . In 1912 it inspired a Hawaiian music craze that lasted for years."[35] Several decades later, Owens also nostalgically credited the original play with initiating his own love affair with the islands:

> Long before I knew the meaning of *Aloha*, I had pictured, in dreams, a land of indescribable beauty . . . My dream-picture, I seem to remember, began to take focus on a night when, in the Opera House in Missoula, Montana, I witnessed a mag-

nificent stage play. It starred Lenore Ulric. It was called "Bird
of Paradise." All through my youth I cherished the dream of
my make-believe world.[36]

While the film version is not technically set in Hawai'i (though parts were filmed there), it owed heavily to the islands' pop tourist iconography. "Native Hawaiians" in the film, argues Desmond, "clearly were positioned as [hula] spectacle,"[37] while Del Rio's pre-Code nude swimming sequence explicitly announced the overt—and permissible—sexuality of the hula girl archetype.

Like the South Seas romances, the hula girl represented the commodified embodiment not only of local heritage, and the islands' overt musical connotations, but also of a native population that is imagined to be passive and nonthreatening—one only interested in pleasing the traveler and thus presenting spaces for (colonial) economic and cultural conquest. Hula, Desmond writes, "provide[d] the most concentrated dose of Hawaiiana. . . . Their spectacular aspects—sound, movement, colorful costumes, lighting, stage design—all appear to provide access to some sort of cultural knowledge without requiring special preparation or verbal comprehension on the part of the audience."[38] The hula girl's unique racial identity at the time—neither black nor white—offered a safely liminal category of race that existed outside more established boundaries on the mainland. And drawing on Hawaiian heritage offset the perception of the dance as little more than an overtly sexualized, unseemly performance that appealed primarily to the baser desires of its (presumed masculine) audience. (*Variety* reported in 1937 that film producer "Harold Hurley [was] back from Hawaii hula ogling."[39]) Thus, she offered an innocent, but unmistakable, sexuality that carefully walked the line of acceptability Hollywood negotiated within the more restrained sexual attitudes of 1930s America:

> The hula girl is sexy, yes, but never aggressively so. The innocence associated with the Edenic trope prohibits knowing, aggressive deployment of sexual allure, making the hula girl nonthreatening to men and women alike. . . . The hula girl image evokes the feminized lushness of the tropics: accessible, hospitable, beautiful, exotic and natural and ties all of these qualities to a cultural distinctiveness.[40]

Whether situated as a (sacred, forbidden) native celebration that the filmic audience can silently observe (*Bird of Paradise*), or as a lavish spectacle explicitly intended for the diegetic audience's consumption (*Honolulu*), many such films of the classical Hollywood era feature at least one prominent hula performance. The first prominent cinematic "star" hula girl was Clara Bow in *Hula* (1927)—the poster tagline called the film the story of "an unconquered Island Girl who comes Face to Face with Love."⁴¹ More often in early Polynesian-themed films, the hula girl was not a leading character but rather a generic secondary figure who was, as in *The Black Camel*, synonymous with "native" girl (just as the beachboy was synonymous with "native" boy).

Even films as reflexive about the clichéd touristic experiences as *Waikiki Wedding, Honolulu, Honolulu Nights*, or *Moonlight in Hawaii* take at face value the idea that the spectacle of hula offered a powerful, if elusive or ill-defined, entry point into local traditions. This is made most explicit in the opening moments of *Waikiki Wedding*, when the white outsiders Tony Marvin (Crosby, in a role originally intended for Danish actor Carl Brisson) and Shad (Bob Burns) quietly observe a "native" hula performance as part of an ostensibly private wedding ceremony. Here the touristic back region is presented as something more authentic, something away from the cycles and stages of touristic consumption and closer to the perceived actual spaces of local Hawaiian culture—a contrast that is then heightened further by the more overt artifice of Tony's "planned" Hawaiian adventure later in the film. A 1937 article on the film's technical director, Louise Beamer (a Honolulu dancing school director), even noted that the goal was to show more authentic Hawaiian dances, "*most of which have never been seen by tourists' eyes*, and some of which date so far into their prehistoric period that they are done solely to drumbeats, since they antedate the introduction of any other sort of music into the islands."⁴²

Over time, the figure of the hula girl gradually moved from the periphery of Hawaiian-themed films, often one among many in the background of a larger dance performance, to the centerpiece of the show by the 1940s—a transition that also coincides with the progressive "respectability" of the dance itself (as connoting "heritage" instead of only "sexuality") and with the increasing use of white movie stars (Bow, Eleanor Powell, Betty Grable), instead of Native Hawaiian performers. One 1937 article on the making of *Waikiki Wedding* claimed that almost no full-blooded Hawaiian women were used for hula scenes because they were perceived by the studios as being too heavy set.⁴³ Both the casting of Caucasian actresses and the mainstreaming of hula performances worked to further "sanitize" (both racially and sexually) the hula girl for a general white mainland audience. An exhibitor in a 1939 issue of

Boxoffice claimed that Powell's hula performance was *Honolulu*'s biggest draw: "A swell teaser trailer featuring the great hula number pre-sold this picture. To back up this promise, *Honolulu* was good entertainment, not strictly grade A, but definitely not boring. Business was above par."[44] The centrality of hula in *Honolulu*'s larger marketing strategy coincided with

> a multi-island hula competition sponsored by Hollywood's [MGM] Studios and the Hawai'i-based Consolidated Amusement Company [to find] a "hula queen." In the "greatest hula contest ever staged in the Islands," nearly 500 young Hawaiian women vied for the title for over a month, going through several rounds of competition. Each hoped to win the grand prize: a trip to Hollywood and a chance at stardom in the United States. . . . [The winner Alice Kealoha Pauole Holt] passed her MGM screen test in Hollywood and spent three months there, touring as an "ambassador of good will" and dancing in the American stage and film productions of *Honolulu*.[45]

To sustain the often-spectacular number of elaborately choreographed hula performances captured on film, studios drew upon the extensive "infrastructure of performance sites and a pool of trained entertainers"[46] who toured the live hula show circuit on the mainland. Adria Imada recounts a story of one such performer who went to Hollywood in search of these roles:

> Another "very charming" hula teacher has returned from Hollywood where she directed hula scenes for a new studio film. Her hula classes kept her going from 8am to 6pm, and "if she [had] had any more it would [have been] the death of her." These profiles could have described a number of Hawaiian women from the 1930s to the 1950s.[47]

Given such developments, hula dancers began to unionize by 1939: "performers would organize to avoid exploitation, especially since Hollywood studios had begun to shoot many films on location in Hawai'i in the 1920s and 1930s."[48] Similarly, since they were performing a version of hula as influenced by Hollywood demands as by local traditions, Native Hawaiian hula dancers saw their performances as a compromised attempt at preserving their own local culture and history in the face of its crass commercialization. Imada notes that "for Hawaiian cultural practices to be perceived as authentic, they could not be tainted by market relations, but in turn were eagerly appropriated and commodified by the tourist industry. . . . Hawaiians found themselves trying to ensure cultural reproduction while participating in capitalist markets."[49]

The Massie Affair

After Vidor's epic appeared in 1932, the old South Seas romance largely disappeared from cinema for over a decade. There were high-profile exceptions, such as Lois Weber's *White Heat* (1934) and John Ford's *The Hurricane* (1937), starring Lamour, one of the first movie stars who publicly supported Hawaiian statehood.[50] Later South Seas films, such as *Hurricane* and *Wake of the Red Witch* (1949), shifted the emphasis away from the US's seafaring exploration to a critique of other colonialist exploitations of indigenous populations (especially, France and French Polynesia), disavowing the US' own imperialist actions in places like Hawai'i and the Philippines. "Texts are always haunted by their ancestors, as much as they are of their time," Jeffrey Geiger writes of Hollywood's disingenuous critique of colonialism, "postwar US fantasies of Polynesia can be seen to have adapted and renewed much older—and primarily European—connotations, myths, and legends about the South Seas."[51] The shift to European characters may also have been to offset mainland (southern) concerns about racial miscegenation between US sailors and native populations. (*Variety* reported in 1942 that there was "color line resistance anticipated throughout the South [to] 'Moon and Sixpence,' . . . which has a Tahitian girl marrying a French artist. . . . This inter-racial union may be resented in some states."[52])

The intersection of racial and sexual tensions on the islands was never more acute in this era than during the Massie tragedy, which impacted both Hawai'i and the mainland during 1931 and 1932. As much as the emergence of more sophisticated forms of mass communication in the 1920s and 1930s, or the decline of agriculture in the wake of the Great Depression, the Massie Affair was a crucial context then that helped shape shifting images of Hawai'i circulating on the mainland. One of the former hula girls whom Imada interviewed, Tutasi Wilson, said she "felt personally responsible for correcting images of Polynesians and Hawai'i when she met mainland Americans. She recalled, "When I got to Hollywood [in 1934], the Massie case was not too far back."[53]

The incidents of the Massie Affair involved a naval officer's wife, Thalia Massie, who disappeared from a party in Honolulu late one night and was later found on the side of the road with a bloody face. She said that she'd been raped by a gang of local Hawaiian men. While Massie had clearly been assaulted, many questions about the events of the night, as well as her racially charged accusations, also emerged. Thus, the initial attempts to prosecute the five defendants—which the US Navy had insisted upon to maintain peace between the military presence and local population—ended in a mistrial.

Unhappy with the outcome and worried about her daughter's reputation, Thalia's mother, Grace Fortescue, recruited her son-in-law, Lt. Thomas Massie, and several other naval men to kidnap one of the defendants—a well-known local boxer, Joseph Kahahawai—with the intention of forcing a confession out of him. At some point during the blotched attempt at an interrogation, Kahahawai was shot and killed. In a panic, they dumped his body in a remote part of eastern Oʻahu, assuming no one would care about a missing Hawaiian (they even reportedly admitted the crime to a police officer after being caught in the act of disposal). All four were charged with homicide and the resulting trial and publicity threatened to plunge the islands into a race riot. While the murder was rebranded by some in the mainland press as an "honor killing"—a justified retribution for an (unproven) act of rape—the local population was insistent upon justice for Kahahawai's death. The resulting Fortescue trial received extensive, often sensationalistic, "yellow journalism"-type media coverage back on the mainland, which attempted to paint Hawaiʻi as both a primitive island of violent brutes and a lawless space of antiwhite discrimination. Ultimately, Fortesque was sentenced to ten years imprisonment for manslaughter, a sentence that was shamefully commuted under pressure from the Navy to one hour served in the territorial governor's office.

The Massie Affair was a powerful symbol in 1931 of the mainland's conflicting attitudes toward Hawaiʻi—a love affair with its natural image of paradise, alongside a fascination (and fear) stemming from the racial, cultural, and political difference it presented to the rest of the United States. "In those days, the 1930s and 40s, they [Americans] thought we were gorillas," Wilson said, "when we [islanders] were on the train, they were checking to see if we were colored."[54] Gavan Daws further describes the effect of the Massie case on the mainland's problematic perception of Hawaiʻi: "It was as if someone walking down a warm and sunlit path had accidently kicked aside a stone and discovered, with a shock all the more frightening because it was unconsciously anticipated, a hidden world of crawling obscenity."[55] More so than the excitement and danger its lurid details evoked, the dramatic illusion of tropical utopia that the Massie case highlighted was a part of its journalistic appeal—the idea that the "Hawai'i" Americans had been sold was never really quite the truth to begin with, and in ways that may have both troubled the touristic construction of, but also reaffirmed the desire for, "paradise."

Retrospectively, the events surrounding the Massie Affair today are noted for the extent to which it showed Hawai'i pushing back against the tradition of white supremacy that marked the American justice system throughout the nation's history. About deeply entrenched institutional racism in the US, which certainly extended to Hawai'i's de facto colonial status in the 1930s, David E. Stannard writes: "What happened in the islands . . . from the 1930s to the 1950s, was an astonishing reversal. In terms of the speed and totality of changed ethnic fortunes and political ideology, it may be unrivaled in American history. . . . Equally remarkable is the fact that pivotal in that turnaround was a connected series of racially charged events . . . that together focused the world's attention on justice in Hawai'i for months on end during 1931 and 1932."[56] Outrage on the islands, he argued, led Hawaiian residents of all ethnic and racial backgrounds to unite against the dominant political oligarchy of the time—a shift also aided by an increasingly potent labor force. This then helped further plant the seeds for Hawai'i's generally progressive policies and laws today. But given the threat these developments posed to racial hierarchies back on the mainland at the time, the Massie case is also remembered for the extent to which US news publishers played up racist assumptions about the islands in order to sell papers. Daws adds that these newspapers played off the idea that "if Hawaii was unsafe for one white woman it must be unsafe for all white women. Thus, for example, the editorial staff of William Randolph Hearst's *New York American* could tell without even looking that the obscenity under the stone was real."[57] One infamous Hearst editorial declared that "the situation in Hawaii is deplorable. It is becoming or has become an unsafe place for white women. Outside the cities or small towns the roads go through jungles and in these remote places bands of degenerate natives or half-castes lie in wait for white women driving by."[59] Yet while the coverage of Massie on the mainland has been usually assumed to be monolithic, not all papers participated in this form of yellow journalism. In some cases, it was exactly the opposite. *Variety* reported in 1932 that "with travel to Honolulu at low ebb, steamship companies are bearing down on coast newspapers to keep out reports of several race riots on the islands. . . . Several newspaper owners on the coast are financially interested in the steamship lines and in Honolulu property. Any space given to the disturbances on the islands will ruin trans-Pacific travel that so far this season has been very anemic."[58] At least on the West Coast, there was a conscious effort to minimize coverage of the events—and undoubtedly many other newspaper owners in the US had a financial investment in some aspect of the many Hawaiian-connected business interests.

Massie was the structuring absence of Hollywood representations of Hawai'i throughout the 1930s—one reason why depictions walked a fine line between the profitable touristic promise of escape, adventure, and romance in an exotic land, and the prevalent awareness that such deceptive utopic sounds and images always also conceal (for better and for worse) as much, and often more, as they reveal. To what degree was the push to reconstruct Hawaii's image in the media a response to perceptions of the islands after the Massie case? The timing of the HTB's aggressive PR push in 1933 wouldn't seem entirely coincidental, though the bureau's documents from the time certainly avoid mentioning the topic directly. Judy Rohrer has also noted how the rhetoric of racial utopia that frames many populist discourses about the islands was first developed in the wake of these same tensions: "Unions were organizing plantation workers in solidarity against *haole* bosses, the *haole* oligarchy was pushing back, trying to maintain their stranglehold on politics and economics, and the infamous Massie affair erupted into national headlines."[59] Many locals embraced a new racial consciousness after the trial was over—a development at least as much rooted in fears about threats to a newer tourist-based economy as to a sudden personal awakening of progressive ideals. Moreover, the reflexive construction in the 1930s of the Hawaiian vacation as carefully planned out in advance, even potentially clichéd in its routines, pushed back against the perception of the islands as not only somewhat uncivilized but even dangerously anarchic. Vacations to Hawai'i became more about the safe (routinized) swoon of romance in a modernized touristic setting and less about the spontaneous, unpredictable, uncontrollable, and thus deeply threatening, perils of adventure.

We can see this not only in the harmlessly reflexive, often comedic, Hawaiian tourist narratives, but also in the rapid decline of the "South Seas" romance onscreen in the 1930s. The Massie trials, by some coincidence, were underway right as the cast and crew of *Bird of Paradise* arrived in Hawai'i to begin production in 1932. *Variety* in February of that year reported in side-by-side articles that cast and crew had arrived in Hawai'i for production at the same time as "many prominent newspaper men from the key cities on the mainland are in Honolulu to cover the coming Fortescue and Massie trials."[60] This, despite the fact that just a month sooner, *Variety* had initially reported that RKO had decided to shoot in Florida instead of Honolulu "because of the reported turmoil over attacks by natives on white women there."[61] Stannard notes that Vidor's film crew spent six weeks in Hawai'i:

> At one point the winds blew so fiercely on the beach where he was filming that they denuded the coconut trees of their palm fronds. The next day he had a small army of local teenagers climbing the trees and nailing them back in place. But at night, when he retired to his suite at the Royal Hawaiian Hotel, the accounts he read in the newspapers of what was happening beyond his small circle, on the mainland and in Honolulu [regarding the trials], must have seemed at least equally improbable.[62]

Schmitt claimed that *Bird of Paradise*'s "filming began in O'ahu, but because of rainy weather was completed in Catalina."[63] While the bad weather was well documented at the time, concerns over the Massie trials were undoubtedly a factor in any change of location as well. The coincidental timing, however, is worth highlighting further—both the more inflammatory rhetoric around the trials and the "South Seas" film itself depended on what even by 1931 would have been viewed as at best anachronistic clichés about Native Hawaiian culture and its population. *Bird of Paradise* was a nostalgic vision of the kind of premodern paradise that was becoming increasingly outdated at a time when Hawai'i was promoting its modern tourism industry and when such "primitive" depictions of the islands too easily lent themselves to the kinds of racist attitudes that helped create and then escalate the Massie situation.

In *Honor Killing*, Stannard recounts the anecdote of Vidor's production leaving Honolulu right before the cast and crew of *The Black Camel*, a flawed but nonetheless more reflexive depiction of modern-day Hawai'i, arrived to film their own production on location. He writes that "no sooner had the cruise ship carrying that cast and crew [from *Bird of Paradise*] departed from Honolulu Harbor, with hundreds of leis tossed from the deck into the surrounding water as custom dictated, than another group actors arrived to receive the equally customary lei greeting . . . to film *The Black Camel*, a Charlie Chan movie, at the Royal Hawaiian Hotel."[64] It should be said that this story cannot be historically accurate—the cast and crew of *The Black Camel* had left Los Angeles for the islands on March 28th, 1931,[65] almost a year before the *Bird of Paradise* production was in town, while a *Honolulu Advertiser* article around the same time corroborates that location filming for *Black Camel* took place during the month of April.[66] (Additionally, *Black Camel* itself premiered on July 5th that same year,[67] months before the fateful September night of the initial alleged attack had even occurred.) However, the anecdote remains worth noting for the deeper truth of its inviting symbolism—how one era of Hawai'i on film was being decisively replaced by another at the beginning of the 1930s.

"A Paradise Streamlined"

Early on in *Waikiki Wedding*, there is a remarkable graphic match dissolve between a line of Native Hawaiian men banging drums during the film's opening wedding sequence as it dissolves seamlessly into a line of local factory workers on a pineapple cannery assembly line. (The reflexive ability to see the work display here gives the knowledge of production an ironic element of *authenticity*—as though seeing, real or imagined, how commodities are produced gives them added value.) The cut encapsulates the entire film's ideological arc—the self-aware veil of Hawai'i's tropical fantasy is brushed aside to reveal the territory's new industrialized realities. The sequence conveys Hawai'i's modernity at the close of the 1930s—having moved on from its "primitive" beginnings amid the music of the jungle to a fully modernized economy immersed in a visible Fordist model of production. This fits with the entire film's attempt to rewrite assumptions about the islands as a retrogressive, premodern wilderness in a post-Massie era. But the sequence in *Waikiki Wedding*—while rejecting that damaging stereotype of a primitive Hawai'i—also retrospectively conveys the depressing vision of a local population that has been reduced to its value as cheap compartmentalized labor to be maximized in a factory (while also eliding somewhat the ethnic and racial diversity of the actual Hawaiian population at this time). And, as the film's later plot twist implies (much of the film's tropical "adventure" turns out to be an elaborate hoax performed for one traveler's benefit), the next step in its economic evolution would be the performative role of Hawaiians within the emergent tourism market. Whatever its ideological shortcomings, the dissolves brilliantly encapsulate the coexistence of Hawai'i's preindustrial (agriculture) and postindustrial (tourism) economies by the 1930s—as well as the spectacle of Native Hawaiian performance (for the camera) being as increasingly important to the territory's economy as actual productivity in the fields and factories.

Waikiki Wedding foregrounds how Hawai'i's transition to a tourism-based industry was the latest shift in the white oligarchy's economic exploitation of the islands' various resources. "From early fur, sandalwood, and whale trade, to sugar and pineapple and then tourism," writes Rohrer, "*haoles* pursued profit with a vengeance."[68] As the Depression called into question the economic stability of some agricultural commodities, tourism instead became the latest commodity—a much more plentiful, even *boundless*, one—for local businesses to exploit as land-based resources were limited. Imada notes how even during such dire economic times, the tourism industry "spent $100,000 on a 'comprehensive campaign' to 'tell the world of Hawaii.'"[69] Desmond adds:

> The stock market crash of 1929 did not put an end to elite tourism in Hawai'i. Ironically, it ushered in a period of massive growth following on the successes of the 1920s, during which

Figure 1.5. In *Waikiki Wedding* (1937), a graphic match dissolve from a line of drummers at a Native Hawaiian wedding ceremony . . .

Figure 1.6. . . . to a line of pineapple factory workers demonstrates the film's attempts at depicting Hawai'i not as a mythical "South Seas" paradise but as a modern site of commercial progress and industry. At the same time, this cut also unintentionally depicts the evolving ways in which the islands and the people were exploited by outside interests for the equally lucrative commodities of both agriculture and cinematic spectacle.

tourist visits had nearly tripled, adding roughly $75 million to the Hawaiian economy for that decade.[70]

As Hawai'i was still perceived as a playground for rich in the prewar days of luxury cruise ship travel, such an ad campaign was not as counterintuitive as it might have first appeared (while the economic impossibility of island travel for most other Americans then may have further intensified its radio and cinematic appeal). Overall, the severe economic situation forced many of the industrialists on the islands to rethink their focus. Pineapple tycoon James Dole, who was himself long an opponent of a tourism industry he felt did not benefit his personal economic interests, "found himself short of funds in the depression of the late twenties and early thirties, and in 1932 the sugar agencies took control of Hawaiian pineapple."[71]

As a story about a failed pineapple-industry-funded public relations campaign, *Waikiki Wedding* reflects these shifting priorities. In some ways, pineapple was especially a victim of its own successful advertising campaign from the previous decades. Prior to the Depression, the Hawaiian pineapple industry successfully sold their canned pineapple to mainland consumers as the "king of fruits," but one which "had now been democratized for the first time."[72] In other words, the produce was represented as a small indulgence for working-class families to enjoy at the end of a hard day's work. (After the war, pineapple companies returned to this same pitch. As a 1962 commercial for Dole Pineapple entitled "Pineapple Country" stated, "Once so rare it was the Fruit of Kings, today pineapple travels throughout the world, and is known as the King of Fruits.") Hollywood played a role in this perceived luxury as well: by the 1930s, as Fran Beauman noted, "the pineapple was soon exposed to a new kind of royalty happy to bestow favour on it: Hollywood movie

Figure 1.7. *Waikiki Wedding* (1937) focuses not only on the islands' hugely lucrative pineapple industry, but also on the ways in which its aggressive promotional campaigns and the larger marketing strategies of Hawaiian tourism overlapped in significant ways.

stars. The pineapple companies made certain to enlist them without delay so that the fruit might bask in the reflected glamour of the early movie business."[73] However, once the Depression hit Americans in the early 1930s, pineapple became one of those modest financial indulgences that struggling families decided they could live without.

Added to those challenges were new laws regarding US agricultural production. In 1934, Congress passed the Jones-Costigan Act. This established "quotas for each sugar-producing area in the American national market," writes Daws. "The effect was to raise the share of the market open to mainland producers at the expense of 'offshore' and foreign producers. Hawai'i lost between 8 and 10 percent of its previous market, and to add insult to injury the islands were classified with Puerto Rico and the Philippines as 'foreign' places where future cuts in the quotas might be made if necessary."[74] In a territory with no direct representation in Washington, DC, Hawaiian businesses were generally powerless to actively change such circumstances. Thus, this new economic and political situation in Hawai'i had two key, interlocking, consequences by the 1930s: the push toward a tourist-based economy, and the first aggressive push toward the possibility of statehood and self-representation. Both goals were united by a common messaging strategy that, moreover, was also motivated in no small part by blunting the negative public relations impact from the Massie tragedy.

Front and center in this campaign to rebrand the islands' economy and its branding was the Hawaii Tourist Bureau, effectively the territory's de facto public relations agency. Rooted in a turbulent period of political, racial, and economic instability, the aggressive push in the early 1930s to promote Hawai'i as a premiere tourist destination also coincided, as Desmond notes, with larger trends in the "concomitant growth in the advertising industry and mass media, both of which expanded in the 1930s and helped spread the destination image of Hawai'i and images of hula dancers as never before."[75] Although the HTB had been around in different forms during the preceding decades, 1933 and 1934 in particular saw the bureau, according to its own records, embark "on an ambitious program of advertising and publicity for Hawaii."[76] The bureau worked closely with the Bowman-Deute-Cummings advertising agency in San Francisco (a group that also featured Matson as one of its prime clients) to circulate its messages directly on the mainland. A crucial figure for this project was one of the ad agency's senior partners, Sydney Bowman, who began by "working from San Francisco with funds supplied by the Matson Line, the Hawaiian Sugar Planters' Association and the Hawaii

Tourist Bureau, [where he] inaugurated advertising campaigns in mainland magazines and newspapers with photographs and copy that were irresistible."[77] Much like Robert Young's character in *The Black Camel* or, to some degree, Crosby's public relations idea man in *Waikiki Wedding*, Bowman was one of those who came to the islands in the 1930s with a plan "to sell Hawaii to the mainland and island monopoly to Hawaii."[78] In 1960, noted journalist H. Allen Smith wrote that "if anybody put Hawaii on the map it was Sydney."[79] He helped establish the Pan-Pacific Bureau, an organization as important as the Hawaii Tourist Bureau itself, helping the latter to consistently and discretely find ways to plant the images and sounds of Hawai'i in a variety of media platforms. As Christine Skwiot notes, the Pan-Pacific Bureau's role was to "coordinate the simultaneous appearance in mainland papers and journals of HTB ads, and the stories, features, and editorials it produced."[80] Bowman accomplished this in part by purchasing extensive advertising space in various publications as a way of encouraging the editors and writers to use the material he would send them. When this strategy eventually wore out its welcome, he began to invite journalists, photographers, cartoonists, and so on, out to personally visit and report on Hawai'i directly, all expenses paid—"the only condition was that they write about Hawaii for their publication."[81] All of them took the same Matson cruise ships, stayed at the same resorts (the Royal Hawaiian or the Moana), and visited all the same tourist spots. As a result, mainland journalists constructed a picture of Hawai'i as "truly the tourist's paradise, that it was thoroughly American, loyal, progressive, worthy of statehood."[82]

In close coordination with Bowman-Deute-Cummings and the Pan-Pacific Bureau, the HTB's presence on the mainland took several forms: exhibits at fairs and centennials; radio programs (most especially, *Hawaii Calls*); their own promotional line of lantern slides and motion pictures, which were widely circulated in numerous theatrical and non-theatrical venues; and, most ubiquitously, print media, which included buying their own advertising space, producing their own literature, and influencing others' various newspaper and magazine coverage. While the cinema was a very powerful medium that the bureau successfully used both directly and indirectly to sell its message, the HTB largely relied during this time on the far more ubiquitous mass media of print and radio. Regardless of the medium, the bureau's message was consistently the same: "selling romance," writes Brown, "not repeating facts."[83] More specifically, the HTB's advertising campaign in the 1930s stressed the ideas of "Hawai'i's romantic history, commercial development, [and] cultural advancement"[84]—consistent with the bureau's larger strategy of balancing the premodern natural beauty with the technological and economic advantages of also being a modern twentieth-century metropolis.

Most Americans during this time would have been most familiar with the HTB's print media coverage. In the 1930s, the bureau produced its own bimonthly *Hawaii* magazine and *Story of Hawaii* booklet, for which 3,716 copies were initially produced.[85] A 1943 article in the *Journal of Marketing* reported that the HTB was one of the leading advertisers among all trade organizations in the entire United States, having spent an average of $49,182 a year on magazine advertisements over the previous

Figure 1.8. A 1942 guide to the islands, *Hawaii USA*, was one of countless examples of promotional print media that the Hawaii Tourist Bureau produced for mainland audiences in the prewar period.

twenty-two years (the Association of Hawaiian Pineapple Canners, meanwhile, was reported in the same journal article to have spent an average of $191,763 over the span of a decade).[86] In 1931 alone, the HTB claimed to have spent over $160,000 on print advertising that reached a subscription base of over thirty-seven million readers (other companies, such as Matson, also assisted with some of the costs).[87] A few years later, the bureau boasted of an "aggressive . . . direct advertising campaign," involving "a majority of the twenty leading magazines that are carrying the Territory's story to nearly six million people of all classes."[88] Such publications included *Vogue, Fortune, Vanity Fair, Time, Travel, Saturday Evening Post, Harpers, Scribner's, Spur, House & Garden, Town & Country,* and *Forum & Century*. In the calendar year 1936, meanwhile, the bureau reported "a total printing of 8,442,915 full-page ads" at a cost of $80,000.[89]

The rhetorical strategy of this campaign was "the 'go now' theme: 'time to quit dreaming about a trip to Hawaii!' Thus the campaign [was] designed to close sales instead of merely planting the desire to visit."[90] Internally, there was debate within the bureau over how much to spend on advertising directly when, with the assistance of partners such as the Pan-Pacific Bureau, they were often able to influence free coverage of the islands in other ways. The bureau claimed in 1936 to have sent 2,584 photographs to publications and agencies, while "some 1,500 newspapers were regularly supplied with an interesting newsletter."[91] Two years later, they sent "news releases to editors of 1,600 leading mainland newspapers, and articles to editors of leading magazines, but most of it resulted in taking, developing, printing and distributing 4,458 photographs. For instance, 31 newspapers used full-page spreads of these photos . . . solely because of the excellent pictures and keen reader interest in Hawaii."[92] The bureau also featured print advertising directly on the cruise ships themselves (a strategy that was directly, if gently, mocked in *Honolulu*).

Another ubiquitous and arguably more powerful medium for the HTB to reach mainland audiences was radio: as direct in its reach into the domestic sphere as print, it was the most intensely intimate and deeply affective medium possible at the time. The bureau's greatest public relations accomplishment was the decades' long success of the *Hawaii Calls* radio program (which also migrated later, with less success, to the newer medium of television in the postwar period). Supported financially, creatively, and promotionally by the bureau, the program was produced by local Honolulu CBS network affiliate station KGMB-AM. (Ironically, the same radio signal that broadcasted out *Hawaii Calls* episodes in the 1930s would be used by Japanese fighter planes to help locate Honolulu during the attack in December 1941.) The show was the brainchild of its host, Webley Edwards, who wanted to promote what he saw as a more authentic Hawaiian sound than what was emerging at the time from the mainland music industry and the Hollywood studio system. In addition to helping to fund the program, the bureau itself actively promoted the show with travel agencies across the US as part of their monthly newsletters.[93] Bowman helped push for the production of *Hawaii Calls* and a similar radio program entitled *The Voice of Hawaii*. Scripts for both radio programs were "written in Bowman's Honolulu office and carefully avoided the pattern of commercial broadcasts, stress[ed] Hawaii's pleasant surroundings and American atmosphere, mingled with charming Hawaiian customs."[94]

Often performed in the Banyan Courtyard of the Moana Hotel, *Hawaii Calls* was an effective demonstration of how the HTB and its partners in the field of tourism were able to coordinate and craft a specific kind of inviting Hawaiian experience and effectively transmit it to a wide and diverse audience across thousands of miles in an age where truly *mass* forms of audio and visual communication were still in their infancy. One radio listener in Ohio wrote their local radio station in 1936 to state, "I want to compliment the Columbia Broadcasting System for presenting *Hawaii Calls* on Monday evenings. This is the most outstanding presentation on the air and I should like very much if it could be permanently continued."[95] A remarkable PR achievement, it sold a certain idea of "Hawaii" to millions over time without necessarily sounding like the blatant sales pitch it was. A series of performances in front of a live audience, and accompanied by (as Edwards reminded listeners every time) "the sound of the waves on the beach at Waikiki," *Hawaii Calls* showcased both the music of mainland musicians such as Owens and a great many local talents, giving the program a greater sense of relative authenticity than "Hawaiian" content being produced in the soundstages of Hollywood during this same time. The phenomenal longevity of *Hawaii Calls* over several decades highlighted how

> Hawaii was well served by radio. Ordinary people of the 1920's and 30's were exposed for the first time to the sounds of the world's faraway places (like Hawaii) and they liked it. The programs they heard from paradise typically included lovely Hawaiian music, the haunting native language being spoken, and lots of evocative descriptions of the many beauties of the islands.[96]

In 1936, Hawai'i's territorial governor, Joseph Poindexter, wrote to the Tourist Bureau to thank them for their successful program, noting, "I've heard many favorable comments during my stay on the mainland, concerning the weekly radio programs originating from here and rebroadcast in California. These appear to me to be an effective method of bringing Hawaii to the attention of great audiences and arousing interest concerning the Islands."[97] In 1938, the radio program was loosely adapted into a film musical about two young American stowaways (one of whom was played by prominent child star Bobby Breen) who travel to the islands and become involved in attempts to steal sensitive Navy documents. Originally called *Stowaways in Paradise*,[98] the film version included music from the show and later changed its title in order to capitalize on the program's popularity. Although only a modest commercial success,[99] the adaptation was one of the few movies at the time to be somewhat well received by at least some Hawaiian critics as relatively authentic,[100] in part because of the original radio program's perception as being a more positive and closely linked depiction of the islands. The film version, however, heavily deemphasized the diversity of the radio program's cast in favor of a more conventional Hollywood story of white kids in peril.

To maximize the general success of its radio presence (in 1938, the bureau claimed to have produced sixty-six programs in the previous few years[101]), the HTB actively produced its own phonographic records of several popular Hawaiian programs with the express purpose of broadcasting them on local stations on the mainland, a "supplementary activity of the Bureau's publicity campaign . . . designed to take fullest advantage of Hawaii's popularity as radio program material."[102] *Variety* reported in 1937 that the agency was

> actively engaged in its endeavor to raise $25,000 for its radio broadcasting activities over the three coast-to-coast mainland networks—NBC, CBS and Mutual—during the next two years. The last appropriation of $25,000 expired last May and the transoceanic broadcasts, extolling the beauties of the mid-Pacific isles, which are presented under the auspices of the Hawaii Tourist Bureau, have been off the air since that time.[103]

The HTB also coordinated with other island businesses to help sell their notion of paradise. "The Hawaiian Pineapple Company [later changed to Dole Pineapple in 1960] was in contact with NBC as early as 1927 to discuss different ideas for programs to help with advertisement and promotion.[104] The network responded in kind: "A very appropriate and popular [Hawaiian Pineapple–sponsored] program," one executive wrote in an interoffice memo, "could be produced in New York under the direction of Raymond Scudder who has written such NBC productions as 'South Sea Islanders' and 'East of Cairo.' Scudder was born in Japan, 'brought up' in Hawaii and lived there fifteen years. His aim is to build some special programs for your company using Hawaiian and Polynesian legends."[105] And these mainland broadcasts encouraged their listeners to write the islands for more information on Hawai'i (correspondence that one way or another would've ended up in the bureau's offices for a reply).[106]

During the 1930s, the bureau also helped with exhibits at such national and international showcases as the Century of Progress International Exhibition in Chicago (1933), the Texas Centennial Exposition in Dallas (1936), the California-Pacific International Exposition in San Diego (1936), the Golden Jubilee in Vancouver (1936), and the Gold Gate Exposition in San Francisco (1939). The bureau even proposed a publicity stunt involving a Zeppelin airship departing the Chicago fair, where they were prominently displayed, for a trip to Hawai'i, and then return "with a Hawaiian delegation aboard."[107] The San Francisco exhibit was the premiere site for one of the bureau's numerous self-produced promotional films, *Hawaii, USA* (1939), which was a collaboration with Paramount Pictures. The response, reported one author at the time, was so strong that "Paramount was encouraged to make two feature shorts from the movie for distribution in 7,500 theatres throughout the country. . . . [The movie] was shown again at the San Francisco fair in 1940."[108] Additionally, the bureau spent $4,000 on its own 16-mm and 35-mm prints for distribution in clubs and other mainland organizations in 1940.[109] *Hawaii USA* was accompanied by a lavish color booklet of the same name circulated by the bureau throughout the US in the early 1940s, and which—just like their films of the time—largely ignored the local population in favor of natural attributes such as flowers, waters, volcanoes, trees, and pineapples, and promoted its ancient legends and mythical histories at the expense of the territory's emergent modernity, which received only a passing notice. The latter is evoked ("fine medical facilities . . . all the public utilities, an unexcelled water supply, radio and telephone communication between the islands . . . *a Paradise streamlined*"[110]) only in so far as it might have alleviated the mainland tourist's concerns over Hawai'i being perceived as too exotic, too dangerous, too remote, for a novice explorer. "The mythical Pacific remained an ideal to be met beyond the frontier's known horizon," writes Geiger, "while

Hawai'i was a safe travel option occupying the realms of tourism and international trade."[111]

Hawaii USA was only one of the more visible of the numerous short promotional films and movie lantern slides that the bureau itself produced from the 1930s and on through the 1950s. In addition to assisting Hollywood cameramen, travelogue producers, and newsreel photographers with finding ideal shots to be used as general stock footage,[112] and discovering local citizens to work as models for the crews,[113] the HTB also "began to produce its own films in the 1930s," writes Desmond, "both to build upon and counter some of the mainland film images of Hawaii."[114] The HTB invested lavishly in both sound and color productions—two expensive and thus rare cinematic luxuries of the time. At the height of its film influence in the mid- to late 1930s, bureau movies were "distributed through the [20th Century] Fox [theatrical] circuit of over 8,000 of the best motion picture theatres of America," in addition to "one complete set for principal steamers [cruise ships], and for strategic centers around the country."[115] Fox agreed to have the films screened in its noncommercial slots at a reduced rate. Because the movies were clearly seen as promotion, which lacked the technical polish of more professional productions, the bureau noted, "we have been able to obtain only a nominal purchase price for these movies, but distribution is far more important than price, and the distribution we are obtaining is of the very best. It will bring all the Islands in their brightest garb before millions of people."[116]

Meanwhile, the bureau felt its "most effective form of promotion instituted during the year [1936] for all the islands was placing [complete five-reel] sets of the Tourist Bureau's new colored motion pictures on all principal passenger steamers coming to Hawaii."[117] The aggressive push was comprised of eighteen ships total (some of which, however, did not travel directly to Honolulu due to the US' protectionist maritime laws). According to bureau records, several Pacific-crossing companies such as the Canadian Pacific Steamship Company, the Union Steam Ship Company, Dollar Steamship Company, and the Yokohama Dock Company also obtained copies of the prints, in addition to Matson.[118] The bureau proclaimed that "these prints won immediate acclaim from local residents and visitors who saw them en route" to the islands.[119] In 1936, Governor Poindexter wrote to George Armitage, the executive secretary of the bureau, to congratulate the organization on this development, and to highlight that "the pictures of island scenery shown on the [Matson's SS] Lurline coming down served as a pleasing introduction to the islands. This is a feature of the Bureau's advertising program that should be continued, and extended, in my opinion."[120]

Figure 1.9. *The Island of Hawaii* (1930) was part of a series of short subject films that the Hawaii Tourist Bureau produced to promote island travel in the 1930s. One of the earliest instances of color footage shot on the islands, these movies were shown to prospective visitors on the mainland as well as to those staying in Honolulu, as a way to encourage additional travel to the other islands of Hawai'i.

During the 1930s, the bureau also exhibited its movies to various audiences on the islands themselves—often in their own screening rooms at the bureau office in Honolulu's Dillingham Building and at the Outrigger Pavilion (which hosted over one thousand spectators for a screening in 1931[121]), or at more public venues such as the Pawaa Theatre, where for a time a HTB film was screened every Monday afternoon,[122] and the Princess Theatre. The latter, in June of 1935, hosted over 1,300 people attending a screening of several of HTB's short films about the islands of Hawai'i.[123] While one purpose behind the screenings on both cruise ships and in local venues was to encourage inter-island travel beyond O'ahu, they also were usually screened for tourists and other regular Pacific travelers with at least one eye on being shown back to those living on the mainland. As early as 1931, the bureau boasted that its "motion picture films were in constant use. Many local people going to the mainland used them for lecturing, or in connection with tour promotion programs. Several thousand feet of excellent all-color, all-sound motion pictures . . . shown in leading theaters throughout the world."[124]

In 1933 and 1934, the bureau committed roughly $20,000 (or nearly half of its "Indirect Advertising" budget) solely to the production and distribution of new films.[125] One such film was *Song of the Islands* (1934), produced eight years prior to the more well-known 1942 Betty Grable Hollywood spectacle of the same name. According to *Variety* in 1941, "Song of the Islands" had been a working title that 20th Century Fox often used for convenience sake with upcoming South Seas–related projects.[126]) In the twenty-minute film, writes Imada,

> white American tourists bid a bittersweet good-bye to Honolulu after a stay in the islands. Draped in long carnation leis on a steamship deck, they are serenaded by a group of strolling Hawaiian musicians. Shown in Fox movie theatres in the United States, such films necessarily obscured the social and political relations that enabled this leisurely experience.[127]

A few years earlier, the bureau produced a series of four ten-minute films about each of the major islands: *The Island of Oahu* (1930), *The Island of Hawaii* (1930), *The Island of Maui* (1930), and *The Island of Kauai* (1930), the first color (Vericolor) and sound films ever made about Hawai'i. Filmed by Hollywood-based Brown-Nagel Productions (who also produced their own Hawai'i-focused travelogues[128]), these promotional films offered individual overviews for each of several major Hawaiian islands. James Mak has noted that one important motivation for a series that highlighted appeals of each of the different islands was that the HTB and its local partners were worried that too much tourist attention was being paid exclusively to O'ahu at the expensive of the others.[129] This was a centerpiece of the "See Every Island" campaign,[130] which was at the time, the bureau boasted, "the most ambitious program of motion picture coverage ever undertaken for the Territory," with "a professional release to class 'A' pictures in all parts of the world."[131] The films themselves were rather simple affairs whose goal was "visualizing the scenic assets of the Islands"[132] (later that decade, the bureau helped promote a radio program called "*Hear* Every Island," as a continuation of that theme).

The films emphasized the juxtaposition of the islands' natural beauty with the emergence of a modernized Hawai'i, which fit the bureau's focus on harmonizing the uniqueness of its exotic appeal with the economic reassurances of a society fully immersed in the various advances of the twentieth century. This contradiction fit what the HTB described in *Hawaii U.S.A.* (1942) as the territory's "paradox of an ancient history still modern."[133] For example, *The Island of Oahu* repeatedly foregrounds the coexistence of the two, such as when the narrator draws the audience's attention to Honolulu as a bustling metropolis, with a "background of primitive beauty," one where "beautiful palms blend harmoniously with modern business structures." The travelogue emphasizes the main paved roads throughout the island that tourists can explore, but also ones that were "free of billboards" that might otherwise ruin the type of eyesore experiences drivers encountered back on the mainland. One sequence emphasizes how the modern processes of canning will help preserve one of the island's most sought after natural commodities, the pineapple. Perhaps nowhere is this harmonious contrast between the natural and the modern more uniquely realized than in the film's prolonged focus on the aquatic inhabitants of the Honolulu Aquarium (now called the Waikiki Aquarium), which was one of the first of its kind in the entire United States.

Like the film itself, the aquarium utilized the latest in modern technology to capture a part of Hawai'i's natural beauty and put it safely on display for the tourist. Neither the film nor the aquarium required the tourist to brave the dangerous elements of the ocean in order to achieve such a view. In contrast, the most distinctive aspect of this early bureau film is that it is devoid of almost any reference to the local Hawaiian population, and no mention of the kind of luaus or hula performances that later came to so dominate such touristic representations of the islands. Surfing is referred to by the narrator as the "sport of kings" over an image of surfers on the waves of Waikiki. A line of "serenaders" is framed distantly in a very long shot, walking across the lawn of the Royal Hawaiian Hotel as they "sing songs of Old Hawaii," which thus serves as a "fitting end to the day." A year later, the bureau had a new, longer two-reel version cut together featuring footage of all the islands "for occasional loan to local residents touring and lecturing on the mainland"[134] (their many films often reused some of the same footage for economy's sake). Their films, according to a 1938 letter to the territorial governor, were shown "at several very popular programs in Honolulu, and continuously on trans-Pacific steamers at least once each trip; also on a long promotional tour made by [Bureau] Executive Secretary, George T. Armitage, the most effective instance being one of the National Geographic Society's popular fall programs in Constitution Hall, Washington, D.C., December 3 [1937], with over 4,000 present."[135]

Turning its attention away from tourism during WWII, the HTB then changed its name to the Hawaii *Visitors* Bureau after WWII and returned to producing its own promotional films. Its first major postwar film was *Hawaii Today* (1948). The HTB spent over $7,000 on twenty new prints of the movie, along with twenty prints of a newer, untitled twenty-minute travel movie, and ten prints of a ten-minute movie that emphasized Hawai'i's culture of sports, hunting, and fishing.[136] Later films included *Hawaiian Holiday* (1951), *Waikiki, Gateway to Hawaii* (1958), and *The Enchanted Islands of Hawaii* (1958)—the last two featuring voice-over narration by *Hawaii Calls* host Edwards (who would also later narrate the HVB's *Hawaii, Never Easier to Sell* in 1961). It spent approximately $8,000 on one dozen color prints and two dozen B&W prints of both *Waikiki, Gateway* and *Enchanted Islands*, with the goal of being "distributed by a major film service to television stations with an approximate audience of 6,000,000."[137] In 1950, the bureau even discussed the possibility of working with legendary documentary filmmaker Robert J. Flaherty (*Nanook of the North*, *Moana*) on a Hawaiian-themed project, probably for the newer medium of television, claiming, "There is a large national firm somewhat interested in sponsoring the film."[138] However, it is unclear how far negotiations on the idea ever progressed, and Flaherty himself passed away nearly a year later.

Since television was first and foremost an advertising-driven medium, just as radio, newspapers, and magazines were, the newer domestic technology in the postwar era proved to be easier for the Visitors Bureau to influence directly than the movies had been. Promotion and sponsorship for such programs as *Harry Owens and His Royal Hawaiians* (1949–1958) and a 1960s syndicated television version of *Hawaii Calls* were only the beginning. The bureau bought extensive advertisement airtime on such high-profile national TV programs as NBC's *Today* show.[139] During this time, the bureau also collaborated with renowned photojournalist Ozzie Sweet and prominent radio and television celebrity Arthur Godfrey on color and B&W film footage that was to "be used on two hours of [Godfrey's] first TV programs in the Fall."[140] Sweet wrote to the HVB himself to inform them that "eight thousand feet of Hawaiian film had been 'edited at last—well worth all the time and hard work we put into the production.'"[141] In 1951, the bureau assisted Franklin Productions on a series of thirteen television shorts, "each of a full half-hour, portraying the real legends and beauty of the islands."[142] The following year it also worked closely with producer Carl Dudley on a location shoot for a TV project called *International Detective*.[143] Meanwhile, many of the HVB's own films—such as *Hawaii Today* and *Hawaiian Holiday*—also found a second life in distribution on the new domestic visual medium.

Meanwhile, as other related companies in the agricultural and transportation industries began to produce their own Hawai'i-related promotional films, the HVB kept a record of the available titles for when the territorial governor's office would "receive requests for films from people on the mainland," adding that "many of the other films listed here are available in regional cities."[144] A 1952 bureau list of then-current and available 16-mm prints included short-subject films on the islands from such companies as the Hawaiian Pineapple Company, the Hawaiian Sugar Planters' Association, United Air Lines, Standard Oil Company, Northwest Airlines, Pan American World Airways, American President Lines, and the Haserot Company.[145] Meanwhile, the bureau's San Francisco office maintained a collection of six Hawai'i-themed films in the early 1950s, and claimed that they'd been shown 146 times during 1954 at a variety of locations throughout the mainland and Canada.[146]

Pre-statehood, the bureau's actual direct influence on high-profile Hollywood films is harder to trace (for example, HTB's director Armitage traveled on the same Matson cruise ship as film producer Samuel Goldwyn in 1938, the year the latter's MGM Studios began production on *Honolulu*,[147] a film in part about traveling on a Matson ship to the islands). This may be in part because location shooting on the islands did not start to become popular until the late 1950s (by 1958, they claimed to have "worked with several movie and television shooting units on location in Hawaii,"[148] such as *South Pacific* and *The Old Man and the Sea*). Back in 1931, the Tourist Bureau took credit for "inducing [20th Century] Fox [Studios] to come with a company to film *The Black Camel*" on location in Honolulu.[149] After learning that 20th Century Fox had acquired the film rights to the Earl Derr Biggers novel of the same name, the bureau sent a cablegram to the studio, writing that "inasmuch [as the] entire setting is Hawaii we strongly urge you to give careful consideration shooting picture here with authentic setting."[150] Cast and crew of the film left Los Angeles on March 28, 1931, on the SS *City of Los Angeles* (operated by LASSCO, which by then had merged with Matson). Gordon Ghareeb and Martin Cox noted the humorous coincidence that two of the stars from *Dracula* (1931), which had previously featured particularly horrifying events that occurred while sailing across the ocean, were also along for the trip—Bela Lugosi and Dwight Fry. "The fact that the 'Count' and 'Renfield' were both on board the liner," they wrote, "filled the crossing with anticipation and awe."[151] The production stayed for a little over a week of filming in and around the Royal Hawaiian Hotel, but by April 17, they'd returned to Southern California—"to be met by the press and photographers eager for the latest scoop on the filming."[152]

Despite featuring a generally formulaic and forgettable Charlie Chan murder mystery narrative involving the murder of a movie star while shooting a movie on Oʻahu, *The Black Camel* is highly distinctive among early Hawaiʻi-set Hollywood films for at least two reasons—for one, it was one of the first studio films shot in part on location in Hawaiʻi, utilizing not only the local beaches as a setting but also the Royal Hawaiian Hotel. While Hollywood crews regularly visited Hawaiʻi throughout the time for background footage of the islands (where they often were assisted by representatives of the bureau), it was rare for significant portions of scenes to be shot there. (Two years later, Weber and her crew would shoot *White Heat* [1935] on Kauai.[153]) Second, *The Black Camel* is also significant as one of the first feature-length *sound* films to be set on the islands—made during a time when many movie theaters back on the mainland US still weren't even equipped for sound projection yet (the delicacy of sound film recording is on full display in the narrative's opening moments, which features a fictional Hollywood crew within the diegetic space attempting to film an oceanside scene with the distracted movie star). With such heavy media saturation across the mainland by organizations such as the Hawaii Tourist Bureau, it is easier to see why slightly more self-aware Hollywood films set in Hawaiʻi, such as *The Black Camel* (in part a movie about movies), might begin to emerge from the prewar studio system.

"I Was Promised Three Romantic Weeks in Hawaiʻi . . ."

Also with the emergence of sound film technology came the popularity of the newly forming musical genre. Many of the most prominent Hawaiian-themed films during this time were also musicals: *Waikiki Wedding, Hawaii Calls, Honolulu, Moonlight in Hawaii, Flirtation Walk* (1934), *Hawaiian Nights, It's a Date,* and *Song of the Islands.* Musicals, adds Brown, "were perfect for the island treatment since they relied on song and romance, both of which Hawaii offered in abundance."[154] One prominent early subgenre of the Hollywood musical was the inherently reflexive "backstage" version, which involved "behind the scenes" narratives, according to Rick Altman, "primarily concerned with putting on a show" within the story logic of the film (diegetic characters performing for a diegetic audience, as well as for the movie's own audience in theaters).[155] Most of these feature at least one sequence of characters explicitly performing for a diegetic audience—while even nonmusicals, such as *Bird of Paradise*, often feature prominent hula musical numbers. The backstage cycle, according to Altman, thrives in part as a reaction against the increasing skepticism of audiences well versed in genre clichés:

> [They] begin each film by recognizing the outdated, reductive, unreal nature of the genre's syntax, thus lulling the spectator's critical faculties to sleep; then use the rest of the film to demonstrate the extent to which that seemingly outmoded syntax is not so devoid of sense after all . . . identifying their plot material, characters and resolutions as banal and stereotyped—but only in order to eventually restore meaning to the very atmosphere that seems devoid of it.[156]

While this "sham distancing device,"[157] as he terms such self-awareness, refers to the backstage musical, the concept also works as an apt descriptor of many Hollywood films about the islands during the 1930s—musical or otherwise—where an initial narrative acknowledgment of the touristic experience's "outdated, reductive, unreal nature," along with the attendant dramatic elements of anticipation and disappointment, serves a similar critical distancing effect. And, in some of these films, elements of the backstage musical overlap with Dean MacCannell's notion of the "back region"[158] of tourist sites—spaces constructed to take their respective audiences "behind the scenes" and create the impression of being somehow more "authentic" than those experiences that are explicitly presented as on a literal or figurative stage.

Citing the same contemporary review of *Waikiki Wedding*, both Okihiro and Desmond imply respectively that at best the critics were more aware of these tropical clichés than the film itself was: "reviews in the islands were even more acidic, the *Honolulu Advertiser* pronouncing it 'the purest hokum,' a 'pseudo-Hawaiian narrative.'"[159] (Owens too admitted that local critics were not kind to *Waikiki Wedding*, though he only noted how they—like he—were upset that the film's slapstick comic relief, a pig named "Walford," had ruined the scene showcasing his "Sweet Leilani."[160]) Meanwhile, Schmitt dismisses *Waikiki Wedding*'s production values, noting that "although a Hollywood crew came to Hawai'i to film background and atmosphere shots, island audiences were unable to detect any in the final print," and "in a typical Hollywood gesture, a California beach doubles for Hawai'i."[161] Brown observes that Crosby's character "spirits Shirley away to an old-timey native village,"[162] while Bailey and Farber add that *Waikiki Wedding*'s "image [of the islands] was pure Hollywood."[163]

While such criticism has merit, it also undersells the extent to which many movies about Hawai'i worked through a more self-aware touristic lens. The very first scene of *The Black Camel* is of film starlet Shelah Fane (Dorothy Revier) shooting a movie sequence on location at a local beach—immediately announcing the artifice of Hawai'i's highly mediated tropical image. Performing for the Hollywood crew and its cameras, her character's interaction with a "native" Hawaiian distances its audience from the conventions of the South Seas romance. Meanwhile, in the same scene, local *haole* businessman Jimmy Bradshaw (Robert Young) calls himself the "publicity director of the whole island and the rotary club and the chamber of commerce and everything." He attempts to woo his would-be love interest with the pitch: "Take a moment to enjoy the palms of paradise!" She cynically replies as she storms away, "*Save that gag for the tourists!*" He insists, however, "I'm sick of the tourists. *I want to sell Honolulu to you!*" Later, the film's hero, Chan (Warner Olan), himself notes that "Hollywood is famous furnisher of mysteries"—acknowledging the audience's awareness of the studios' reputation for fantastical storytelling.

Likewise, the comedy musical *Honolulu* starts out as a movie-within-a-movie as well (although that particular sequence is not set in Hawai'i, it reinforces a similar commentary on the artifices of Hollywood's cinematic fantasies). In the latter film, Hollywood star Brooks Mason (Young again) attempts to flee his obsessive fan base by switching places with a pineapple plantation owner who just happens to look exactly like him (played by Young as well). When he first meets his would-be love interest (Eleanor Powell) on the Matson cruise ship to the islands, Mason attempts to use Hawai'i's romantic reputation to woo her. However, having never visited there, he must fake firsthand knowledge of the islands in order to fool her. At first, Mason uses vague and evasive descriptions such as "it's really so beautiful that I can't describe it," or "it's the most beautiful place you ever saw." When pushed by her to describe Hawai'i in more detail, Mason nervously looks around, finally spotting a tourism promotion poster hiding over her shoulder. Ever the accomplished performer, the movie star has found his script, and begins reading the advertising copy verbatim:

> Uh, tell you about it? Well, uh . . . (sees poster) there's "sunny days. Romantic nights. Where gentle breezes sway the spreading

Figure 1.10. In *Honolulu* (1939), a famous movie star (Robert Young) tries to impress a woman (Eleanor Powell) while traveling on a cruise ship to the islands. He pretends to be intimately familiar with the islands by . . .

Figure 1.11. . . . seductively reading the romantic copy off a promotional poster hiding over her shoulder—an instance of an actor simply following the (touristic) script.

palms against the sky of softest blue." (pauses to look again) The, um, "fragrance of the night—the rhythmic movement of the surf to excite the senses" . . . Where, uh, "the stars and moon gleam through vast pineapple patches. An ideal vacation. A romantic honeymoon."

Such an example of the "sham distancing" device overlaps here with a certain post-touristic irony. "Hawai'i" as it's come to be understood within contemporary popular culture is a space, *Honolulu* acknowledges, explicitly defined by the rhetoric of tourism, and the idea of an inherently romantic experience on the islands is a skeptical one that the film knows audiences have been sold relentlessly through media of all kinds. However, as Altman points out, the generic narrative goal of *Honolulu* remains, as with most other classical Hollywood films (regardless of tone or setting), the desire to reaffirm for commercial interests the deeper "truth" of still finding love in Hawai'i in spite of that—"eventually restor[ing] meaning to the very atmosphere that seems devoid of it."

Similarly, *Waikiki Wedding* is the story of a pineapple company employee, Tony Marvin, who specializes in genius public relations campaigns, only to find his latest idea backfire. After a Midwestern woman, Georgia Smith (Shirley Ross), wins his "Pineapple Girl" contest, she's flown out to Hawai'i, where she's promised "three romantic weeks in Hawai'i." But, as she points out to the pineapple executives, "I'm here and I'm not getting them." The problem for local business interests is twofold—her experiences directly challenge the romantic myth the islands are selling, but it also means her syndicated letters describing the disillusionment back home will be a major PR disaster for them. *Waikiki Wedding*'s prize contest highlighted the cinematic fantasy of a transition from such "elite" tourism to one that catered to the broader, more democratic, segment of middle- and working-class tourists.

Some reviews of the time, however, did mention the film's ironies. One noted that Georgia risked "destroy[ing] the illusions about the island of those back home."[164] Thus "it is up to Crosby," wrote a 1937 *San Francisco Examiner* review, "to 'sell' beautiful Shirley Ross on the fact that Honolulu is the most romantic spot in the world."[165] The first time Tony attempts to woo her, in one of the film's many "backstage" musical moments, he brings along a band and sings "Blue Hawaii" from outside her hotel room (only to mistakenly seduce Martha Raye's character instead as she listens inside). In order to provide Georgia with her promised "three romantic weeks in Hawai'i," Tony himself concocts an intricate

Figure 1.12. The phone line in the Native Hawaiian village in *Waikiki Wedding* (1937) is one of several ways in which the film attempts to show how Hawai'i is more modernized than popular media representations of the time often suggested. That it must be hidden from the tourist outsider (Georgia Smith) is not only a sight gag but also a reflection on the careful ways in which Hawai'i's elaborate tourist fantasy must be consistently maintained.

scheme involving his local Hawaiian friends to act out an elaborately fabricated exotic and primitive "adventure" not too far removed from many of the same clichés that *Bird of Paradise* perfected. The "erupting" volcano, for example, turns out to be an extravagant effects show put on by the Hawaiians off in the distance ("Tony wants more smoke!" says one). Meanwhile, the locals must conceal from Georgia the fact that they possess the same modern conveniences, such as phones and wrist watches, as most people do. One review added that Crosby's character "proceeds to make Waikiki glamorous for Miss Ross. . . . The climax comes when reality clashes with fantasy and Bing has to *produce a Waikiki which doesn't exist*. Being a resourceful press agent, he produces it."[166] Another felt that the film reached its comedic high point when Tony "is forced to extricate himself from an entirely synthetic Hawaii that he had himself created."[167]

A *Baltimore Sun* review, meanwhile, felt that "the idea behind the story is an excellent one and had it been presented as a straight company it would have scored heavily."[168]

Waikiki Wedding, writes Houston Wood, is a "romantic adventure that reenacts many of the moments previous films about Hawai'i had transformed into cliché. . . . What had previously been 'authentic' has now become a commercial performance directed by and for non-Natives."[169] However, Wood reads this twist on the tired South Seas formulas, and the tourism industry that in part helped create and perpetuate them, differently. The increasing reflexivity in a movie such as *Waikiki Wedding*, he argues, worked as an endorsement of the need for US intervention into Hawaiian culture and politics by suggesting that the local population was directionless and passive, and thus in need of guidance from outsiders in the form of Crosby's character. While *Waikiki Wedding* acknowledges the modernity of the Hawaiian population, their knowing complicity in Tony Marvin's extremely elaborate tourist "show" reinforces the stereotype of their desire to do little else but perform for the pleasure of white visitors, while also unquestioningly promoting the notion that tourism was the only available next step in Hawai'i's economic evolution as a postindustrial territory.

Paradise under Attack

Unavoidably, the highly stylized nature of the hula performance, the elaborate artifice of the Hawaiian dream vacation, the grinding clichés of the ubiquitous big band versions of Hawaiian music, and the waning genre cycle of the musical, would eventually plunge these tropical cinematic romances into pastiche by the end of the decade. By then, most Hawai'i-themed films were falling flat with critics and audiences, regardless of how self-aware they seemed to be. In a review of *Hawaiian Nights*, the *New York Times* remarked that "reports from the Coast are that Hollywood is in the grip of an economy wave, but we had no idea things had grown so bad that Universal would have to use the leftover straw from the hula skirts as plot material for its new musical comedy."[170] Meanwhile, *Moonlight in Hawaii*—a similarly reflexive film—was rejected by *Variety* in 1941 as "good talent goes sour in a tiresome musical."[171] Likewise, an exhibitor dismissed *Hawaii Calls* as "not as good as previous Bobby Breen pictures,"[172] while *Charlie Chan in Honolulu* had "No Draw."[173] Far from the more reflexive days of *The Black Camel* several years earlier, the title *Charlie Chan in Honolulu* was a transparent attempt at playing up

Hawai'i's appeal at a time when Chan's own popularity (to say nothing of the problematic racial politics) was also waning. Despite the title, the film isn't really even set in Hawai'i but instead on a freighter docked in Honolulu harbor as a result of the murder investigation (but the title is oddly redundant anyway, given that the character of Chan was already based out of Honolulu in the first place).

Shortly after the Japanese attack on Pearl Harbor, 20th Century Fox released the ill-timed big-budget Technicolor spectacle *Song of the Islands*. (*Waikiki Wedding* had originally been intended for Technicolor production several years earlier, specifically because of its tropical setting.[174]) A Betty Grable musical, the lighthearted film told the story of a land feud in Hawai'i between a plantation owner and a cattle baron. Although "footage of authentic tropical scenery and native hula dancers" was filmed on location in Hawai'i,[175] the film retains an otherworldly artifice in keeping with its mostly soundstage-shot footage and glossy genre production. With Grable assuming center stage as the hula girl of the show, with Owens and "His Royal Hawaiians" providing the music (as they had in *Hawaii Calls*, *Cocoanut Grove*, and *It's a Date*, as well as two short subjects), and with Hilo Hattie as the "buxome [sic] native maid,"[176] the movie comes across—intentionally or otherwise—as a last gasp parody of Hawaiian-themed films of the 1930s, an excessive pastiche of aloha musical, South Seas romance, tropical travelogue, and plantation drama.

Song of the Islands' irrelevance, in retrospect, highlighted not only the exhaustion of Hollywood's "current Hawaiian vogue" by the start of the 1940s but also stood in stark contrast to America's participation in the Second World War with its unfortunate debut four months (March 13th) after the Pearl Harbor attack—the first Hawaii-themed film to be released by Hollywood on the mainland after December 7th. Brown claims that the film "bore the misfortune of terrible timing. . . . No one wanted to be reminded of the Pacific when it seemed that all the news coming from there was scary, and the film did poorly."[177] WWII brought into even fuller relief the disconnect between touristic fantasy and geographical realities—between the mainland's image of paradise on the islands and the violent realities of a world at war right at a time when the Hawaiian craze had exhausted itself into clichés. Yet, while the film's performance may have been underwhelming, Grable's presence in *Song of the Islands*—(she, "in abbreviated Hawaiian attire, displays a particularly formful [sic] figure to hold interest of the male section," said one review[178])—suggests the extent to which the hula girl would go on to fit well within the wartime culture of the "pinup" model.

Despite the prevalence of ironic and reflexive Hawaiian-themed films in Hollywood during the 1930s, and the evidence that at least some embraced the artifice, there remains the issue that opened this chapter—how such idealized depictions of life in paradise, promoted as much by the likes of the Hawaii Tourist Bureau as by the Hollywood studio system, negatively affected soldiers' expectations about Hawai'i and the larger Pacific once they began to arrive on the islands in the wake of December 7th. Military personnel, write Bailey and Farber, expressed an "anger born not of suffering, but of disillusion and frustration. Part of the problem was that many of the men had believed the myth of Paradise. They'd seen the movies and they expected, as the Morale Services Section of the Central Pacific Base Command discovered, 'a hula girl under every palm tree.'"[179] They add: "Judging from the response of the wartime arrivals, a great many of them had taken the films at face value. 'I expected . . . hula girls running around,' said one soldier, 'And I expected to find grass huts here,' said another."[180] While at least some of this frustration could have been expressed with a knowing irony (meaning, some may have to some degree wanted to, but never really did, believe the myth in the first place), no doubt much of this irritation and resentment was legitimate—especially under the duress of combat.

There would seem to be at least three plausible explanations for this reaction—the most self-evident one, as Bailey and Farber noted, was that "those of less reflective temperament" could have been easily inclined to take the silver screen fantasy at face value. The other reasons, though, are just as worthwhile—for one, notes Lewis, the tourists before the war "expected song and dance in the hotel to reflect the image and ethos of islands they had been 'sold' by commercial interests—and that is what they got."[181] But the tourism industry that spent so many years and dollars promoting the myth of paradise was not waiting in Honolulu with hula girls and leis to greet the incoming hordes of soldiers with the same urgency and intensity as they had previously with the paying tourists (and easily persuadable journalists). Although representatives of the bureau played a modest role in supporting the war effort, the realities of global military conflict took center stage on the islands over the pleasures of leisure. Moreover, connected to that, was the inevitable nostalgia that overtook a country during war—the desire to imagine a return to a more "innocent" time before the engagement with Japan. Seen through this hazily retrospective lens, it becomes easier to imagine a Hawai'i that really *was* as carefree and laidback as some media in the 1930s sometimes claimed. The *New York Times*' review of *Song of the*

Islands suggested, "Twentieth Century-Fox is rediscovering the lisping innocence of a time when the world was young"[182]—a not-so-subtle reference to the events of December 7th. It was not only military targets in the territory of Hawai'i that were under attack during WWII—it was the Edenic myth of a simpler time in their own personal lives that many mainlanders (and soldiers) also wanted to hold on to, and that a prewar Hawai'i effectively symbolized for them after the fact. And, just as importantly, it would be this kind of nostalgia that would only intensify in the decades ahead—though one always in tension with other postwar and statehood-era developments.

2

Twilight of the Past, Island of Utopia

December 7th and the Contradictions of War Nostalgia

> The object of romantic nostalgia must be beyond the present space of experience, somewhere in *the twilight of the past, or on an island of utopia where time has happily stopped,* as on an antique clock.
>
> —Svetlana Boym, *The Future of Nostalgia*

Even before the Japanese aerial attack of December 7th put the US naval presence in Hawai'i squarely within the collective American imagination, Hollywood had been depicting the military as a major presence on the islands. Robert C. Schmitt noted that "movies about the armed forces [in Hawai'i] have been particularly popular, accounting for 33 titles between 1898 and 1959."[1] *In the Navy* (1941) was another entry into the popular series of Bud Abbott and Lou Costello comedies, following on the heels of the extremely popular *Buck Privates* (1941). Grouped with *Keep 'Em Flying* (1941), these military service comedies were intended in part to sell the idea of the 1940 peacetime draft, at a time when the US was quietly preparing for likely entry into World War II. Along with tourist narratives, Hollywood films about the islands most commonly focused on the military presence there, though in ways that elided the implied colonial occupation contexts therein. *In the Navy* was no different—managing to capture, retrospectively, the naïvely comical image of a tropical paradise unburdened by the specter of war, in spite of its military setting. The film tells the story of two enlisted men, Smokey (Abbott) and Pomeroy (Costello), stationed on the USS *Alabama* on its way from California to Honolulu. Upon arrival to the islands, they are greeted with such cinematic cliché as luau dinners and hula spectacles. More than other Hawai'i-themed films of its era, *In the Navy* explicitly perpetuated a warped utopic view of military life on the islands—the fantasy of an exotic heaven that was nowhere to be found once thousands of soldiers began arriving in the wake of the Pearl Harbor attack.

The military aspect was only one way in which *In The Navy* was typical of the kinds of movies Hollywood had long been making about Hawai'i. The film's primary plot, in an echo of Robert Young's movie star journey in *Honolulu* (1939), also concerns the attempts of a famous celebrity—in this case, popular singer Russ Raymond (Dick Powell)—to avoid his excessively adoring crowds of fans by fleeing to Hawai'i in yet another variation on the islands as playful site of escape for media stars. Having been fed up with the obsessive attention his celebrity drew, Raymond disguises himself as a regular enlistment man with the Navy's knowing assistance. The Alabama's voyage to the islands also echoes Hollywood's focus on the journey to Hawai'i being as narratively central as the destination itself, while Raymond's role as celebrity crooner plays up an element of the backstage musical genre influencing the comedy's hodgepodge of occasional music sequences. In many ways, the film was symbolic of an era that was soon to be romanticized in memory—which its military context eerily, if unintendedly, foreshadowed.

As Beth Bailey and David Farber succinctly put it, "it's hard not to begin with Pearl Harbor."[2] On December 7th, 1941, Japanese air forces attacked US naval installations in Pearl Harbor, Hickam Field, Schofield Barracks, and other strategic military sites throughout the island of O'ahu. The events were the catalyst for the United States' full immersion into the Second World War—a conflict already underway throughout Europe, Africa, and Asia. It needn't be belabored that December 7th fundamentally changed the mainland's relationship to Hawai'i in ways that the earlier discourses of touristic advertising and travel narratives did not. As *Tora!*

Tora! Tora! (1970) producer Elmo Williams put it, "Pearl Harbor was a milestone in everyone's life. People remember exactly what they were doing when they learned about the Japanese attack."[3] Instead of casting Hawai'i as a faraway exotic destination (one which, at the time, many Americans did not even know was a US territory), the events highlighted the role of the islands as a first line of defense, and thus very much a part of a nation suddenly under attack. And, increasingly over time, December 7th, the ensuing combat, and the nation's collective memory of both also added an important layer of emotional and material complexity to what had been up to that point a fairly one-dimensional, clichéd, and superficial touristic depiction of the islands—entangling the islands and war in ways that affectively complicated both. Orvar Lofgren notes how "discussions of tourism rarely mention the fact that masses of working-class men got their first experience of the exotic during the war, albeit in rather strange circumstances."[4] Norman Douglas and Ngaire Douglas add that "the effects of the war in the Pacific were paradoxical. Those parts of the region which experienced direct conflict underwent enormous culture shock and suffered massive social dislocation. . . . But there were opportunities to be seized and sometimes profits to be made."[5] Memories of WWII ultimately provided the subsequent postwar travel industry with a gravitas and focus lacking in the prewar tropical fantasies.

The same could be said for Hollywood going forward. WWII—and, in particular, Pearl Harbor—was the specter haunting all mass media representations of Hawai'i for the next few decades, both for the films and television shows set in the islands (regardless of whether they acknowledged that history) and for the generation of media audiences who had some personal connection (themselves, friends, family) through military service to the islands. And added to this were the still millions of other Americans stateside who watched countless hours of newsreels and war movies that brought that conflict to life. Indeed, that mediated memory—the *archival afterlife* of Pearl Harbor footage—would be as central to America's negotiation of the event's legacy, and its intensely nostalgic aftermath, as memories of the war itself. For those particular audiences, it really all did "begin with Pearl Harbor," with the vague memories of *Honolulu, Waikiki Wedding, The Black Camel, In the Navy,* and so on at best relegated to the imaginary space of a simpler time and place that even the more reflexive movies themselves had never really promoted. To this generation, Japan had, as the famous quote goes, "[awoken] a sleeping giant and fill[ed] him with a terrible resolve" on the seeming path toward America's self-proclaimed destiny of revenge and victory.

Figure 2.1. A censored scene from the end of the WWII government propaganda film, *December 7th* (1943), which featured the ghosts of soldiers from combat past wandering a military cemetery and debating the value of endless war. The original version of the film was a far more ambivalent take on the kind of wartime nostalgia often promoted in later representations of WWII and the Pearl Harbor attack.

That famous line is worth revisiting further—for one, it is largely a Hollywood invention, promoted by one of the more well-known cinematic recreations of the Japanese attack on Pearl Harbor, *Tora! Tora! Tora!* (And, in classic pastiche fashion, the same misquote was further perpetuated by Michael Bay's *Pearl Harbor* [2001] decades later, which reportedly drew on the 1970 film for much of its own "historical" research.) At best, the line loosely interprets Japanese Marshal Admiral Isoroku Yamamoto's thoughts on the possible negative repercussions from the attack. It's a powerful reminder of the extent to which some of the most memorialized aspects of American history—even for the generations that lived through it—were, and still are, shaped and reshaped by Hollywood myths that retrospectively reflect what hegemonic audiences want to believe about the past. These types of historical films bring "to spectacular life the sweeping themes of the historical past," writes Robert Burgoyne, and have "played a decisive role in articulating an image of America that informs, or in some cases challenges, our sense of national self-identity, an image of nation that is then projected to the world."⁶

Unlike other chapters, this one focuses more on representations of the lingering memories of a particular time period than the period itself, with an eye toward better understanding the nostalgic impulses surrounding the constant specter of war underlining every depiction of Hawai'i in the post-WWII period. Aside from the 1942 documentary, *December 7th*, "mostly a recreation of the surprise attack filmed on a studio back lot," wrote military historian Lawrence Suid, "Hollywood did not again portray Pearl Harbor [directly] until after World War II. December 7 appears very briefly in the 1949 film, *Task Force*, an epic rendering of naval aviation and in the 1953 film, *From Here to Eternity*, which well captured the initial shock of the attack among the soldiers at Schofield Barracks."⁷ In addition to movies such as *December 7th*, or *Remember Pearl Harbor* (1942), the attack is also often mentioned, or implied, in what Robert Eberwein has called Hollywood "retaliation films,"⁸ fictionalized or loosely nonfictional war movies released during WWII that boosted morale by emphasizing America's successful military response to Japanese aggression. Meanwhile, depictions of the Pearl Harbor attack itself became more fascinating and complex in the postwar period as the need for documentation and wartime propaganda faded, and the rose-colored glasses of time's reminiscence were donned.

Nostalgia is one impulse in touristic and Hollywood depictions of Hawai'i that might match, in affective power, other complementary desires of romance, adventure, and escape. December 7th is most acutely the moment when nostalgia—that love affair with a simpler time—enters fully into media representations of, and audience reactions to, the mainland's complex relationship with Hawai'i. Pearl Harbor–related movies and television shows, with their delicate subject matter, retrospectively adopt a nostalgic lens—sometimes literally (i.e., using archival footage, or black and white cinematography in a media age increasingly gravitating to color)—when looking back at that time period. One trend was the Hollywood historical film, period pieces made years, even decades, after the conclusion of WWII that attempted to recreate life in Hawai'i before, during, and/or after the Japanese sneak attack. Another trend—more fantastical in narrative, but no less illuminating thematically—was the use of the "time travel" story, particularly on the newer medium of television, where characters literally travel back to December 7th. Pearl Harbor nostalgia films and TV shows straddle a fascinating line between traditional nostalgia texts and the popular genre of the war movie. As

Arthur McClure writes, war movies traditionally have "had an importance that was two-fold; to give unity of purpose for the war itself, and to give strength of purpose to the people on the home front. Films that dealt with the [second world] war tried in their own way to define the objectives of the war and the way in which these objectives were to be achieved. They also sought to show somehow why it was necessary to make sacrifices."[9] While some war movies can certainly contain a nostalgic element in so far as romanticizing the past, or using an idealized vision of history to affirm cultural and nationalistic values in the present, what distinguishes these Pearl Harbor texts is not only the yearning for the past but also foregrounding a sense of regret, which complicates those other, more straightforwardly propagandistic, militaristic depictions of triumph. And yet though they contain elements of wishing events could have unfolded differently (though they never quite do in these narratives), they ultimately also work to reaffirm the righteousness of America's involvement in WWII by going right back to "where it all began."

Nostalgia for War

The most famous of these texts certainly would be *From Here to Eternity*, a novel (1951) and later Oscar-winning film (1953) that was the first high-profile Hollywood project to tackle the subject. (MGM had planned at one point in the mid-1950s to make a film about Pearl Harbor [then called *East Wind, Rain*] based on the book *Day of Infamy* written by Walter Lord.[10]) The very title, *From Here to Eternity*, follows a nostalgic logic by juxtaposing a specific time/space (here) with its absence (eternity)—the urgency of wartime Hawai'i with the timeless infinitude of death, something that maintains an often unspoken and uncomfortable relationship with nostalgia (as in, the looming specter of humanity's finite end evokes a desire to look back instead). In addition to that film, other postwar period pieces set in the early 1940s—such as two very different all-star Hollywood military epics, *Tora! Tora! Tora!* and *In Harm's Way* (1965)—are equally worthy of analysis. These cinematic looks back were just a few of the numerous "films made during the Cold War," writes Eberwein, "that continue to reassert the [nationalistic] values of World War II . . . in a context that very much privileges historical truth."[11] While often claiming a cinematic "realism" greater than the more propagandistic movies made during wartime, these movies also operated paradoxically as "nostalgia memory" films. These texts, writes Pam Cook, "conjure up a golden age, which is both celebrated and mourned, providing an opportunity to reflect upon and interrogate the present. Past and present are conflated, as contemporary concerns are superimposed on earlier historical periods in the process of reconstruction."[12]

I would also argue that the appeal of the "sleeping giant" line is not simply in how it reinforces a particular strand of American exceptionalism and resolve, but also for the specific dreamlike motif of sleeping, and waking, that runs throughout many nostalgically direct and indirect depictions of Pearl Harbor. This metaphor also more subtly plays up the notion of Hawai'i itself as little more than a lovely little dream shaped by discourses of tourism. Going forward, the desire to "return" to Hawai'i literally and through mediation becomes synonymous with a desire to return to that state of innocence, the desire to hold on to and preserve such a dream in the wake of the inevitable passage of time and the crushing weight of history's inevitability. The title of the song "Hawaii Sang Me to Sleep" from the 1939 film *Hawaiian Nights* seems eerily prophetic in hindsight. Americans, on O'ahu and the mainland, were literally and symbolically "asleep," the stories often go—further foregrounding the imagined nostalgic naïveté of an "innocent" country on the eve of war. Pearl Harbor is thus framed "as a place of violently and tragically betrayed innocence," writes Vernadette Gonzalez, which "additionally obscures any instance of America's own acts of treachery"[13] (such as the initial overthrow of the sovereign Hawaiian government). Shortly after the attack, *Variety* correspondent Mabel Thomas painted just such a melancholic image for industry readers back home. Her job was usually to report on such matters as celebrity sightings and theatrical exhibition practices in Hawai'i. Prewar, Thomas had sold the islands as a peaceful place, even as "the safest place in the world to shoot scenes of naval warfare"[14] (a statement ironically written less than two weeks before December 7th). But, in the immediate aftermath of the attack, Thomas looked back wistfully:

> [I] shall always regret more Yanks were not able to visit Honolulu before the transformation took place, changing a city that was well on its way to being considered the world's ideal playground to a mighty fortress. . . . This hateful condition is not going to last as long as many think, and again the seas of the world will be safe for travelers to come here and again we will be the old beautiful Hawaiian country, ready to greet all comers from all lands, in the true traditional manner of the real Hawaiian Aloha.[15]

Figure 2.2. "Uncle Sam" (John Houston) is literally asleep on the morning of the Japan military attack in *December 7th* (1943). In the original, uncensored version, we see Sam wrestling with his conscience over the looming specter of world war, undercutting the narrative of an innocent country peacefully oblivious to larger global events that this version, and later representations of Hawai'i pre–Pearl Harbor, would reinforce.

That this romanticized vision of life on the islands may not have corresponded to many first-person accounts from the time was less important than how this nostalgic vision increasingly gained hold in the American imagination. Yet, precisely, nostalgia for what? While there was always a nostalgic urge implied in earlier depictions of the islands as a premodern paradise (erasing the colonialist history therein), such yearnings for yesterday took on a more immediate and powerful pretext in the wake of December 7th. Fantasies of nostalgia itself are never that innocent to begin with. They do not exist for their own abstract sake but are always inseparable from some kind of personal or collective upheaval, even at times trauma, which called nostalgia into being and which nostalgia in turn works to conceal. The troubling event can be a major one (the horrors of global warfare) or a relatively minor issue (the awkward transition to adulthood)—but it is always at the core of the desire in the first place to look back to, and thus romanticize, the time in life prior to that change. Thus, the imagined innocence implied in Hawai'i's reputation as a tropical paradise in the second half of the twentieth century is always intertwined with how it was perceived romantically to have existed before the horrors of December 7th—the events of WWII being the central component of the nostalgic impulse. It is, in other words, not only a nostalgia for prewar life, but also, in a sense, *nostalgia for war* itself.

Beyond just its clear conservative and nationalistic connotations, the perverse contradiction that is nostalgia for war—the suffering that not only initiates but *perhaps more importantly sustains* the longing—begins to make sense. There may be no better example of this than the hugely successful *From Here to Eternity*, which managed to reconcile the grim realities of prewar military life it represented onscreen with the postwar nostalgia to which it simultaneously appealed. As such, this dynamic is especially acute in depictions of the Pearl Harbor attack, since they most forcefully highlight the inherent, though often repressed, nostalgic juxtaposition between utopia (paradise) and dystopia (tragedy). However, this contradiction also hangs over the entire modern history of Hawai'i as the staging ground for numerous US military conflicts in the Pacific region. "Pearl Harbor's hallowed place in U.S. historiographies of World War II," writes Gonzalez, "is further secured by the ways its narratives of sacrifice and heroics operate to lend a mantle of righteousness to contemporary US militarism in the region."[16]

Another contradiction is that "nostalgic love," as Boym notes, "can only survive in a long distance relationship,"[17] meaning that one can only look back longingly on that which one cannot ever reexperience immediately and directly, and which also implies the possibility that such remembered moments never quite existed as such in the first place. Boym is defining "long distance" here both temporally (the more common sense of the word "nostalgia" now) and geographically (the original definition as a form of homesickness). The source of nostalgic love is impossible to attain not only because one cannot ever literally go back in time (despite so many mediated fantasies to the contrary), but also because a physical return to the actual location or locations as they exist in their current state will invariably contradict the idealized fantasy that has been constructed in the nostalgic's mind. In this respect, the safe distances of mass media such as film and TV could sustain those geographic and temporal boundaries in a way that the immediacy of tourism and actual travel could not.

But, of course, the travel industry in the postwar period worked aggressively to sell this fantasy, nonetheless. "Before their own ranks became depleted," wrote Douglas and Douglas, "the survivors of the Pacific War—allies and enemies alike—would be encouraged in large numbers to revisit the sites that they had hitherto been so anxious to leave. Nostalgia has long been a potent factor in tourism. The incorporation of the war's legacy into Pacific travel not only rekindled interest in some destinations, it was largely responsible for creating interest in others."[18] Attractions such as the USS Arizona Memorial had to evoke memories of war delicately and somewhat abstractly—paying respects to the men and women who died on December 7th, while also evoking the contradictory nostalgia, the aforementioned sustained longing, at the heart of Hawai'i's touristic appeal. And yet, aside from the financial restrictions of travel, the military nostalgia of the time had limited appeal. As Paul Craig observed in a 1963 report on Hawai'i tourism: "Many veterans got their first contact with overseas areas (Hawai'i included) during World War II. There was doubtless some tendency for them to want to return to these places in peacetimes; but after 15 or 20 years this effect has probably worn off substantially or been satisfied."[19]

More so than any particular tourist attraction (whose very physical act of memorialization embodies a decisive separation between the "then" and the "now"), a more effective vehicle for such sustained longing, ultimately, was mass media—particularly those with the capacity to faithfully recreate the nostalgic period in question and then endlessly recycle and repackage it over the subsequent years. Aural and visual media are inherently nostalgic to begin with—they possess the unique ability to capture moments in time, which then, going forward, confront audiences with the presence of an ever-increasingly distant past. This then becomes especially magnified by how WWII was the first war to be thoroughly captured on film, thus possessing an especially and uniquely potent indexical power through its archival afterlife. In this regard, such nostalgia is inevitable—and what may be even more relevant for present purposes is how that archival function (as well as period recreations) can sustain the nostalgia by also *denying* the passage of time. Nostalgia media texts embody that elusive liminal space—the one that is so central to nostalgic impulses in the first place—between the desire both to live in the past and to acknowledge the passage of time, which necessitates that same desire to begin with. In the case of Pearl Harbor nostalgia, which involves a coexistence of both the war and the imagined simplicity of life before that conflict, film and television's mediation of the past helps to postpone the homecoming (the "long distance relationship"), in order to maintain in the present the fantasy of what that time and place was like, and what it meant to Americans of that generation.

December 7th

The first prominent film representations of Pearl Harbor were in government-funded documentaries, such as Frank Capra's *Why We Fight* series (1943) and the John Ford–Gregg Toland-directed *December 7th* (1943)—wartime propaganda that both challenged but also at times perpetuated the kind of prewar nostalgia that would later define such images to a greater extent. In *Why We Fight*'s final installment, "War Comes to America," the Pearl Harbor attack is acknowledged briefly as the decisive climax of events leading up to the US' inevitable involvement in WWII (some of the reenactment footage appears to be reused from the Ford-Toland documentary). Attempting to boost the country's morale, *Why We Fight* lays out extensively its reasons for how and why America was already leaning away from isolationist policies long before December 1941. This narrative of preparation undercut the imagined naïveté (a country "asleep") that other representations would either imply or outright show. For example, *December 7th* begins with "Uncle Sam" (played by Walter Houston) depicted as a sleeping tourist on the islands on the morning of the attack, while the rest of Hawai'i is depicted as oblivious to imminent military combat.

Produced by Hollywood veteran Ford's Navy Reserve filming unit, *December 7th* won the Academy Award for Best Documentary Short Subject in 1944. The half-hour film offered a largely factual account of the attack on Pearl Harbor and its immediate aftermath through a mixture of available actuality footage from the day itself and extensive recreations and effects shots of the attack staged later, along with new additional documentary material of the military rebuilding its naval fleet and of the new civilian life in Honolulu under martial law. While in Hawai'i, Ford "bought out the opening night of 'How Green Was My Valley' at the Waikiki Theatre, and gave every man in uniform the preference, just for them and their officers."[20] While Ford received codirecting credit on the film—in particular, for reportedly reediting the first cut after government censors strongly objected—famed cinematographer Toland (*Citizen Kane*, *The Grapes of Wrath*) was largely responsible for overseeing the original production, the sole such credit in his brief but storied filmmaking career.

"I helped him along," Ford told Peter Bogdanovich years later, "I was there, but Gregg was in charge of it."[21]

Befitting its somber expository tone, *December 7th* sought to fulfill the War Department's desire to "present factually" the events before, during, and after that day, leading up to an account of how the Navy quickly regrouped, rebuilt, and prepared to take the fight back to Japan. What is striking about the documentary's straightforward account of events is how much it adopts a traditionally touristic perspective on the Pearl Harbor attack, aligning its point of view with what mainland audiences would most likely recognize. Establishing Oʻahu on the eve of battle, the opening shots of the documentary ironically privilege and reinforce the established touristic visual clichés of the territory. During a staged Sunday morning seaside service (a location evocative of the Kodak Hula Show), the priest interrupts his weekly sermon to remind the group of soldiers gathered before him to remember that Christmas is soon to arrive and that they should buy what would be considered typically touristic souvenirs (i.e., hula dolls) to send back to loved ones on the mainland as a holiday present (a similar seaside religious service in Bay's *Pearl Harbor* was also perhaps inspired by this scene). Most explicitly, the initial arrival of the Japanese air forces themselves are framed from a touristic lens—the planes arrive at 7:50 a.m. "according to the clock on the Aloha Tower" (the first sight most tourists would see while arriving on a cruise ship, and referenced repeatedly in the film), and then travel across the usual sights of Nuʻuanu Pali, Diamond Head, and Waikiki Beach—almost as though on a guided tour—before the bombing of military installations commenced.

Toward the end of the documentary, the narrative pauses to pay respects to those servicemen who died during the attack. An elaborate ceremony is staged on beautiful Hawaiian beaches as enlisted men lay flowers on a long line of crosses, surrounded by American flags, meant to honor the dead. The most striking aspect of this sequence was not only the memorial itself, but its stunningly symmetrical juxtapositions—tropical beaches with war memorials, religious crosses with palm trees, mourning with paradise. Most notably, the sequence ends not on the religious markers or the faces of the other soldiers, but on a low-angle shot looking up as the camera tracks along an endless row of palm trees. Pointed skyward, the image confers on the Hawaiian islands an almost heavenly aura while reiterating the dominant visual motif of the documentary—a tropical paradise under attack.

The final moments of the film include a sequence about how loyal Japanese Americans responded by expressing their devotion to the United

Figure 2.3. A single cross on the beach in *December 7th* (1943) is matched graphically . . .

Figure 2.4. . . . with a palm tree, as the low angle reinforces both a heavenly aura upon the islands and the juxtaposition of tropical peace with wartime horror.

States of America by changing the names of their businesses to more patriotic ones ("Keep 'Em Flying Café"), closing religious temples and language schools, and removing written uses of the Japanese language. This narrative of racial harmony avoids the concurrent and hypocritical history of internment occurring on the mainland but is consistent with the rhetoric of cultural and racial harmony that war propaganda of the time used to promote national harmony (and echoes the tourism rhetoric of the previous decade). Along those lines, another patriotic appeal to unity occurs when the documentary asks some of the fallen to "introduce" themselves to the viewer from beyond the grave—the roster of dead soldiers is a thorough mix of ethnic and geographic diversity, where men from several backgrounds announce—in the mildly progressive rhetoric typical of the time, that they are "all Americans" now. The documentary announces near the end that "war has come to '*Hawaii USA*'" (a phrase aggressively promoted in the prewar period by the Hawaii Tourist Bureau), highlighting the islands not as a remote tropical destination, but as another part of the United States of America.

However, there was originally a longer, much different version of *December 7th* that was hidden from public view by government censors for nearly fifty years. Before Ford himself edited down Toland's more ambitious but quite flawed first cut, this roughly eighty-minute movie provided more context for the attack itself, exploring in heavily allegorical fashion what the documentary saw both as the warning signs prior to December 7th, and skepticism toward what lessons would be learned from engaging in yet another bloody conflict as the reality of war now loomed for America again. This cynicism was expressed very explicitly in the original version's much bleaker ending (see figure 2.1), which featured the ghost of an unnamed sailor (played by Dana Andrews), one presumably killed on December 7th, wandering through a military graveyard alongside the ghost of another soldier who died back during the First World War. While wandering the seemingly endless landscape of tombstones, and pointing out all the different men buried there since the days of the American Revolution, the two spirits talk back and forth about the endless cycles of death and destruction in which the world always finds itself. Such a depressing note was not the message the US government was trying to convey to the country on the outset of war. Although the young sailor tries to stay positive, believing that this time the world will learn from its mistakes and come out of this newest conflict finally committed to lasting global peace, the older soldier remains highly skeptical.

The other significant difference in the censored version was a much longer opening sequence in which Uncle Sam, before he went to sleep, contemplates the status of Hawai'i prior to the attack. In this cut, Sam is merely on "vacation" in Hawai'i, looking out across the landscape from the vantage point of his guest villa, and waxing poetic about the islands' considerable charms while a steel guitar plays softly in the background—Hawai'i was "the territory of heaven," he says, one whose "air is choked with the fragrance of a million flowers." However, he is soon visited by Mr. "C" (Mr. "Conscience"), played by Harry Davenport, an enigmatic figure who challenges him to look beyond his own superficial understanding of prewar Hawai'i to see the signs of trouble quietly brewing. The racism displayed here was another aspect of the film that troubled government censors, as Mr. C tries to convince Sam that each Japanese American living in Hawai'i—from hairdressers to taxicab drivers to those living near the military bases—was a disloyal spy reporting everything they saw or overheard back directly to Tokyo through the Japanese Consulate in Honolulu. Sam, though, does not want to believe it, arguing that most Japanese Americans were honest and loyal—over footage of Japanese American children singing "God Bless America" and reciting the Pledge of Allegiance—and continuing to insist on the multicultural "melting pot" harmony and natural beauty of Hawai'i. Failing to convince Uncle Sam of the severity of the situation, Mr. C. finally leaves him, suggesting that Uncle Sam's touristic clichés reflect how his head is too "buried in the sand" to see what is really happening. At this point, exhausted by wrestling with his conscience, Sam tries to go to sleep, only to have his peaceful thoughts of this "Paradise of the Pacific" now haunted by nightmare visions of a world at war—previous footage of the islands' charms juxtaposed with archival footage of the Axis powers as he tosses and turns.

As the film moves toward that fateful Sunday morning, the effect now is very different from the shorter version. The censored 1943 edit picks up at this point in the narrative—with Sam engaged in what, for decades, the average viewer would have assumed to be a perfectly harmless, relaxing rest, instead of being overwhelmed with a guilty conscience presented by looming war in the original cut. In some ways, the longer version of *December 7th* was much more skeptical of the nostalgia for prewar Hawai'i, which the censored version perhaps unintentionally reinforced for wartime and postwar audiences. While the latter suggests that Uncle Sam, like every American back then, was innocently and obliviously asleep on the eve of December 7th, the longer version resists such naïveté—in terms both of what life was like before then, and of what dark consequences still lay ahead. In short, the two versions of *December 7th* collectively reveal an underlying tension that framed many subsequent mainstream media accounts of the attack—how to be somber and honest about the actual events of that day, while also still hoping to imagine some nostalgic space of innocence that might have preceded it.

From Here to Eternity

The fact that *From Here to Eternity* was the first significant feature-length narrative film about Pearl Harbor to emerge out of Hollywood only partially explains its popularity. More so than *December 7th*, the movie perhaps best typifies the contradictory attitudes of many Americans toward memories of that day—the need for wartime "realism" in its depiction of military life's cruelties and dangers along with a need for the nostalgic prewar fantasies of tropical paradise. A *Boxoffice* review of the time suggested as much: the movie offered "the clear, arresting, atmospherically authentic insight into life in America's peacetime army, the aura of which is brought into further sharp focus through the use of the Hawaiian backgrounds against which the novel was written."[22] Both the location shooting and the use of actual archival footage from the Pearl Harbor attack in its spectacular finale ("integration of actual combat footage" from the raid, wrote *Variety*, "adds a tough wallop to the climactic scenes"[23]) were cited as adding to the film's sense of realism. However, it was the source material that gave *From Here to Eternity* the most oft-noted sense of authenticity. The hugely popular film was based on James Jones's equally successful novel of the same name, which broke records by selling out its first round of paperback printing (more than a half million copies) in the wake of the film's appearance.[24] The book's popularity was all the more intriguing given that it was, as Bailey and Farber noted, "one long testament to the despair Hawai'i could inspire,"[25] and was often banned in certain cities[26] (its notorious reputation in that regard no doubt furthered book sales as well).

From Here to Eternity is the melodramatic story of several intertwined military lives in Honolulu in the immediate days leading up to the Japanese attack—two enlisted men (Montgomery Clift and Frank Sinatra); their first sergeant (Burt Lancaster), who carries on an affair with the wife (Deborah Kerr) of his superior officer; and a "hostess" (Donna Reed) who works at a nearby Gentlemen's Club. Director Fred

Zinnemann noted that "there are really four or five stories going on at the same time. They were all written very skillfully by Dan Taradash and woven into a progressive thing that kept moving all the time."[27] It is the specter of WWII that gave the film its coherence and urgency. "This picture is filled with sudden tragedies, often ghastly and the kind that can only be linked with war or the threat of it," wrote one review. "There is a big doom ever lurking over what happens."[28] The Hawai'i of *From Here to Eternity* forsakes almost all the usual tourist clichés of the islands, save the occasional beach location backdrop, in favor of—by early 1950s Hollywood standards—a much grimmer depiction of life in paradise filled with dehumanizing military barracks, (implied) brothels, violent back alleys, and seedy bars—"a small world of rough men and prostitutes, of drinking, gambling, sex, violence, and despair."[29] As an *LA Times* review from the period observed: "To say that it is rich in compassion would be false. There is far more of bitterness about the story as it is told."[30] The sadness and desperation of this world ends in tragedy for some, but also in a renewed era of selflessness and common cause in the immediate aftermath of the attack and the United States' headlong plunge into the Second World War, with Alma (Reed) declaring in the film's final line that Hawai'i was "the most beautiful place in the world," despite the personal tragedy and the imminent arrival of war. Even during war, the film believes, the islands retained a sense of peace.

Despite the implied optimism of the ending, such cynicism about life in Hawai'i prior to December 7th was met both with the ire of film industry censors—given its depiction of what for the time was seen as immoral sexuality—and of a United States military that was more interested in the jingoism of the censored *December 7th* and *Why We Fight* than the harsh light of Jones's novel. As Claudia Sternberg wrote, "Two major censors were actively involved: the Breen Office [in Hollywood] and the Department of Defense. The conflict was twofold: on the one side were the moral issues, prostitution and adultery; on the other, the harsh criticism of the leadership of the American Army, thin ice for a studio in the McCarthy era."[31] Indeed, the aforementioned *LA Times* review even implied its anti-US military ideology could be used as subversive Communist propaganda.[32] *From Here to Eternity* was often compared in media coverage of the time to the Otto Preminger film *The Moon Is Blue* (1953), another controversial film about military life. Yet, as such increasing challenges to censorship practices of the time (which Preminger in particular was well known for) would imply, restrictions had relaxed considerably in the decade since war. "I could make the picture without

Army approval," the film's producer Buddy Adler explained to the *New York Herald Tribune*, "but it's cheaper and more realistic to use actual locales, which the Army would provide."[33] Ultimately, numerous changes were made, such as the depiction of Maggio's (Frank Sinatra) torture at the hands of the military stockade officers (scenes from the book were later turned into a New York City play called simply *Stockade* that appeared about a year after the film[34]). Despite the changes, however, the Navy still refused to show it to sailors on naval ships and shore stations, while one representative claimed that "the Army, having cooperated in making the picture, was 'stuck' and had to use it"[35] at their bases.

The film was also a stylized reimagining of Hawai'i on the eve of war, with a cinematic "realism" that even in the 1950s was met skeptically by some. "You know the formula," wrote one reviewer dismissively in a 1953 issue of *Picturegoer*, "conventional melodrama made to look like realism by serving up stock characters who drink, cuss incessantly, complain of their inner workings and make love as casually, and about as sensitively, as they eat ham sandwiches."[36] Meanwhile, the film's visual aesthetic was more in keeping with contemporary styles than with those of 1941 Hawai'i. *From Here to Eternity* "dressed its principle male actors in a succession of aloha shirts," writes DeSoto Brown, "that more accurately reflected the fashions of the year in which the film was made."[37] Only in the postwar period did the so-called "aloha" shirts become

> a hot commodity and travelers often took aloha shirts home with them. Textile designs included words in the Hawaiian language, historical sites, flowers, and cultural motifs. Kamehameha Garment Company accomplished an impressive feat in 1951 by producing the seven-color reproduction of the Eugene Savage Matson [cruise ship] menu painting for prints on sportswear. With the movie *From Here to Eternity* aloha shirts exploded on the fashion scene since the actors were dressed in aloha shirts, and many other films set in Hawai'i followed.[38]

Outside the barracks, Honolulu in the film largely resembles images from a postwar tourist brochure. The depiction of its "gritty" nightlife at times feels like little more than a long string of tropical, bamboo and grass, cloth-covered "tiki bars"—another mostly postwar and distinctly mainland phenomenon that somewhat undercut the otherwise grim depiction of the islands pre-WWII.

This collage of prewar ugliness and postwar stylization reflects a juxtaposition of the dark depiction of prewar Hawai'i with the inevitable nostalgia it spoke to in its postwar audience—its noted reputation then for a kind of stark cinematic realism contrasting with, but also complementing, the sentimentalism it simultaneously evokes. Bailey and Farber tell the story of a soldier from Cleveland Heights, Fred Borgerhoff, who spent the final days of his military service largely wandering the less reputable streets of Honolulu:

> One rainy afternoon . . . Borgerhoff struck up a conversation with a young, attractive woman, a highly unusual occurrence for him and for most every other enlisted man in Hawaii. He does get the feeling that she's a prostitute but that means little to him. . . . She says that she's going to be a very well-known woman someday because a guy is writing a book that's got her in it. . . . *For the next couple of hours, engrossed, he reads a series of sketches and parts of stories about army life in Hawaii. Sure enough, there are descriptions of Hotel Street and several prostitutes figure in; much of the action takes place just before and after the attack on Pearl Harbor. Borgerhoff thinks it's terrific stuff, true to life, enough so that he'd rather keep turning the pages than talk up the good-looking and maybe obliging woman who gave it to him.*[39]

The manuscript, according to the soldier, was an early draft of Jones's novel. The anecdote highlights the ambivalence of the often dreary, seedy wartime days in Hawai'i coexisting with nonetheless fond memories partially grounded in its stylized representations. The film—for all its Hollywood artifice—retained an affective power for those with direct and indirect memories of war. Undoubtedly, much of this intensity was tied to the forceful realities depicted in the more historically accurate novel, to which the compromised film could only superficially gesture.

Finally, another aspect of *From Here to Eternity*'s nostalgic appeal had no necessary connection to memories of WWII but were instead tied up in its place within technological shifts in the industry. Numerous commentators of the time (and parent studio Columbia's own promotional rhetoric) contrasted the film's "old-fashioned" qualities with emergent trends in television, widescreen ratios, and color photography. As early as 1953, the film's black and white, boxy Academy size aspect ratio (1:33:1) aesthetic was already on the verge of being an anachronism in the face of impending change (while also harkening back to the cinematic look of WWII footage). Studio chief Harry Cohn reportedly wanted to shoot the movie in color to ensure another million dollars at the box office, but director Zinnemann insisted otherwise,[40] while the *New York Herald Tribune* reported that the film was also at least considered for 3D exhibition.[41] The novelty of its quaint technology thus played a major part in its popularity and promotion. One audience member, Bob Downing, wrote a sarcastic letter to the entertainment editor of the *New York Times*:

> It seems a pity that fuddy-duddies are attempting to demean the marvelous technical improvements in new movies by pointing out that *From Here to Eternity* is simply an old-fashioned 2-D picture, with good script and splendid direction and acting. Shucks! Some folks prefer the horse and buggy, too![42]

Taking a longer historical view, Ivan Spear wrote in *Boxoffice* that "the film is irrefutable testimony to the oft-voiced contention that, regardless of all the current new developments in photographing and projecting celluloid entertainment, the cardinal requirement of good pictures has changed but little—and still includes the best in story, acting, production and direction."[43] Similarly, the *Daily News* published an editorial (featured prominently in Columbia's advertising):

> This smasheroo flicker, we noticed, doesn't have any 3-D gimmicks or even Technicolor. It's just plain, old-fashioned theatre—and the audience loves it. . . . We don't believe theatres have changed much since [the days of Shakespeare]. Stage and camera stunts are dandy, but the spine-tingling story is what the paying customers craved centuries back and still do. So, it's tough about those federal admission taxes, boys, and TV's probably here to stay. But *Eternity* proves you've still got a salable product.[44]

The last point, finally, also acknowledged the looming specter of television. Frustrated with the lack of business at a Newark, New Jersey, movie venue, one theater owner offered a free showing of the movie to patrons, which resulted in numerous moviegoers "lined up in front of [the] theatre before 7 p.m. opening. Hundreds more had to be told there was no room for the 9 p.m. show."[45] This caused one *Variety* article to derisively note that "people will leave their television sets to see a film for free, especially if it's *From Here to Eternity*."[46] The theater owner himself, meanwhile, hardly disagreed with the sentiment: "It creates good will and it's the only way to get people who are glued to their seats at home."[47]

The Revolt of Mamie Stover

The seedy ugliness of wartime Hawai'i as depicted in parts of *From Here to Eternity* find even greater expression in another December 7th-set film released a few years later: *The Revolt of Mamie Stover* (1956). Set in the early 1940s, *Mamie Stover* is about a San Francisco call girl, Mamie (played by Jane Russell), who flees police attention by hopping onto a freighter and heading to Honolulu. The first part of the movie is a throwback to the Hawai'i stories of prewar Hollywood with its emphasis on the long journey to the islands by cruise ship (moreover, in the original novel of the same name, Mamie is a failed movie actress who only succumbs to prostitution out of desperation in a critique of the industry that was too biting for 1950s Hollywood). After Mamie finds increasing business success as a club hostess in Honolulu, a past love interest becomes jealous and resentful about her career and, in an act of self-righteousness, attempts to save her by offering to take her away from that life. She refuses and, disillusioned, she heads back to her hometown in Mississippi. As with the finale of *From Here to Eternity*, the film depicts the Pearl Harbor attack as a dramatic reprieve from the seemingly petty concerns of daily life. However, the morally ambivalent tale is also a deeply cynical take on December 7th—prominently so as one of the first Hollywood films on the subject. After the attack, Mamie uses all the cash money she'd made as a hostess to buy up considerable amounts of property on the islands at extreme discounts—exploiting the momentary panic of landowners who now find themselves living in the midst of a war zone. Similarly, Mamie and her partners are also quick to exploit the sudden waves of GI soldiers now stationed on the islands after December 7th and anxious for female companionship. *The Revolt of Mamie Stover* rejects any 1950s-era sentimentalism for events surrounding the December 7th attacks, or for life on the islands pre-WWII, in favor of an honest look at ruthless forms of war profiteering by someone who had spent her whole life exploiting others' weaknesses.

Hell's Half Acre

By the mid-1950s, the popular trend of "film noir" came to Hawai'i in the form of *Hell's Half Acre*, a B-movie mystery that, like *From Here to Eternity*, straddles a fascinating line between the seedy backstreets of Honolulu and the heavy weight of WWII memories. Although much of the film follows a fairly conventional genre storyline, the Hawaiian backdrop is key. Donn Beach (originally born Ernest Beaumont-Gantt) was listed as the film's technical advisor under his well-known pseudonym "Don the Beachcomber." Beach is credited as one of the originators of the "tiki bar" aesthetic after opening his own tropical-themed lounge in Hollywood in 1937: "a South Seas hideaway that was to become the blueprint for the many entrepreneurs who would follow in his footsteps: like an island in the urban sea, the Polynesian paradise that Donn designed was meant to be a refuge from the teaming metropolis that surrounded it."[48] In the postwar period, after returning from his own stint in the Air Force, Beach aggressively promoted his own brand of "Beachcomber" hospitality: "Donn had also created an image, a figure: that of the twentieth-century urban beachcomber, an individual somewhere between well-traveled connoisseur, beach beatnik, and marina swinger."[49]

Not surprisingly given this, *Hell's Half Acre* opens with a luau show being performed at a Honolulu tiki bar ("Chet's Hawaiian Retreat")—two developments (hula shows, tiki bars) that exploded in popularity in the aftermath of WWII and in the shadow of looming statehood. What distinguishes the hula show in this film, in addition to its tiki bar setting, is its somber conclusion, when it takes on the overtones of a spiritual ceremony and pays respects to the memory of world war and of Pearl Harbor. Performers debut the song "Polynesian Rhapsody" for the audience, about "a man's great love of Hawai'i." In voiceover, the bar's owner (a tiki entrepreneur like Beach), Chet Chester (Wendell Corey), waxes poetic about his relationship to the islands as the song plays. "Hawai'i, I came unwilling," he says, "a stranger to you, sick and weary, bitter and tired, all hope dissolved, all heart despairing . . ." In that moment, Hawai'i symbolized for him the opportunity to start over from the mistakes he made as a wartime military deserter turned criminal racketeer. Reflecting on the postwar popularity of tiki bars, Francesco Adinolfi writes that it is tempting to think that

> soldiers back from the Pacific brought fond memories of their lives overseas, turning entrepreneurs and opening restaurants

that "reproduced" the places they visited during war. But this isn't really the case. . . . It becomes very difficult to imagine that these "exotic businessmen" were motivated *solely* by nostalgia. Rather, the Pacific represented a vast, unexplored space to be mined. Ex-soldiers dedicated themselves to its commercialization while disavowing their traumatic wartime memories.⁵⁰

In *Hell's Half Acre*, disavowal of traumatic wartime memories—specifically, wartime cowardice and the legacy of December 7th—is crucial to the narrative. Fleeing the Army at the outbreak of war years earlier and immersing himself in Honolulu's criminal underworld, Chet (whose real name was Randy Williams) allows everyone, including his wife (Evelyn Keyes) and son back on the mainland, to think that he died on that tragic day. (After the war, the real-life Beach also left for Hawai'i to avoid his ex-wife and former business partner, Sunny Sund—in this case over legal matters connected to "Beachcomber" naming rights.) Eventually, Chet's wife comes to believe that he may be still alive and living secretly in Honolulu, causing her to make for the islands. In its own film-noirish way (fatalistic narratives often focused on trying to undo crucial decisions in the past), this plot device foregrounds the lingering collective trauma of the Pearl Harbor attack. With a narrative that revolves around the idea that the dead may not be dead after all, the film reinforces the desire to believe that December 7th might not be as tragic as it was perceived to be, or that there was still the chance to undo somehow what had been done. (*Hell's Half Acre* also uniquely anticipates *Hawaii Five-O*'s [1968–1980] gritty "trouble in paradise" crime genre set-up—a Honolulu overrun by tourists during the day, and crawling with shady criminals at night.)

In Harm's Way

On the eve of the so-called "New" Hollywood's invasion of the old studio system in the late 1960s, Paramount Pictures attempted one last big-screen nostalgic look back to the attack on Pearl Harbor, a move that invited criticism from some of the more youthful voices within the industry: "Hollywood should be devoting more attention to purely contemporary themes," one executive told *Variety*, "rather than dredging up old wartime stories."⁵¹ A star-studded spectacle of the first degree, *In Harm's Way* follows *From Here to Eternity*'s model of looking back to the events of December 7th and recreating them as a sprawling, melodramatic historical epic about, as one review of the time put it, "the personal crises of some few who rose from the rubble of the Pearl Harbor disaster."[52] In a review that lamented the film's lack of creativity and bloated pacing, *Monthly Film Bulletin* noted that "it is particularly sad that this kind of film is still being made more than ten years after *From Here to Eternity*"[53] (another reviewer added, none too subtly, that "like some of its male stars, Otto Preminger's *In Harm's Way* is noticeably overweight"[54]). Being made with generous support from the US Navy (who offered locations, extras, and military equipment for the Hawaiian shoot), and evoking relatively little controversy over its depiction of sexuality and the military (despite similar potentially controversial subject matter), says much about how cultural attitudes had changed in the dozen years since *From Here to Eternity*. Perhaps more than any other Pearl Harbor–related film released during the first couple of decades after the war, *In Harm's Way*'s stunning Panavision frame makes good use of location footage of the islands as a backdrop to another story of tragedy, action, and melodrama in the early days of America's immersion into WWII. (The Hawaii Visitors Bureau coordinated with mainland theaters for promotional tie-ins, providing one hundred vanda orchids that were given away on opening night.[55])

The Preminger film is even more of an anachronism than its more famous Pearl Harbor cinematic predecessor, since it stands as one of the last big-budget black and white films to emerge from the remnants of the old studio system. What had been aesthetically reassuring to some with *From Here to Eternity* was simply outdated by 1965. Film critic Elspeth Grant wrote at the time that the film was "so old-fashioned in tone and treatment,"[56] despite Preminger's reputation for boundary-pushing. The film was part of a renewed cycle of old-fashioned war films in the 1960s, which reemerged because "both movie and television executives believe that the public appetite for Westerns has been satiated, and they are therefore turning to war for their action and adventure"[57] (clearly unable then to adapt to changing cultural attitudes by doing anything other than going back into genres of the past). One unnamed prominent studio executive was quoted by *Variety*'s Peter Bart at the time as also saying that "we shouldn't have to turn back the clock 20 years to find subjects for pictures."[58] The film's stunning Oscar-nominated visual contradiction—an expansive widescreen frame still holding on to black and white cinematography—serves as an apt metaphor for the coexistence of past and present that the Pearl Harbor attack represented in American consciousness by the mid-1960s, the technological ambitions of widescreen Panavision in tension with its monochrome pastiche recreation of history. Content-wise, only Barbara Bouchet's risqué striptease on the eve of December 7th, or the intense depiction of sexual assault by Kirk Douglas's character late in the movie, would cue modern audiences to the film's status as a product of the post–Production Code era.

Besides the use of black and white cinematography, the film's impressive roster of a "Who's Who" from the days of old Hollywood reinforced that sense of a throwback to another time—Douglas, John Wayne, Patricia Neal, Henry Fonda, Dana Andrews, Franchot Tone, and Burgess Meredith. Even Wayne's subdued and slightly saddened performance (rumored to have been influenced by his lung cancer treatments) offers the film an uncharacteristically quiet presence that seems especially haunted by the inevitable weight of time's passing. On the power of nostalgia, Vera Dika wrote about Wayne's later career appearances (specifically his performance in *The Shootist* [1976]):

> We are being referred back, not to a lived reality, or even a diegetic one, but to a specifically cinematic past. *Our memories of old movies come into play and now serve as an ongoing double*

Figure 2.5. In addition to a roster of aging movie stars from the waning era of classical Hollywood, *In Harm's Way* (1965) also featured black and white cinematography and many original WWII-era military filming locations that were in real life due for the wrecking ball, adding another layer to the film's nostalgia for wartime Hawai'i.

exposure to what we see onscreen. The effect is jolting. Age and death rupture the surface of the image.[59]

At the historical closing of the "classical Hollywood" era in the mid-1960s, *In Harm's Way* is a film that subtly, but unmistakably, equates the old (WWII-era) military with the old (pre-1960s) Hollywood in the contrast between its stable of aging megastars with its equally impressive lineup of then promising young actors (Brandon De Wilde, Jill Haworth, Paula Prentiss, Arthur Kennedy, Carroll O'Connor, Slim Pickens, Larry Hagman). The parallel between old military and old Hollywood is perhaps most directly addressed in the film through the character of Commander Egan Powell (Meredith), a former LA screenwriter turned military intelligence man with a dubious reputation for marrying and divorcing movie actresses.

Ironically, the film's most fascinating temporal contradiction is its implied nostalgia for the WWII-era generation, its aging core audience, that narratively it also seems skeptical of—at least as portrayed in the story's tensions between old (experienced but worn out) and young (inexperienced but more energetic). As Christine Sprengler and others have argued, nostalgia films—particularly, war movies—are often allegories for contemporary conflicts.[60] Not always intentionally so, but many such films carry—and seek to alleviate by reassurances from the past—the weight of contemporary issues. In the case of *In Harm's Way*, meanwhile, that connection is highlighted in particular by the casting of Wayne, a cinematic icon of American might, veteran of numerous war films, and a well-known conservative who vocally supported the Vietnam War, which was well underway by 1965. This subtext of the Indochina conflict haunts the film—particularly in the arguments between the arch conservative Wayne's Torrey and his estranged public-relations-focused (read: "liberal") son over the value of "trumped up" wars. This implies a general suspicion throughout the film over youth's ability to take seriously, and be ready for, the fighting ahead (then and now).

Benefiting the veteran cast of *In Harm's Way* then, the narrative—beyond just the anachronistic look and period setting—is also a story *about* nostalgia, in sharp contrast to the earlier Zinnemann epic where such impulses are instead mostly implied. *In Harm's Way* was made in Hawai'i during a time of rapid urban changes in the wake of statehood, and many of the locations used were soon after demolished to make way for redevelopment by the Hawaii State Agency[61] (which may partially account for some of the film's ambitious sequences of urban destruction during the Japanese attack). In this sense, the film literally offers a window visually to remnants of Honolulu's actual wartime metropolis (in contrast, for example, to Elvis films of the 1960s, which emphasized the islands' touristic modernity, or historical epics such as *Hawaii* [1966], which privileged the natural settings). Many of the film's central characters—Capt. "Rock" Torrey (Wayne), Commander Paul Eddington (Douglas), and Lt. Maggie Haines (Neal)—are people haunted by the wisdom of their choices in the past, facing the threats and tensions of dealing with an ambitious younger generation (literally, in the case of Torrey's estranged son), and generally struggling with—as Eddington puts it early in the film—the feeling of "obsolescing like this old crater boat." Torrey and Eddington command a naval cruiser referred to, appropriately, as the "old swayback," which evokes not only age and a potentially debilitating medical condition, but also the idea of something and someone from "way back" (appropriately, the USS *Saint Paul* was used for these scenes precisely because it was one of the few old naval ships that still retained a 1940s-era design). During the Pearl Harbor attack, one young ensign (fittingly played by Robert Mitchum's own real-life son, James) thoughtlessly refers to Wayne's Torrey as the "old man" (earning an apprehensive glance from the other young men)—before catching himself, apologizing, and properly referring to him as the "captain."

Already fighting a sense of irrelevance on the eve of war, these older characters then struggle to find a role in the new military world brought on by the events of December 7th. After the attack is over (featuring not only more archival footage but also logistically ambitious recreations of destruction), Torrey initially takes the fall with a military anxious to point fingers for failing to follow military protocol during the attack. Meanwhile, Eddington's adulterous wife (Bouchet) dies in a car accident caused by her and her lover's attempts to outrun the Japanese attack—a tragic event that haunts the deeply disturbed and doomed character throughout the remainder of the film. That, plus Torrey's humiliating demotion, foregrounds the extent to which the Pearl Harbor attack serves as the central trauma, personal as much as collective, haunting and motivating the remainder of the film—despite the fact that the sequence itself comprises only a small fraction of the nearly three-hour-long epic, wherein the veterans eventually help lead America back to victory. In ultimately showing the value of leaders like Torrey to help win WWII by the story's end, *In Harm's Way* is both a romantic look back in time and a fantasy looking forward, advocating for the continued relevance of an older generation facing cultural obsolescence in a new moment of American history. For all its logistical ambitions and small moments of gravitas, *In Harm's Way* was the ultimate anachronism, a nostalgia *for nostalgia*—as in, one generation looking back to, and trying to hold on to, that moment fifteen or twenty years earlier when the feeling of looking back wistfully at Pearl Harbor was still fresh and engaging in people's minds.

Tora! Tora! Tora!

Ironically, the one film about Pearl Harbor that is somewhat infamous now for its largely manufactured quotation about awaking "the sleeping giant" is the one that, to a fault even, is also known for its excessively dry attention to "exceptional historical accuracy for a Hollywood movie."[62] Wrote military historian Lawrence Suid, "Within the limits of the special effects artistry of 1970, the Twentieth Century Fox epic rendered the actual attack with surprising believability. More important, it provided audiences with a good understanding of why the Japanese embarked upon the attack and what actually happened in the early morning of December 7."[63] However, this strategic authenticity alone did not lead to any deeper desire on the part of audiences for yet another such tale. "Beyond such impressive logistics, with their promise of eye-popping action scenes and dazzling special effects, lurks the big question," asked one *LA Times* reviewer, "why and to what purpose is this picture being made? Do you really need still another World War II spectacular?"[64] The call to authenticity was perhaps at least in part about product differentiation with an otherwise exhausted topic.

One of the last of a dying breed (the Hollywood historical epic), *Tora! Tora! Tora!* sold itself as the corrective to nearly all earlier Hollywood accounts of December 7th. The *Independent Film Journal* called it a "jumbo documentary telling it like it was,"[65] while another stated that it was "a documentary filmed in the Hollywood, multi-million dollar spectacular style—a style which is impressive but not really helpful in making history 'come alive.' "[66] The film tells both Japanese and American perspectives on the attack, which ironically only seems to highlight further the impossibility of an "objective" depiction when so many points of view must be taken into account. The desire to document in detail the actual events of the attack also betrays an anxiety that the collective memories of December 7th were quickly fading. Priding itself on a factual approach to history, the dry movie ended up being heavily criticized for its lack of narrative tension and dramatic engagement. Even Suid conceded that "in working so hard to tell an accurate story and recreate the actual attack with visual authenticity, the filmmakers forgot Hollywood's prime directive: a movie must entertain to bring audiences into the theater. As a result, *Tora! Tora! Tora!* succeeded as history, but failed as drama."[67] And, importantly, the history lacked drama precisely because there wasn't that much suspense in what had happened on one of the most infamous and well-known (and well-documented) moments in American history.

One could also argue that deemphasizing the typically nostalgic lens through which these events had long been mediated may have explained the indifferent response among audiences as much as the matter-of-fact documentary-like approach did. Gone is the emphasis on first-person narratives of regret. In their place, wrote Vincent Canby in a scathing review of the time, is an attempt

> to dramatize history in terms of event rather than people and it just may be that there is more of what Pearl Harbor was all about in fiction films such as Fred Zinnemann's *From Here to Eternity* and, as the *Variety* report pointed out, Raoul Walsh's *The Revolt of Mamie Stover* than in all of the extravagant posturing in this sort of historical mock-up.[68]

At the same time, there's little doubt that the movie—for all its dry procedural storytelling—still had the potential to affect audiences with a direct memory of that day, which 20th Century Fox tried to exploit. Real-life veterans of the war were invited to many local screenings in an effort to boost publicity, even serving as greeters in the lobby in at least one theater.[69] According to a report in *Boxoffice*, moreover, one Orange County media outlet even interviewed local Pearl Harbor survivors about their memories of the attack as part of their coverage of the film's release.[70]

The nostalgic appeals of the film, such as they existed, were left to veterans, who filled in the emotional gaps that gave this history its power. In a *Washington Post* article appropriately titled "Remember Pearl Harbor? Now It's a Movie," Gary Arnold wrote that "it's impossible to deny that the subject matter of the film has special emotional interest, a real emotional resonance for most Americans. I've never met anyone old enough to have memories of Dec. 7th, 1941, who didn't recall precisely what he was doing when he heard reports of Pearl Harbor. . . . By the same token, it risks wholesale disenchantment if it proves to be 'just another' king-sized war movie."[71] In the end, the film's only real audience was the small number of military officials, scholars, and general history buffs who were never satisfied with the accuracy of earlier cinematic depictions of December 7th. Another problem with *Tora! Tora! Tora!* (as with all war movies by 1970) besides its lack of drama was also quickly changing attitudes about the glorification of the military—which arguably the nostalgia for Pearl Harbor had been enabling for decades—in the midst of a deeply unpopular conflict in Vietnam, at which the generational tensions in *In Harm's Way* had first hinted a few years earlier.

"A New and More Naïve Public"

In contrast to the sporadic representation of Pearl Harbor on the big screen in postwar decades, images of Hawai'i more generally spread with the emergence of the new medium of television during this same period. This included both new programming and the recycling of older films. Christopher Anderson describes the platform of early television as "the unofficial archive of the American cinema, in which [classical] Hollywood's past resurfaced in bits and pieces, like fragments of a dream."[72] Despite its then-cutting-edge technological innovations, television was an inherently nostalgic experience on a number of levels. A politically and aesthetically conservative medium in its infancy, most TV programs avoided delicate matters such as the statehood question and memories of WWII by instead retreating to older genre tropes. The explosion of Hawaiian vacations in the postwar period was—as with the massive popularity of television—the beneficiary of the same middle-class prosperity that enabled the financial opportunities for both. Yet, in contrast to the ambitious tropical travelogues and war epics of the big screen, early TV's depiction of the islands retained a heavy dose of familiarity in its evocation of well-worn tropes from prewar Hollywood.

Such similarity echoes Rick Altman's point that one of the few ways to revive the popularity of an exhausted creative trend was to "transfer the genre to a new and more naïve public (e.g., the western's move to television since the 1950s)."[73] Appropriately, popular programs such as *The George Burns and Gracie Allen Show* (1950–1958), *I Love Lucy* (1951–1957), and *The Jack Benny Program* (1950–1965) featured—as their star-persona-driven titles implied—similarly reflexive stories about celebrities taking long luxury cruises to the islands, where they often encountered even more celebrities, such as Marilyn Monroe. Dominated by images of pineapples, hulas, and luaus, these stories often felt like a lazy rehash of such prewar movies as *Honolulu*, *In the Navy*, *Waikiki Wedding* (1937), or

It's a Date (1940) (in contrast, warmed-over theatrical texts then like *Ma and Pa Kettle at Waikiki* [1955] and still another version of *Bird of Paradise* [1951] were more coolly received at the box office). Another iteration of the inherently reflexive early days of television, they regurgitated the long fascination with the artifices of the "classic" Hawaiian vacation, while also offering the at-home audience a heavy dose of nostalgia that made the newer medium feel more accessible.

However, television didn't completely shy away from the delicate topic of December 7th. One such particularly powerful experience was a nostalgic 1958 episode of NBC's *This Is Your Life* (1952–1961) that focused on the memories of the Pearl Harbor attack and the legacy of the sunken USS *Arizona*. Like many early TV programs, *This Is Your Life* was an adaptation of a previously successful radio program of the same name. Hosted by Ralph Edwards, *This Is Your Life* offered retrospectives of celebrities and other famous people by bringing back friends, family members, and other past acquaintances to meet them face-to-face—often to the surprise of the guest of honor. Although the show was sometimes lighthearted in tone, it often took on more serious topics, such as the atomic bombing of Hiroshima and legacy of the Holocaust, and also sometimes used its platform for important fundraising initiatives. Airing around the time of the seventeenth anniversary of the attack, the episode on the USS *Arizona*—filmed in part at the site of the wreckage itself with cooperation from the US Navy—was an example of both. The retrospective in this case focused on then–Rear Admiral Samuel G. Fuqua, the highest-ranking officer to survive the attack on the USS *Arizona*. Taking command after the bombing, Fuqua directed rescue efforts, gave the order to abandon ship, and stayed aboard until all other survivors had successfully escaped. For his actions that day, he was awarded the Medal of Honor by the United States government. The half-hour episode begins with Fuqua participating in a flag ceremony at the existing memorial, before being approached by Edwards and invited to attend an event at Pearl Harbor's Bloch Arena, where he is greeted warmly by people from his personal and military past in front of an appreciative live audience. It closes, meanwhile, by returning to footage of the wreckage. The episode was reported at the time to be "such a striking and significant program that it was televised nationally twice in the same week—on December 3 and 7—the first time this has been done for a major network program. The total viewing audience was estimated at around 90-million persons."[74] Additionally, an audio tape version was produced for broadcasting on radio channels as well.[75]

The purpose of this episode was not only to honor the rear admiral, but also to raise funds for a new USS Arizona Memorial. Far from the iconic Alfred Preis–designed structure that sits above the wreckage today, the original memorial at the time was a very simple and modest metal platform, to which a ten-foot plaque was later added honoring the sailors who sacrificed their lives that day. Host Edwards claimed to have taken "an especial personal interest in the 'Enshrine the Arizona' project and made arrangements to produce the show at Pearl Harbor."[76] Made at an estimated cost of approximately $83,000, the idea for the episode began in the summer of 1958 with a series of conversations between representatives of Hawai'i's Pacific War Memorial Commission and executives from NBC.[77] Established on May 17, 1949, the commission, "an official agency of the Territorial Government of Hawaii, [had] undertaken to raise the necessary funds for [a newer, permanent USS Arizona Memorial], by means of voluntary public contributions."[78] Shortly after the first broadcast, one NBC executive wrote to the commission and told them, half-jokingly, that "there is nothing left to do but sit and count the money."[79] Within several weeks of the broadcast, "almost $90,000 was received at Pearl Harbor, mostly in contributions, as Mr. Edwards suggested, of $1.00."[80] Later reports put the total as high as $150,000.[81] Fundraising included non-media activities as well, such as a campaign within the state of Arizona to raise money, dedication ceremonies, a reenactment of the USS *Arizona*'s 1915 christening, exhibits that displayed mementoes from the *Arizona*, and the production of plastic scale-models of the battleship through the Fleet Reserve Association.[82] The commission was so pleased with the results of the *This Is Your Life* broadcast, which had helped initiate the state of Arizona fundraising efforts, that it passed a special resolution in 1959 honoring the program's efforts: "Undoubtedly, the single biggest impetus thus far for the campaign has been provided by Mr. Ralph Edwards and his television program, *This is Your Life*."[83]

Many celebrities participated directly and indirectly in the fundraising—two years later, Elvis Presley would do a benefit concert in Honolulu while in town shooting *Blue Hawaii* (1961), and Jack Paar (a WWII veteran) did a series of three *Jack Paar Tonight Show* episodes (1960) shot in Honolulu, one of which featured a segment on the memorial. (Paar was also one of many NBC TV hosts in both New York and Burbank to plug the Pearl Harbor episode of *This Is Your Life* on their own shows.[84]) Upon seeing those Honolulu broadcasts, Pacific War Memorial Commission chairman H. Tucker Gratz noted that Paar's "was a striking presentation, sincere and touching, and I'm sure it brought home to millions of viewers the need for a suitable and permanent memorial for those heroic dead."[85] He lamented, however, that Paar did not directly ask his audience to send money to the campaign. He wrote to Eddie Sherman, a well-known Honolulu newspaper columnist with deep ties to Hollywood celebrities, to ask, "If you're in correspondence with Jack, would you please, Eddie, ask him if he'd give his viewers that message . . . to mail a dollar to the Arizona; the need is urgent and immediate."[86] NBC also worked with the War Memorial Commission in 1961 to include promotional spots for the fundraising drive on local radio affiliates in places such as Seattle, Portland, San Diego, and Minneapolis.[87]

Early Television as Time Travel

As an archival repository for older films—both fiction features and documentaries—there was always an inherent experiential element of time travel in the newer medium of television. Sean Redmond has noted this kinship—by archiving and rebroadcasting older visual media, the newer medium confronts audiences with visible evidence of the past.[88] For instance, the nostalgic power of Fuqua and others recalling memories during the *This Is Your Life* broadcast was magnified immensely by the broadcast's juxtaposition with archival war footage and with photographs from decades past. By providing the presence of past indexical images and sounds, TV allowed audiences in its early days an unprecedented ability to generate the feeling of traveling back in time. The appeal of time travel, writes David Lowenthal, often reflects "the desire to alter what has happened," which is "a common if futile response to a dilemma that confronts us all: past events have determined the world and ourselves as we are; yet we know that these events were not pre-ordained but simply contingent, that matters might have turned out otherwise. From that might-have-been we fantasize reaching back to make it so."[89] Thus, adds Dika, nostalgic time travel narratives rarely present a purely utopic depiction of the past, but instead one "that is flawed and that ultimately yields no security. . . . The past is refashioned to explain ongoing cultural concerns to contemporary audiences. . . . The past is indeed a foreign country, and it cannot be used to erase history and the present."[90]

The core contradiction of time travel as a genre is the same contradiction that structured the United States' collective memories of the Japanese sneak attack—the desire to relive a romanticized memory of the past coexisting with a competing desire to somehow change a moment in time that is actually, beneath the surface, filled with horrors and defined by regrets. An episode of CBS's *Westinghouse Desilu Playhouse*, called "The Time Element," more famous today as an unofficial "pilot" for the now iconic series *The Twilight Zone* (1959–1964), is useful to revisit in the context of nostalgia, television, and time travel, as well as a fascinating reconfiguration of the US' collective memory of December 7th. Both that show and a subsequent episode of *The Time Tunnel* (1966–1967) focus on men who, in different ways, find themselves literally transported back in time to the moments immediately preceding the Pearl Harbor attack (a similar narrative device was later used in the 1980 sci-fi adventure *The Final Countdown*, which saw a modern naval aircraft carrier sent back to 1941 and confronted with the existential dilemma of whether to prevent the tragedy).

The connection between visual screens and time travel was most explicit in the short-lived series, *The Time Tunnel*, an episodic television show on ABC that told the story of two scientists, Tony Newman (James Darren) and Doug Philips (Robert Colbert), who traveled randomly through time, arriving at a different point in history each week. During their journeys, the two men are observed by a group of scientists in the present who study the data (their narrative role, ultimately, is to do little but provide expository information to the show's audience). The time "tunnel" is literally a screen, which allows scientists to watch history, but never participate—a temporal contradiction of both being in the presence of, but also decisively separated from, the past. As one scientist notes, "All men have to live with their past . . . it can't be changed"—an apt statement that summarizes the popularity of time travel as a narrative device, as a fantasy of wanting to think the past still could be changed (a desire that almost all depictions of Pearl Harbor directly or indirectly reflect). The images they watch are a mix of archival material from the given period, when available, combined with the new footage of scientists on their quest. This highly reflexive plot device calls attention to the increasing ubiquity of new mediated versions of history in the latter half of the twentieth century, while the newsreel footage of the Pearl Harbor attack carries a much more powerful sense of history revisited than some of the same footage used decades earlier in *December 7th*. And implied in that visual archiving for subsequent generations of audiences is how the enormity of historical events and their inherently simplified mediations have become increasingly intertwined to an unprecedented degree. "This isn't just a picture," one scientist must remind his colleagues (and the audience).

During the fourth episode of its only season, "The Day the Sky Fell In," the scientists arrive the day before the Japanese attack. What distinguishes this one from other episodes of the series is that Tony was also a child living in Honolulu on December 7th, giving the story a much more intimate dimension. Here, he meets his long-lost father, someone who had been reported missing during the attack (his mother, meanwhile, had died a year earlier)—and a subtext to the entire episode is that this event represents the core disturbance of his childhood. The element of trauma in "The Day" is most directly played up in Tony's initial inability to remember what he was doing that day after the Japanese planes had begun their attack. "It must have been the shock of the bombing . . . ," he tells his time-traveling partner, "it wiped out everything [in my memory]. All I can remember is running and running. . . . I ran towards my father." The desire to prevent the attack, then, not only takes on a more personal element, but becomes acutely symbolic of larger cultural attitudes—the opposed desires to both remember and forget the tragedy. In the end, he cannot change the past but at least is able to find some emotional closure with what happened, coming face-to-face with his dad before his death: "It's good to know my little boy will survive," he says. His father, it turns out, radioed the aircraft carrier USS *Enterprise* before dying, in a bit of historical license, in order to ensure they did not sail into the attack—giving him a heroic end. Japanese planes then bomb the radio room after Tony and Doug flee, leaving "nothing left" of the building: "That's why my father was never found." In its own melodramatic and fantastical way, *The Time Tunnel* acutely dramatized the reoccurring trauma of Pearl Harbor in the collective American imagination—how to accept that history cannot be changed, while also managing to find something still unknown within that same story to finally provide some semblance of closure.

The latter, meanwhile, is a little harder to come by in a different time travel episode of the early TV anthology series *Westinghouse Desilu Playhouse*, produced by Desi Arnaz and Lucille Ball. Written by Rod Serling, "The Time Element" foregrounded the aggravated sense of regret, as well as the pangs of nostalgia, that memories of December 7th evoked—but without the easy emotional (or narrative) answers that many of these other texts provided. Debuting on November 24th, 1958, the episode is now regarded as an unofficial pilot for *The Twilight Zone* because its positive reception pushed the network into greenlighting Serling's ambitious, but unconventional, project. Set in the present-day late 1950s, "The Time Element" is the story of a man, Peter Jensen (William

Bendix), who has the same reoccurring dream of awaking in the fictitious "Imperial Hawaiian Hotel" in Honolulu on December 6th, a story he relays in detail to his skeptical psychiatrist (Martin Balsam). The dream, however, is so real that Peter is persuaded to believe that he is traveling back in time. The story of time travel follows a predictable genre pattern here—Peter is initially convinced either he or the people around him are going crazy. Eventually, though, he begins to settle in and embrace the situation—in this case, happily placing bets on sporting events for which he already knows the outcome. Soon, though, the inevitable guilt of knowing what will occur settles in—spurred by his encounter with a young naval ensign (Darryl Hickman) and his new bride (Carolyn Kearney), the former being stationed on the infamously doomed USS *Arizona* (we also learn, as a final twist of the dramatic knife, that the wife will also be killed by Japanese fighter planes). Aware of the sensitive subject at hand, he remarks to a flippant hotel maid that she's "on the threshold of a deep wound." Predictably, Peter then proceeds to try and prevent the attack, with equally predictable results—everyone from newspaper editors to the barman to the other sailors become convinced he is insane (similarly, the two scientists in *The Time Tunnel* are accused of telling "crazy stories that no one would believe").

Resigned to the events of fate, Peter retreats to the hotel bar. Surrounded by young sailors dancing with girls while on shore leave, the scene suggests the imagined innocence of life in Hawai'i before the attack. Meanwhile, the imagery of Peter sitting at the counter while drowning in his sorrows evokes the common idea of reminiscing that one might associate with middle-aged men having a solitary drink at the bar (this is echoed by the film's twist ending, when the psychiatrist also visits a bar for comfort, only to be confronted with unsettling details about the past). Yet instead of simply waxing sentimentally about memories of life before the war, Peter finds himself literally reliving it. The overtly nostalgic element to this sequence is highlighted when he notes in a first-person voiceover, "It was kind of a crazy feeling though to watch these kids relax over their dates and their drinks when tomorrow morning there'd be a couple of thousands of them taking a miserable route through hell . . . to get to heaven." The symbolism of youth here becomes self-evident, as the sailors and their dates embody the war generation's lost innocence and the future gone with it as much as actual historical individuals—the way life could have gone but did not. The entire diegetic space here is a nostalgic fantasy—the joy and warmth of the Imperial Hawaiian (the kind of exclusive tourist destination that in real life would have been generally off-limits to servicemen prewar) is far removed from the grim, seedy Honolulu of the same era in *From Here to Eternity*. Meanwhile, actual war brides in Honolulu during that time were fairly uncommon—wives generally remained stateside, and physical companionship, when desired, was most often pursued with prostitutes (with the military's knowing ambivalence).[91] Yet even the aforementioned melancholic moment of recollection is disrupted, as Peter cannot stop insisting to anyone who will listen that the attack will take place—taunting the irate soldiers with the war song "Let's Remember Pearl Harbor as We Go to Meet the Foe!" (the same song was also used as historical shorthand in *The Time Tunnel*). In the end, he is killed during the attack by a Japanese plane strafing run, which leads to a surprise conclusion where the psychiatrist—stunned after witnessing his patient disappear suddenly back in the present—is told by one of Peter's old friends at the bar that he actually died during the attack on Pearl Harbor.

Despite its indulgent fantasies of time travel, "The Time Element" serves as a sobering bookend to so much of the nostalgic fascination with Pearl Harbor that had dominated many such media representations in the postwar decades. The episode's narrative is not simply a sentimental look back, but one struggling against the forces of inevitability and destiny. Peter ultimately cannot change history for the better—and his frustration in the end ("Why wouldn't anybody listen to me?") symbolizes the collective regret over the inability to alter the past or the legacy that came with it. Less a shocking twist than historical affirmation, Peter's tragic fate completes the episode's thematic insistence on the inability to change the past without risking disastrous consequences for the present. The final melancholia of "The Time Element" is not the lost innocence of the prewar period it briefly wallows in, nor the inability to prevent the tragic loss of life on December 7th, but the larger need to accept historical events as they happened.

The use of time travel narratives on television by the 1960s suggested how tenuous it was becoming to keep on telling the same story of December 7th in straightforward and/or unironic ways. At the same time, the endlessly deferred desires of time travel fantasies—that if only the audience could just travel back to that fateful Sunday morning one last time, then they could finally understand what really happened, accept it, and move on—was not too far removed from the goals of more historically accurate cinematic accounts such as Ford and Toland's *December 7th* or *Tora! Tora! Tora!*, as well as more melodramatic ones such as *From Here to Eternity* or *In Harm's Way*. At the heart of all these representations was the need to believe that there was still some fundamental misunderstanding, some mystery, about the events of December 7th. *Tora! Tora! Tora!*'s own producer promoted this idea: "While everybody remembers Dec. 7th, 1941, many people are still in doubt as to what exactly happened that day and how it came about."[92] While many complicated chronological, geographical, political, and logistical details surrounding December 7th were still being uncovered in research and debated by historians through the subsequent decades, there was little left to reveal (particularly within the limited scope of conventional Hollywood narratives) about the deeper significance of those events—not so much what happened but what it meant—for audiences that had already spent decades endlessly revisiting it.

3

You're Still Talking about Class?

Adapting for Statehood in *Diamond Head* (1963)

> After the passage of the National Labor Relations Act, a good many members of west coast maritime unions found it worth their while to spend time [in Hawai'i]. . . . To these Californians labor unions based on race or nationality were worthless. The idea might succeed in isolated instances on remote plantations, but that was the limit of its possible effectiveness, and because blood unionism could easily set one group of laborers against another, it finally played into the hands of management. The new slogan was simplicity itself: Know your class and be loyal to it.
>
> —Gavan Daws, *Shoal of Time*

☙

EARLY IN THE COLD WAR ESPIONAGE film *Big Jim McClain* (1952), two FBI agents in Honolulu (John Wayne and James Arness) take a moment from chasing suspected Communists to pay their respects to the fallen sailors of Pearl Harbor by visiting a makeshift memorial for the sunken USS *Arizona*. The sequence reinforced how by the 1950s "the war [had] wiped out all possible objections to admitting Hawaii as a state . . . the civilians of the territory suffered the ignominy of martial law with good grace; and the 442nd Regiment and the rest of Hawaii's thirty thousand servicemen met every demand made upon them."[1] Far simpler than the more elaborate, now iconic version built a decade later, the original memorial site was a modest series of metal railing platforms situated above the remnants of the wreckage. "By making hypervisible the histories of war violence, reinforcing familiar narratives of innocence and sacrifice, underscoring ideologies of multiculturalism and statehood, and crafting moments of intense sensory and affective identification with a defining moment of war," writes Vernadette Gonzalez, such references to December 7th "undertake the important cultural labor of recruiting sympathy for U.S. visions of security and for the measures the United States must take to achieve them."[2] Small moments in propaganda such as *McClain* tie that cultural labor and collective memory to contemporary political and social challenges in ways that elided important historical differences in favor of simplistic narratives of nationalism.

As the agents observe the sunken ship, we see a troubling conflation between memories of WWII and emerging tensions with Communist nations such as the USSR and China through appeals to an abstract notion of what was at stake in America's perpetual conflict in the Pacific. More than another war memorial, *McClain* may ultimately be more significant for how its silly spy melodrama and broad anti-Communist propaganda played out the tensions centered around labor disputes between Hawai'i and the mainland often elided in other fictional representations of the islands on the eve of statehood. The film takes its reactionary rhetoric straight from the likes of Republican US senator Joe McCarthy—even going so far as to open the story with a hearing at the House Un-American Activities Committee (HUAC) in Washington, DC, where McClain (Wayne) becomes increasingly irate at how—as the film depicts it—one disingenuous and smarmy union representative is able to weasel out of revealing his obvious Communist ties by hiding behind the Fifth Amendment. Not coincidently, *McClain* appeared in theaters just a couple of years after the 1949 International Longshore and Warehouse Union (ILWU) strike at the Honolulu shipping docks, a successful 177-day-long strike by union workers to demand greater pay. Many pro–Big Five organizations such as the "Broom Brigade" blamed the work stoppage directly on Communist influences, and shortly after the strike ended, members of HUAC were sent to the islands to investigate the origins of several recent labor strikes there.

Similarly, in *McClain*, the FBI travels to Oʻahu to track down the Communists they believe have infiltrated local unions and manipulated the worker population. A propagandistic cliché of the Cold War era, the film promoted a popular belief of the time that every union representative was a subversive un-American who took his orders directly from Mother Russia, and whose only interest in helping the rights of the working class was to sow disharmony and destroy the US from the inside. "In the spring of 1947 the chief of Army Intelligence in Hawaii and his commanding general came privately to [Hawaiian Territorial] Governor Ingram Stainback," writes Daws, "to warn him that the ILWU was a nest of Communists and that the infestation was spreading."[3] US Senator Hugh Butler of Nebraska visited the islands in 1948 and "convinced himself that there were unbroken lines of influence running all the way from Moscow to the Honolulu waterfront and back."[4] Similarly, a 1954 NBC television special, *Hawaii—49th State*, argued that "a major part of the control of Hawaii rests not in the islands but . . . in San Francisco, at the headquarters of International Longshoremen's Union—a union which was thrown out of the CIO [Congress of Industrial Organizations] for following too closely the Communist line."[5]

As this TV special suggested, the rhetoric around Communism in the islands during the 1950s was also related to the statehood movement—as opponents would often raise the possibility of inviting an openly communist-friendly outpost into the union. This threat was a convenient excuse for the ruling *haole* elites in Hawaiʻi to explain why they were losing the fight with labor unions, and who had resisted the new "industrial and political forces that were redistributing power, and to a lesser extent wealth, in the once-stable island community. For many members of this group, disruption, instability, and uncertainty were obviously the result of the un-American and conspiratorial activities of subversive communist elements."[6] Fearing the potential to further perpetuate concerns about Communist influence, few films and television shows about Hawaiʻi in the pre- and post-statehood era engaged with class and labor struggles. Those that did, such as *Big Jim McClain*, were unambiguous in expressing Hawaiian patriotism. The local Honolulu police are depicted (by real-life officers) in *Big Jim McClain* as eager allies in the fight to root out any and all Communist presence in Hawaiʻi.

What was also only partially implied in anxieties about Communist influences lingering throughout Hawaiʻi—as depicted in films such as *Big Jim McClain* and *Hell's Half Acre* (1954)—was that the tension was not only labor-based but deeply intertwined with questions of race, given a diverse population of Asian descent on the islands that was perceived by some conservative texts as being possibly involved with, or at least complicit in, Soviet influence, given the closer physical proximity to the Far East. Opposition to statehood on the islands themselves was organized by groups such as Imua (the nickname for the ironically titled "Hawaii Residents Association"), which was "both an anti-communist and anti-Japanese organization, and its publicity and very existence accentuated tensions between labor and employer groups, as well as across ethnic lines. It was the last resort of *kamaaina haoles* [longtime white residents] unwilling to accommodate to Hawaii's more flexible political and racial climate."[7] The issue of statehood in the coexistent shadows of WWII and the Cold War framed racial relations for both Hawai'i and the mainland in more urgent, and more ambivalent, ways. "Racism," wrote Roger Bell, "was a crucial factor in the protracted statehood dispute."[8] Instead of the touristic South Seas fantasy of primitive natives welcoming white travelers with open arms, the idea of Hawai'i actually becoming a coequal part of the country forced many Americans to reconcile the islands' distinctive racial identity with the US' often unspoken white supremacy, and moreover how the challenge of America adapting to Hawai'i, and vice versa, both reflected, troubled, and intensified similar issues and tensions already long at play in the mainland.

The most overt and ambivalent cinematic representation of the many intertwined issues of race and class in Hawai'i during this era might be the steamy Hollywood melodrama *Diamond Head* (1963)—the story of one wealthy plantation family's struggles with its own racial attitudes, set on the eve of statehood. *Diamond Head* would most clearly reflect on the big screen how the push for statehood appealed to the United States' liberal principles of freedom and tolerance, but also awkwardly forced the country to confront older mainland prejudices it wasn't necessarily invested in acknowledging. For all its hokey racial melodrama and typical Hollywood clichés, *Diamond Head* remains a distinctively illuminating film from this period, as it offers a unique and usefully problematic take on the intersections of race, class, politics, regional identity, and national identity in the era of statehood. That it is incapable of reconciling these complex contradictions at the core of aligning Hawai'i's unique identity with the established self-proclaimed utopic ideals of American democracy makes it no less a fascinating snapshot of this moment in Hawai'i's history.

Adapted from a very different novel by Peter Gilman, originally entitled *Such Sweet Thunder* (1960), the film version of *Diamond Head*

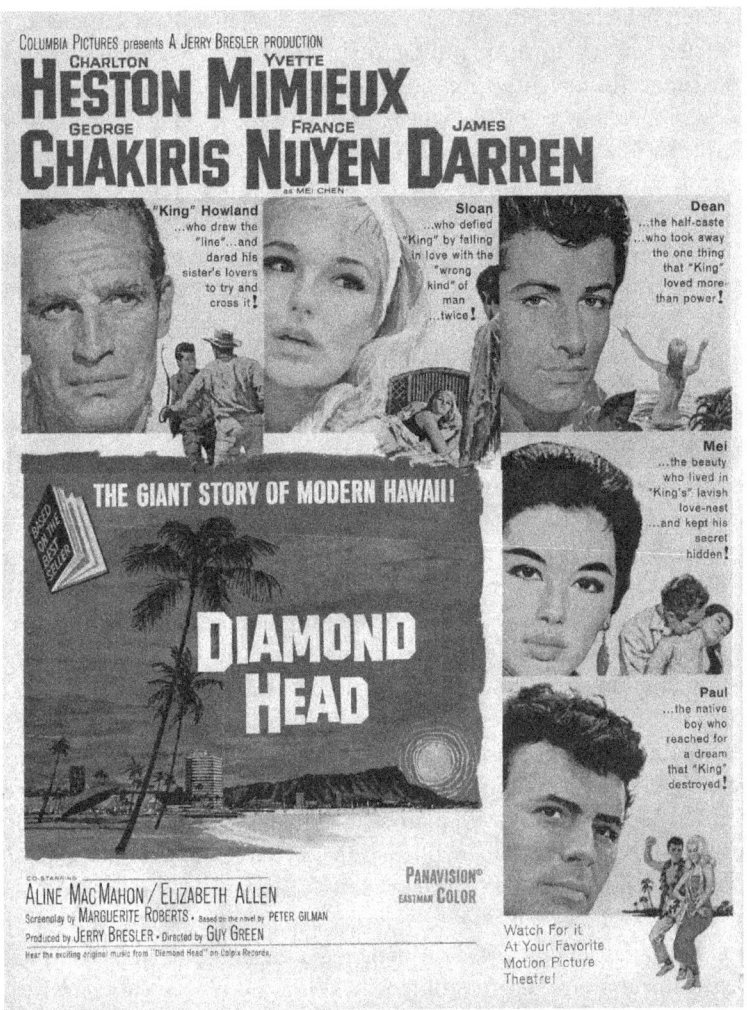

Figure 3.1. In some ways, *Diamond Head* (1963) was little more than Hollywood's awkward attempt at cashing in on the 1960s' trendy subject of statehood by taking the old genre formulas of the Southern racial melodrama and mapping it onto the very different political and cultural dynamics of modern-day Hawai'i. Yet the uneven end result still was uniquely illuminating for its time as a commentary on the politics of literary adaptation, the US' statehood-era negotiation of its own self-professed global democratic ideals as they clashed with a longer internal history of prejudice and intolerance, and—perhaps most illuminating—how a particular strand of "aloha multiculturalism" intersected with neoliberal notions of race and class in the postindustrial age.

promoted a form of post-racial whiteness[9] that elided white privilege by embracing the rhetoric of multicultural tolerance, while also removing a coexistent history of labor consciousness and economic exploitation by equating class prejudice with racial prejudice. Hegemonic rhetoric about Hawai'i's reputation for multiculturalism has long been used to erase a history of economic exploitation, where any labor agitation was seen through touristic frames as betraying the lovingly romantic spirit of "aloha"—despite the fact that it was class consciousness that in part helped to unite diverse working-class workers behind support for statehood. As early as the 1920s and 1930s, writes Lori Peirce, "the *Haole* ruling class constantly depicted Hawai'i as a racial paradise, a place where the Hawaiians, *Haole*, Japanese, and Chinese lived cooperatively. . . . The message being communicated was that ethnic diversity was not a threat to the *Haole* ruling class"[10] in the way that working-class unity would be.

Diamond Head is the story of a wealthy plantation owner, King Howland (Charlton Heston), who is encouraged by local authorities to run for US senator once the plans for statehood go through. (The role was originally intended for Clark Gable before he passed away, the star of that most well-known of all plantation melodramas, *Gone with the Wind* [1939], and whose real-life nickname was also "King.") Given his considerable industrial power, King finds a few disgruntled union workers to be one of the many obstacles he encounters while running for office. As the patriarch of a prestigious white family with immense wealth and influence on the islands, his name, "Howland," also sounds uncannily like *haole*. Meanwhile, his younger sister Sloane (Yvette Mimieux) falls in love with a Native Hawaiian, Paul Kahana (James Darren), while off at college in California. Alan Marcus notes, meanwhile, the relative rarity that—while not discounting the unfortunate whitewashed casting—the major Hawaiian characters "are depicted not as beach boys [*sic*], but as college educated and cosmopolitan."[11] When Paul and Sloane return to the islands with intentions to marry, King is forced to confront his own prejudices about whites marrying Hawaiians and how those attitudes may or may not align with America's self-professed ideals of equalitarianism—an issue that the coming status of statehood brings to a head. Further complicating matters is Howland's own secret love affair with an Asian woman, Mai Chen (France Nuyen), who is pregnant with his child, the potential male heir to his fortune. (*Variety* at the time pointed out how "one of the oddities of *Diamond Head* [is] that no one, from conception on, ever seems to consider the possibility that the unborn child might turn out to be female."[12]) Meanwhile, Mai's brother Bobbie (Marc Marno) expresses open resentment at not only Howland's power and status but at being unable to find work as anything other than a "beachboy" for tourists. His personal and professional anger brings to the surface the history of exploitation that informs his frustration, though his villainous status ultimately undercuts audience sympathy. Moreover, his bitterness fits squarely with a neoliberal statehood-era mentality that depicted some Hawaiians as unwilling to adapt to the reality of modern times (earlier in the film, a different Hawaiian notes that, due to statehood, opportunities will expand now for locals to do "things besides play a ukulele").

Both the film and its original novel reveal much about the political and cultural implications of literary adaptation—a common industrial practice for studios always looking for the next safe bet. The process of adapting an idea from one medium to another had long been an important component to mainland representations of Hawai'i. Plays (*Bird of Paradise*) adapted into movies. Songs used in one context (*Aloha Oe, Blue Hawaii*) were adapted for another. Radio programs (*Hawaii Calls*) evolved into movies (and later TV shows). And, oftentimes, as with many Hollywood films then and now, the adaptation was from popular novel to big-screen spectacle (*Diamond Head, South Pacific, From Here to Eternity, Hawaii*). Issues of what was and was not adapted often focus on topics such as censorship pressure (as was the case with *Eternity*), or narrative length (*Hawaii*), and so forth. By and large, decisions made in the adaptation process are rarely purely aesthetic in consideration—as in, "What's the best way to tell the core story?" Adaptation is not only a creative act, but a political and historical one. Any changes made to the "original" say more about the larger historical climate, about changes in industry trends and cultural attitudes. Artistic intentions are often secondary to commercial and ideological goals, as well as the assumed mood of the contemporary audience.

Diamond Head had the advantage of not only its timely Hawai'i subject matter, but also being a sensationalistic racial melodrama that appealed to a mainland negotiating the historic implications of the US civil rights movement. In the film, as Marcus notes, the location of "Hawaii, where mixed marriages were commonplace, provides the artificial setting for a verbal exchange that was more indicative of debates relating to racial attitudes in mainland America. This approach is germane to the film and the book, rather than a subtext imposed by the filmmakers."[13] The casting of Heston, a highly visible activist at the time, he argues, further supports this reading. "In an interview with the actor published in 1974 he reflected on that era," Marcus writes, "stating that 'the social comment implied in [certain films] was important to me.' "[14] As Judy Rohrer notes, "Race is not the taboo subject in Hawai'i that it is in the dominant white culture of the continent. In fact, race gets talked about constantly in Hawai'i. It is now an everyday part of island culture, a tool people use to navigate a very multiracial environment."[15] The numerous interracial relationships throughout both novel and film bring to the fore troublingly unanswered questions for some Americans about racial tensions in ways that earlier sentimental depictions of hula and beachboys avoided. Both texts clearly position these interpersonal relationships as symbolic of larger local and national discourses converging on the eve of statehood.

In attempting to navigate the lucrative commercial popularity of Hawai'i in the era of statehood, the film version avoids the book's spirited depiction of Hawai'i's intense labor strife and class tension (except for a couple of minor, but crucial, sequences) in favor of the much more profitable and commercially safer tradition of the interracial romance. For all the tensions with censors and certain geographic regions (and perhaps because of those tensions at times), the subgenre of the interracial melodrama has proven to be consistently, historically viable. Early in the film, Howland's sister tells Sloane that interracial marriage "happens all the time [in Hawai'i], but not to people of our class." To such a blatant display of bigotry, the young woman angrily responds, "'Class'? You're still taking about class? If I believe anything it's that all people are the same." Here concerns over class differences are explicitly equated with concerns over racial differences—and thus to focus on class, within the logic of the film, is the equivalent of being racially intolerant. The film's melodramatic narrative of interracial love, and the enlightened acceptance of all people that it promotes, in effect attempts to override the collective history of class differences and crucial labor struggles in Hawai'i.

Diamond Head's dismissal of class consciousness reflected a neoliberal, postwar desire to promote racial (or even, in Sloane's case, post-racial) harmony at the expense of older prewar labor struggles, the complex history of collective bargaining and strong government support that had once worked to buttress it. Hawaiians of wide ethnic and racial backgrounds united in the 1930s, 1940s, and 1950s, not simply out of a utopic desire for racial harmony, but out of economic and political necessity. Allowing the population to be divided along racial lines, like on the mainland, undercut common class struggles for better economic equality and opportunity. "'Trade not aid' and 'vacations not donations' arose in the context of business and government leaders' rejection of New Deal projects to redistribute wealth and income through progressive taxation and government spending," wrote Christine Skwiot, "and embrace of the notion that private investment and enterprise would fuel sustained economic growth and the upward mobility of most people."[16] Just as the Hawaiian tourist industry promoted consumption over production, and exploitation of local workers in the service of "leisure," the "aloha spirit" reinforced the centrality of interpersonal relations in a racially diverse world over the equally messy, conflicted labor history through which that spirit was intensely fought for.

Selling Statehood on the Big Screen

The statehood movement began in earnest in the 1930s—as white industrialists became increasingly nervous about losing control over how they were taxed and other economic disadvantages, realizing they needed more stable political clout through self-representation, rather than as a territory at the mercy of the federal government. Yet the road to statehood took an ironic turn—for one, the same economic and cultural elites initially pushing for statehood would eventually find themselves opposite a rapidly growing local working-class population that saw the possibilities of statehood as a way to gain increasing political power to combat those same powerful few. While many weren't particularly enamored with the US' colonial presence, some did recognize the political pragmatism of statehood as a means to greater agency. After WWII, writes Gonzalez, "statehood, in this case, was understood as a just reward for the suffering sustained by the islands and its peoples."[17] By the end of the 1940s, there was serious discussion on both sides of the Pacific about the prospect of Hawaiian statehood.

Yet despite the aggressive propaganda campaign by the Hawaii Statehood Commission and Hawai'i's appreciated role during the war, "the proportion of mainlanders willing to accept either [Alaska or Hawai'i] as a state also declined significantly" during the 1950s.[18] Opposition was both racial and political in nature: "The only significant variable which might have influenced the differences in mainland opinion was the composition of Hawaii's population. The issue of communist influence appears to be the only other variable."[19] Many conservatives were resistant to the idea of adding a state with not only liberal political and social views, but also one where people of European descent were not the majority. Writes Skwiot, "The beauty of mixed-race women and youths figure prominently as a reason U.S. citizens should visit Hawai'i," but many at the time felt "interracial marriage and procreation was not a model for the mainland to adopt."[20] On the other end, however, were some Americans who saw the admittance of Hawai'i to the union as a testament to the nation's increasing sense of racial tolerance and equality. "Statehood would enable the United States to improve relations with Asia," she adds, "and to demonstrate to the world that it accepted people of color as equals."[21] As Max Lerner wrote in a 1965 article on Hawai'i in the *New Pittsburgh Courier* (a paper that targeted African American readers): "A visitor to Hawaii can afford at least a touch of pride at the thought that the 50th state, which has rounded out the American union, is not even a close facsimile of any other state, is very much itself, has made America ethnically richer and more diverse, and is a living example of what the [civil rights] marchers at Montgomery [Alabama] were marching for."[22]

Daws documented an anecdote of one Hawaiian, in the immediate aftermath of statehood, "sitting in a bar, the perfect image of the local boy, a blend of any number of racial strains. Looking at himself in the wall mirror, he said with some satisfaction: 'Now we are all *haoles*.'"[23] Like many early historians of Hawai'i's past, Daws painted an image of Hawai'i as always destined to elevate itself as a part of the US, to symbolize America's desire to imagine itself as an increasingly "post-racial" society. But as Bell notes:

> It is highly misleading to claim that Hawaii's peoples were 'all haoles,' because the term had definite economic and social connotations; it implied that Hawaii was a broadly egalitarian society ... the overwhelming support for statehood as an index of widely shared political aspirations and democratic values resulting from pervasive Americanization over almost a century. It did not, however, reflect broad structural unity, the dissolution of ethnic diversity, or uniform patterns of acculturation.[24]

The term *haole* in this context meant that entrance into a democratic United States erased the profound racial, economic, and cultural differences that provided Hawai'i with its own distinctive identity. To get to statehood, representatives of the islands had to spend the better part of two decades repeatedly selling the US on the idea that Hawai'i was undeniably loyal to the nation, that it was racially diverse (but not dangerously so), that it was exotic (but not foreign), and—connected to all of that—that it was, despite its physical distance from the mainland, not overrun by Communist influences that so troubled much of the nation during the Cold War.

Hawai'i's advocacy for statehood was as much a touristic endeavor as a political one—in so far as it was the former that helped move public opinion in their favor over the course of decades. Descendent of early missionaries, prominent Honolulu newspaper executive and early advocate of the tourism industry Lorrin P. Thurston "helped coordinate the Hawai'i visits of US media and government officials and ensured that virtually all arriving and mainland-bound tourists received literature asking them to write their congressional representatives 'urging favorable action on Hawaiian statehood.'"[25] Postwar, the same economic islands interests that had worked so aggressively to sell Hawai'i as a vacation destination in the prewar years had now been mobilized in a more direct push for statehood—though entrance into the union, desired by many sometimes conflicting local groups, had always been one goal of the tourist industry. The Hawaii Visitors Bureau "boasted that in 1958 its press office 'directly arranged' 102 pages of tourism-statehood articles published in mainland magazines, including 'all of the stories' in [publisher Henry R.] Luce's *Time*, *Life*, *Fortune*, and *Sports Illustrated*."[26]

Postwar Hollywood also occasionally played a role in the effort as well. In 1947, the US House of Representatives passed a statehood bill by a vote of 196 to 133 (which was subsequently ignored by the Senate). To help exploit this timely news, RKO Pictures produced a propaganda film entitled *Hawaii: The 49th State* as part of the studio's successful "This Is America" short subject documentary series.[27] Featuring 112 titles released from 1942 to 1951, "This is America," writes Richard Barsam, presented "a unique reflection of American history and American values" throughout the period, with an emphasis on (according to promotional brochures of the time) the fact that "the films were 'the real thing—not Hollywood make-believe.'"[28] To help promote the film, RKO encouraged movie theater managers to start a contest to see who locally could design the best new US flag featuring forty-nine stars. "You can't have better publicity on any film," boasted RKO's theater exploitation guide, "than that supplied *free* by Congressional investigation and debates."[29] An unabashed advocate for Hawaiian statehood, the documentary was marketed as a rejection of the "romantic picture of Hawaii familiar to every American who's ever unwrapped a travel folder or seen a South Seas movie."[30] In a publicity guide sent to theater managers, RKO wrote:

Figure 3.2. To help promote the postwar cause of Hawaiian statehood, RKO Pictures produced the documentary *The 49th State* (1947) with heavy input from the Hawaiian Statehood Commission and the Hawaii Press Bureau. Like the Tourist Bureau films of the prewar era (and, to a lesser extent, *Diamond Head*), the film preferred to play down old tropical stereotypes in favor of presenting Hawai'i as the site of a modern economy with thriving commerce and a diverse and industrious population.

The allure and charm of Hawaii are no myth. The hula is genuine, the climate marvelous, but today the people of the islands are out of patience with mainlanders who regard Hawaii merely as a languorous place of enchantment. For Hawaii is also a dynamic American community of half a million people, a vital force in American economy, one of the busiest crossroads of commerce.[31]

Similarly, an exhibitor's sale guide added that the Hawaiian people had "abandoned dreamy native ways for business, industry and education."[32] The Statehood Commission, meanwhile, played an active role in the production and promotion of the film. In January of 1947, one member of the commission, George McLane, along with Otto Janssen of the Hawaii Press Bureau, traveled to New York City to consult with RKO on the content of the film. Some of the suggestions made were to include a scene that takes place in Washington, DC, to strengthen the impression of Hawai'i's connection with the federal government, and a sequence that would "locate Hawaii by a diagrammatic map showing the westward expansion of the United States" in order to situate Hawaiian statehood as part of the larger rhetoric of US manifest destiny.[33]

On October 7, 1947, the commission hosted an advanced screening reception in Washington, DC, in the Chinese Room of the Mayflower Hotel. The event was attended by both filmmakers and politicians, including Hawai'i's then-delegate to the US Congress Joseph R. Farrington, who was himself referenced in *The 49th State*. Farrington was the "son of a territorial governor, a rich man, and a liberal Republican (or as liberal as Republicans got in Hawaii)."[34] One of statehood's most visible proponents, Farrington was credited for giving "firm guidance to the early postwar drive for eventual admission,"[35] providing interviews for a variety of print and later TV programs in support of the effort. At the screening, United States Secretary of the Interior Julius Albert Krug introduced the film, stating, "I have had the feeling that if we could take the American people out there to see the islands for themselves, there would be no question in anyone's mind that the Territory is ready for statehood. Unfortunately, we can't do that, but through the medium of the movie camera, we can do the next best thing. We can bring Hawaii to the American people."[36] In contrast to this, the film's producer, Philip Reisman Jr., preferred to downplay the propagandistic nature of *The 49th State*, saying that filmmakers "are in the entertainment business . . . we do not consider ourselves as educators." Later, he added, "We don't feel it is the purpose of the documentary film to tell people *what* to think. Our purpose will have been served if we have encouraged them *to* think."[37]

A decade later, in 1958, Hawai'i's territorial governor William F. Quinn attempted to use the Washington, DC, premiere of the Cinerama travelogue film *South Seas Adventure* (1958) as an opportunity to influence lawmakers into supporting statehood. The film was originally titled *Cinerama South Pacific* but the title was changed to avoid confusion with the popular James Michener adaptation, *South Pacific*, released that same year. Cinerama was an early form of widescreen film that used three separate 35-mm cameras lined up shoulder-to-shoulder-to-shoulder to capture a cinematic image three times wider than a typical movie of the time. The original Cinerama films, under the ownership of Stanley Warner Theatres, were travelogue films that featured some basic scripted scenes, but largely emphasized thrilling point-of-view shots (riding a bobsled, landing on an aircraft carrier, riding a rollercoaster) and especially the impressive scenery of exotic locations to maximize the new format's visual potential. Such locations included Niagara Falls, the American West, Europe, and the so-called "Seven Wonders of the World."

Promoted by the company as "your Cinerama dream vacation" and featuring voiceover narration by Orson Welles, *South Seas Adventures* was an epic journey across many parts of the Pacific Ocean. Running over two-and-a-half hours in length, the film opens aboard Matson's SS *Lurline* as it begins its final sail into Honolulu. Much of the first part of the film is largely a more visually ambitious version of the same older vacation clichés. Hula girls greet visitors beneath Aloha Tower, while "Aloha Oe" and "Song of the Islands" play in the background. We see surfers at Waikiki, along with the usual depictions of swimming and fishing. Images of tropical flowers and pineapples abound. A more modern phase of Hawai'i tourism is highlighted in the film by a greater emphasis on Honolulu's postwar nightlife, the centerpiece of which is a sequence where tourists visit Don the Beachcomber's famous restaurant and watch the Polynesian-themed floor show. After the O'ahu scenes, most of the film moves on to other, sometimes more remote, regions in the South Pacific: Tahiti, Tonga, Fiji, Pentecost Island, New Zealand, and Australia.

Sensing a promising public relations bonanza, the territorial governor's office (along with the Statehood Commission[38] and the Hawaii Visitors Bureau[39]) had hoped to host a "Hawaii Night" at the film's premiere on January 21, 1959, in Washington, DC. (Meanwhile, approximately seventy-five well-connected people in Honolulu, including Big Five representatives, were invited by the bureau to a sneak peek screening the previous July at the Princess Theatre,[40] which was converted for Cinerama projection for the film's debut.) The plan in DC included inviting not only President Dwight Eisenhower, members of the US Congress, the Supreme Court, and other government agencies on one night, but also having a second night's screening for congressional aides and secretaries.[41] Quinn's original draft for a letter inviting the president to the premiere included two explicit references to Eisenhower's support for Hawaiian statehood, as well as the importance of having members of the new incoming session of Congress view the film themselves.[42] Other potential plans for "Hawaii Night" included Hawaiian entertainers provided by Aloha Air Lines and Hawaiian Air Lines, lobby displays courtesy of Pan American Air Lines and United Air Lines, orchid leis from Kei Yamato florists, and TV clips and newspaper clips sent from Hawai'i to DC media outlets.[43] Other ideas included a Hawaiian orchestra and "girl dancers and others to assist in distribution of leis, about 12 girls in all."[44] The Hawaiian Pineapple Company (which a little over a year later changed its name to "Dole") also "agreed to provide pineapple juice without charge to be served to guests during intermission."[45]

However, in late November of 1958, the DC film premiere was moved up a full month by Stanley Warner to December 16, forcing the governor to cancel the "Hawaii Night" portion of the event. On December 4, Quinn personally wrote to the White House's secretary of the cabinet, Robert Gray, to express his frustration:

> I am sincerely sorry over this development, as I feel that the premiere would provide a wonderful opportunity for Hawaii to bring its statehood message to a large and important audience soon after the Congress convened. A premiere before the opening of the new Congress featuring Hawaii would naturally not have the desired effect.[46]

As late as November 14, the plan was still in place to invite the president, but was put on hold until the day had been confirmed.[47] The reason given for the sudden change in exhibition dates was that the prior Cinerama film playing at DC's Warner Theatre, *Windjammer* (1958), was reportedly "losing approximately four to five thousand dollars a week,"[48] according to Carl Dudley, *South Seas Adventure*'s producer, in an apologetic letter to the governor. As a result, the box office losses forced the theater chain to move up the opening of *South Seas Adventure* in an attempt to begin reviving lagging ticket sales.

From print coverage to the local movie theater, at the center of this media push for statehood was a familiar image. Ever present in advertising, the hula girl became central to Hawai'i's pitch for statehood as a symbol of the unconditionally affectionate, benignly colonized and excessively inviting, all wrapped up in the warm and safe nostalgia of a prewar paradise. Hula performers also "saw themselves making a contribution to the statehood effort that was as significant as that of politicians."[49] (It's worth noting that one of the more noted silver screen "hula girls," Dorothy Lamour, was a prominent supporter of statehood.) One big difference was the increasing presence of hula dancers on the mainland, crossing media boundaries and oceans to sell statehood up close. While hula circuits in the United States had toured successfully for decades, they became increasingly visible in the 1950s. "As ambassadors of aloha on the continent," wrote Imada, they "promoted Hawai'i as a friendly American outpost in the Pacific. Their movements were critical for the colonial territory to become a state."[50] And as skilled performers, they also benefited from the mediated memories they evoked for audiences.

The imagery of the passive and inviting female also, argues Skwiot, reaffirmed a "patriarchal authority to reassure white U.S. citizens fearful of admitting a multiracial state into the Union that continued to equate national belonging with whiteness."[51] In the end, Adria Imada adds, the push for statehood in Washington was literally sealed with a kiss: "If [Virginia congressman Howard] Smith authorized a vote in the house, [Hawaiian politician and later state governor Jack] Burns promised him he would arrange to have a 'beautiful . . . Hawaiian girl' give Smith a kiss and a flower lei. . . . Two days later, the House passed the statehood bill, making Hawai'i the fiftieth state."[52] As this implies, the element of the forbidden interracial romance remained at the colonial center of Hawai'i's allure to the US: "The larger project of state incorporation over several decades [was] a process that relied on the imagined sexual rapport between islander women and American men. . . . Their hula performances offered the United States a fantasy—a fantasy of intimate possession—and eventually helped to produce the fiftieth star in the American flag."[53] Similarly, as Jane Desmond notes, the fantasy of American women with island men—particularly in the prewar era—was a potent one too.[54] And the threats it posed to both patriarchal authority and older racial hierarchies were at the heart of interracial melodramas such *Diamond Head*.

Diamond Head and the Racial Melodrama

In the dead of another brutal Midwestern winter, a hula show accompanied by a Hawaiian band was performing outside the Chicago Theatre (warmed by heaters) to promote the opening of *Diamond Head*, complete with distinctive food delicacies flown in from Hawai'i.[55] Advertising for the film included producing a one-hour travelogue documentary about Hawai'i for local television that included footage from the film and interviews with the stars, and cross-promotion with local travel agencies and department stores—the latter of whom offered themed fashion model shows that tellingly showcased the latest trends in high-end *travel* outfits, *not* Hawaiian garments.[56] Such aggressive promotion was needed to offset the costs of such an ambitious epic. One way *Diamond Head* saved money was as one of several so-called "runaway" film productions that increasingly gravitated to Hawai'i and other offshore locations in the postwar era—movies and TV shows that were shot outside Hollywood to avoid some of the union labor requirements and heavier tax policies that raised the costs of shooting in LA. Ironically, Heston was himself a vice president for the Screen Actors Guild at the time of the production—voicing objection in union solidarity to the rise of runaway productions, even as he was himself often a participant in them (even more ironic given *Diamond Head*'s negative depiction of union workers). Dubbing him the "No. 1 Jet-Age Star," the *Los Angeles Times* noted in 1963 that Heston "has done more acting overseas than in Hollywood during the past five years."[57]

The film began shooting on the islands on March 15th, 1962,[58] hoping to utilize the stunning locations at a time when widescreen technicolor films set in Hawai'i were a rare novelty. The cast and crew shot on Kauai and O'ahu for five weeks, before heading to Hollywood for another six—most of the film, even its centerpiece outdoor luau sequence, was shot on soundstages. The *New York Times* reported that "photography on Honolulu's docks was done behind picket lines and within the desired harbor bustle,"[59] but didn't expand on the labor strife at hand, preferring to focus on the one thing that most often concerned the industry with Hawai'i shoots—the unpredictable weather. The picketing may have been connected to the rumor *Variety* reported on in 1962 that the film had been shot on location "to take advantage of [cheaper] pay for extras," which the film's producer Jerry Bresler denied.[60] A separate article of the time spun the topic differently: "Possibly the chief advantage of utilizing these locations, in [the film's director Guy] Green's opinion, is the availability of many racial types on all the islands. He also has employed a number of citizens for bit parts and found a majority of them to be 'naturally expressive.'"[61] The film turned out to be Bresler's most expensive to date, costing $2,500,000,[62] even as he had previous experience shooting in Hawai'i with *Gidget Goes Hawaiian* (1961), which also featured James Darren in a central role. "For the sake of authenticity and, of course, economy," Bresler told the *Times*, "there has been no construction of sets."[63] Given such location authenticity, the film was actively embraced by Hawaiian tourist businesses, "who generally agreed Kauai island has never looked lovelier,"[64] according to *Variety*. The Hawaii Visitors Bureau assisted with the film's Honolulu world premiere, since they "unofficially [saw] *Diamond Head* as the biggest booster for Isle tourism since *Blue Hawaii*" two years earlier.[65] The embrace by local industry was ironic given that the film, as with the novel, painted an often unflattering and inaccurate depiction of the islands' political and racial dynamics, which already had irked some locals.

As its tangled web of melodrama would suggest, the film fit safely within the subgenre of the interracial romance, whose track record of commercial success took something of the risk off its delicate subject matter. The industry trade paper *Boxoffice* predicted that "although there is sex aplenty, including two illicit love affairs, the film will intrigue teenagers even if it's too torrid for the kiddies."[66] The interracial romance, writes Marcus, "had its own benefits for tackling issues associated with race relations, allowing the filmmaker to make certain moral and ethical points that in any other genre might be less effective."[67] Hollywood depictions of Hawai'i and other visions of the South Seas romance had long embraced this model, though not always with a clear emphasis on moral didacticism. While *The Hurricane* (1937) used interracial love as a means to criticize the racism of (European) colonialism, *Bird of Paradise* (1932) largely sidestepped any direct questions of bigotry. Within the geographical context of Polynesia onscreen, this trend had perhaps reached its popular apex just a few years earlier in the love doomed by prejudice at the heart of the musical *South Pacific*. By the 1960s, even stars with a generally conservative audience, such as Elvis Presley (*Blue Hawaii*, *Paradise Hawaiian Style*) and John Wayne (*Donovan's Reef*), appeared in tropical-set narratives that at moments explicitly questioned and even at times outright rejected old racial prejudices of the mainland.

In an intense knife fight, instigated by Mai's drunken brother, Howland mistakenly kills Paul at a luau celebration of the impending wedding. Marcus reads this moment as symbolizing the racial violence of the time, as an example of "signposting our on-going obsession with cultural and ethnic difference, theories of racial superiority, and a desire to imagine the Other's landscape as an exotic site to be controlled."[68] In despair, Sloane shuns King and ends up in the arms of Paul's half-brother, Dean Kahana (George Chakiris). As Marcus notes, "Dean is a doctor—another device used to legitimate the worthiness of Sidney Poitier's character, Dr. Prentice, as a suitor for Joanna Drayton in *Guess Who's Coming to Dinner*."[69] Yet Dean is treated with a passive racial contempt by King because of his *hapa haole* roots—"half-white, half-brown," he derisively notes. While the plantation owner looks down on people of mixed descent, statehood rhetoric valorized such people as increasingly assimilated and thus more "American." Skwiot adds that the mainland's justification of occupation and acceptance of Hawaiian statehood was based in part on "denying the modernity and maturity of 'pure' Hawaiians while praising that of 'part'-Hawaiians."[70] After his secret lover dies in childbirth, King rejects the child—only to have a last-minute change of heart that suggests that the old bigot might finally begin to see the error of his racist ways. (The *Guardian* pointed out that "death is the universal let-out in pictures where miscegenation threatens to become too embarrassingly real . . . ," and commented derisively that "*Diamond Head* has a couple of Hawaiians to dispose of in this way before bringing the story . . . to a bearable conclusion."[71])

Since the nineteenth century, a plantation mindset rooted in the social hierarchies and labor practices of the agrarian South had shaped European attitudes on the islands—a white minority asserting its own sense of racial superiority through the exploitative labor of the nonwhite majority. However, Native Hawaiians were not forced into labor as African slaves had been, and many openly expressed disinterest, and even hostility, to the type of compensated physical labor whites expected them to perform in the fields. This is what in part initially opened Hawai'i to a greater influx of nonwhite labor from other parts of the globe and planted the seeds for its multicultural population. Hawai'i's reputation for diversity, writes Lori Pierce, was "not an accident. It was the deliberate policy on the part of *Haole* plantation owners to import a cheap, exploitable labor force, largely from Asia."[72] The fact that *Diamond Head* frames the racial tensions on the islands in ways that seem more closely aligned with the white supremacy of old Southern plantation melodramas—misrepresenting the more complex and fluid racial dynamic of Hawai'i—would support the idea that *Diamond Head* was allegorically speaking more about the mainland racial tensions than the islands. "If this turbulent melodrama is to be believed," wrote film critic Mae Tinee at the time, "the color of a man's skin can be as much a stigma in Hawaii as in Mississippi."[73]

Marcus adds that "despite his high standing as a wealthy white rancher, King represents a backward and rural past."[74] An Atlanta paper offered one of the few film reviews of the time to sidestep King's overt bigotry, describing him instead as a "ruthless empire builder [caught in] a bitter struggle between two self-willed people"[75] (the phrase "ruthless empire builder" appeared in other newspaper coverage of the time, suggesting it was taken from studio press releases). Marcus also points out that one of the original posters for *Diamond Head* showed the plantation owner "King with a whip, as he attacks a native Hawaiian, echoing the whipping of plantation slaves in the south, and of Afro-Americans in later years by the Ku Klux Klan"[76]—an offensive image that bears no connection to any scenes in the actual movie, but is clearly meant to evoke the setting and themes of old Southern melodramas.

At the same time, the old-fashioned model of the racial melodrama (echoing the "social consciousness" films of the 1940s) highlighted how unambitious culturally classical Hollywood really was by the 1960s. The *Boston Globe* observed that "unfortunately, the roles the actors are asked to play seem to have little to do with real life. At times the picture resembles an old-time serial rather than an up-to-date drama,"[77] while also adding that "if the story sounds a trifle unconvincing, that is just what it is."[78] The *New York Times*, meanwhile, noted that Heston was stuck playing "that old standard villain in plantation fiction, the big landowner who wants to rule the roost and keep his sister from marrying the young fellow whom he considers her social and racial inferior."[79] Tinee noted the cliché in such narratives that "people of mixed blood are generally far more decent than our hero, who is surprised that his money cannot purchase popularity for him."[80] *Variety* added simply that *Diamond Head* was "a contrived and banal melodrama of bigotry and bloodlines in modern, heterogeneous Hawaii."[81] Undoubtedly, the film still made some conservative pockets of audiences uncomfortable. One exhibitor in North Dakota wrote that it was "one of those films that [the audience] either liked or hated. Very divided. They came to see Hawaii and were disappointed, as it is a family racial picture."[82] Alternatively, the *New Pittsburgh Courier* was one of the few to acknowledge its superficially progressive impulses: "It is laid in the islands and the photography is splendid; the story is just as exciting for it is interracial from many angles."[83]

More than effectively contest older social attitudes about race, *Diamond Head* instead brought into relief the explicit notion that Hawai'i's entry into the union forced the country to address its own unsolved internal issues. This is made most direct early in the film when King considers the language of the speech he plans to give upon acceptance of the nomination for senator once Hawai'i becomes a state (the very idea that one powerful white person could be single-handedly selected by other powerful locales to become senator in the first place grossly overlooks the political realities of the time). His half-sister Laura accuses him of pandering to the locals through disingenuous ideals of equality. "You know what these people want to hear," she says in a more blatant display of bigotry that takes some of the edge off King's own prejudice, "tell them they're as good as you are. Or tell them that they're better. They'll believe it." Laura's status as an outsider, only visiting Hawai'i for a short time, highlights the notion of old mainland prejudices intruding on the islands. King then invites Dean to visit him, hoping to appeal to his own mixed racial background to help dissuade the impending union between his white sister and Dean's Hawaiian brother. Implying that his own notion of democracy and tolerance has its limits, King offers his guest a rough draft of the acceptance speech:

> I know what this should say: "These islands are the showcase of the United States. The place we prove to all the races of the world that all men are equal in all things. This is where we open all doors to everybody" . . . I've told other men to make [that speech]. But I don't think I can, because I don't believe it. I thought I did, but I don't. I find I don't mean "all doors," not the door to my sister's bedroom. . . . It had to come into my home before I knew what I really believed.

Dismissing these egalitarian ideals, King crumples up the paper and tosses it to the ground in a transparently symbolic gesture. In this one speech, the complex racial-political dynamics of Hawai'i's claim to statehood become reduced to a mere family melodrama. Like King, the US wanted to see itself as a global model for racial inclusion and equality, but the notion of Hawai'i entering the national "family," as it were, forced some Americans to think more carefully about the sincerity of such rhetoric. Tinee pointed out the tired trope that King "really believes that he's of a superior breed. Some of his best friends are Hawaiians, but as in the cliché—when it comes to marrying his sister—wow!"[84] Marcus reads the moment of "not to my sister's bedroom" (which also has overtones of incestual desire made more explicit later in the film) as a "fear of black penetration"[85] in so far as it echoes mainland rhetoric on the subject of miscegenation as a key flashpoint for anti–African American attitudes.

The single biggest objection to statehood in Congress was argued by a core group of "Dixiecrat" senators—"Southerners [who] provided the backbone of all opposition to Hawaii."[86] Despite the possibility of Hawai'i's strong Democratic majority further empowering their own overall political influence in DC, their prejudices on this issue made them align with Northern Republicans. Sometimes the racial resistance was referenced indirectly in speeches about "far off" locations, such as when Texas Congressman Kenneth Regan stated:

> I fear for the future of the country. If we start taking in areas far from our own shores that we will have to protect with our money, our guns, and our men, instead of staying here and looking after the heritage we were left by George Washington, who told us to beware of any foreign entanglements. I think he had this outpost in the Pacific Islands in mind at that time.[87]

Often, it was more direct, as with South Carolina senator Strom Thurmond's belief that Eastern Asian cultures and Western European ones were not meant to mix. For politicians like him, argues Daws, "the clash of values . . . was one of a much more ancient origin, expressed in culture but rooted in biology. Hawaii could never be incorporated as a truly American state. The national body politic would reject it like some unassimilable alien substance."[88] Their concern was also the prospect of having a person of Asian descent in either chamber of Congress—given Hawai'i's hugely influential Japanese population. This was an important part of the islands' racial dynamic that *Diamond Head* all but ignores in its assumption that the white oligarchy would continue to be the political face of the islands. Finally, the film's tired plantation formulas highlighted how the fight over Hawai'i's claim to statehood was also a symbolic replay of the Civil War for those in the South who a century later still refused to concede defeat (and which was exacerbated by the political momentum for African American civil rights in the aftermath of WWII). The idea of statehood was conflated by opponents with an expansion of federal powers, and the old "states' rights" argument was, as Bell notes, "a direct, if slightly muted, echo of the rationale for succession advanced by the South before the Civil War."[89]

Post-racial Whiteness

The complex question of Hawai'i's admission into the union was dependent upon a key contradiction that defined the mainland's own loaded perception of the islands' racial dynamic—a post-racial whiteness, a celebration of racial enlightenment that paradoxically denied the very idea of racial difference to begin with, and thus silently reinforced white hegemony as the unspoken norm. As Rohrer notes, the "discourse of racial harmony has been given decades of play by academics, politicians, writers, and the Hawaii Visitors Bureau."[90] Back in 1937 (in the shadow of the Massie Affair), the Reverend Sidney L. Gulick wrote about what he called "the coming Neo-Hawaiian race," a prediction that the unique mixing of different backgrounds among the diverse people living on the islands would result in a new race of people that will transcend the old categories and boundaries. This bit of futuristic utopia is likewise echoed by Sloane in the film, who declares that "one day all races will be mixed." In Hawai'i, wrote Gulick, "a remarkable synthesis of the most diverse races is going forward. Here a Hawaiian-Caucasian-Chinese-Japanese-Portuguese-Puerto Rican-Korean-Filipino race of enthusiastic Americans is in the process of 'becoming.'"[91] Later, he added: "A polyglot population of many races, each racial group possessed of its own marked mental, social, moral and spiritual traditions and customs mutually and profoundly different, is being transformed into a unified people."[92] This old narrative of racial harmony, Rohrer notes, "represents Hawai'i as an idyllic social paradise where there is no racial conflict or inequality. Frequently contrasting the islands with the 'racist mainland,' this discourse circulates among many communities."[93] This is only one of many racial narratives about the islands, she adds, and is in sharp contrast to the competing notion of whites and other nonlocals feeling they are the subject of a kind of reverse racism at the hands of Native Hawaiians. The latter rhetoric pops up in *Diamond Head*, where the Hawaiian grandmother (Aline MacMahon) tells King at the luau that she is as disappointed in her grandson's decision to marry Sloane as King is in her. When he expresses surprise, she asks him rhetorically: "Do you think prejudice only goes with white skin?" Similarly, King's bias is limited largely to the mixing of races, in an echo of "separate but equal" forms of prejudice: "White's good, brown's good," he says, "but you mix the two together, you know what you get?" Superficially, the grandmother's attitude reinforces the perceived indiscriminate racism promoted by the film (that racist attitudes exist on all sides), but also works through false equivalency to erase the history of colonialization, discrimination, and extermination that underlies her desire to "protect" the last traces of full Hawaiian blood that remain in her family lineage (a far different position than King's attempts to maintain the purity of white privilege and exceptionalism). In this context, the unintended by-product of Gulick's "coming Neo-Hawaiian" race—originally promoted as a means to combat old prejudices of the mainland as well as the deep-seated white fear of Asians—was instead to elide the institutional effects of white supremacy historically.

In order to become a state, Rohrer notes, "Hawai'i would again have to be represented as white as possible" by ascribing to US ideologies and values.[94] For all its superficial addressing of racial prejudice, *Diamond Head* was complicit in this project of whitewashing. The casting of the film suggested as much—with two white actors (Darren and Chakiris) cast in the central parts of the Hawaiian brothers. "Darren, despite a rich tan," joked *Variety*, "seems about as 100% Hawaiian as Paul Revere."[95] Meanwhile Chakiris, already a veteran at playing different ethnicities in doomed interracial love stories, "should have stayed in *West Side Story*—he is totally lost in *Diamond Head*," wrote the *Boston Globe*.[96] On the subject of casting, the *Los Angeles Times* noted a common criticism of the plot: "An especially strange vagary is the casting of Chakiris not only as a doctor but also as—for purposes of plot, obviously—the only one on the island."[97] The *New York Times* noted derisively that "the cast of Hawaiians are as hackneyed as the surf at Waikiki . . . Only the scenery in Hawaii looks real."[98]

Diamond Head struggles to erase the specter of whiteness in favor of foregrounding Hawaii's multicultural dynamics to articulate spaces for a "post-racial" society. At the same time, the islands' own complex racial dynamic undermines the film's post-racial logic. This comes to a focus in particular on the use of the term *haole* in the movie as a generally derogatory term (another instance of the film's apparent depiction of reverse racism). *Haole* is distinctive in the context of US race relations—both mainland and islands—as the only consistent time historically when white Americans were forced to acknowledge their own racial position. The word *haole* "reminds us," writes Rohrer, "that race . . . can be as much about culture and behavior or performance as about skin color."[99] In earlier films, such as *Waikiki Wedding* (1937), *haole* is deployed as a generally affectionate term—the verbalized welcoming of the (white) outsider into the local native community. Historically, however, the term's everyday usage on the islands is more ambivalent—sometimes following a similar expression of acceptance but more often used in the negative to express displeasure at the white presence in Hawai'i.

In populist texts such as *Diamond Head*, the word *haole* works to muddle and even elide, rather than clarify, the process of Othering that historically constructed racial dynamics in Hawai'i from a European perspective. Whiteness is an elusive concept because it is "a form of racialization produced largely through the racialization of 'others'"[100]—and in the process remains present but often invisible within mediated spectacles of racial difference. While the hula girl and beachboy images work to reify and objectify Native Hawaiians as exotically different for the unacknowledged white gaze, *haole* on the other hand calls out the silent observer as also racially marked. But the difference is that—as with the Hawaiian grandmother's own prejudices—its usage minimizes the profound cultural and economic hierarchies just beneath the surface. In this problematic equivalency, whites become as much a victim of racial bias as historically marginalized groups such as Native Hawaiians. And the deeper prejudices are overlooked as being simply a matter of outdated perspective born only of generational difference, which the interracial love of a younger, more innocent generation (Paul, Sloane) will eventually overcome. In the film's neoliberal logic, Hawai'i's modernity is dependent upon the local population's embrace of the twentieth century as much as on older white prejudices (King's generation) being left behind. And the mostly simplistic binary of *haole*s versus Hawaiians seen in *Diamond Head* also largely marginalized the robust cultural and economic presence that people of Asian descent—especially Japanese—provided as a vital part of the territory's contribution to the nation during the push to statehood. In this regard, *Diamond Head* betrays a nostalgia for a moment long since passed—the era of white domination of Native Hawaiians by the ruling elite class first ushered in during the days of the missionaries in the early nineteenth century.

Such Sweet Thunder

Ultimately, if the film was unsuccessful in articulating the islands' complex racial dynamics—or in navigating the anxieties about racial difference with which the question of statehood confronted its mainland audience—choices in its adaptation from the source material was crucially symptomatic of the increasing erasure of a class struggle and labor strife that rested just beneath the surface of Hawai'i's "aloha" brand of multiculturalism. By tying the question of statehood to the issue of racial tolerance, while at the same time depicting class as an outdated aristocratic concern and union workers as angry and intolerant, *Diamond Head* posits the nation's democratic ideals as being beyond the seemingly petty struggles of class exploitation and economic disparity. In the original book, *Such Sweet*

Thunder, the question of race and class are deeply intertwined, albeit in ways that still to some degree, as in the film, reduce such complex issues to the small-minded squabbles of inter-family melodrama. This is complemented, however, by a considerable amount of space dedicated to detailed, if utterly unrealistic, speeches and other digressions explaining Hawai'i's political and labor histories. Unlike the film, the novel openly challenges the narrative of inevitable statehood. The book acknowledges both "local statehood opponents and commonwealth advocates [who] comprised a small minority in Hawaii after 1945. Yet during the protracted campaign for admission they exerted an influence disproportionate to their small numbers. They retarded the statehood drive by opposing the official campaign, supplying material to congressional opponents, and promoting Commonwealth status as an alternative to immediate statehood."[101] The book is a none-too-subtle allegory for America's historical presence in Hawai'i—white businesses (missionary descendants) increasingly intertwined with a local population it never fully understands but tries to control. Immediately, reviewers saw the book's cinematic potential. The *Los Angeles Times* observed that "the forthright unsubtle plotting will endear this yarn to Hollywood film directors. These Hawaiians don't discuss, they clobber or knife each other. Volcanoes don't look pretty, they erupt and incinerate the villain [in reference to the original's very different ending]. Every scene is designed to shout 'Camera!' "[102] The *New York Herald Tribune* added that "undoubtedly our fiftieth state is our most exotic, and this novel, appearing almost simultaneously with Hawaii's star on the flag, ignores none of its dramatic potentialities. . . . Against that background is played out a present-day story of the fight for statehood, the conflicted of the privileged few and the 'Big Five' industries and the workers, and above all, the impact of racial intermingling."[103] Yet only half of that story would reach the big screen.

Such Sweet Thunder was written by a newspaper reporter (Gilman) who had spent decades researching the islands. For all its cheesy melodramatic and sexual indulgences, the book revealed a detailed journalistic understanding of Hawai'i's complex politics throughout the first half of the twentieth century, which the *Los Angeles Times* aptly referred to as "a scientific blend involving statehood, social stratification, slaying and sex."[104] Based out of Honolulu, Gilman covered news across the Pacific for the Associated Press after WWII. He also later assisted with writing the film adaptation. The *Chicago Daily Defender* wrote at the time that the film rights were "sold in the six figures. And Columbia Pictures paid him a more-than-handsome stipend for the right to make a film version."[105]

In the wake of statehood, wrote the *Los Angeles Times*, "any novel about Hawai'i is hotter than the lava in Mauna Loa."[106] Clearly, Columbia was hoping to cash in on the popularity of James Michener's *Hawaii* (1959), another bestseller that shared a few similarities with *Diamond Head* in so far as it was a provocative depiction of sex, race, and violence on the islands that used personal stories and struggles as relatable stand-ins for Hawai'i's more complex cultural and political history. The *New York Times* wrote that the purpose of the book was "to capture the magic of the islands, once a palm-frond frontier and now going tame under the onslaught of stateside capital. Call it a Hawaiian handbook, a reporter's grab-bag, an old-fashioned regional novel, but please, in Mr. Gilman's name, do not confuse the novel at hand with James Michener's *Hawaii* just because both stem from more or less the same impulse to report, reveal and romanticize."[107]

Although both film and novel generally focus on the modern, melodramatic twists and turns of a powerful *haole* family on the eve of statehood and a pending interracial marriage, there are important differences between the two versions of the Howlands' story. In the book, the family patriarch is an older man named Willard Howland, and Sloane is his daughter, not niece. He is still pushing for statehood and for being the first US senator, and still objecting to the marriage between her and Paul, but he is much more overtly and abusively racist and unsympathetic. The book "stirred a certain amount of controversy" in Hawai'i, wrote *Variety*, "because the key figure is, by Hawaii's standards, a bigot and 'racial purist' "[108]—someone unlikely to have had the political success that Howland achieves in the novel. More bizarrely, Howland repeatedly refers to Native Hawaiians as "black." As Marcus points out, "As a contemporary drama set in Hawaii around the time of the book's publication in 1960, it would have been out of keeping for a Hawaiian born white man to refer to a Native Hawaiian as being 'black.' It is more likely that the author is using the premise of racial conflict to reflect mainland black/white relations."[109] He adds that such "rhetoric in the book is substantially toned down in the film, and the direct association [of nonwhites in Hawai'i] with Afro-Americans made more discrete."[110] Meanwhile, his younger son, Aaron, is a hapless, middle-aged alcoholic who is secretly carrying out an affair with an Asian mistress and ends up killing her brother at the luau scene. Thus, Heston's character was a combination of both Willard and Aaron, mixing Aaron's illicit romance with the elder's position of power and prejudice.

While Marcus rightly notes that the novel's "main characters and essential themes of cultural difference, interracial romance and social acceptance are transferred to the screen version,"[111] this overlooks one important aspect. In the novel, the leader of the local union, one opposing King's political ambitions, is the patriarch's secret illegitimate son, Ward Akana, the result of an affair Howland had with a woman of Hawaiian and Japanese descent decades earlier. The son's antagonistic attitude toward his father is partly the result of class loyalty, and partially of personal resentment at being shunned by his parent. The book foregrounds labor struggles, but also in its typically melodramatic way implies that worker tensions may partially be the result of an abandoned son's bitterness. While the line distinguishing personal and political animosity is vague, the dynamic between the two allows the book to explore more explicitly in-depth the history of labor and politics on the islands, as Ward becomes a (compromised) advocate for a racially diverse working class in the face of an angry and bigoted white industrialist. He is also one of the book's more vocal advocates for commonwealth status. The book also addressed the inaccurate perception that, as Bell wrote, "Communists had captured and retained political and economic control of the islands."[112] Still Ward struggles with a personal desire to obtain his father's attention and approval on the one hand, and with a desire to stay loyal to labor's uncompromising demands on the other.

Whereas the book lays the blame of class tensions both on the shoulders of the Big Five and the sometimes-shady politics of local labor leaders, the film version takes a more ambivalent approach toward the Howland family's position of power, while depicting union workers much more harshly and unsympathetically. While Gilman explained at length in the novel the political viewpoints of figures such as Ward, union representatives in the film only get one scene wherein they are depicted as little more than an angry mob. Late in the movie, Howland goes to give a political speech to workers in a warehouse in order to win support for his senate candidacy. Claiming he has known many of the people there for years, he is repeatedly drowned out by a few of the men in the union crowd who interrupt him by clapping rudely. Some of the workers are also depicted as intoxicated. As all the men join in to clap over his speech, Howland says defiantly, "I feel I have a right to be here. This is my home ground." Finally, he storms out of the meeting, only to be confronted by the same worker who started the outbursts. When asked why he's running out on his old friends, Howland punches the man and leaves. Shortly thereafter, Howland withdraws his candidacy to be the state's first US senator. The sequence in the warehouse depicts Howland (and symbolically the white "Big Five" oligarchy he descends from) as a reasonable man of integrity with deep ties to the people and the lands of Hawai'i, while the union workers are depicted as lazy, drunken, disorderly antagonists who oppose Howland perhaps simply because their union bosses directed them to. While the original novel was hardly pro-labor propaganda, it made a more visible effort to detail the histories and stakes involved for individuals such as Ward's and others' struggle for economic justice.

Undoubtedly these changes made in the adaptation were partly about the fear that any sympathetic depiction of labor in 1963 might incite accusations of Communist sympathy at a time when Hollywood was still recovering from the blacklist witch hunts of the 1950s. But by erasing Ward and the history he represents, the film version of *Diamond Head* puts forth a vision of Hawai'i (and by implication the mainland) where class and labor rights are no longer an issue due to the newfound progressive enlightenment of a rich white man and his racially diverse family. In the film, race and sexuality come to symbolize individualism and the future, while labor comes to symbolize conformity and the past.

Figure 3.3. Unlike the original novel (*Such Sweet Thunder*) it was adapted from, *Diamond Head* ignores the complex politics and histories of labor that played a significant role in pushing for statehood and in shaping Hawai'i's identity. In its place is a single scene depicting union workers as an unruly and ungrateful mob that fails to express sufficient gratitude for industrialists like Howland's primary role in building the islands' modern economy.

This also fit within a broader postwar United States where the choices of consumerism become more important than the rights of production, where the consumer's options become the definition of freedom and opportunity while labor unions become the face of mindless and selfish rigidity. The modern economy of Hawai'i benefited from this culture as much as any, rhetorically conflating the act of tourism with the spreading of American ideals of freedom, tolerance, and economic opportunity across the globe. Statehood became the final affirmation of tourism's perceived democratic impact. But if the film version of *Diamond Head* ignored much of the cultural, economic, and political histories shaping its cheesy melodrama, the two adaptations of Michener's *Hawaii* (a book that was part of the final push to win over support for statehood on the mainland) would attempt more explicitly to merge drama with history—in ways that become more and more problematic as its timeline works its way back to the present day.

4

Founded on Truth but Not on Fact

Pastiche Narratives of Modernity in Adaptations of James Michener's *Hawaii* (1959)

> Historical texts have identified Hawaiians as both primitive savages and a generous people. . . . Tourist venues continue to represent Hawaiians as a people never meant to exist into modernity and as "dead" in tours of empty, archeologically framed cultural sites and homes of past *ali'i* [monarchs].
>
> —Rona Tamiko Halualani, *In the Name of Hawaiians*

❧

THE ADMISSION OF HAWAI'I into the union predictably sparked a deeper interest among many Americans in the islands' long histories and their native population. Many reviewers noted the convenient timing of James Michener's *Hawaii* (1959) in the wake of statehood, leading one reviewer to observe that it "should be a popular book in spite of its shortcomings."[1] The ugly historical realities that surfaced as a result of this new fascination with pre-annexation Hawai'i were mostly glossed over by popular media—though occasionally navigated, as in Michener's historical novel, in more detailed, if still not particularly satisfying, ways. "Until the early 1990s," writes Judy Rohrer, "official Hawai'i history was based on scholarship done by *haole* historians who strung together a linear narrative of Western progress starting with Captain Cook's 1778 'discovery' and marching through the 'civilizing' campaign of the missionaries, the 'success' of plantation agriculture, the 'unfortunate' demise of native people and power, and the 'inevitable' Americanization of the government, which continued until the government was American with the culminating act of statehood in 1959."[2] Haunani-Kay Trask notes that "a few authors—the most sympathetic—have recorded with deep felt sorrow the passing of our people, but in the end, we are repeatedly told, such an eclipse was for the best."[3]

These populist histories, from authors such as Michener, Gavan Daws, and Lawrence Fuchs, exploded in post-statehood US literature. Daws's *Shoal of Time: A History of the Hawaiian Islands* (1968), and Fuchs's *Hawaii Pono: A Social History* (1961), while still promoting "inevitable" narratives about statehood, worked as more academic, nonfiction alternatives to the popularity of Michener's historical novel, which dominated bookshelves during that same decade. His balanced a generally conservative depiction of history with a dose of revisionist liberal fantasy—a retrospective ambivalence—meant to superficially allay collective national guilt over the American annexation of Hawai'i and the slow destruction of much of its culture and people even prior to that. His work claimed that "it is true to the spirit and history of Hawaii, but the characters, the families, the institutions and most of the events are imaginary."[4] Historians "were very much like missionaries," writes Trask, "they were part of the colonizing horde. One group colonized the spirit; the other, the mind."[5] For these historians, the end game of statehood—with its neoliberal connotations of political empowerment, national freedom, and modern progress—was necessary to minimizing, and even largely erasing, the ugly histories of colonialism and annexation that defined the white presence in Hawai'i since the days of Euro-American traders and New England missionaries in the early nineteenth century.

Hawaii went on to be one of the most widely read novels of the 1960s. Its popularity also meant that Hollywood quickly came calling, knowing that such a timely topic, plus the book's built-in readership, translated to lucrative box office potential. The group sales manual for the film version stressed selling the book's popularity first and foremost.[6] Michener was "the best known of US popularizers" of Hawaiian statehood,[7] while the *New York Herald Tribune* dubbed him "Hawaii's non-political representative"[8] in 1959. The book sat on the list of top-selling books for eighty-six weeks,[9] with a readership that was claimed to be "well over 100,000,000."[10] Producer Walter Mirisch paid $600,000 for the book rights before the novel had even been released, and immediately began promoting how "this extraordinary novel will be made into a motion picture which will begin production in 1960."[11] However, the challenge of adapting such a mammoth thousand-page book into a more economical cinematic form—plus the physical logistics involved with filming such an globally ambitious historical epic—meant that it would be several years before production even began. The producers' original plan was to make at least two separate films out of *Hawaii*'s massive literary girth—but even then, the challenge became which parts of the book to include, which ones to leave out, and where to put the break from one to the next. After many different ideas, drafts, and revisions over several years, the end result was *Hawaii* (1966) and then *The Hawaiians* (1970)—the former focused primarily on missionary experiences of the nineteenth century, while the latter recounted the plantations' development and the Asian immigrant experience, leading up to the US annexation of

Figure 4.1. Attempts at adapting James Michener's hugely popular and mammoth historical 1959 novel on the big screen resulted in two ambitious cinematic epics that reflected the US' sometimes well-intended but deeply flawed attempts to reconcile the ugly histories of genocide, colonialism, and exploitation with post-statehood rhetoric of tolerance, democracy, and opportunity. Tensions between a sense of retrospective liberal guilt and the inevitable march of neoliberal notions of "progress" become harder to conceal as the stories move closer to the present and the moment of annexation.

the islands. The considerable time and investment in the end proved to be worth it. While *The Hawaiians* was not particularly successful at the box office, *Hawaii* went on to do massive business—indeed, it was the highest-grossing film of 1966.

The success of the film, meanwhile, followed closely on the notable popularity of another Michener book, *Tales from the South Pacific* (1947), which was successfully adapted as the simply titled *South Pacific* to Broadway in the late 1940s and then to film in 1958. (The filming of the movie on the islands was incorporated into a Hawaii Visitors Bureau full-page advertising campaign that was featured in the *New Yorker*, *Times*, and *Sunset*.[12]) "For an American audience newly conscious of a global destiny," writes Rob Wilson, "*South Pacific* conjured up Pacific space into a settler's paradise of enchantment, racial harmony, and (to be sure) military necessity."[13] By the end of the 1960s, both *South Pacific* and *Hawaii* were in the top thirty-five highest grossing films of all time (not counting inflation): *South Pacific* had grossed $17.5 million, while *Hawaii* had topped out at $16 million.[14] It's not inconsequential to note that *Hawaii* was the most financially successful Hawaiian-themed film in the 1960s (though given its immense production costs not nearly as lucrative as it could have been), out-grossing even the tropical travelogue musicals of megastar Elvis Presley by a clear margin. While much of this could be traced back to the immense success of Michener's novel and other industry factors (Julie Andrews's emerging star persona; the overall, if quickly waning, popularity of widescreen Technicolor historical epics; relaxed production standards that allowed for modest representations of nudity), the film was also the first of its kind to attempt a negotiation of complex historical questions in the post-statehood era.

Both the novel and the two film adaptations have received scarce scholarly attention despite their prominent populist presence in the 1960s. This chapter explores how these movies addressed, and unsuccessfully alleviated, tensions and contradictions in the US' populist understanding of Hawai'i's contentious colonial history in the wake of statehood, producing conflicted texts that reflected equally conflicted mainland ideas about America's colonialist invasion of a sovereign nation. These films divorced codependent concepts of colonialism and modernity, white hegemony and multiculturalism, industry and religion—marginalizing the former while foregrounding the latter—in order to construct a narrative that both reveals and hides the historical forces informing the white European and American conquest of Hawai'i. The vision of history put forth was in a way *retrospectively* post-racial, in the sense of imagining a future time when race and ethnicity would not matter (even as it reinscribes whiteness as the unacknowledged norm). Michener's book attempted to reconcile Hawai'i's colonial history of Native Hawaiian dispossession and *haole* hegemony with the "harmony" model of race relations that, describes Rohrer, "constructs Hawai'i as exceptional in its lack of racial prejudice, its egalitarian relations, and its opportunities for nonwhite upward mobility."[15] Expressing an ambivalent attitude toward the long-promoted colonialist belief, as Jeffrey Geiger notes, that promised "economic rewards for those industrious enough to resist falling too deeply into reveries of Polynesian indulgence,"[16] the two films also manage to be both capitalist and anti-colonialist—positing new economic freedoms of the West as directly opposed to the old monarchal oppression—instead of seeing the former as a natural outgrowth of the latter.

By investing in a meticulously researched and detailed mise-en-scène (costumes, sets, props, and so on), the films employ a spectacularly stylized realism that conceals deeper historical inaccuracies—depoliticized history visualized through pastiche, the surface-level imitation of an older style with less interest in the contexts that originally informed it. Michener's book was, according to the author himself, "founded on truth but not on fact."[17] On the one hand, this suggests that the author was less concerned with historical fidelity than what he saw as deeper symbolic truths about Hawai'i. On the other, it also suggested that the negative facts of genocide, colonialism, and annexation were sublimated by more affectively "positive" truths regarding modernity and multiculturalism. In the original 1966 press kit put together for the promotion of *Hawaii*'s theatrical release, the filmmakers emphasized that the historical authenticity of the film was based on a mix of "Michener's undoubted great story telling [with] the *great visual realism* of the story."[18] The close attention to authentic mise-en-scène added to Michener's own years of historical research, creating a film that prided itself on unprecedented realism (as opposed to the frivolous artifice of touristic depictions of the islands). Yet by Michener's own admission, the epic novel was not intended to be an entirely factual textbook account of Hawaiian history but rather a dramatic version of the past that was faithful to his own populist interpretation of it. As such, the significant cinematic adaptations of the novel not only perpetuated that understanding for a mass audience but also emphasized an attention to authenticity that was more stylistic than substantive, more visual than dialectical. Like the book, the movies were fascinated with the artifacts and geography as often as with the people.

Pastiche depictions of history depoliticize the past as a series of stylistic gestures—meticulously researched period costumes authenticate more romantic myths being sold. In *Legendary Hawai'i and the Politics of Place*, Cristina Bacchilega notes the islands' popularity at the dawn of the twentieth century coincided with the increasing dissemination of "photographs of faraway places and peoples," which were seen to "provide more powerful 'evidence' than words, and their coded realism was read as mechanical or objective reproduction."[19] Delia Malia Caparoso Konzett adds, "Cinema had barely learned to walk during the 1890s when it was able to convey direct images of US expansion into the Pacific to home audiences, thereby naturalizing these new acquisitions," which required "violent acts of translation via cinema."[20] The result, Bacchilega adds, was the construction of a history visualized through images, and a people robbed of agency and self-determination through the reified passivity of being objectified symbols of their culture and history. The concept of "legendary Hawai'i" involves, she writes, "Hawaiian stories labeled as 'legends' [that] have been translated to produce a *legendary Hawai'i* primarily for non-Hawaiian readers or audiences."[21] This imaginary space allowed audiences "to experience, via Hawaiian legends, a Hawai'i that is exotic and primitive while beautiful and welcoming. This new product of the imagination was at the turn of the twentieth century valorized through the ubiquitous colonial practice of translation and the new technology of photography."[22] Cinema had the power to magnify further that perceived visual realism, particularly in a postwar period where location shooting and technological advances (color, widescreen) were able to enhance the spectacular potential for what was captured onscreen.

The intersection of photographic indexical realism, meticulous historical research, and "legendary" stories about Hawaiian history came to a head in films such as *Hawaii* and *The Hawaiians*, which offered epic but superficial accounts of the past that largely reinscribed, through contradiction and elision, neoliberal narratives of capitalist progress. While *Hawaii* sentimentalized the islands' lost culture, destroyed by the presence of white explorers, *The Hawaiians* celebrated the historical emergence of Hawai'i's robust multicultural society. Both films thus promote a liberal notion of racial relations, but one predicated on what Robert Stam and Louise Spence noted as the affectionate racism of colonial narratives that express an outwardly benign and even "positive," but condescending, view of nonwhites. "The insistence of 'positive images,' finally," they write, "obscures the fact that 'nice' images might at times be as pernicious as overtly degrading ones, providing a bourgeois façade for paternalism, a more pervasive racism."[23] The depictions of Native Hawaiians in film,

Figure 4.2. *Hawai'i*'s (1966) interest in historical authenticity had less to do with any of its narrative details than with the meticulous research that went into constructing its visually spectacular mise-en-scène (period-specific costumes, settings, props) and a musical design that consciously rejected touristic cliches, reflecting the ways in which stylistic pastiche both intensifies and depoliticizes representations of history.

especially in historically based pictures, is not far removed from the original attitudes of missionaries themselves, "who could not see their own contradictions. . . . The discourse of the 'noble savage' (transplanted from encounters with native peoples on the continent) collided with notions of the Kanaka Maoli as 'heathens,' creating a tension in which Native Hawaiians were simultaneously worthy of saving and inherently damned."[24] They are presented through this colonial lens as goodhearted (if in need of guidance), with a more primal, "authentic" status through their imagined position away from "modern" society and closer to the natural world. And their status as spectacles of the premodern by necessity meant they are incompatible with the forwarding-looking historical narratives so many of these texts ultimately wish to tell. Hawaiians are depicted as well-meaning but helpless (while people of Asian descent are represented in *The Hawaiians* as more useful in so far as they successfully adapt to the demands and values of Western capitalism).

Thus, a key contradiction expressed through these populist histories is a nostalgia for Native Hawaiians and Hawaiian culture that awkwardly coexists with the unspoken belief that they are victims of their own inability to adapt and modernize—perhaps most directly suggested in the films by the equation of "progress" with American democracy and of "tradition" with royal monarchies. Another important historical contradiction emerges, especially in *The Hawaiians*—modern capitalism posits that the inherent dangers of all royal monarchies justify both the US' independence from one (the United Kingdom) *and* simultaneously its conquest of another (Hawai'i). "Michener deemed irrational the Hawaiian desire for self-determination," argues Christine Skwiot, "which he championed for other Pacific Islanders under European rule but which he could not fathom for Hawaiians, given his belief in the nonimperial nature of U.S. expansion."[25] In his vision, colonialism was informed by oppression, racism, and the negative weight of history, while capitalism was based on at least the *future* potential for tolerance and equal opportunity, if one is willing to work hard enough. The exploitative, destructive possibilities of both become elided in narratives that imagine replacing colonialism's backward ways with capitalism's forward motion, and wherein the destruction of the Hawaiians and their culture unintentionally becomes a tragic but necessary by-product.

Perhaps most illuminating is the divorce of religion from industry. Both historically maintained a mutually beneficial relationship in building modern sites of capitalism—especially in those colonial spaces most ripe for exploitation. But in the films, both are presented as mostly pursuing different, even competing, civic agendas. While Captain Cook and crew are generally credited as the first Europeans to land on the islands, the start of the permanent *haole* presence in Hawai'i traced back to the arrival of New England missionaries in the 1820s, intent on spreading the word of God to the "heathen" natives. "Upon the heels of British explorers and their diseases," writes Trask, "Americans came to dominate the sandalwood trade in the 1820s. Coincident with this early capitalism was the arrival of Calvinist missionaries, who introduced a religious imperialism that was as devastating a scourge as any venereal disease."[26] The prominent depiction of a Christian work ethic in both Michener adaptations ignores its primary economic function—to accumulate land and wealth—and instead reimagines it simply as a by-product of a selfless and single-minded devotion to God and the teachings of Jesus Christ. Historically, missionary efforts in Hawai'i were intertwined with the pursuit of long-term economic benefits extending from that work ethic. "When the money to be made in sugar and pineapple became apparent," adds Rohrer, "many missionaries, and missionary sons, became planters."[27] By New England ideals, wrote Daws, "the islanders' style of life seemed unhealthy and sluggish, and Hawaiian women in particular thought work 'rather a disgrace.' Yet when it came to a frivolous diversion such as a hula they would practice energetically in the hot sun for days on end."[28] As much as promote Christianity, missionaries also stole land from the Hawaiians and helped build the economic and political infrastructure that dominated the islands well into the twentieth century. Throughout both Michener films, however, religion is depicted as naïve, often well intentioned, and generally ineffectual against the forces of history. In *Hawaii*, missionaries can be cruelly judgmental, deeply ignorant, and for a small few ultimately greedy, while in *The Hawaiians* their descendants are depicted as merely passive and perhaps even inept. But in both films they are often presented as the thoughtful and righteous antagonists to such industries as shipping and agriculture, instead of their most consistent ally, with the intent of allaying guilt over economic exploitation with an appeal to the good intentions of Christianity.

All these elisions and contradictions are enabled by the safe buffering of centuries passing. The "contemporary" part of Michener's original story ("Golden Men") is the most prominent one left out of the adaptations, as the simplified, idealized interpretation of history becomes harder to sustain the closer the narrative moves to the observable realities of the present. It is, in a sense, history itself that becomes objectified in the cinematic spectacles of *Hawaii* and *The Hawaiians*. Becoming removed through representation from its contemporary audience as something safely in the distant past, the ugly historical truths of genocide, rebellion, annexation, and others (either explicitly acknowledged, or lingering in the shadows but awkwardly unrecognized) remain carefully contained within the pastiche aestheticization of history. Statehood forced complicated questions upon the country not just about the present (as *Diamond Head* struggled to negotiate) but also about the past—America's own ideals as a site of tolerance, freedom, and opportunity could only be reconciled with the intolerant, restrictive, and exploitative history of its own colonialist project in Hawai'i within the safe spaces of historical allegory and abstraction—the reassurances of "truth," not the aggravation of "facts."

Postwar Hawaiian "Histouricism"

Written accounts of pre-annexation and pre-statehood Hawaiian history, such as Michener and Daws (the latter of whom largely ignores tourism), saw themselves as modern *correctives* to the kitschy, artificial representations of Hawai'i presented through decades of touristic discourse and superficial Hollywood depictions of romance and adventure. The *Los Angeles Times* wrote in 1960 that *Hawaii* was "not a tourist paradise song like 'I Wanna Go Back to My Little Grass Shack in Hawaii,'"[29] but presented itself instead as a more factual account of the islands and its inhabitants. Yet these more historically detailed narratives were every bit as touristic a frame as much of the media that preceded them—a kind of cinematic "back region" (to use Dean MacCannell's term) meant to appear more authentic than other more obvious tourism spaces such as the Kodak Hula Show. Halualani writes that Hawaiian "historical" sites such as Iolani Palace "compel visitors to peer into and experience native life from supposedly a native Hawaiian perspective . . . [that] serves to authenticate and differentiate tourist spaces from the excessively artificial and touristy feel of other sites."[30] Similarly, the film version of *Hawaii* begins with a voiceover from the film's primary Native Hawaiian character, simulating for the audience the film's "experience of native life from supposedly a native Hawaiian perspective." Michener in particular, writes Paul Lyons, exemplified what he terms "histouricism": "a conflation of the authority of history writing with the agency-mystifying and glossing qualities of touristic writing."[31]

Many of these narratives promoted "the by-now familiar rhetoric of anti-conquest [that] dominated the explosion of representations of the islands that followed. James Michener's *Hawaii*, . . . still widely read, roots its narrative in the supposed genetic differences among races, which Michener conceived to be much like the essentialized racial types that Twain, London, Von Tempski, and other earlier writers used."[32] Such "anti-conquest" rhetoric had less to do with a respect for self-rule and more to do with an infantilizing sense of Native Hawaiians as inherently innocent and naïve. Mark Twain's *Letters from Hawaii*, originally written during his trip to the islands in the 1860s and finally published in 1947, also became increasingly popular in the following decades. Twain's correspondence provided a dual function—not only providing a unique (and celebrated) first-person artistic perspective on Hawai'i, but also retrospectively suturing American history to that of the islands in ways that affirmed their mutual destiny together (and conveniently leaving out the intervening period of rebellion and annexation). Far from a simple endorsement of paradise, Twain's project, writes Stephen H. Sumida, "embodies a complex pastoral view [that was] masked, however, by the allure of the very clichés Twain first parodied, then pondered, yet failed to subvert in a fully consistent way."[33] Preceding *Shoal of Time* as one of the first populist nonfiction accounts of its kind, Fuchs's *Hawaii Pono* focused on the period from annexation to statehood, painting a picture of the islands' multicultural assimilation that the *Hawaii Five-O* (1968–1980) producers identified—along with the last two chapters of Michener's book—as "strongly recommended reading" for their scriptwriters looking for research.[34] Also popular was *Hawaii: A Literary Chronicle* (1967), which offered a combination of new and classic Hawaiian-themed essays, poems, travelogues, and so on, by mostly American writers.

Most of these narratives echoed the idea of "legendary Hawai'i." By translating these ancient stories of volcano demons and shark gods for a modern audience, these "legends" celebrated Hawaiian heritage as an important part of their identity, but the emphasis on an oral or anecdotal tradition posited them as incompatible with both "official" history and modern society. The idea of a "legend" in these populist mainland texts, writes Bacchilega, "is interpreted as fanciful or undocumented history. This has resulted in erasing the meaning of 'history' carried in the Hawaiian word and genre, with *mo'olelo* being translated and understood only or primarily as 'story.'"[35] The very act of documenting Hawaiian tradition serves a colonializing function, not only in preserving (and thus separating) the past from the present but also enacting a new kind of historical violence, which "is at the core of the rupture of tradition, a rupture that, at the hands of a new power, may take the form of translation (as recontextualization and recodification) or unequivocal suppression."[36] Visual media—particularly in the self-contained diegetic worlds of Hollywood historical epics—reaffirm that rupture of translation by taking one loose, albeit ideologically loaded, reinterpretation of tradition (Michener) and recontextualizing and reifying it as pure visual spectacle (*Hawaii, The Hawaiians*).

The land of "Bali Ha'i" in the different versions of Michener's *Tales of the South Pacific* typifies the kind of "legendary" space many of these stories promote. In the original, Michener described the mythical island as "a jewel of the vast ocean. It was small. Like a jewel, it could be perceived in one loving glance. It was neat. It had majestic cliffs facing the open sea. It had a jagged hill to give it character. It was green like something ever youthful, and it seemed to curve itself like a woman into the rough shadows. . . . Like most lovely things, one had to seek it out and even know what one was seeking before it could be found."[37] Here its personified landscape is foregrounded over the inhabitants, while the locale's geographical inaccessibility symbolizes the more elusive nature of the South Seas in the US imagination. "Musicals like *South Pacific*," writes Francesco Adinolfi, "had paved the way for Polynesian fiction. It was as if the gods of the Pacific accepted, for a night or so, being a part of the great American exotic dream."[38] In the musical version, Bali Ha'i is presented as a mythical vision off-limits from stationed WWII sailors. A local native, Bloody Mary (Juanita Hall), praises the location in song:

> Most people live on a lonely island,
> Lost in the middle of a foggy sea.
> Most people long for another island,
> One where they know they will like to be.
> Bali Ha'i may call you,
> Any night, any day,
> In your heart, you'll hear it call you:
> "Come away . . . Come away."

As a potent symbol of postwar South Seas pastiche, the song unsurprisingly "quickly entered the repertoires of many American tiki restaurants."[39] Bali Ha'i, like much of the novel, was inspired by Michener's own time serving in the Pacific during WWII. Rooted in the mystery of the South Pacific, enabled precisely by the sense of geographic and temporal distance associated with "legends" and "traditions," Bali Ha'i visualizes the impossibility of lasting peace, romance, and happiness. It was essentially a fitting stand-in for the touristic construction of Hawai'i in the mainland imagination—a mediated paradise that some always desired to experience from a geographical and temporal distance, but which could rarely be attained in person for any extended period of time.

While *Tales of the South Pacific* was Michener's breakout success, his career thrived for the four decades as the author of more than forty books on a range of geographic locations. A former newspaperman, he had a talent for translating nonfiction material into an engagingly readable literary format. But he was always first and foremost associated with Hawai'i. He carved out a space for himself as the islands' primary mainland storyteller on a variety of platforms—promoting his work as going beyond the hula shows and travelogue descriptions of Waikiki Beach to tell a deeper tale of Hawai'i, past and present. A *New York Herald Tribune* article from late 1959 speculated that the timing of his book's release with the admission of statehood "has led to rumors that Mr. Michener has political aspirations in the islands."[40] However, by 1961, Michener left Hawai'i because of what he claimed was racial discrimination against his wife, who was of Japanese origin: "Friends said restrictive covenants denied him the right to buy a home in the exclusive Kahala area because his wife is not Caucasian."[41] (years later, he ran unsuccessfully for Congress in Pennsylvania). Even for Michener, "Hawai'i" (like Bali Ha'i) was more appealing as an idea seen from a distance than an actual location blemished like everywhere else by the sometimes-harsh realities of everyday life. Beyond the books, Michener had his own anthology TV show, *Adventures in Paradise*, which ran from 1959 to 1962 (the show was a compromise after network executives failed to get the rights for *Tales of the South Pacific* back from Richard Rodgers and Oscar Hammerstein II in order to do a television version). He wrote prefaces for everything from Hawaiian tour guides (*Hawaii 1966*) to Hawaiian-themed cookbooks (*Hawaii Cookbook and Backyard Luau* 1964). By the 1970s, he was even a prominent pitchman in United Air Lines advertisements for Hawaiian travel, reinforcing the company's self-described role as the official airline of the islands.

As Michener's dual role through the postwar decades as both storyteller and pitchman suggests, his work straddled the fine (if common) line between political propaganda in support of statehood and blatant tourism promotion: "While Michener urged 'every American who can possibly do so' to visit Hawai'i," writes Skwiot, "he was aware that most would only be able to read about its 'glory.'"[42] In a 1959 letter to the editor of the *New York Times*, Michener pushed aggressively in support of statehood:

> The varied people of Hawaii, starting from a Polynesian base and augmented by stalwart missionary stock from New England, to which have been added oriental strains, form an amazingly cohesive group. They are well educated in fine schools and a strong university. They are trained in democratic procedures. They have a very advanced culture built out of many compatible strains.[43]

This advocacy for statehood was, as Houston Wood notes, based on "Euroamerican, pseudo-scientific classification systems focused on blood [that] continue to dominate constructions of the islands. They ground Michener's own influential fictions representing Hawai'i and the Pacific, as well as most of the histories and advertising that are associated with Waikiki."[44] Michener concluded his statehood sell with a "common sense" appeal: "All I had to say could be summed up in one sentence, which I know Americans feel to be correct: 'Hawaii ought to be given statehood now because it is the right thing to do.'"[45] This letter summarized Michener's populist view of Hawai'i—a wonderfully diverse population, grounded by an old missionary work ethic, committed to learning American history and values, thoroughly modern in all civic respects (thus immune from any potentially negative influences from Asia or the spread of Communism), and deserving of statehood by virtue of its long unquestioned loyalty to the US.

"Perceived in One Loving Glance"

Michener originally had an idea for a different book in mind, complete with "outlined plot-sequence and character-biographies," but in an apt bit of symbolism the notes reportedly were lost in a plane crash in the Pacific Ocean.[46] Starting over, he spent seven years total on the book—four researching, three writing.[47] Across a thousand pages and more, *Hawaii* tells the story of the islands' journey from volcanic formation to the eve of modern statehood. Cramming so many stories into one novel, characters become thin symbols of Hawai'i's history more than three-dimensional humans. But what the book lacked in character depth and complexity, it made up for with historical research and sheer narrative scope. It is, first and foremost, a story of geography as much as people—the opening chapter, "From the Boundless Deep," tells of the islands' initial geological formations, which perhaps unintentionally delegitimizes the inherent Native Hawaiian claim to sovereignty by showing how the land predated them. The novel's dedication—"To all the peoples who came to Hawaii"—reinforces this further, implying there is no one type of "Hawaiian." The book, writes Wood, "constructs the division between Hawaiian lands and the Hawaiian race in an especially effective way. There are six sections to the novel, and the first, 'From the Boundless Deep,' offers a narrative of the islands without including any people whatsoever."[48] The next chapter, "From the Sun-Swept Lagoon," tells the story of the islands' earliest inhabitants who migrated from Bora-Bora. The third, "From the Farm of Bitterness," details the New England missionaries' experiences, essentially serving as the primary source material for the 1966 film. *The Hawaiians*, meanwhile, was based largely on the next two, "From the Starving Village" and "From the Inland Sea," which tell the tales, respectively, of the Chinese and Japanese immigrant experiences from the earliest colonial days, up through annexation, and culminating with the Pearl Harbor attack.

The last chapter, "The Golden Men," is a celebration of Hawai'i's contemporary status as a thriving modern city and beacon of multicultural coexistence, promoting the oft-repeated populist notion of Hawai'i as a symbol of America's post-racial future. The "Golden Man" was someone who, wrote Michener, was "influenced by both the West and the East, a man at home in either the business councils of New York or the philosophical retreats of Kyoto, a man wholly modern and American yet in tune with the ancient and the Oriental."[49] Thus the book ends in much the same way it begins—with a Hawai'i that is not defined by the presence of Native Hawaiians, but by "all the peoples who came to Hawaii." Native Hawaiians, writes Wood,

> are represented as a distinct race with certain, blood-determined characteristics. But, just as important, they are also depicted as a race whose time of prospering has passed. In the competition among races that Michener claims characterizes contemporary Hawai'i, those with a predominance of Hawaiian blood are handicapped by inherited characteristics that are supposedly of little use in the modern industrial age.[50]

Book reviews of the time noted this as well, though not framed in critical terms. *Hawaii*, wrote the *New York Herald Tribune*, tells the story of "how a society grew—how the native population, at the point of expiration, was revived by the influx from the Orient, how great planters and traders reigned as a feudal barony until comparatively recent times, how democracy has arrived, and what may be expected of Hawaii's 'golden men,' who by heritage stand between East and West."[51] Michener, added the *Los Angeles Times*, "sings of the earth-shaping of his Golden Man (he wants no racial connotation) from primitive Polynesians who canoed here more than 1,000 years ago, from earnest American missionaries and predatory American sea traders in the early nineteenth century and from, among others, Chinese, Japanese and Filipinos."[52] This review brought into relief the ways in which the Golden Man was a fitting post-racial contradiction—someone whose insistence on "no racial connotation" could only exist within the pronounced context of Hawai'i's distinctive diversity. But still it is "Hawaii [who] is the hero" of the book, another adds, "from the time the first of its islands raised its volcanic head above the waters some sixty million years ago (and sank back to reappear another day), almost to the eve of statehood."[53]

The book's excessive length, meanwhile, was the source of both praise and criticism—on the one hand, Michener's impressive research lent the project a largely unquestioned air of authenticity. This was positioned by some reviewers as being the opposite of popular tourism rhetoric at the time with its emphasis on history instead of hokey "tourist-paradise song[s]."[54] But, adds another, "in its details it is of uneven interest, as if its author could not bear to omit anything at all of what he had been at such pains to learn of industry, religion, politics, morals."[55] These slow stretches "represent the difference between the enduring work of art *Hawaii* might have been and the semi-documentary it is, thoughtful, informative, dramatic in the grand scale of perspective"[56] (another similarly called it a "long, quasi-documentary novel"[57]). Whatever its shortcomings, however, Michener's accessible writing style and deep interest in the popular subject combined to ensure a major readership for the book, while the author's "semi-documentary" approach to history would offer a template for something distinctly unlike any other take on Hawai'i to emerge from old Hollywood.

Three years after the film version was first announced and still over a year away from actually starting principal photography, the *New York Times* observed in 1963 that "the story of how 'Hawaii' is made into a movie may turn out longer than the mammoth novel."[58] How to adapt such a massive book was exactly the problem for filmmakers. Even Michener himself was skeptical: "I doubt if it can be serialized or made into a movie. . . . The characters are too numerous and they change too fast."[59] The hopeful plan was always to do multiple movies (though the specifics changed greatly over the years): "each of them a multimillion-dollar project in color and on a screen large enough to do justice to panoramic views."[60] Many of the important character and narrative details for what would become *The Hawaiians*' plot was already structured in the early drafts of *Hawaii*, and one early plan was to have the second film be largely set in the twentieth century. *From Here to Eternity* director Fred Zinnemann was the first choice to direct,[61] and was committed to the project for years. "Intoxicated by the wealth of material," the *Los Angeles Times* reported in 1966, "Zinnemann wanted to shoot the whole book, which covered the growth and development from the Middle Ages to 1956."[62] The "purpose of the book was only partly adventure and scenery," he told the *New York Times*; instead he saw "the movie as a chance to show how different races can be integrated peaceably."[63] To adapt the novel, Zinnemann turned to his *Eternity* collaborator, Daniel Taradash, and together they worked on the script for two years.[64] As early as 1961, "they were ready to go before the cameras, [but] they had a script so vast that it would have required two showings of four hours each on successive nights to see it all."⁶⁵ Peter Bart added in 1965 that "it was Zinnemann's concept that filmgoers would buy a ticket, say, for Monday and Tuesday nights to see two sections of the movie,"⁶⁶ which Mirisch quickly nixed.

The problem was not just a question of historic scope, narrative pacing, and exhibition limitations, but of the incredible production costs that were implied in the script's various ambitions. Despite the popularity of the topic and book, United Artists initially balked after the costly fiascos of *Mutiny on the Bounty* (1959), *Cleopatra* (1963), and *It's a Mad, Mad, Mad, Mad World* (1963). There was simply no way to make the film from a financial standpoint—regardless of running time—that did justice to Zinnemann's original plans. Ironically, one of the filmmaker's ideas to save money, the *New York Times* reported in 1963, was to "completely eliminate . . . the missionaries from New England"⁶⁷ (essentially the only subject of the final film version). He instead found the more complicated racial dynamics of the later parts of the story far more fascinating. The long process of writing the scripts was costly by itself—the first script cost $200,000, before being abandoned.⁶⁸ It was reported in 1963 that over $2 million had already been spent on the project,⁶⁹ while later reports claimed that the Mirisch Company was over $4 million in the hole by the time shooting even began.⁷⁰ In total, the film would end up costing over $14 million to make,⁷¹ $8 million over budget.⁷² UA's concerns over a *Cleopatra*-level fiasco were hardly unfounded by the time the movie appeared in theaters.

But that end was still far from fruition in the early 1960s. Taradash was replaced by Dalton Trumbo, who worked on the script for another eighteen months (one of the countless memos that he sent to Mirisch and Zinnemann in January of 1963 was titled humorously "Guess What?" in sarcastic reference to the indeterminable number of correspondences regarding the project). Trumbo took the authenticity of the project seriously, drawing on his own experiences with Calvinism to help shape his interpretation of the missionary experience, while being assisted by Leila Alexander with additional research. He also revised the pidgin dialect after consultation with the University of Hawaii.⁷³ When Trumbo came on board, the plan was 22 pages on Bora Bora, 117 pages on the missionaries, 104 on the Chinese immigration, and 213 on the Jap-G-Men, with the intention of breaking up the story somewhere to make two separate films.⁷⁴ The problem he initially noted was "*where to cut Film One*. Five months ago, on September 17 [1963], I raised this question at great length. I'll not repeat myself here. But the importance of this question cannot possibly be exaggerated at this moment."[75] His suggestion involved combining the missionary material with the first half of Chinese immigrant stories, using Whip Hoxworth's (Charleston Heston's character in *The Hawaiians*) departure as a boy to conclude the first film, except that "the imbalance in pages, film length, elapsed historical time, characters dramatized and events occurring is colossal."[76] Another idea was to end the first film on the lowering of the Hawaiian flag after US annexation, and to then begin the second with the raising of the American flag.[77] Ultimately, the two biggest changes made to the original scripts were to cut the first two chapters down to a brief montage sequence that opened *Hawaii*, and to abandon all of the twentieth-century material (and many of the Japanese stories with it). By the time writing was more or less finished, director Zinnemann had lost interest and moved on to other projects, leaving the film to George Roy Hill, who was just near the start of his own accomplished career.

In April of 1964, an actual production schedule was finally announced—"it will have been five years when, next spring, *Hawaii* finally gets rolling."[78] And yet, as production finally moved closer, there was still too much material. As a result, Trumbo went to Hawaii as shooting was underway for one last revision. The plan was "to unwrite his script by hindsight. With the film being shot in continuity, he started at the last page and worked backward, eliminating characters who had not yet been established and telescoping events that had not yet taken place. By the time Hill's shooting met his edited pages, about 20 years had been trimmed off the story and two prominent Oriental stars, Jeannette Lin Tsui and Peter Chen Ho, had become instantly available for employment."[79] It was reportedly Hill who suggested limiting the story of the first film to just "the attempts of Boston missionaries to establish their church there in the years between 1820 and 1867"[80]—the intention for his part being at least partly ideological. Andrew Horton argues from an auteurist perspective that "from the beginning Hill saw more than mere entertainment in the project. Made at the time that Vietnam was just becoming a major issue, *Hawaii* as Hill presents it becomes not merely a tale of missionaries in a pagan land, but by extension a metaphor for Vietnam and the 'rape' of any culture by another."[81] Hill reinforced this interpretation, telling the *Los Angeles Times* in 1965:

> What happens in Hawaii has enormous application today. Americans go into a foreign land with their ideas of religion, of government, and their notions of what is right—believing

that these are bound to be superior to those of anyone else. They confront traditions as old if not older than theirs. Yes, they learn, we learn, but in some cases too late. If, while watching this picture, you substitute political philosophy for religion, then Abner Hale [the film's main missionary character] becomes the United States. You'll find he makes a great many of the mistakes we are making right now.[82]

To what extent that allegory might have been picked up by audiences of the time, though, is unclear—particularly at a moment when the emergent war in Southeast Asia had yet to turn unpopular. Undoubtedly the box office success of the final product was predicated in part on merging the competing ambivalences of the US' past colonial transgressions with its continuing present ones—acknowledging a certain historical truth without alienating contemporary audiences who would've been still supportive of modern military intervention during the depths of the Cold War. The film's historical buffer offered a safe cushion—mistakes made in the past could be reconciled for contemporary audiences by virtue of the fact that the US' modern imperial mission would have been seen by some as spreading freedom (the exact opposite of the missionary agenda depicted in the film) in the face of Communist aggression.

At the same time, focusing on any intended ideology within the narrative ignores the fact that the film worked primarily as spectacle. Critic Vincent Canby noted at the time of its release that "although the film tells the sadly ironic story of the extinction of one culture upon invasion by another, one comes out of the theatre not so much moved as numbed—by the cavalcade of conventional if sometimes eye-popping scenes of storm and seascape, of pomp and pestilence, all laid out in large strokes of brilliant De Luxe color on the huge Panavision screen."[83] (In a separate article later, he added that "the story of a fundamental missionary . . . is too small and austere to compete successfully for our interest with the film's flora and fauna."[84]) Ultimately, Canby recognized that "you don't spend that kind of money [on movie rights, period mise-en-scène, and location shooting] and wind up making an 87-minute black-and-white art film about some schnook missionary, involuntarily and unknowingly involved in the extermination of a culture he does not yet understand. Yet that is precisely the kind of film that *Hawaii* should have been."[85] Another critic, meanwhile, added that Hill "wisely lets his cameras linger on the warmth and gayety of the islanders, who undoubtedly come across as the brightest feature of the movie"[86]—implying that even the extras were little more than another part of the spectacle. "In the interests of realism, Hill wanted to use only unknowns and correct ethnic types, regardless of previous experience"[87]—leading to one of the many tensions between him and Mirisch. One prominent local actress, Elizabeth Logue (who played the key role of Noelani), was a former Hawaiian Airlines employee and well-known "hula girl" who "appeared in countless advertisements promoting South Pacific tourism"[88] and later made an appearance in the opening credit sequence of *Hawaii Five-O* (1968–1980). The depiction of "natives," and laxed industry censorship, allowed for a fairly generous depiction of nudity for a mid-1960s Hollywood production—"rumors began drifting in from location that so many nude scenes were being shot, not only in the water but on the land and in the huts," joked one reporter at the time, "that the finished picture could only be shown at a stag smoker."[89] Canby also noted the historical significance of "the spectacle of beautiful native maidens (for the first time in a Code-approved Hollywood spectacle) who do not wear bras."[90]

The production team's attention to realism was less based on character or narrative accuracy and largely stylistic. Authenticity for the filmmakers—as stressed throughout the film's original press kit—was defined entirely by its meticulous mise-en-scène. Extensive research on period-appropriate and geographically specific costumes, props, sets, and so on, were done at Honolulu's Bishop Museum. Most of the physical materials that would have existed in Hawai'i during the film's early nineteenth-century setting no longer remained. As a result,

> the film's craftsmen found it necessary to import thatch from Japan, since the pili leaves normally used for thatching huts in the era of the story are no longer to be found on the Hawaiian islands. Rooster feathers had to be imported from the Philippines for the colorful costumes. Red and gold royal cloaks came from Hong Kong. Imitation tapa cloth was woven in Ireland. Silk maile leaves came from Japan, straw mattings from Mexico, boar's teeth necklaces and bracelets from India and original tribute silk from Taiwan.[91]

Similarly, composer Elmer Bernstein was committed to finding out what authentic Hawaiian sounds were known to have existed on the eve of the New England arrivals: "The missionaries brought their music, running to hymns and folk songs of the period. The question which confronted Bernstein was: what, if any, was the native Hawaiian melodic contribution to that confrontation? It wasn't *Sweet Leilani, Little Grass Shack, Aloha*

Oe or the like: of this, Bernstein is certain. Yet Bernstein's score for the film needed to embody—or at least be suggested by—the music indigenous to the place and the period."[92] To find these answers, Bernstein did research at the Bishop, the University of Hawaii, and by contacting the descendants of old missionary families.[93] This meant that "there were no ukuleles in *Hawaii*. Ukes were first introduced to the islands long after the period of the film."[94]

Shooting for the film was done across the globe. Filmmakers went to a "living history" museum in Massachusetts for the film's New England portions, where real antiques instead of cheaply manufactured replicas were used for set decorations. In Hawai'i, much of the film was shot on location at Makua Beach, where the production built a "remarkable setting showing the grass huts fashioned of pili grass, the magnificent grass palace of Queen Malama and the early clapboard houses built by the religionists from New England and the ships chandlers who served the whaling fleet."[95] As in New England, filming was a popular attraction for tourists, who were "milling around that desolate stretch of beach and thatched huts at Makua at 2 a.m.," noted one reporter. "I shouldn't wonder if some of them show up in the picture."[96] Meanwhile, the sea voyage sequences were shot in Norway, where production was delayed because the weather was too nice for the kind of winter conditions for which they were searching.[97] These changes added to the exploding budget and intensified tensions between Hill and Mirisch. In the span of three days, Hill left the production and was replaced by Arthur Hiller, before being reinstated. News trickled out that he'd been fired over the production's slow pace, but was saved by the local Hawaiian actors who threatened to strike if he was not brought back—"175 of the native extras circulated a petition asking that the director be rehired."[98] Also protesting, "the film's casting director, Marian Daugherty and her staff of three quit, taking their files with them."[99] Mirisch joked later, "We actually welcomed the lost weekend. I think everybody but the movie people have become used to the five-day week."[100] Upon Hill's return, the Mirisch Company sent out a not-so-subtle announcement that "Mr. Hill would now return to the picture, but presumably would sharply accelerate his shooting pace."[101]

Destroying a "True Paradise"

"The arrival of American Calvinist missionaries in 1820 accelerated the erosion of the Kingdom of Hawai'i's political autonomy and cultural integrity," writes Vernadette Vicuña Gonzalez, "criminalizing Hawaiian cultural practices and imposing Western gendered norms of domestic behavior. As an extension of this legal hastening of cultural death, the settler elite alienated Native Hawaiians from their land through legislative maneuvers that allowed foreign land ownership in Hawai'i by midcentury, which destroyed the foundations of Native political and economic self-determination."[102] Attempting to mitigate this through a belated form of *haole* social consciousness is at the ideological core of *Hawaii*'s historical revision. The film focuses on the life of Reverend Abner Hale (Max Von Sydow), who courts a wife in New England primarily so that he may be allowed to begin life as a missionary—the belief being unmarried men should not be around the "corrupting" sexual influences of native women. "Despite [Michener's] disclaimer," wrote one book reviewer, "one seems to recognize such early-day carriers of the Word as Hiram Bingham, Asa Thurston, Samuel Ruggles and others"[103] in the fictional representation of missionaries. Hale in particular was influenced by Bingham, one of many who brought an antagonistic attitude to the islands:

> For all that [the missionaries] liked to describe themselves as humble servants of the Prince of Peace, they humbled themselves only before God, and they came to the islands prepared for war—far outnumbered, yet clothed in invulnerable self-righteousness and convinced that against the Truth they preached no enemy, however powerful or high born, could stand.[104]

Through Hale, the movie presents an unrelentingly critical depiction of Christianity's aggressive intrusions up until the film's final moments. "Not since the Rev. Mr. Davidson went after Sadie Thompson," wrote Canby, "has Protestant Christian proselytism come off so poorly onscreen. . . . The film finally lumbers to its close to find Mr. Von Sydow, now a widower, stooped and crooked and looking a little like the witch in *The Wizard of Oz*, back at screen center, still a figure of unexplored pathos."[105] Terry Clifford of the *Chicago Tribune* noted: "How well you like [the near three-hour running time] depends upon how long you can take the hellfire-and-brimstone rantings of a nineteenth century Calvinist creep. . . . The rest of the movie mainly concerns the clash between the happy, simple, charming natives, and the stern, humorless, unforgiving, tactless 'mangy scarecrow' of a minister."[106] Abner, Von Sydow himself added, "just has no idea how to behave in the real world."[107]

His wife, Jerusha (Andrews), accompanies him despite her lack of affection, and her secret desires for a ship captain, Rafer Hoxworth (Richard Harris), she believes had abandoned her for a life at sea. Upon the actress's arrival in Honolulu, Andrews visited the local wax museum and recalled being shocked to discover that "there was a wax figure of the first missionary lady, and if that lady isn't the very image of me.... I have an eerie feeling that I was destined by fate for this part."[108] Beyond the standard love triangle drama, however, her role in the film involves little more than offering a sympathetic ear to the Hawaiians and, ultimately, a more humanizing side to Abner. The missionaries are accompanied by a young Hawaiian-born divinity student, Keoki (Manu Tupou), who hopes to find his calling by helping convert his fellow islanders to the teachings of Christ. Keoki's voiceover begins the film, suggesting, as Horton argued, that by "framing the story from a Native Hawaiian's point of view . . . the story ultimately belongs to Hawaii and not to Hale."[109] Facing racial discrimination at Abner's hands, Keoki returns to his roots and helps lead the revival of Hawaiian culture and costumes in defiance of the missionaries. The Hawaiians are led by the Ali'i Nui (supreme leader), Keoki's mother Malama (played by Jocelyne LaGarde). She attempts to adapt to the new outsider ways so that she can learn to read and write. The sense of a "legendary Hawai'i" is made explicit in a scene late in the film when Malama's brother, Prince Keolo (Ted Nobriga), canoes out to the sea and seeks guidance by talking to a shark god.

The film uses the selfless, merely God-loving, central figures of Hale, Jerusha, and Dr. John Whipple (Gene Hackman) to divorce the Christian missionary agenda from its proactive role in exploiting "the horror of mass deaths during this period; the role religion played in fortifying Western social, political, and economic ideologies and structures; and the foundation religion laid for subsequent control of the islands by a missionary-planter oligarchy."[110] Instead, all of these destructive elements are presented in *Hawaii* as an unfortunate by-product of good intentions. In addition to bringing "capitalism, Western political ideas (such as predatory individualism), and Christianity," writes Trask, Cook and his men "introduced diseases, from syphilis and gonorrhea to tuberculosis, small pox, measles, leprosy and typhoid fever."[111] Even before the seizing of land, the original island population decreased by 95 percent due to foreign diseases within the first century after contact with Captain Cook's crew.[112] In specific regard to disease, *Hawaii* is unambiguous in its indictment of the early settlers' negative impact—culminating in Dr.

Whipple's angrily didactic speech to Reverend Hale, spurred by a measles epidemic that claimed thousands of native lives, about the "true paradise" that's been destroyed by the arrival of Europeans. Yet Rohrer points out that the actual missionaries only exploited this crisis further by insisting that converting to Calvinism was the only solution:

> At the heart of this crisis [of spirituality] was the horrific depopulation of Native Hawaiians described as "the Great Dying" and primarily attributable to multiple diseases brought by foreigners to which Kanaka Maoli had no immunity (the Hawaiian islands are the most "isolated" land masses on the planet, making their biodiversity unique and fragile).[113]

The film's further promotion of liberal guilt is brought to the surface by Jerusha's equally didactic deathbed plea to Abner to see what a loving and selfless people the Hawaiians are—thus beginning the Reverend's belated conversion to a more compassionate man willing to help the local population instead of simply condemning them. Hale's journey is consistent with other Hawai'i colonialist texts that, as Christine Higgins and Gavin Furukawa argue, "involve dichotomous characterizations of 'the savage and the civilized' as white protagonists voyage to 'exotic' locations and reflect on their experiences, thereby creating west-based visions of the enlightened self and inscrutable other."[114] The depiction of the Native Hawaiians—with their mix of enduring innocence, aggressively open-minded attitudes about sexuality, and ultimately antiauthoritarian stance that embraces racial difference rather than conceals it—has echoes of the American counterculture generation of the 1960s. In many ways, the Hawaiians—not Hale—are the heroes of the film, struggling to make peace with the aggressive outsiders but ultimately embracing their own heritage as a rejection of the European presence.

Reflecting the liberal sensibility of its filmmakers (Trumbo, Hill), *Hawaii* is in some ways surprisingly progressive for a big-budget 1960s Hollywood historical epic, exactly that which some critics such as Canby liked about it despite its big-budgeted, bloated spectacle. On the other hand, the profound historical gap between the 1820s represented onscreen and the 1960s audience buffers some of the deeper implications of this critique. Implicitly contrasted with the belated embrace of Hawaiian heritage in the contemporary wake of statehood, this historical narrative implied that such deep wounds have since been healed—instead of considering that the exploitation of the Hawaiians by outside interests continued unabated well into the twentieth century. Moreover, the colonialists' economic interests on the islands are almost completely elided in favor of a complicated, but generally negative, depiction of Christianity's purely religiously motivated presence (any financial investment in Hawai'i instead is restricted mostly to the brutish misogyny of the merchant sailors). The movie culminates with the development that, against Abner's protests, one or two unsavory missionaries will now begin to take the land as a justified reward for their generations of hard missionary work—"God's Way," says one. However, if Daws's interpretation is true ("they came to the islands prepared for war"), then an element of conquest (and not merely a spiritual one) was always at stake as well. In the film's end, Hale's sudden change of conscience (fighting for Hawaiian rights in the face of encroaching sugar plantation industrialists) is represented as the inevitable manifestation of his own personal conviction in God, regardless of institutional affiliation, and reinforces the movie's belief that the intent of the original missionaries was never financial gain.

Moreover, the film's depiction of the Hawaiians is generally condescending in the "affectionate racism" kind of way that Stam and Spence describe. While represented as an unrelentingly loving and generous people, the Hawaiians' naïveté also facilitates the perception throughout the film that they are utterly helpless without colonial oversight. They are closely equated with the landscape and with nature—the opening montage of *Hawaii*, much like the opening of the book, is a celebration of the simple beauty of a land of paradise and not of the people, which makes ironic the end concern in the film about stealing their land. The native/nature union is magnified particularly late in the film, where the dramatic death of Queen Malama causes a major thunderstorm to come plowing through the islands. The entire depiction of the native population fits comfortably within the older touristic lens of Hawai'i as populated only by welcoming hosts—in the beginning, they seek not independence but only the approval of the white missionaries and sailors, while the staging of a sacred hula performance late in the film is presented as a celebration of Native Hawaiian heritage and history instead of its affirmation as one of the islands' primary tourist spectacles. Rev. Hale immediately condemns the heretical proceedings upon discovering them, which fits the larger historical narrative of white outsiders initially trying to destroy the Hawaiian way of life—but ignores that the retrospective touristic celebration of this culture was spurred entirely by the post-missionary, post-annexation realization that that way of life was already almost entirely irreversibly lost.

The depiction of the Hawaiians in the film symbolized a core paradox in the mainland's collective attitude toward the islands—the desire to romanticize the imagined innocence of the land, its people, and its culture was dependent upon the deeper reality that the US had no desire to acknowledge, let alone grant, Hawai'i its independence. Like Hale, the nation had simply come to understand, embrace, and respect Hawaiians as one part of its own existence—but not one separate from it. On the other hand, Hale's motivations aren't entirely clear in the end either (particularly as such a maddeningly one-dimensional character for much of the film). In commenting on final revisions to Hill and Mirisch, Trumbo expressed concern that "our audience may be perplexed by Abner's persistent racism. . . . I like the idea that from the time of the measles epidemic to the end of his life Abner becomes increasingly convinced that these people are doomed (naturally by God, since no other power exists), and that it is this very conviction of their doom that softens his heart toward them and makes him their champion."[115] If Trumbo's interpretation is be believed, Abner's conversion in the end has less to do with a disavowal of the missionaries' destructive behavior and more the complete embrace of a spiritual ideology that gave birth to it in the first place. Despite the film's mildly liberal politics, *Hawaii* fits perfectly within the tradition whereby, argues Bacchilega, the islands were often represented as little more than "an exotic landscape that has provided a (self-) redemptive site for missionaries."[116] In the end, Hale's conscience (and to some extent, contemporary audiences) has been relieved in so far as he will now take up the "right" side of the fight (the same fight already lost to history)—and what had been done to the Hawaiians historically feels secondary to the alleviation of a national guilt in the wake of statehood.

The Hawaiians

When the *haole* elites were pushing for annexation with the United States by the end of the nineteenth century, one of their biggest pitches to an ambivalent mainland was valorizing the work of the original missionaries as a crucial civilizing presence in the distant and unfamiliar territory of Hawai'i—the strongest evidence, they felt, to support their claim that the islands were not a lawless tropical isle overrun by dangerous natives. Such a narrative was self-serving since many of those elites were also the children and grandchildren of those same lauded missionaries. Annexation of the islands was always an inevitable goal of the whites who first landed in Hawai'i in the nineteenth century, because they felt "deeply insecure in the face of their physical isolation, ethnic separateness, and small numbers. These white settlers looked anxiously to Washington for assurances of support in the event of political or economic difficulties."[117] But urgency for an official union with the United States ultimately rested on "the rapid growth of Hawaii's sugar industry and its substantial dependence on American markets after the 1850s."[118] The US traded duty-free rights to markets on the mainland with the *haole* elites in exchange for exclusive military access to island harbors. However, the McKinley Tariff of 1890 in Washington put heavy restrictions on foreign trade in order to help support domestic industries—and since Hawai'i was still categorized as a "foreign" country, the tariff put a significant strain on the local agricultural industry. "More than any single event," writes Roger Bell, "the McKinley Act spurred local support for annexation, especially among the dominant white business and sugar groups."[119] In addition to the need for security, they felt joining the United States would be the only way to secure favorable market conditions.

Although the film covers much more historical ground than just the immediate period leading up to annexation, *The Hawaiians* had for itself the task of rewriting these rebellious historical actions as an unfortunate and desperate last resort to an ill-fated clash of idiosyncrasies, cultures, and values, putting the blame entirely on the Hawaiian monarchy instead of fully acknowledging the relentless *haole* push of economic and political greed that led to the overthrow. The fact that *The Hawaiians*, a film that generally paints a gentle picture of the annexation (led reluctantly in part by descendants of missionaries), follows *Hawaii*, a film that generally criticized the outsider and missionary influences on the islands, is only one of the many historical contradictions that the sequel struggles to negotiate, and with even less success than its predecessor. Halfway through the film, Noel Hoxworth (John Phillip Law) confronts his powerful plantation-owning (and former slave-ship-running) father, Whip Hoxworth (Heston), about his dubious past, which includes rumors of several criminal acts, up to and including murder. Whip eyes Noel cautiously and, with a slight grin, says to his son, "You're trying to decide whether your father is a son of a bitch?" In essence, this is the key line of the entire film—one which struggles to balance the late 1960s Hollywood commercial imperatives of white hegemony, star-driven narratives, and retrospective celebrations of statehood with the nineteenth century's unrelentingly ugly plantation and annexation histories.

Figure 4.3. The son of Rafer Hoxworth (Richard Harris's character in *Hawaii*), Whip Hoxworth's (Charlton Heston) central role in *The Hawaiians* (1970) as both hero and villain in Hawai'i's economic development and in the specific fight over royal sovereignty and hostile annexation encapsulates the inability of the film to reconcile ugly colonial histories with the US' self-image of freedom, industry, and progress.

That Heston's character is repeatedly both hero and villain over the course of the two-plus-hour narrative reflects this uneasy, and ultimately unsustainable, balancing act—through him, the United States itself becomes both protagonist and antagonist in Hawai'i. Hoxworth was in many ways an exact repeat of the actor's character from *Diamond Head*—the (at best) ambivalent antihero, widower (in the film's second half), ruthless plantation owner, a hypocritical bigot (with another secret Asian lover), and someone whose family bonds are ultimately challenged yet again when the prospect of interracial marriage enters into his home. However, Hoxworth, as a businessman first and foremost, is ultimately more practical on the subject of race than Howland was, seeing the economic benefits in what he views as an otherwise unfortunate union between two powerful families—one of European descent and the other Chinese (and, as in *Diamond Head*, the other family is equally unhappy, reinforcing the false equivalency of reverse racism that the earlier film also promoted). A symbol of an earlier era, Hoxworth's prejudice suggests simply another obstacle to overcome in the capitalist march of "progress," yet the value of his pragmatic business sense ensures his continued survival and even eventual triumph. He must learn to accept, and even negotiate with, the waves of Asian immigrants brought to Hawai'i in the nineteenth century. And, like *Diamond Head*, *The Hawaiians* is as much about the mainland's collective memory of the American Civil War, and the legacy of slavery, as about the history of Hawai'i. The actions of *haole* business interests in nineteenth-century Hawai'i to ensure safety and security through annexation in the face of overwhelming minority numbers was informed by the long-standing fear of slave uprisings in the American South (they named themselves the "Committee for Safety"—the very people causing the overthrow saw themselves as the ones maintaining peace and order for their own economic benefit). *The Hawaiians'* narrative of indiscriminate economic opportunity amid nineteenth-century plantation culture rewrites the history of slavery without the discrimination, violence, and restrictions of actual slavery, where enterprising nonwhites are imagined as having the same freedoms and opportunities as *haoles*.

A sequel to *Hawaii* was announced soon after the original premiered (though reports said it wouldn't be released for four years to give "the current film a lengthy engagement"[120]). Ironically, the *Boston Globe* speculated then that the two Michener chapters on which the sequel would be based, "From the Starving Village" and "From the Inland Sea," were "obviously not suitable at the present time. . . . So it will undoubtedly be the last section, 'The Golden Men,' in which all nationalities mingle, which will make the most up-to-the-minute film."[121] The very idea that Hollywood would tell the epic story of Chinese and Japanese immigrants for a mainstream (white) audience was inconceivable for this journalist—guessing that the only acceptable story instead would be of a modern, presumably post-racial Hawai'i. Yet, as the aforementioned Trumbo and Mirisch notes indicate, the plan always was to tell that earlier historical story, and indeed *The Hawaiians* is strongest, in contrast to *Diamond Head* and *Hawaii*, in its acknowledgment of the emergent Chinese population on the islands—from being brought to Hawai'i as forced labor and eventually building their own considerable and somewhat independent economic presence (the subsequent Japanese wave of immigrants receives less attention). The extent of Whip's personal distinction between the two sets of immigrants—apt both for its racism and for its economic focus—is that in his eyes the Japanese "work cheaper" and are "tamer" than the Chinese population.

The Hawaiians foregrounds how the islands' reputation as a uniquely multicultural society was less the result of some abstract notion of an "aloha spirit" and more the explosion of agricultural plantations that created the need for a larger labor force than the local population could sustain. The immigrant story is embodied in the resilient figure of Nyuk Tsin (Tina Chen), a Chinese slave who is brought to the islands first by Hoxworth's own slave ship, eventually survives the Molokai leper colony, raises several children, helps Hoxworth initiate a pineapple economy on his own land, and eventually achieves her freedom. In the end, she emerges as an extremely powerful member of the Hawaiian business community. Symbolizing the rich history of Asian contribution and innovation in Hawai'i, Tsin is a classic testament to American notions of its own exceptionalism based on the Protestant work ethic—the simplified belief that anyone, regardless of their origins, can achieve great success if they are willing to work hard enough for it. She inspires her children with the conviction that they can "make more money, get more land." When they say it is impossible for Chinese to achieve such influence and power, she responds proudly that "impossible come back from Molokai," meaning that if she was strong enough to return from the infamous leper colony, she is strong enough to do anything. Sumida notes the long history of many writers using the leper settlement as a symbol of "the dark side of Hawaii"[122]—and Tsin's return in this regard symbolizes a larger historical overcoming of the islands' brutal past.

At the same time, the film's rich tapestry of different races interacting on a daily basis—plus Tsin's conviction that nothing is "impossible" for Chinese immigrants—erases how "solid class barriers separated a relatively small oligarchy of whites from much larger groups of nonwhite laborers"[123] in the nineteenth century. It also ignores a fundamental truth about the *haoles* who overtook Hawai'i—their "deep-seated belief," writes Bell, "in the inherent right of white men to rule over the uncivilized native races of such a tropical outpost [that] led to growing demands that Hawaii be a de facto, if not actual, protectorate of the United States."[124] Finally, class barriers and white supremacy contributed to a key aspect of the immigrant experience elided in *The Hawaiians*: "both Asian groups were vital to the economic life of the community; but being foreign-born and denied the vote, neither participated in the political turmoil which brought Hawaii into the United States."[125] Moreover, given that immigrants were "vital to the economic life," this celebration of multiculturalism perpetuates a deeper issue that to a lesser extent marred *Hawaii*—whatever their origin or background, residents of the islands had to adapt to the arbitrary and unquestioned rush of enterprise that was rapidly transforming society in the wake of missionaries, shipping industries, and plantation economies.

Tsin's triumphant economic story affirms the righteousness of the colonialist project—the larger goal of converting Hawai'i from an untapped land full of lucrative natural resources, but populated by unproductive "workers," into a modern economic state that maximized its various commodities for a global market. Her resiliency resides primarily in her savvy business sense—for example, having one of her sons marry a local Hawaiian girl for the primary purpose of acquiring the other family's land. Then, in the end, after much of Honolulu's Chinatown section is burned down (the result of fighting the bubonic plague and inspired by a real-life tragedy in Honolulu in 1899), and she has lost all her property, Tsin successfully negotiates with Whip to receive a substantial amount of money to both rebuild her business and to purchase the cheap land left by the fires. Tsin seems conveniently indifferent to Hoxworth's suggestion that some *haoles* have been accused of setting the fires intentionally in order to run off the Chinese and then buy up the momentarily worthless land afterward. Instead, she prefers ultimately to exploit the tragedy just as much as her white counterpart had. In the end, Hoxworth's dubious morality is offset by his gracious financial gesture, rooted in the liberal guilt that haunts both films—and by the fact that, despite leading the earlier rebellion against Queen Lili'uokalani (Naomi Stevens), he had vocally opposed the burning of Chinatown in the first place, albeit out of his own economic self-interest.

But Hoxworth still carries that specter of rebellion. His contradictions reflect the collective history of the United States' long involvement in the Hawaiian islands, and thus he becomes the focal point of its most contentious moment. The industrialists like him "saw an unreasonable queen on one side and irresponsible agitators [other Native Hawaiians and *haole* sympathizers pushing for independent Republic status] on the other, and they concluded that the only course that offered any hope at all for the future was annexation to the United States."[126] In the film, the rebellion is not depicted for what it was—a deliberate, organized, and long-term plan on the part of the white oligarchy to discredit the Hawaiian monarch and promote annexation by the United States in order to ensure greater control over the local population and greater political voice in Washington (though it does briefly acknowledge the long campaign on Hoxworth's part to change public opinion against Queen Lili'uokalani long before the moment of annexation). Instead, the rebellion is represented as a small *haole* insurgency motivated primarily by the queen's undemocratic rejection of a previously agreed-upon constitution. This "Bayonet Constitution" (so-called because King Kalākaua was forced to sign it under threat of violence) was pushed upon the monarchy in 1887 by the *haoles* to ensure "citizens" had a democratic say in the governance of Hawai'i. But this only benefited whites by putting severe voting restrictions (such as land ownership) on nonwhites. Lili'uokalani "had sworn an oath to uphold the constitution of 1887, but she did not take this to mean that she could not rule the country."[127] Thus, the rejection of the Bayonet Constitution was a belated attempt to do just that. The queen's intention was to install her own constitution, which acknowledged the marginalized rights of Native Hawaiians: "The procession symbolized the wish of her loyal subjects for a new constitution," writes Daws, "but the document itself was her own; she had been working on it secretly for months. In future only true Hawaiians would be allowed to vote, and they would not have to be rich men to cast a ballot or run for office."[128] But tearing up the old constitution wasn't quite a rebellious act in the face of *haole* demonstrations of power so much as it walked straight into a devious trap, since "her ambitions merely provided powerful opponents with an ideal opportunity to end the monarchy and concentrate political power even more directly where economic power already lay—in the hands of white settlers."[129]

In *The Hawaiians*, however, the white power structure is depicted as a diverse mix of viewpoints—some have benevolent intentions toward the monarch, some do not (nonwhites are generally absent from the conversation altogether). While Hoxworth plants the seeds of overthrow by painting Lili'uokalani as a power-hungry tyrant, his brother-in-law Micah Hale (Abner's son from the previous film), who is now in charge of family business interests, repeatedly voices the legitimate critiques of the rebellion's subversive and illegal behavior, insisting on a common ground that must exist between the two opposed parties. In the film, the eventual annexation is represented as an unfortunate and entirely defensive gesture against a stubborn queen (played by a white actress) who not only rejects the *haoles'* demand for democracy but also insists on beheading Hoxworth and other traitors for treason. Earlier, Whip argued that Lili'uokalani "thinks she's the Queen of England"—implying that fight in Hawai'i is historically identical to the US' Revolutionary War against Great Britain, and thus rewriting the hostile political overthrow of a sovereign nation as instead being analogous to a fight for freedom. Although the queen did threaten to execute leaders of the rebellion, there's less definitive evidence that she had such serious intent, let alone that much power. A large part of the tension in the first place was that the monarchy was mostly a symbolic presence in the day-to-day life of

1890s Hawai'i, something Lili'uokalani sought to challenge (Hoxworth suggests as much when he says she is a "luxury the islands can't afford"). The story of "beheadings" effectively works to reinforce the notion of a "primitive" Hawai'i that justified annexation and modernization. In *The Hawaiians*, white conquest of the islands is distorted and misrepresented as the unfortunate compromise between two violent extremes—the queen's brutal, backward monarchy and Hoxworth's armed militia. The compromise falls to the weak-willed Hale, who tries and mostly fails to be a voice of reason yet ends up the "father of his country" (Hoxworth says with a hint of mocking contempt) after the rebellion despite his own wavering inaction and painfully reluctant support of the queen's removal. Micah was based loosely here on the far more assertive Sanford Dole (another son of missionaries), the first "president" of Hawai'i (in its brief Republic phase), who not only supported the rebellion but was one of the first to push for it (in many ways, Hoxworth's ruthless business sense and political ambition is more closely aligned with Dole's biography—another ugly truth the film seems uncomfortable with acknowledging). The most the film can muster in commenting directly on the morality of rebellion and annexation is the queen's equivocating comment to a passively ambivalent Hale, "It is a sad day for the both of us."

Such a messy history is compressed into one long drawing room sequence in the Iolani Palace where the queen, Hoxworth, Hale, and others debate the different sides of the rebellion (similarly, Halualani notes that the palace itself acts as a tourist site whose very function is to "discursively excise nativism from modernity"[130]). In reality, Lili'uokalani did step down to avoid bloodshed, but also thought the US would intervene and reinstate her once it was informed of the illegal overthrow. "Facing an occupying US military force across from her palace, Lili'uokalani ceded her authority," writes Trask, "not to the provisional [*haole*] government but to the United States."[131] While US president Grover Cleveland initially supported her position, calling the coup an act of war, he was undermined by a more conflicted Congress uninterested in meddling with "foreign" affairs, and eventually opposed annexation while recognizing the new Hawaiian republic under Dole's control. This Constitutional Republic (1893–1898) was intended as a short-term solution since annexation did not immediately take place. As with the Bayonet Constitution, voting rights were again heavily restricted. "The alleged 'republic' was actually an oligarchy," writes Trask, "with a franchise limited by property and language requirements [to exclude the Asian population as well] and a loyalty oath that effectively excluded most Natives."[132]

Figure 4.4. The complex history of annexation at the end of the nineteenth century is simplified down in *The Hawaiians* to a single extended scene where representatives of the *haole* island oligarchy confront the queen (Naomi Stevens) over the limits of her authority as the head of the royal Hawaiian monarchy, ultimately (and, as the film tries hard to suggest, reluctantly) concluding that she needs to be removed. In the process, the scene obfuscates one very simple fact—the United States stole Hawai'i from the Hawaiians (adding an unintended irony to the film's own title).

In one subtly remarkable edit, the film then cuts instantly from the rebellion of 1893 to the annexation of 1898—as the queen is marched away under guard, a medium shot of an ashamed Hale is quickly replaced by a single triumphant image of the American flag flying above Hawai'i (the now-erected reverential stone statue of Hale himself beneath the flag serves an ironic contrast to the immediately preceding sequence). This not only erases the long and complex politics on both sides of the Pacific that connected the separate moments of rebellion to annexation, but it also hides one of the film's great structuring absences—the profound conflicts and ambivalence *within* the mainland toward the idea of annexing Hawai'i at all (another structuring absence was permanent Republic status—*The Hawaiians* allows no room for the possibility of a truly "independent" Hawai'i). The initial attempt at annexation was "not a fait accompli, given widespread Hawaiian and U.S. opposition [exactly the sequence of events elided in the film's abrupt cut]. Resistance emerged at sites official and cultural, political and performative. The queen led the way."[133] Saying the United States overthrew the Hawaiian monarch is true, but also incomplete. Some Americans wanted Hawai'i to be independent to respect its autonomy and/or to stay out of the European practice of colonial politics, while others didn't want who they perceived as a primitive and immature people becoming a part of the (white) United States. Limited military and financial resources also restricted major expansion for the United States, as did dealing with the political and cultural aftereffects of the American Civil War domestically (even though that conflict also made the US more conscious of the need for military stability and security in places like the Pacific).

Annexation remains the key historical moment in *The Hawaiians*, since it best "symbolized and ensured the triumph of foreign influences which had transformed the islands so radically in the preceding century. The eclipse of Hawaiian culture, traditions, and political authority was also reflected starkly in the fact that less than one in every four people living in the islands in 1900 was descended from Hawaiian or part-Hawaiian ancestors."[134] The perceived righteousness of annexation the film promotes depends not just on the retrospective inevitability of Hawai'i having always been destined to be a part of the United States, but on the equally important myth that America's interest was always unconditionally mutual. "The biggest push toward annexation," notes Trask, ". . . did not come from the continent but from *haole* sugar planters in Hawai'i."[135] The colonial history of nineteenth-century Hawai'i was less an aggressive imperial force encroaching directly and relentlessly onto the islands, and more like several decades of *haole* business interests pushing hard to get the United States' attention and support. Generations of whites living in Hawai'i (of both American and European descent) were the more forceful advocates for annexation, creating a messy political situation locally, and then trying to force America's hand to intervene. The US, in turn, was ultimately more interested in the strategic possibilities for its naval forces in the Pacific, especially after Japan's victory over China in 1895, than in pleasing the islands' ruling elites for their own sake (France, Britain, and Japan also expressed interest in control of the islands at various points in the nineteenth century, thus speeding up the question of US annexation).

The film's final structuring absence is the lack of representation for the indigenous population. As nearly the only prominent Native Hawaiian character in the film, Queen Lili'uokalani is alone in her opposition to the future—depicted simply as a stubborn old woman representing an outdated and unacceptable past (not just the primitiveness of precolonial Hawai'i, but also the elitist, undemocratic era of royal monarchical rule). Beyond that, *The Hawaiians* perpetuates the myth that Native Hawaiians were generally passive on the subject of annexation, ignoring the much larger culture of resistance on the islands kept at bay by the US' overwhelming military presence—"[US minister to Hawai'i John] Stevens ordered 150 marines ashore from the USS Boston on the pretext of protecting the United States Legation and Consulate in Honolulu and securing the safety of American citizens."[136] This harsh critique of the Hawaiian monarchy is established earlier in the film, meanwhile, when Hoxworth's Hawaiian-born wife (Geraldine Chaplin) becomes increasingly mentally unstable, implied by the narrative to be the result of centuries of royal inbreeding. This plot point both undermines *Hawaii*'s greater respect for the Native Hawaiian population, and—as with the queen—implies that ultimately royal Hawaiian lineage was a destructive one that had to be left behind in an era of political, racial, and economic modernization. Beyond these two characters, Native Hawaiians are completely absent from the film, replaced not only by whites but by Chinese and Japanese populations. Perhaps the final and most obvious irony of a film called *The "Hawaiians"* is that—with one royal exception—actual *Kanaka Maoli* play no part at all in the epic story.

Coming Storms

The popularity of Michener's novels and cinematic adaptations were only the beginning of America's fascination with Hawai'i as the islands moved into the post-statehood era. To film one of *Hawaii*'s severe sea storms that ravaged the missionaries on their way to the islands, the production built a giant ship replica on hydraulics in a Hollywood soundstage. As Von Sydow and cast were being thrown about in front of the cameras, crew "let loose a torrent of water on wincing actors, taking pains to splash an occasional make-up man or wardrobe lady who wanders too close to the set."[137] At the same time, another—much bigger—star, also associated closely with Hawai'i, was preparing to shoot a very different movie in the soundstage next door. All the commotion being caused by *Hawaii*'s elaborate production was distracting him, and so he "dispatched some hard-eyed young emissaries to announce that 'the boss' was disturbed by the noise created by the rocking boat."[138] The star in question was Elvis Presley, and "since Elvis's bid is Hollywood's command, the young men were assured that the 'storm' would soon be over."[139] Although ironically *Hawaii* would go on to be a monumentally larger critical and commercial hit that same year than the rock 'n' roll icon's own *Paradise Hawaiian Style* (1966)—an underwhelming attempt to cash in on the success of *Blue Hawaii* (1961)—the anecdote is nonetheless revealing. Not only were the islands themselves receiving unprecedented attention from movie studios by then, but even *Hawaii*'s considerable impact at the time could not overshadow how the new state's tropical connotations of music, romance, and adventure in postwar American pop culture would be, in the long run, most strongly identified with the figure of Elvis.

5

Business or Pleasure

The Touristic Contradictions of the Elvis/Hawai'i Experience from *Blue Hawaii* (1961) *to Aloha from Hawaii* (1973)

> Elvis is the classic example of a star who makes movies but is not really a movie star. . . . His movie career was more a tribute to his popularity than a major contributor to it.
>
> —Mark Feeney, "Elvis Movies"

&

Late in the last of three Hawaiian-set feature films to star Elvis Presley, *Paradise Hawaiian Style* (1966), his romantic interest / secretary Judy (Suzanna Leigh) informs pilot Rick Richards (Presley) that he has a phone message from another woman. "Business or Pleasure?" he asks. "I'm beginning to wonder if there's a difference with you," she dryly replies. The gag is apt in context, given Elvis's characters' constant womanizing in movie after movie. Yet it also draws into relief how many Elvis films in the 1960s reflected the emergent baby boomer desire to hold on to the carefree days of youth (pleasure) during the transition to the responsibilities of middle-age adulthood (business). "It seemed to have been a unanimous opinion among Elvis scriptwriters," observes Feeney, "that, when not singing, he was good only for girls and cars (or something else with an engine in it), as if he were the ultimate teenage boy."[1] This was perhaps never truer than in his Hawai'i-set films. Between 1961 and 1966, Presley made three films in the islands—*Blue Hawaii* (1961), *Girls! Girls! Girls!* (1962), and *Paradise Hawaiian Style*. The first two films appeared at the height of Elvis's cinematic popularity—in 1962, he had three major box office hits alone, with *Blue Hawaii* topping the list.[2] The star also returned to Hawai'i several years later to shoot a historic TV concert special, *Aloha from Hawaii* (1973), which was broadcast live across the globe.

Paul Hooper has argued that *Blue Hawaii* in particular "had a greater impact upon popular impressions of the islands than any film ever made. In a sense, this is regrettable, as its portrayal of Hawaiian society, while blandly complimentary, is a blurred amalgam of Hawaiian, Samoan, and Tahitian culture overlaid with borrowed Southern notions of hospitality, aristocracy, leisure, and race."[3] In a 1962 letter to the Pacific War Memorial Commission (after Elvis had performed a hugely successful charity concert in Pearl Harbor to help raise funds for construction of the USS Arizona Memorial), an associate of business manager Colonel Tom Parker, Tom Diskin, made the claim, "I understand from some of the business people in Honolulu that they consider Elvis one of their best good will ambassadors as a result of his performance in the picture *Blue Hawaii*."[4] While Diskin's statement was undeniably self-serving, it also retained more than an kernel of truth. *Blue Hawaii* in particular dominated the marketplace with box office numbers ($4.7 million, according to a 1970 list of all-time box office champs[5]) and soundtrack sales. Despite failing to match the lucrative transmedia popularity of *Blue Hawaii*, the other two films are just as revealing for how their very presence reflected the kinship of Elvis's persona to the islands in particular.

Despite spending relatively little time there, the star continues to be historically associated in popular culture with the islands of Hawai'i. Presley's commercially successful and culturally relevant, if aesthetically forgettable, Hollywood career, which Feeney refers to as "the black hole of Elvis's career" between the more prominent Memphis and Vegas periods,[6] has led to less consideration of his onscreen cinematic presence. Certainly, his movies were safely formulaic. A local Memphis entertainment editor insisted in 1963 that "with due deference to his fans, I still think the Presley film image and formula are wearing thin, and the box office indicates quite a few people seem to feel the same way. I don't suggest he start spitting on the flag, taking candy from babies, and pushing old ladies down the stairs. I do suggest that he and Colonel Parker start looking more closely at the scripts and casts of pictures submitted to him."[7] Unlike his stage career, argues Feeney, "there's no comparably resplendent egregiousness to the movies, no thrill of excess. They're flat, mechanical, bored."[8] In a 1965 letter to the *Boston Globe*, one woman wrote:

> I do not understand why Elvis Presley should be among the top moneymakers of the screen. He is only a moderately good singer—and to many people's taste not even that. He is scarcely a handsome young man of the Gregory Peck, Rock Hudson tradition. His pictures are usually produced along the same dull lines and sometimes there is not even much change in plot. Please tell me why he is said to be so rich as a result of his acting. I don't see it.[9]

The *Globe*'s response pointed to "teen-age enthusiasm for Elvis . . . [that was] not interested in subtlety nor versatility." Yet by the mid-1960s, the teenage appeal was arguably waning—Elvis himself seemed to believe as much. Recognizing his aging demographic, he told Hedda Hopper: "I've got to make good as a movie actor if I want to stay on top. I can sing in the films, of course, and I will. I have a dozen numbers in *Blue Hawaii*, which I have just completed, but the old wiggle is on the way out."[10]

The more likely explanation for Elvis's movie success was the lucrative soundtrack market that went with it—the same *Globe* piece added at the end: "Presley's records and his music publishing business swell his annual receipts. Some people have estimated that Elvis might get between $4,000,000 and $5,000,000 in 1965, which is Big Business."[11] A mere month and a half after its debut, one trade paper reported that "sales of Elvis Presley's *Blue Hawaii* LP have now topped the 600,000 mark, and that the album sold 350,000 copies in the first week of release."[12] Six months later, the same periodical observed that *Blue Hawaii* is "believed to be the fastest selling LP to reach the million mark in recording history."[13] The soundtrack "shot to number one on the LP charts, far outstripping any studio album Elvis had released to date (with sales of over one and one-half million, it sold close to five times the number of [his comeback album] *Elvis is Back*, for example) and further confirming the wisdom not just of [film producer] Hal Wallis' strategy but of the Colonel's grander plan"[14] to synergize theatrical film release with soundtrack album and a range of other ancillary merchandise in an age that saw movies competing with an increasing number of other leisure alternatives.

Feeney argues that *Blue Hawaii* was "the first [Elvis] picture in which *travelogue supersedes storytelling*."[15] In these travelogues, we see a perfect convergence of two separate discourses—the well-known one of Elvis as perpetual teenage boy, and the deeper rhetoric of tourism as negotiating an inherent tension between work and leisure, business and pleasure. *Blue Hawaii*'s original title was *Hawaiian Beach Boy*.[16] As Jane Desmond notes,[17] Native Hawaiian beachboys and surfers were the original tourist guides in the islands' emergent leisure-based economy, offering not only information about the territory but also more sensual experiences associated with the permissive sexuality of the beach (though, ironically, surfing is nearly completely absent from the film). *Blue Hawaii* is the story of a military veteran, Chad (Presley), returning from life in the Army to his family's home in O'ahu. Rob Wilson writes that *Blue Hawaii* "at least tried to turn Elvis Presley into a place-bound Pacific resident."[18] Rather than embrace his father's pineapple business, Chad just wants to hang out on the beach with his local friends and of course fellow band members. He is able to solve this tough dilemma by using his local knowledge to become a tour guide who coordinates the interests of his travel business with his father's successful agricultural company in a replay of Hawai'i's own pre-WWII economic history. *Paradise Hawaiian Style* follows a similar path, but without the generational angle—as Richards, a washed-up commercial airline captain, unites his familiarity with Hawai'i with his skills as a helicopter pilot to build a business with his friend that transports tourists around the islands. Meanwhile, the film in between, *Girls! Girls! Girls!*, was shot in Hawai'i—and technically set there—but without utilizing much of the same Hawaiian iconography. In this film, too, Elvis's character, Ross Carpenter, works in the leisure industry, taking tourists out to the ocean for deep-sea fishing adventures.

The explicit emphasis on the travelogue in Elvis's movies echoes a common complaint about the star's post-military cinematic body of work—its heavy attention to location shooting as the primary appeal and, related to that, its indifference to the conventions of plot and narrative in favor of leisure spectacles involving colorful visuals and musical shows. In 1966, critic Diane Thomas wrote about the kinship between summer movies and summer vacations, citing *Paradise Hawaiian Style*: "Summertime is fun time and Moviedom has rolled out a raft of fun films for the vacation audience.... The only opening scheduled this week is an Elvis Presley comedy geared, of course, to the summer vacation teen set."[19] Elvis films in particular seemed to reify the idea that

Figure 5.1. Chad (Elvis Presley) takes a tour group to a nearby pineapple plantation in *Blue Hawaii* (1961). Most noted today for its lucrative soundtrack (Elvis's highest-selling album during his lifetime), *Blue Hawaii* was also the beginning of the star's "travelogue" cycle of movies, which were more interested in exotic locations (and music) as spectacle than in any remotely nuanced narrative storytelling. What also distinguishes *Blue Hawaii* (and *Paradise Hawaiian Style* five years later) is that it is also a highly reflexive narrative about the travel industry—wherein his character Chad single-handedly modernizes Hawaiian tourism by collaborating with his father's pineapple company (a bit of synergy that in real life had existed for decades by then).

summer movies were a form of virtual tourism. Indeed, reactions most often focused on the scenery. After watching *Blue Hawaii*, one exhibitor remarked, "[I] wish I could leave for Hawaii next week."[20] Hawaii, Wallis told *Variety* in 1964, "is just a wonderful place to make movies."[21] Later, he was quoted as saying that with Elvis, "I looked for original stories with colorful backgrounds and situations which lent themselves to musical numbers, like *Blue Hawaii* and *Hawaiian Paradise*—that sort of thing."[22] Elvis's biographer Peter Guralnick adds:

> There was no doubt in Hal Wallis' mind what image of Elvis *he* intended to convey. He would give the public what it wanted, Elvis the entertainer over Elvis the actor—a course that in his mind was only reinforced by the relative failures of Twentieth Century Fox's *Flaming Star* and *Wild in the Country*.

His own *Blue Hawaii*, by way of contrast, had gone straight to number two on *Variety*'s weekly list of top-grossing films upon its Thanksgiving release and continued to do business well into the new year.[23]

At the same time, the narrative/spectacle binary elides how the overall cinematic experiences of Elvis's Hawai'i films were, as Rick Altman argued, profoundly *affective*: "There is no question about the nature or intensity of the experience [in his films]. In fact so intense is the experience that the tourists, like the film audience, soon discover that Elvis' singing is what they have come to see and hear."[24] John Connell and Chris Gibson add that the mass-marketed sounds of Hawai'i carry the impression of a greater degree of intimacy than visual media do: "through recourse to nostalgia and claims to authenticity," music more fully embodies the affective appeals of tourism and touristic escapes.[25] Elvis created a richly layered experience for the viewer that complemented but also transcended the confined spaces of the cheesy narratives and inconsistent production values. His films "exude a sense of life present in few other musicals of the period," Altman adds, "Approximately split between allegiance to the show motif (get the girl, get the singing job) and fairy tale exoticism in a resort setting (Miami, Acapulco, Las Vegas, Hawaii), the films lay increasing emphasis on the role of Elvis (and his new music style) as misfit."[26]

Rather than dismiss Elvis movies as only "travelogues," or as star-driven narratives that really only served as advertisement for the soundtrack, I would argue that the three Hawai'i-themed films, as well as his 1973 TV special, were part of a much larger postwar touristic fantasy—one fed by the affective intensity of Elvis music and the actuality value of location shooting. The narratives of these films were not incidental—Elvis's role in *Blue Hawaii* and *Paradise Hawaiian Style* as *literal* tour guide brought into relief how the "experience" of Elvis (as performer) and the "experience" of Hawaii (as tourist fantasy) could be very much one and the same. "Playing on the latent identification of travel and romance which underlies not only the fairy tale musical tradition but the travel business as well," writes Altman, "*Blue Hawaii* is only fulfilling an archetypal plot by making Elvis into the tour operator, the one who can provide tourism and romance."[27] Elvis's character introduces his diegetic and nondiegetic audiences to the adventure, romance, and fun of the islands, even as he himself also embodied similar fantasies for both a younger generation of baby boomers and the older generation of adults transitioning into middle age and older. Elvis bridged the childlike energy of one generation with the warm nostalgia of the other. Hawai'i did as well—the youthful vigor of fun in the sun merged seamlessly with postwar memories of stars like Bing Crosby (the first singer to perform "Blue Hawaii" in *Waikiki Wedding*, 1937) and the imagined simplicity of island life pre- December 7th.

The potent experience of Elvis/Hawai'i performed complex ideological work that is typical, as Richard Dyer argued, of the classic Hollywood musical—alleviating competing tensions in real-life anxieties.[28] "The Elvis canon has one axiomatic principle: respectful, respectable hedonism (a.k.a., good clean fun)," Feeney writes, "Yet that principle subsumes two reoccurring themes: class and multiculturalism."[29] Elvis's characters blended the youthful frivolity of a perpetual teenage boy in his quest for frivolity, adventure, and sex with a simultaneous commitment to a self-starter work ethic. For both those generations, then, the aural and visual experience offered by Elvis merged the competing desires of working hard and yet still managing to have fun constantly. They effectively erased the tension between, and choice of, "business or pleasure." This was the very same tension that, as Dean MacCannell argued, was exacerbated by tourism's fundamentally flawed promise to visitors to "get away from it all."[30] The ultimate fantasy of the Elvis/Hawaii experience may have been the ideal that work would still somehow remain central to the tourist adventure.

This touristic dream of living out a different existence than the day-to-day routine is also both race- and class-based. The issues are closely interrelated—"the limited dramatic tension produced in [*Blue Hawaii*]," writes Houston Wood, "arises from Elvis's parents worrying he will become a 'beach bum' and fail to follow in his father's footsteps as a white man profiting from the labor of Asian immigrants and of the Natives in their ancestral land."[31] The idea of Elvis as Hawaiian "beach bum"—or more accurately, the "beachboy" in his established tourist identity—effectively collapses racial and economic questions into an ideal role that not only alleviates work/leisure tensions but also does so under the youthful guise of a post-racial fantasy that attempts to transcend the older boundaries of mainland race and class elitism embodied by Chad's bigoted Southern mother (Angela Lansbury). Elvis's character in *Blue Hawaii* was a rare example of "a non-native [Hawaiian] local" in Hollywood films of the time,[32] one who "flirts with the danger of going Native and gratifying his various 'primitive' lusts."[33] Elvis's Hawai'i films—especially *Paradise Hawaiian Style*—are, as Feeney argues, mildly progressive as Hollywood goes for the time period in their depiction of a multicultural society.

The imagined innocence of Chad's leisurely baby boomer naïveté allows him to not only dismiss older prejudices but also remain ignorant of the institutional histories of economic exploitation that shaped those prejudices and from which he continues to benefit personally and professionally. The utopic emotional power of that post-racial fantasy that Chad and his local friends embody is quite real—a key affective component to the classical musical's ideological work, as Dyer noted. Yet it also conceals what Joy Taylor has called *Girls! Girls! Girls!* and *Blue Hawaii*'s "exotic whiteness"—where these films "demonstrate White supremacy in the casting of Euro-Americans in the lead roles while also promoting depictions of racial harmony between White and non-White characters; to portray racial progressivism, the White characters temporarily don the markers of color and culture."[34] As with other Hawaiian-themed texts of the time, this multiculturalist fantasy imagines racial difference as no longer significant, even as it also puts forth the equally troubling agenda that class no longer is either.

Synergistic Opportunities

With "Hollywood . . . on a big-budget musical kick again,"[35] Elvis's emergence onto the movie scene coincided with the convergence of two industry trends: the growing push of films to sell soundtracks, and then, to facilitate that, the increasing use of musical talents in the cinema. Prior to this time, movie music albums were not as central to Hollywood's creative decisions or business strategy: "Though they rarely were used in big production numbers," *Billboard* reported in October of 1961, "film themes have been best sellers. Consequently, diskery execs expect the new movie musical trend will pay off even bigger"[36] by designing the films themselves with a greater eye toward this ancillary market. And it wasn't just that studios realized soundtracks were becoming a valuable additional stream of revenue in partnership with record companies; the soundtracks on their own helped push ticket sales in return. Earlier that year, *Billboard* also reported that "movie executives are continuing to dig deeper and deeper into the ranks of hot record artists in both the singles and album fields in their never-ending search for box-office properties. . . . Meanwhile, the current success of movie themes of records and the importance of these disks in helping to create excitement about the movies, has caused a scramble on the part of producers."[37]

With Elvis, in *Variety*'s words, "a one-man disk industry,"[38] producer Colonel Parker saw the transition to movie star as his next logical step in cementing Elvis's value as a music icon, even if ironically it meant ceasing to do any concerts or independent albums. In a 1962 article named "Films Keep the Presley Legend Alive," music critic Ren Grevatt argued that "if his records are no longer the magic spellbinders they used to be . . . the Presley movie career has turned him into a sensational record album artist, via his soundtrack LPs."[39] In Presley, Parker had a particular opportunity for media convergence:

> Nothing could be simpler or more logical: the soundtrack album promoted the movie release, the movie release guaranteed a certain level of sales and publicity for the album. And as the Colonel perfected his own brand of synergistic opportunity . . . it began to become apparent that there was no real need for anything *but* the soundtrack music.[40]

This sentiment was shared in 1968 by Albert Goldman of the *New York Times*, who looked back at Elvis's remarkable financial success that decade with a great deal of envy. The twin pillars of film event and soundtrack album were just the tip of the iceberg for the most lucrative display of market saturation this side of Walt Disney's *The Mickey Mouse Club*. "With the Colonel exploiting the merchandising gimmicks by each new [film] role (everything from mannish sweatshirts to girlish pink teddy bears)," Goldman wrote, "with the royalties pouring in from Elvis' 30 gold records, and with residuals and replays and remakes and reissues from all the golden years, when Elvis and the Colonel grossed as much as $35-million in a single year, why should anyone ridicule the old Colonel and his cigar?"[41]

The Colonel's promotional efforts were notoriously relentless. Immediately upon arrival to Honolulu to do location shooting for *Blue Hawaii*, Elvis was made to do a charity performance to help raise funds to complete construction of the USS Arizona Memorial in Pearl Harbor. The concert was held on March 25th, 1961, only two days before production on *Blue Hawaii* began. At one point, Parker had even pushed for a second concert.[42] Sailing on the S.S. *Matsonia*, the Colonel arrived in Hawai'i several weeks before Elvis, largely to help finalize the details of the benefit concert, which he closely oversaw. He was particularly aggressive in pushing special $100 VIP tickets, which he considered to be "collectors' items,"[43] as well as "the only way we can get this much money" needed to fund the memorial.[44] In attendance at the concert were Wallis, director Norman Taurog, and friend Jerry Wald, along with prominent representatives of Hill and Range (Elvis's music publishing company), the William Morris Agency, and RCA records, who were also expected to donate to the cause.[45] Then–vice president Lyndon B. Johnson was invited to attend but, writing to Memorial Commission chairman H. Tucker Gratz, "As you can imagine, my position as Vice President carries many heavy responsibilities. My schedule for the next few months is so busy that I am not able to take on any more engagements, no matter how attractive they are."[46] Outwardly, the nonprofit charity concert was a smart bit of seemingly selfless self-promotion, though Parker did unsuccessfully try to entice NBC early on into broadcasting the concert on television, which was in part about creating an opportunity for his team and Elvis to see long-term profits off reruns.[47]

Although the Colonel himself originally wanted the concert in a larger venue in downtown Honolulu, it was eventually staged at the insistence of the US Navy and the Pacific War Memorial Commission at the Bloch Arena in Pearl Harbor[48]—the same location where most of NBC's *This Is Your Life* charity episode had been filmed a few years earlier. Even Parker conceded that "it will give the USS Arizona Memorial a much more fitting association by having the show at Bloch Arena."[49] The connection to the USS *Arizona* also, as with Elvis's own military service (both off screen and onscreen), appealed to the nostalgia of an earlier generation of Americans, couching the star's youthful appeal within a larger history of sacrifice: "You know," Parker reportedly told local papers, "Elvis is twenty-six and that's about the average age of those boys entombed in the Arizona. I think it's appropriate that he should be doing this."[50] However, not all reactions to this fundraising were unconditionally supportive. While not criticizing the concert itself, one Honolulu citizen wrote the local paper to argue that the money raised could be better used elsewhere. "Why not use this fund for a 'living memorial,' a scholarship at the East-West Center, or other endeavor for those in need?" the person wrote. "It could [be] restricted to members of the families of the men of that ship [USS *Arizona*] or broadened to include others. I am wondering how members of the families of the men of the Arizona feel about a 'living memorial.'"[51] When the concert was over, the Hawaii House of Representatives and the Pacific War Memorial Commission presented Elvis with a plaque at a press conference at the Hawaiian Village Hotel (one of the shooting locations for *Blue Hawaii*). They thanked him in a resolution, which stated—probably at the Colonel's urging—that the concert was the "biggest single gate [ticket sales] in the history of Hawai'i."[52] In total, the commission claimed that, by April 24, 1961, the performance had netted $67,000, a check for which

Figure 5.2. In Honolulu for the shooting of *Blue Hawaii*, Elvis did a charity concert at Bloch Arena to help raise funds for the new version of a memorial for the sunken naval ship, the USS *Arizona*, in Pearl Harbor—the last concert he gave for many years. Although Elvis's association with Hawai'i is largely remembered in terms of film musicals (and the Hollywood phase of his career more generally), it both started and ended with two of the more high-profile concerts he ever gave, as his live Hawai'i television special a decade later was a ratings bonanza.

they had hoped Elvis would personally make an appearance with.[53] Elvis, however, had already left the islands by then, having spent less than a month total on location shooting the iconic film.

Blue Hawaii

Elvis had recorded the entire *Blue Hawaii* soundtrack in California over the course of just three days prior to leaving for Hawai'i. After completion of the soundtrack, which was released before the movie itself, Presley reportedly sent a copy to music critic Jonah Ruddy "with a note from Colonel Tom Parker—'Remember, for the price of a ticket to the cinema, a holiday in Hawaii, the world's lushest paradise of fun—heaven of song—Eden of romance!' "[54] Elvis at the time was less enthusiastic about the islands' culture or history than Parker, who possessed a somewhat nostalgic relationship with Hawai'i, having served there in the US military during the 1920s. "It seemed as if Hawaii had brought out all of his impishness," wrote Guralnick, "and he interviewed tourists, using the aluminum tube from his cigar as a microphone and identifying himself as representative of Radio Pineapple."[55] Parker's fascination with doing something Hawai'i-themed went back to his very first Elvis movie pitch to Wallis after the star returned from his military service:

> In Colonel's scenario, the action would take place on the Hawaiian Islands, because Hawaiian music looked like it might be the coming trend and Elvis clearly had the voice for it. The story line focuses on a gang of promoters who con Elvis into singing with some Native Hawaiians—he is running away from his fans perhaps, his record company is frantically looking for him because they need material—but the promoters snow Elvis into singing for free, then surreptitiously record and bootleg the performance, to the natives' (and Elvis') financial disadvantage. . . . Wallis, it must be noted, remained patiently forbearing throughout, acknowledging the appeal of the Hawaiian angle but suggesting that the story line might be a trifle melodramatic.[56]

Aside from "backstage" element, this initial plot idea was itself a nostalgic throwback to similar stories of the 1930s and early 1940s, such as *Honolulu* (1939) and *In the Navy* (1941), which featured Hollywood celebrities fleeing their fans by heading to the islands, only to get caught up in a series of comedic misadventures. The final version of *Blue Hawaii* would invert this tired outsider's perspective on the islands by making Elvis a local-born son of the islands instead of a fish-out-of-water traveler, while also maintaining a tourist framing through the plot convention of the travel guide. Yet other parallels to the earlier Hawai'i-themed films remained, such as the schoolteacher (Nancy Walters)—in an echo of the Georgia Smith character in *Waikiki Wedding*—who comes to Hawai'i hoping to find the oft-advertised romance, only to be quickly disappointed. "You know I've taken a vacation every summer," she tells Chad, "looking for romance."

As the film's most overt nostalgic signifier, *Blue Hawaii* opens with Presley singing the title song over the credits, reiterating not only the tranquil, romantic mood of the islands typical of touristic rhetoric, but also the decades of commercial media that sold it—in this case, Bing Crosby and *Waikiki Wedding* especially, the classical Hollywood film from which this iconic song originated. Many articles from the time frequently compared 1960s crooning Elvis to Crosby, who was regarded as Elvis's "foremost vocalist-predecessor in Hollywood."[57] Crosby also had a history with islands' themed music that included not only cinema but also albums such as *Favorite Hawaiian Songs* (1944) and *Blue Hawaii* (1950). By the 1960s, he like everyone else was cashing in on the Hawai'i trend by going "all Hawaiian with 'Adventures in Paradise,' 'Keep Your Eyes on the Hands,' 'Lovely Hula Hands,' and 'Beautiful Kahana.'"[58] The music supervisor on *Blue Hawaii*, Joseph Lilley, had himself worked on numerous Crosby musicals at Paramount, and imagined himself "a stickler for an authentic Hawaiian sound."[59] When the music was completed for *Blue Hawaii*, "Hal Wallis was convinced that he finally had what he had been looking for all along: the soundtrack for a Bing Crosby picture, starring Elvis Presley."[60]

The nostalgic connection between *Blue Hawaii* and Crosby's generation reaffirms how by the early 1960s Elvis's core audience consisted increasingly of young parents and aging adults as much as teens. The evocation of "Blue Hawaii" in the latter film suggests a rather unironic love affair with the islands, consistent with the nostalgic postwar rewriting of pre-WWII Hawai'i, whereas the original Crosby film—while affirming Hawai'i's reputation for adventure and romance—was more self-aware about its touristic artifices. *Waikiki Wedding* posits the touristic experience as a collusion between the locals and the pineapple company, thus erasing the actual tourism industry's presence. In Elvis's film, tourism is depicted as an emergent, marginalized industry—rendering it as little more than an economic afterthought on the islands rather than its central economic force, second only to the US' massive naval presence. While Chad's veteran status acknowledges the role of the military—and the relationship between veterans and Hawai'i tourism—his "return" (escape) from military duty to the islands elides the military's massive presence there. The running joke about his mom's desire to believe that Chad saw some real combat during his peacetime tour of duty defuses the very real dangers at stake in the military's continuing presence in Hawai'i.

Blue Hawaii also shares some affinity with the "backstage" musical genre tradition. Certainly, this is consistent with many Elvis films, where the star must invariably perform, willingly or otherwise, in musical acts for others (nightclubs, lounges, parties, etc.). While the Crosby film situated its version of Hawaiian music as the product of diegetic performance in so far as the natives performed for the white visitors—and more clearly the entire "show" of Georgia Smith's touristic adventure—Chad's friendship with other local beachboys manifests itself as an aspiring band. "They've gone professional," he tells his mother, implying that they are not just lazy beach bums. Ironically, though, this is exactly where we first meet them, when they ride in on a canoe as though a preformed musical act, performing a version of "Aloha Oe" to which Chad quickly hops on board and joins in. This well-known Queen Lili'uokalani song ("sung in at least half the Hawaiian films ever made"[61]) highlights *Blue Hawaii*'s pastiche nod to the collective mediated version of Hawaiian heritage being defined by a specific song, and wherein the local population provides the expected conduit.

When Elvis performs "Rock-a-Hula" with his friends at a family function, the star's objectified position, physical hip movements and *'uli'uli* props, situate Elvis in a reversed "hula girl" role—a particularly pointed instance in a narrative that blurs the boundaries and assumptions about the sexual objectification of bodies. "In the film's rhetoric," writes Wood, "Elvis's singing and dancing construct the familiar, idealized, Hawaiian freedom and sexuality."[62] Guralnick reads "the familiar movements that Elvis has always claimed are natural to his music [as being] appended to silly songs, as if there were a joke."[63] Elvis's highly sexualized appeal for audiences of the time was intensified by the film's more sexually permissive beach settings. As one critic of the time wrote of the "Slicing Sand" musical number:

> Though this lacks meanness, and so would probably displease some of Elvis's critics, it has a blatant sexuality up to anything in the older movies: wearing nothing but a shirt and a revealing bathing costume, Elvis leads some equally undressed girls in a

Figure 5.3. Long noted for aggressive, sexually suggestive, hip movements during his concert performances, Elvis assumes the objectified position of the "hula girl" in *Blue Hawaii*, complete with *'uli'uli* (rattle) in hand. The staged performance at his parents' house, for the amusement of family guests, also serves as a touristic "front" region (a space consciously intended for tourists) that contrasts with his more informal, relaxed performance of "Can't Help Falling in Love" within the "back" region (thus coded as more "authentic") of his girlfriend's family home.

bout of ferocious sand-kicking in the eye of the camera. Out of the context of clubs and one-night stands, Elvis's particular gifts appear to be innocently exploited by a Hawaiian setting. I'm not at all sure that the innocence of the setting doesn't make the performance more exciting. There are similarly "innocent" scenes in the film.[64]

Chad's own ambitions as a tourism professional not only offset that classist perception of him as being little more than a beach bum, but also highlighted how the "beachboy" stereotype was itself situated in the 1960s as a more attractive—even more "authentic"—leisure choice than following the usual tourist trappings (a point also reinforced by the surf documentaries of the time). In a 1966 article for the *Chicago Tribune*, columnist Ed Sheehan wrote:

> The tour directors will frown on this, but here I go. Do Hawaii, Hawaiian Style. Bring money, but be a beachcomber.

> Skip the air-conditioned rooms, schedules, and guided tours. Get some sand between your toes and some miles between you and civilization. . . . Kailua is the place where people came to shoot marlin scenes for "The Old Man and the Sea." John Wayne and Lana Turner filmed "The Sea Chase" here. Elvis Presley and entourage came for "Girls, Girls, Girls."[65]

The reference to Hollywood movies highlighted the irony that going off the beaten path in order to find the more authentic, more natural Hawai'i that Sheehan championed was no less a product of mediation than Diamond Head and Waikiki. The appeal was not to truly go seeking out new, exciting, and potentially dangerous spontaneous adventures, but to live out a more abstract sense of the Hawaiian experience than the "guided tour" route provided, a desire that Elvis's movies narrativized for them.

Despite the use of diegetic performances to establish musical front and back regions, there is little in the way of a "front" stage for Hawaii tourism in *Blue Hawaii*. The closest are the hula girls greeting travelers with leis at the airport, used to set up an easy sex joke for Elvis. Chad is a tour guide who privileges less traditional spots for visitors, while the tourism industry in the film is depicted as less elaborate and sophisticated than it actually was. When Chad takes his visitor group unplanned to the local pineapple fields, the agricultural site becomes another stage for touristic consumption in an apt demonstration of what MacCannell termed "work displays"—the commodification of one's physical labor is not the material good produced but the immaterial spectacle of its performance for the tourist, thus alienating the traveler from the value of their own everyday work.[66] The happy ending of *Blue Hawaii* is not simply that Chad has found true love with his life partner, Maile (Joan Blackman)—it's also the less acknowledged fact that he needn't worry about whether work will ever cease to be fun for him.

Yet even as the tourism industry plays little part narratively in distinguishing the front and back regions of the film, other aspects of the film reinscribe those boundaries in subtler ways. The most self-evident instance is the contrast between his parents' home, which he refuses to visit at first, and the stunning (apparently private) beach to which he instead insists on going after arrival. The differences between Chad's family mansion and the more secluded home of his girlfriend's Hawaiian grandmother also evoke such an effect. Maile's mixed heritage, and the mostly unspoken tension this creates with Chad's mother, is the closest the film comes to acknowledging Hawai'i's complex racial dynamics. Guralnick suggests that her character was "half Islander but, perhaps in a bid to mitigate any suggestion of miscegenation, also half French."[67] (South African–born-and-raised actress Juliet Prowse, Elvis's *GI Blues* costar, was originally cast in the part but was suspended because she insisted that "her make-up man was hired for the picture, her secretary's fare to the Hawaiian location was paid and her billing clause was improved."[68]) At his parents' place, Chad constantly expresses discomfort within a space that feels too proper and manufactured, and in which there is always the expectation for him to "perform" for others, formally or causally. However, when he retreats to the grandmother's home, he feels much more relaxed and "off-stage," as it were—even as, while there, he offers to sing "Can't Help Falling in Love" for the diegetic audience.

The scene at Maile's grandmother's home becomes a replay of the opening of *Waikiki Wedding*, where the local celebration is situated as an exclusive presentation of native culture for the benefit of the welcomed *haole* observer and implied to the nondiegetic audience to be a more "authentic" Hawaiian experience (the luau dinner scene in *Diamond Head* [1963] performs a similar back region function). To highlight the connection further with back regions, the family just happens to be performing an informal hula dance for each other when Chad arrives to visit—conflating his narrative perspective with an overt touristic gaze. Elvis's iconic performance of "Can't Help Falling in Love" at this family gathering is, for Altman, the pinnacle of the star's cinematic charisma. Before he has even finished a verse, Altman writes,

> the music box [Chad gives as a birthday present to the grandmother] has been joined by a full [nondiegetic] orchestra. Soon, in fact, the tinny Middle-European sound of the music box disappears entirely as a large chorus is added to the orchestra. Imperceptibly we have slid away from a backyard barbeque in Hawaii to a realm beyond language, beyond space, beyond time. With the disappearance of the music box sound we have moved into a world of pure music, divorced from this or any other specific plot. We have reached a "place" of transcendence where time stands still, where contingent concerns are stripped away to reveal the essence of things.[69]

Given the song's diegetic "back region" setting, Altman's point about the transcendent musical space of this moment echoes the ultimate, abstract "experience" at the core of the Hawaiian vacation—as "a 'place' of transcendence where time stands still, where contingent concerns are stripped away to reveal the essence of things." Meanwhile, the staging of the scene calls attention to the performance as a performance—Chad/Elvis sings at first to the grandmother, then shifting seamlessly to Maile (to the older woman's apparent discomfort) and by implication to the nondiegetic audience.

The film's depiction of the tourism industry is an effective inversion of its own actual historical trajectory. In a moment of classic entrepreneurial creativity, Chad decides that he can merge his love of laidback, "hidden" Hawai'i with a practical job as tour guide for the local "Hawaiian Tourist Guide Service." Importantly, Chad is having a picnic with Maile at the popular tourist site, Mount Tantalus, overlooking the city of Honolulu. In the story, Tantalus is represented as a relatively secluded, depopulated, and perhaps even hidden space that only true locals know about. Then, in an added moment of brilliance, he has the inspired idea to join his own business interests with those of his father at the Great Southern Hawaiian Pineapple Company—pitching his elder on the idea that both industries could collaborate on coordinated business vacations for their mutual economic benefit, which reflected the postwar shift in 1960s Hawaiian tourism toward encouraging trade convention tourism. Chad's idea, though, was a reversal of how the islands' tourist industry came into being—the industries of sugar, pineapple, coffee, and so forth turned to tourism to help survive economically decades before Chad came along with his seemingly innovative ideas. This works to somewhat obscure, or remystify, what Hawai'i tourism was by the 1960s—an extremely well-choreographed and experienced business operation involving the coordination of numerous local interests. Chad's affinity with the beachboys not only works as the film's modest attempt to express deference to local Hawaiian culture, but also to symbolize the possibility of a remote space on the islands still waiting for tourists to explore. His tours of the pineapple fields acknowledge Hawai'i's current economic state as more than just untarnished tropical paradise, but in a way that posits the tourism's primary role in the state's economy as little more than a quiet, incidental observer.

Chad's self-identified status as little more than another Hawaiian beachboy serves the function of eliding the history of exploitation of the local population and land—he and other locals are actively taking the lead in constructing the touristic experience for the visitor, rather than passively being oppressed and abused by it. Here, the tensions with his elitist mother again become crucial. She expresses a condescending attitude toward tourists as simple commoners—"Tourists aren't people. They're . . . tourists." This dismissal aligns tourists with the working class with which Chad identifies, obscuring the fact that tourism in Hawai'i was still a relatively luxurious experience for those with the time and money to enjoy it. His mom's patronizing attitude toward the intrusion of visitors also reaffirms *Blue Hawaii*'s recontextualizing of tourism as an intimate experience of the islands hand in hand with members of local culture rather than a shrewd, lucrative exploitation of it (her elitism also elides her family's own *haole*, outsider status in Hawai'i). If anything, tourism then survives in spite of the wishes of the ruling wealthy classes of Hawai'i.

More than any other Elvis Hawai'i film, *Blue Hawaii* received significant attention from theatrical exhibitors. To advertise the film in Fort Worth, Texas, one theater manager "promoted ten cases of Hawaiian leis to be given away the weekend before opening to teenage girls who promised to wear them to school" in exchange for free admission to the film.[70] "All theatre employees," *Boxoffice* reported, "also wore leis and the box office was decorated with them. The record albums were used extensively as intermission music before and during the engagement and over the outside PA system, which could be heard about a block away."[71] Such instances of stunt advertising only scratched the surface of some exhibitors' ambitions in promoting *Blue Hawaii*. One movie theater exhibitor in Missouri believed

> that he has a potential goldmine in "Blue Hawaii." . . . He tied up with nearby McHenry's Appliance Store for the Elvis "Blue Hawaii" album and also for special lobby music which accompanied "hula girls" for the Paul Zimmerman Dance School. These girls appeared nightly for a week in advance of the film, putting on a twenty-minute hula skit on stage and also making lobby appearances for 30 minutes each evening. Stark also hooked up with the neighboring Ben Franklin store for tropical flower arrangements for the lobby. He added fishnet and extra grass skirt decorations and ordered several dozen paper leis in gay colors which he put to a particularly ingenious use. [After selecting a girl from the crowd] he would put the lei around the "queen's" neck and tell her that she would be admitted to "Blue Hawaii" the following week if she would wear the lei and tell her friends about the picture.[72]

While one exhibitor dismissed the film as merely "corny,"[73] others were more enthusiastic. Though lamenting the aesthetic quality of the film itself, one said that "Elvis is a wonderful business getter and is helping us small towners to stay in business."[74] However, as another made clear, his appeal was largely limited by genre: "The ticket buyers want Elvis in musical company—not in drama like the last two from Fox."[75] Overall, their emphasis was as much on Hawai'i as Elvis: "The color and the beautiful Hawaiian scenes are breath-taking along with Elvis and a supporting cast of beautiful girls. Played to better than average business and the comments from our patrons were very favorable. Many said it was his best picture."[76] Added another from Oklahoma: "Although I played this one very late, it brought in one of the biggest box office grosses I've had to date. Good color, beautiful scenery, lots of pretty girls, and Elvis. What more do you need?"[77] Finally, wrote one North Dakota exhibitor: "A beautiful title and a show that is colorful and in color. . . . Just the right length and a nice, clean story."[78]

Girls! Girls! Girls!

Back on the islands, production on *Girls! Girls! Girls!* began before *Blue Hawaii* was even in theaters. Elvis worked with a lot of the same crew, including studio director Norman Taurog. Presley had developed a comfort zone with the veteran filmmaker, who was "a big hit with Elvis and the guys for his relaxed tolerance of their hijinks in *G.I. Blues*. . . . Elvis had clearly loosened up enough to try some conventional bits of comedy at Taurog's instigation—there are playful double takes, lots of brisk and energetic business, and even some genial self-mockery to go with the spectacular Hawaiian sights and sounds and 'production values' that are the hallmark of any Hal Wallis picture."[79] Elvis's working relationship with Taurog and others helps explain the more playful tone of his post-military film career. But the partnership was also practical—they already had experience shooting on the islands while filming *Blue Hawaii*, and there was little in the way of established production facilities or experienced talent indigenous to Hawai'i in the early 1960s. The plan with the film, as with all Elvis projects, was to get a film out as quickly as possible, but without looking overtly repetitive. Hence, *Girls! Girls! Girls!*—despite some logistical commonalities—came out looking very different than its predecessor.

Saying that the film is one of Elvis's "Hawaiian" films is a bit misleading—at least in relation to the image that Hollywood had usually constructed to sell the islands onscreen. One Elvis biographer notes that "Hal Wallis took the company to Hawaii once again for beautiful vistas, beautiful sunsets, and needless to say, beautiful girls. It was a highly forgettable production, a decided step back artistically not just from the two United Artists films that immediately preceded it but even from *Blue Hawaii*. . . . Even the soundtrack seemed somewhat of an afterthought."[80] What's fascinating is how little of Hawai'i's "beautiful" visual attributes ended up on the screen—and presumably by design. *Girls! Girls! Girls!* was originally supposed to be set in the Gulf of Mexico, with the working title, according to a trade paper of the time, of "*Gumbo Ya-Ya*, the Creole expression which means 'Everybody talks at once.' " The article went on to add that "it seems that the executives concerned feel that *Girls! Girls! Girls!* is a more lucid and down-to-earth title—and I must say it strikes me as having considerably more box-office appeal!"[81] At least one existing song in the film hints at the original setting—Elvis talks to a fellow fisherman while out on the sea about his times in Louisiana: "New Orleans. . . . Man, I wish I was there now," he says, before beginning to sing the "Song of the Shrimp" (second only to the tuna fish in "We're Coming in Loaded" as a prime example of Elvis's ability to seduce even seafood through the power of song).

At some point in the production process the decision was made to switch the film's setting to Hawai'i, at least in part as a result of *Blue Hawaii*'s success. As a result, *Girls! Girls! Girls!* highlights just how arbitrary the "paradise" depiction of Hawai'i in Hollywood films is—even shooting "on location" requires a high degree of artifice, framing, and arrangement in order to match existing mainland expectations for what Hawai'i "should" look like cinematically. Thus, the film may be most useful for what it *does not represent* onscreen—it gives us the actual islands of Hawai'i but in a fascinatingly "de-Hawai'i-ed" way that runs counter to decades of mediated imagery. The movie avoids almost all the aural and visual clichés of the islands—Diamond Head and Waikiki, steep tropical cliffs, leis, colorful shirts, and luau shows. Much of the film retains a generic seaside mise-en-scène of shipping docks and fishing ports as equally at home in Southern California, or the Florida Keys, as in Honolulu. The geographical confusion was highlighted by some audiences at the time. One viewer in Elvis's hometown of Memphis remarked, "The scenery is not as magnificent as in *Blue Hawaii*, and although [they believed] it is supposed to be set in the Caribbean, I recall that it was filmed in Hawaii. Several of the shots are very familiar to those in *Blue Hawaii*."[82] Indeed, there are no direct references to Hawai'i anywhere in the entire film, save the brief appearance of hula dancers in the film's conclusion. The *Variety* review dismissed it as standard formulaic Elvis material, and lauded the color photography at several points, but made no reference to the Hawai'i setting.[83] Similarly, the *New Musical Express* review made no reference to the movie's setting either, though it did highlight the presence of "native girls" in a caption to a publicity still of the hula dance sequence.[84]

As with his tourism jobs in both *Blue Hawaii* and *Paradise Hawaiian Style*, Elvis's character's work on the seas (as both fisherman and sport fishing guide) serves as a means to unite the labor/leisure tension in his life, to still have fun and work at the same time—a point further played up during numerous moments when he playfully sings *while* working. A nightclub called the "Pirates Den" replaces *Blue Hawaii*'s tourist company for the narrative's overtly performative front region, where he performs songs such as "Return to Sender," while the private home of his Greek friends replaces the grandmother's house as the back region (in both cases, Elvis brings a gift to the elder woman, which then serves as a transition immediately into song). Perhaps, the more prominent back region is "Paradise Cove," a geographically vague island that is home to his Chinese friends. The term "paradise" is about as close to the usual clichés of Hawai'i on film as *Girls! Girls! Girls!* moves, and the location aptly serves as the setting for the spectacular musical finale where the hula girls make their appearance. During an evening beachside party that could easily be mistaken for a luau dinner show, Elvis and the rest of the cast cease any pretense of narrative and engage in an elaborate musical number where the star returns to singing the film's title song while a series of dancers enter the frame dressed in an array of costumes that evoke numerous races, ethnicities, and cultures—Hawaiian, Spanish, Thai, Chinese, Filipino, and so on. The scene works most effectively as a concise and transparent celebration of Elvis's cinematic identity—non-narrative musical spectacles that involve him performing songs while traveling the globe in search of female companionship.

Isle of Paradise

The backstory to *Girls! Girls! Girls!* highlighted just how interchangeable Elvis movies really were. It was also not the last attempt to cash in on the popularity of situating the King in tropical paradises. This became magnified later when Allied Artists started to negotiate with Colonel Parker for the star's next film. In 1963, *Variety* reported that Allied Artists "President Steve Broidy closed with Elvis Presley to star during 1964 in 'Isle of Paradise.' This will take inspiration from 'Blue Hawaii,' one of the best of the Presleys and will put the singer-actor down amid the sheltering palms again, with the girls, girls, girls. [But] not necessarily Hawaii."[85] Similarly, *Boxoffice* quoted Broidy as saying that "one of Presley's biggest grossing pictures has been 'Blue Hawaii,' and 'Isle of Paradise,' which will be photographed in color, will provide this extremely popular young star with the same type of romantic, tropical vehicle."[86] In the end, the only movie Presley made with AA turned out to be *Tickle Me* (1965), a bull riding movie set in Texas. An April 1964 report from Honolulu in *Boxoffice* even claimed at one point that *Isle of Paradise* "switched locales and is now scheduled for shooting in Acapulco"[87]—an unrealized possibility presumably inspired by the success of *Fun in Acapulco* (1963).

The latter film, meanwhile, had a fascinating, preproduction history of its own. For a time, *Blue Hawaii* had been banned in Mexico, leading *Variety* then to speculate that "since the outbreak of hoodlum demonstrations at the Americas theatre during the screening of *GI Blues*, with rock 'n' roll fans tearing up seats, breaking windows, etc., the so-called 'King of Rock' is on the Mexican 'nervous' list."[88] Elvis was not allowed into Mexico as a result, so all his scenes were shot on a Hollywood backlot while a separate crew went south of the border for location shooting. The trade paper suggested that *Fun in Acapulco* (then called "Vacation in Acapulco") was pitched in part to curry favor with Mexican authorities.[89] In any event, the tangled industrial mess of *Isle of Paradise*, *Tickle Me*, *Vacation in Acapulco*, *Fun in Acapulco*, and others highlighted just how incidental and interchangeable Elvis projects were as Colonel Parker and various studios negotiated one formulaic property after another. As long as Elvis and the soundtracks were secured, the content truly didn't seem to matter much. However, all the properties in this case did draw their roots back to the considerable popularity of *Blue Hawaii*.

Paradise Hawaiian Style

Echoing the struggling, though ultimately profitable, Allied Artists project, *Paradise Hawaiian Style* was called "Hawaiian Paradise" at one point.[90] As the generic title implied—just insert Elvis into "paradise" of one kind or another—the film did feel like an easy, if still lucrative, recycling of *Blue Hawaii*. Even the exploitation strategies for local exhibitors sounded overly familiar by then: "Play the new RCA Victor records of Elvis' songs in the lobby and alert record shops as to playdates," *Boxoffice* suggested. "Use paper leis as decorations. Stage a dance contest for girls in grass skirts, [with] one of them given as a prize."[91] Elvis's character was "intended to recap some of the rugged qualities of his *Roustabout* role. . . . [With most of the same crew in tow] and the third Hawaii location shoot in five years, the feeling was more one of extreme déjà vu than the mere revisiting of familiar ground."[92] To a point, *Paradise Hawaiian Style* was certainly more of the same, though there was "some talk," reports Guralnick, "about trying to get the Beatles to sing one song with Elvis at the conclusion of *Paradise, Hawaiian Style* until Hal Wallis discovered that their United Artists movie deal precluded that."[93]

There's a sense that, in contrast to his experiences shooting *Blue Hawaii*, Elvis himself may have been invested in Hawai'i as more than just another generic tropical shooting location. He had arrived back in Honolulu with the touristic attitude of "beef[ing] about the [media] circus that always surrounds him, and how he'd hoped to be able to *get away from it all* in Hawaii."[94] The singer for the first time visited the new USS Arizona Memorial, the one his charity concert years earlier helped pay for. Elvis "found himself fascinated," notes Guralnick, "by the lessons in Hawaiian customs, music and culture provided by the Polynesian Cultural Center, a Mormon-founded college and retreat in Oahu that served as both a location and a cultural adviser to the film."[95] The *Boston Globe* reported too that "when he returned from Hawaii, Elvis brought back a *toere* log and pairs of *deruas, autas, puilis* and *uli ulis* (all members of the drum family)" (in an article lamenting the abandonment of Elvis's iconic guitar in his latest film).[96] Later, in 1969, Elvis made a point of vacationing in the islands "after finishing his film 'Change of Habit' for Universal in Los Angeles. Presley stayed at the Ilakai. . . . It was all rest and recuperation: no interviews, no pictures, no phone calls, no comment."[97] In each case, Elvis bought into the same nostalgic myth—Hawai'i as a simpler place, filled with simpler people, and thus that to which one could retreat in search of simpler times. In this respect, Elvis seemed invested in the same fantasy that he himself had been so actively involved in selling to the public for the better part of a decade, and which did not necessarily bring him the peace of mind he sought.

In *Paradise Hawaiian Style*, Wood writes, "once again Elvis is caught between the demands of conventional business practices and his desire to yield to the [sexual] temptations that the islands are offering him."⁹⁸ While far from ideologically unproblematic, *Paradise Hawaiian Style* is a much more modern depiction of the islands than Elvis's earlier films. Whereas *Blue Hawaii* seemed to depict a nostalgia for an earlier pre- and postwar Hawai'i, *Paradise Hawaiian Style* was, in its own admittedly kitschy way, more in tune with the islands' current state. *Blue Hawaii* rehashed the older narrative of the GI coming home from military duty (i.e., war) to push Hawai'i's tourism industry into the twentieth century through innovations in business synergy and cross-promotion. In the earlier film, the tourism industry is depicted as one, slightly eccentric, old-timer working out of a small office, with the rest of O'ahu reimagined as a still largely untamed frontier known only to locals. In *Paradise Hawaiian Style*, tourism is depicted as a fully modern operation—of which Rick and his partner are just trying to get their piece of the pie—that has colonized numerous spaces throughout the state. This is seen not only the many elaborate private resorts that Rick flies to but also in the extensive use of the Polynesian Cultural Center for location shooting—a location the *Los Angeles Times* dubbed "Oahu's Disneyland" in 1965.⁹⁹ This center, Rob Wilson adds, is "the real star" of the movie.¹⁰⁰ Elvis's character visits there not once, but twice, in order to perform with the cast as part of a touristic spectacle that *Variety* noted was "Presley's most impressive number . . . with about 70 native singers in a colorful South Seas ritual, effective and holding considerable eye-appeal."¹⁰¹ Wood reads the inclusion of Hawai'i's fully modernized tourist industry in the latter Elvis film as a final rejection of Native Hawaiian sovereignty:

> They have become much like what they remain for tourists today—a people to be found exclusively at hotels and in Polynesian shows. . . . The once idealized and dangerous Hawaiians seem in this film to be safely administered, rather like the once-wild animals one views at a zoo. . . . By 1966, all Hawaiians are depicted as having submitted so thoroughly to Euroamerican management that visitors buy tickets for versions of the tour pioneered by Crosby's Pineapple Girl [in *Waikiki Wedding*].¹⁰²

The film was by far the most extensive use of location shooting in any modern-day Hawaii-set film to that point, which reviews of the time noted. *Variety* remarked that "seldom has the panorama and terrain of Hawaii been utilized to such lush advantage, beautifully caught in the finest tints of Technicolor and providing star with an atmospheric backdrop."[103] The *Washington Post* added that "Hawaii, in fact, shares billing with the accommodating Elvis"[104]—an admittedly common observation about many of his films, but one that seems particularly apt for the visual ambitions of *Paradise Hawaiian Style*.

Such extensive travelogue photography narratively centers on the use of aviation, especially helicopters, as the primary means of transportation—remapping the Hawaiian landscape as a more navigable, conquerable terrain, as well as a more mobile manifestation of the touristic gaze that frames Elvis's Hawaiian films. During this time, "helicopter tourism in Hawai'i, as elsewhere in the United States, was first established during the [Vietnam]' war and took off in its aftermath."[105] The military—briefly nodded at in *Blue Hawaii*—emerges as a structuring absence in the latter film. "Helicopters in the age of modern tourism," writes Vernadette Gonzalez, "generate mobilities, fields of vision, and structures of feeling that produce landscapes for tourist pleasure but are also profoundly interconnected with past and present military violence."[106] In *Paradise Hawaiian Style*, "perspective on place and culture," writes Wilson, "is rendered through the gaze of United Airlines and tourist company helicopters (piloted by a singing Elvis) sweeping over vast native-emptied rain forests of Kaua'i and over the tourist-thick resort hotels and azure Pacific waters."[107] In the movie, Rick is literally able to move in and out of different picturesque scenes, unencumbered by the usual laws of gravity and lateral physical movement. Vehicles in motion embody the cinematic movement of the touristic gaze throughout the Hawaiian landscape.

This is most acutely realized in the sequence when Rick first arrives at the Polynesian Cultural Center. At first, he hovers above the tourist destination, providing the audience with a gratuitous series of shots of its many attractions—both human and object—and no doubt assisting the center in its quest for conspicuous promotion. Almost immediately upon landing, his character trades vehicles for a boat that traverses the canals of the center—the more traditional mode of transportation for visitors through the park, meant to simulate the ocean travels from one Polynesian culture (Samoan, Hawaiian, New Zealand, and so on) to another. With both boat and helicopter, a virtual Hawaiian-themed amusement ride, Rick is transformed into a mobile, but passive, spectator, for a stunning touristic vision that passes before his (and our) eyes. Further collapsing the distinction between diegetic (Rick) and nondiegetic (movie audience) spectator, his romantic companion (Linda Wong) invites him for the ride because it's "part of the show." The question of a show for whom is answered when Rick arrives at his destination and immediately joins the center's cast in a performance of "Drums of the Islands"—here, diegetic/nondiegetic, narrative/spectacle, boundaries again dissolve. In *Paradise Hawaiian Style*, the wandering touristic gaze pauses only for a musical performance.

Beyond the depiction of tourism, *Paradise Hawaiian Style* pays modestly greater attention to the contemporary culture of the islands than either *Blue Hawaii* or *Girls! Girls! Girls!*—in so far as Hawai'i is depicted as a location defined by more than just its geography and instead as a fully modernized economy positing itself as a model of post-racial sensibilities in the United States. Island resorts in the postwar era were, as Christine Skwiot writes, designed as symbols of assimilationist ideals. "Whereas designers of the interwar-era Royal Hawaiian Hotel had built an architectural fantasy of white colonial rule in a tropical pink paradise," she wrote, architects in the postwar period "blended Asian, Caucasian, and Polynesian styles to convey interracial harmony and cooperation."[108] Part of *Paradise Hawaiian Style*'s depiction of interracial relationships was reflected in the greater commitment to local casting, featuring "Island talents who made good in Hollywood, Jimmy Shigeta and Donna (Eleu) Butterworth,"[109] the latter of whom "was discovered when she appeared at the Royal Hawaiian Hotel."[110] Feeney retrospectively highlighted this latter film in particular for its emergent, if hardly radical, multicultural cast:

> [Elvis is] semi-adopted into a Chinese-American family in *Girls, Girls, Girls*, and in *Blue Hawaii* has a half-Hawaiian girlfriend and sings with an all-Hawaiian band. . . . In *Paradise Hawaiian Style*, this motif of cultural diversity receives its most prominent treatment: one of Elvis' former girlfriends is Asian; his best friend and business partner is of Hawaiian descent and married to a Caucasian. Unfortunately, any blow for enlightenment is undercut by the casting of a Japanese-American (James Shigeta) as the Hawaiian partner—to the filmmakers, apparently, they all really do look alike.[111]

Feeney sees this as typical of Elvis's larger body of work, which is the "frequent—and, more to the point, utterly matter-of-fact—dealings with members of the other races and the implicit message of racial comity his movies send."[112] Even mainstream periodicals of the time picked up on the film's mildly progressive depictions. While criticizing Presley's seemingly bored performance and this film's unremarkable storyline, the

Washington Post observed in a 1966 review titled "Elvis Presley's Latest Has a Point" that

> the plot and its characters also reveal a sociological influence worth comment. . . . In short, the integration which was a sharp current in Michener's "Tales of the South Pacific" has been accepted as a natural commonplace, not an alarming phenomenon. The genial Mr. Presley ignores racial differences in female and male. Slight as they may be, such casual acceptance for the mass level is a welcome statement and Mr. Presley makes it with matter-of-fact grace.[113]

Taylor, on the other hand, sees Elvis's films as the kind of condescending racism typical of many tourist narratives that feature white characters embracing interracial friendships in exotic locations to express a superficial, and paternalistic, racial enlightenment:

> At first blush, the Elvis Presley movies promoting tolerance through a tourist gaze that is predicated upon the binary of Self/Other may appear to be minor and even trivial, especially in the face of historical events that involve the dispossession of the land. . . . That Hollywood movies are simply entertainment is myopic, however, precisely because the cinematic texts direct attention to a dynamic of racial discourses that circulate widely within U.S. cinematic society defined by [quoting Dale Hudson] "consumerism, patriotism, and ahistoricism."[114]

Despite the representation of a more racially diverse Hawai'i, its colonial history is largely ignored, with the exception of an exchange between Rick and his business partner Danny (Shigeta): "Where would we be if Captain Cook never took a chance?" "My people would still own the islands and you'd probably be in a stew pot somewhere." The attempt at humor highlights an awareness of the lingering legacy of colonialization, albeit in a way that further undercuts the political and cultural questions that such a history also raises—while also naturalizing the racist assumption that Europeans "civilized" the local natives.

Despite some praise for *Paradise Hawaiian Style*'s locations and moderately progressive cultural and historical sensibilities, reviews of the time were generally negative. Typical of such attitudes was the *Monthly Film Bulletin*, which opined:

> This is Elvis Presley right back in the old rut, parading his talents as a man of action while women swoon at this passage. The script is rather worse than routine, and the songs and choreography are undistinguished: which leaves very little but Wallace Kelley's colourful photography of the strictly tourist-eye view of the islands.[115]

In another review, the *New York Times* added similar thoughts—while also evoking the ghost of *Waikiki Wedding* as Elvis's most immediate cinematic predecessor:

> If it weren't for the fact that "Paradise, Hawaiian Style" is in glowing, brighter-than-life Technicolor, one might reasonably expect the late Bob Burns and his bazooka to turn up in his supporting cast. The newest Elvis Presley vehicle . . . is the kind of formula film that in the black-and-white thirties used to star Bing Crosby. . . . There have, of course, been changes in the formula over the last 30 years: The song lyrics now tend to be more explicit . . . and today's Hawaiian backgrounds are often the real thing, not just a decorated backlot jungle.[116]

Variety, meanwhile, found so little of quality to admire that it was reduced to acknowledging the impressive aerial stunt work during the otherwise regrettable "Dog's Life" musical number.[117] Even positive reviews of the film tended to embrace the formulaic kitsch of it all, while again putting the location, more so than the star, front and center. In a thoroughly positive review, *Boxoffice* noted:

> Alan Weiss and Anthony Lawrence wrote the screenplay from an original by Weiss—if one can call original something that uses all the usual cliché props of a Hawaiian setting: Leis galore, flowers worn in each native girl's hair, and of course a luau and hula dancers in grass skirts. For Elvis fans, this should be a sellout—and is relaxing summer fare for everyone but chronic cynical sophisticates.[118]

While failing, like all of his films, to match the box office numbers or record sales of *Blue Hawaii*, *Paradise Hawaiian Style* was nonetheless a genuine success—albeit one with enough of the "usual clichés" for both the setting and the star to foreshadow the formula's rapidly closing commercial window.

"At Last—A REAL Elvis Film"

As much as his music, television too would play a key role in the final chapters of Elvis's career—both its ontological claims to immediacy and authenticity as a more "live" medium than cinema, and as another venue through which to recycle Elvis's existing material. As *Billboard* reported in 1967: "Television's growing romance with feature films can now be regarded as a force in moving catalog soundtrack sets."[119] Certainly, the medium's archival function here also served a powerfully nostalgic function by evoking memories of accomplishments past, but it also kept the star visible for a mass audience. When *Paradise Hawaiian Style* was released in 1966, the televisual recirculation of *Blue Hawaii* was front and center:

> A full-scale advertising and promotion campaign is being launched by RCA Victor in conjunction with the Sept. 13 showing of the 1961 Paramount film, *Blue Hawaii*, on NBC-TV. In addition to the soundtrack starring Elvis Presley, Victor is promoting [the] Presley single, "Can't Help Falling in Love," from the film. The album, which contain 14 songs, also is available on 8-track cartridge.[120]

Though the new film was a more modern take on Hawai'i than its predecessors, the promotion of Elvis's last Hawaii-themed film was a richly nostalgic affair—nostalgic for something (*Blue Hawaii*) that was itself already loaded with melancholic and wistful attributes and connotations. And, in retrospect, what made Elvis such a continued lucrative success through much of the 1960s was also what made his longer-term prospects so suspect—recycling his music and his formulas for their very real, but quickly dwindling, affective and nostalgic commercial value. The aesthetic aspect was nearly uniformly dismissed: the mid-sixties "were almost uniformly dire," observed *Melody Maker* at the time, "and it's safe to say that pap like 'Bossa Nova Baby,' 'Viva Las Vegas,' and 'Do the Clam,' will not figure in one's definitive history of popular rhythm music."[121] While this commentary underestimated the long-term cultural impact of his music, that point was not without merit. By the 1970s, Elvis was mostly living off the considerable profits of his past. As Guralnick noted, the star produced "a hodgepodge of leftovers [in 1973] titled *Burning Love and Hits from His Movies*, which, in a marketing coup defying all logic of aesthetics and taste, had gone on to sell nearly one million copies."[122]

There remained a genuine attraction to the star for millions of audience members, and Elvis reinvented himself onscreen one more time by stripping away the pretense of conventional Hollywood narratives, and cutting straight to the "experience" of Elvis as performer that had made his music and early films so hugely successful. Following in the wake of the "Direct Cinema" trends in documentary filmmaking of the 1960s, which elevated the stardom of performers such as Bob Dylan, Elvis appeared in numerous television concert specials and documentary films: in addition to *Aloha from Hawaii*, he starred in *Elvis* (aka, the "Comeback Special") (1968), *Elvis: That's the Way It Is* (1970), *Elvis on Tour* (1972), and *Elvis in Concert* (1977). Much of this was tied to his resurgence in Las Vegas as an in-demand concert performer again after nearly a decade of exclusively making movies. Although they were mostly comprised of straightforward live concert footage, there were also moments that carried the impression of an in-the-moment spontaneity and behind the scenes intimacy that caricaturized the aesthetics of cinema vérité. In a 1970 article appropriately titled "At Last—A REAL Elvis Film," *Melody Maker* observed in regard to *That's the Way It Is* that

> for the first time in 30 odd Elvis [movie] epics there will be no exotic locations, no Hawai'i, or the Caribbean. . . . The Las Vegas show will be the highlight of the entire picture, but there's more, says Colonel Parker. "There will be the real Elvis worrying about putting the show together, Elvis backstage relaxing, interviews with Elvis—and with Elvis fans."[123]

Building on this newfound success, *Aloha from Hawaii* managed to both capitalize on the intimate and intense liveness of Elvis as stage performer that this new aesthetic constructed, while also reinvigorating the nostalgic legacy that grew out of his entire body of work. By working back to Elvis's basic musical appeal as stage performer, these texts allowed audiences to briefly forget just how canned and mass-produced much of his whole career had been—the formulaic and generally interchangeable films, albums, merchandise, concerts.

There's a nice symmetry to the Hawai'i stage of Elvis's career—it both began and ended with high profile concerts on O'ahu. More than a decade after he had performed the benefit concert for the USS Arizona

Memorial at Bloch Arena, Elvis performed a concert in Honolulu that was broadcast via satellite to much of the entire globe simultaneously on January 14th, 1973 ("except those that haven't got TV,"[124] one periodical quipped). As with his films, the record album was arguably more important. "The RCA soundtrack, a double quadrasonic package," reported *Billboard*, "has gone gold less than three weeks after its initial release."[125] Although not Elvis's first television special, it was arguably the most historically significant:

> All the historic landmarks that this broadcast would establish: the first time that a full-fledged entertainment special would be beamed worldwide via satellite; the largest audience ever to see a television show, "in excess of one billion people," who would view it "on successive evenings beginning January 15, 1973"; "the first time in the history of the record industry" that an album (the follow-up soundtrack) would be released simultaneously on a global basis.[126]

The broadcast was the fifth highest-rated one of any show in the US that year: with a 33.8 rating, 51 percent market share, it was behind only the Academy Awards, a pair of Bob Hope shows and, interestingly, a Bing Crosby special.[127] Later, a longer ninety-minute version was broadcast as well, which added video material that, reported *Billboard*, "incorporates lush, panoramic views, shots of the island of Oahu, accompanied by Elvis crooning songs from his '61 feature film *Blue Hawaii*."[128] At the heart of this elaborate spectacle remained the "King," fragmented through multiple screens and representations:

> First of all, there's Elvis himself, entertaining, on camera, for the whole 90-minute concert. Then there are the mirrors, reflecting Elvis. Then there are the signs, spelling Elvis' name in seven different languages, flashing on and off. Thirteen of them. Finally, there is the 16-by-20-foot silhouette of Elvis in action, outlined in flashing lightbulbs.[129]

The technological ambitions of the broadcast—the split screens, the quickly timed cuts, the endless mirrors reflecting Elvis infinitely into space—contrasted and complemented the nostalgia of all the old songs. *Variety* noted that "the staging was pretentious in an old-fashioned show business way, but with the knowing wink that Presley so warmly inserts

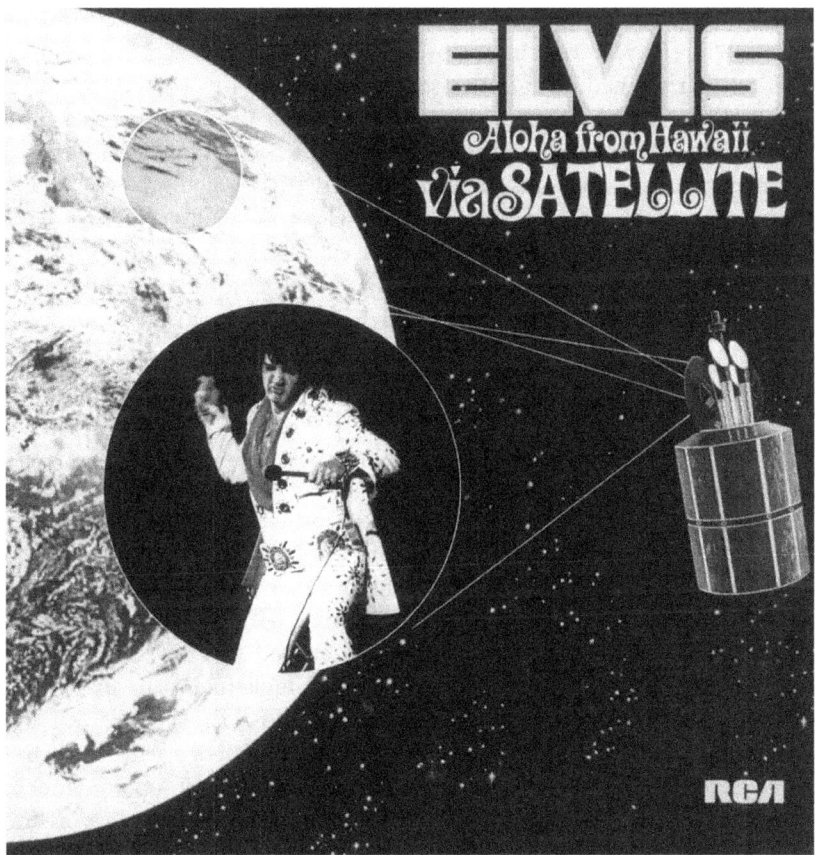

Figure 5.4. Although not nearly as remembered as movies such as *Blue Hawaii*, Elvis's 1973 live performance from Honolulu featured record-breaking TV viewership numbers, while the real-time concert format better captured the affective power of his mystique as performer—the sense of fun and romance he embodied in his prime (not unlike Hawai'i's touristic appeal)—than many of the "mechanical and bored" (Feeney) efforts he gave within the soundstages of Hollywood during the 1960s.

into his performance."[130] Even mistakes didn't seem to distract from the overall effect. TV critic Loraine Alterman observed that Elvis's "Early Morning Rain" was accompanied by a shot that "follows a pink shirted Hawaiian walking along a dazzling sunlit beach. I guess it doesn't rain in Hawaii."[131] But narrative logic was never a key part of Elvis's appeal.

Aloha from Hawaii stripped the Elvis/Hawai'i experience of any narrative pretense, stripping it down—as much as the relatively younger and still garish medium of television would allow—to something of its purest essence. Discussing a rare existing audio recording of the 1961 Pearl Harbor concert that perfectly captured the energy and enthusiasm of the performer onstage, Guralnick observes: "Listening to the recording, though, raises a question: you wonder why this quality couldn't have translated for Elvis into film."[132] The live performance from Honolulu highlighted that sense of an immediate, more intimate connection between viewer and the experience Elvis provided. It foregrounded the same transcendental space that Altman argued briefly emerged in *Blue Hawaii* despite its cheesy narrative and uneven production values—while also reminding viewers of that same affective experience all over again. The real-time effect of the live broadcast was both the energy of the performance as Elvis gained momentum throughout numerous musical numbers and the sometimes-unscripted performative flow as he appeared to improvise from moment to moment. At one point, his microphone cord becomes tangled up in his lei, leading to a small, embarrassed smile as he attempts to untangle it. One critic for the *Washington Post* observed then that "it's always fascinating to watch an audience react to a genuine superstar, in this case devoutly offering handkerchiefs to Presley so he can wipe his sweaty brow."[133] During the show, Elvis plays with the crowd, joking, "OK, I'll do all 439" songs after someone yells from the audience. He adds the line "I hope this suit don't tear up too much, baby" to "Suspicious Minds" in a playful nod to the spectacularly gaudy and tight jumpsuit he wore.

In contrast to the "mechanical" and "bored" nature of his big screen studio performances, *Aloha from Hawaii* captured an energy gradually building in the performer himself as he goes from a feeling of routine and boredom in the first part—"thank you," he says dutifully, unenthusiastically—"you're a good audience. Thank you very much"—to by the end feeding off the enthusiasm of his collaborators on stage, the energetic crowd before him, and the thrill of the performance itself. The show approximated for its distant viewers the pure spirited appeal of Elvis as a live performer in a way that the more formulaic Hollywood movies only occasionally hinted at. Reviewing the album later, one music critic observed in 1973: "I'm sure that if I were to see him on stage—and not just hear him—I'd be enthralled by his charisma, captivated by the electricity of his presence which certainly has a mnemonic effect on the women in the audience."¹³⁴ Whatever (or however illusory) that elusive affective experience was—which so many Elvis critics have attempted to describe—it's clear that moments in *Blue Hawaii* and *Aloha from Hawaii* captured it as well as any Elvis movie or television special ever did.

6

Shoot All Winter, Show All Summer

Frontier Mythologies and the Hipster Tourism of Surf Documentaries

> Surfers are nomads. To surf is to seek, and to seek is to roam. To find a good wave might require traveling a good distance. To find a great, uncrowded wave might take you to the ends of the earth. Bruce Brown's *The Endless Summer* actually recapitulated and promulgated the core ritual of surf culture: the search for the perfect wave.
>
> —Drew Kampton, *Stoked: A History of Surf Culture*

&

AT THE END OF BRUCE BROWN's independently produced documentary, *The Endless Summer* (1964), the filmmaker remarks through first-person narration that "if one had enough time and money it would be possible to follow the summer around the world, making it endless." It's an important qualification, but also somewhat ambiguous—is it acknowledging the near logistical impossibilities of such a trip, or simply indulging in the fantasy? *Endless Summer* is an account of two surfers, Michael Hynson and Robert August, who travel around the globe in search of the so-called "perfect wave"—traveling from their home in Southern California to tropical locations such as Hawai'i, Tahiti, South Africa, and Australia. Surfers, wrote Kampton, represent "the core culture of escape."[1] The film builds off of, and reinforces, the age-old white masculine American myth of the "frontier," of new opportunities always left to explore—a motif strongly evoked in its first shot of two young surfers starring off into the ocean's horizon, flooded with the bright red sun of that mythical "endless" season. Writes Joan Ormrod, "The main premise of the film . . . was attractive to American culture in the period, articulating a re-enactment of the conquering of the American frontier."[2] Brown himself often spoke about new surfing sites around the globe as the latest "frontier" to explore. When asked why surfers were always looking for new locations in a 1965 episode of the television series *True Adventure* called, "Hangin' with Bruce," Brown said, "One reason is just plain escape the crowds that have developed here in California surfing. The other reason, probably the most important, is it's a challenge. There's a new kind of frontier there." Beneath the surface, the idea of an "endless" summer wasn't just about escaping the oppressively cold confines of winter or being able to surf 365 days a year. It was symbolic of the youthful desire, rooted in a teenage "baby boomer" demographic of the postwar era, to never have to return to the everyday life of responsibility. (Similarly, John Engle has argued that these films also appealed at the time to an older generation of WWII veterans, since these exotic travelogues across the Pacific "also spoke to the buried wartime memories, daily anxieties, and awakening desires of the dads with their VA loans."[3])

Thematically, this helps explain the popularity of Brown's surprising smash hit in the mid-1960s, one of the first crossover commercial hits for both a documentary and a no-budget quasi-amateur independent production in the mainstream American theatrical marketplace. But such textual analysis does not begin to account for the historical contexts which enabled its appearance in the first place, while also insufficiently highlighting why the sense of "freedom" implied in that frontier mythology resonated at the time it did. Rather than "conferring upon [*Endless Summer*] an Edenic innocence with which it has been associated ever since," adds Ormrod, "it is impossible to wrest the film from its consumerist roots."[4] The appeal of Hawai'i was one key part of the surf movie's success—the islands were idolized by California surfers as the ultimate surf destination in ways that are only partially explained by its actual wave conditions. In his 1964 film, Brown twice notes that Hawai'i in particular "is truly

Figure 6.1. The image of the setting sun off in the horizon of *Endless Summer* (1964) aptly visualized the frontier mythology of a white masculine baby boomer generation both benefiting from yet also looking to escape the privileged material comforts of a prosperous new leisure culture of the post-WWII, pre-Vietnam, era.

the land of the endless summer." Earlier, in *Slippery When Wet* (1958), he notes that Hawai'i was a "pretty exotic trip" and the ultimate "dream" for surfers. Later, in *Barefoot Adventures* (1960), he remarked that "the dream for most California surfers was to go to the islands."

Images of surfing on the islands, usually depicted as a "native" activity, had been seen in Hollywood films since the beginning of the Hawaiian trend itself—*Waikiki Wedding* (1937), *The Black Camel* (1931), and others, offered stunning location footage of local surfers riding the big waves of Waikiki. The use of surf actuality footage could be traced back to cinema's origins, when Thomas Edison's cameramen "filmed surfboard riders at Hawaii's Waikiki Beach."[5] But surfing was always at best in the background in many of these early films—another superficial signifier, like the appearance of Diamond Head, hula girls and pineapples, of a Hollywood film's general *Hawaii-ness*. Although surfing had historical roots in local Hawaiian culture, its modern popular rebirth was located in teen subcultures of Southern California where, Engle writes, "a small, almost exclusively masculine community of briny fanatics suddenly discovered surfing and, in the process, helped turn an elegant, age-old islands tradition into a pop culture craze."⁶ This trend gravitated back to the islands during the burgeoning consumer culture of the postwar period. Engle continues:

> In the 1950s, a building Hawaiian buzz suddenly made Oahu a necessity for Californians with serious surf chops. From Honolulu they inevitably headed up to the island's rural North Shore. There, it was soon clear, were seven miles of absurdly concentrated high-quality surf breaks. . . . Two or three dozen *haole* mainlanders essentially ruled the Shore, outnumbering the small handful of Native Hawaiians on the scene and a few earlier arrivals-gone-local.⁷

Several historical factors were at play in explaining the sudden explosion of such movies—over seventy surfing-related films in the 1960s. This included both what Douglas Booth has called the so-called "pure" surfing films—the kind of actuality-based documentaries, made by and for actual surfers, for which Brown and his peers were known—and the Hollywood "beach stories," such as *Gidget* (1959) and *Gidget Goes Hawaiian* (1961)⁸ (dismissive references to female beachgoers as "Gidget," such as in *Slippery When Wet*'s voiceover narration, also reinforced overtones of sexism and sexual objectification which pervaded these films). For "real" surfers such as the ones Brown documented, these cheesy romantic comedies pumped out by the industry made convenient rhetorical punching bags for their different levels of perceived inauthenticity. "None captured anything remotely real about surfing or its culture," writes Kampton, "but the films worked at the box office, and every year there were thousands of new surfers buying boards and wetsuits."⁹ In "Hangin' with Bruce," Brown said that "I think the impression people have gotten about surfers that isn't really true is from Hollywood movies which are based like most Hollywood movies not on fact but on fabrication."

The surf documentary's critique of soundstage inauthenticity echoes long-established criticisms of how Hollywood had failed to capture the "real" Hawai'i on film. The lack of such realism gave an easy opening to amateur surf filmmakers who were prolific at both the sport itself and at relatively new home movie technologies such as 8-mm and 16-mm film, which became more widely available after the Second World War. "Drawn into the surfing boom and, in turn, feeding the building crescendo was a new generation of surf filmmakers," writes Kampton, "following the blueprint pioneered and proven by [the first high-profile surf filmmaker] Bud Browne: *shoot all winter, show all summer*."[10] Booth adds:

> While Californian surfers, including Doc Ball, John Larronde, and Don James, began filming themselves for "home movies" in the 1930s, commercial production only began in the 1950s. . . . Bud Browne was the first serious producer. A lifeguard at Venice Beach, teacher, diver, and surfer, he began filming surfers in 16mm color in the late 1940s. In 1953, at the invitation of fellow teacher and surfer Dave Heiser, Browne showed *Hawaiian Surfing Movie* to an audience of 500 at the Adams Junior High School in Santa Monica.[11]

Since the heart of the surf film was the power of its raw footage, amateur filmmakers had an advantage in creating cinematic experiences that would find a considerable audience in spite of the genre's low-budget production values and flimsy to non-existent storytelling, and in non-traditional spaces such as a junior high auditorium. These unique exhibition venues not only offered opportunities for upstart amateurs, but also those perceived as outside the fake, corrupting influences of commercial Hollywood. However, the latter quickly followed the former: "In hindsight it's clear that," writes Engle, "celebrating the stoke in Elks Halls or rented auditoriums, those grainy sequences of young guys on hot Hawaiian breakers were kickstarting the larger surf boom that would soon fill every transistor with the Beach Boys and every theater with *Beach Party*."[12] Adds Orvar Lofgren, "Surfing attracted attention in novels and later Hollywood movies, but the big breakthrough came when 'surfing music' was transformed into an international success by some southern California musicians."[13]

The mythical story of Bruce Brown (no relation to Bud Browne) and *Endless Summer* emerges out of this history. The romanticized tale of an ambitious and resourceful young filmmaker who simply told the stories of personal friends on a surf safari and singlehandedly reached a previously untapped frontier urge in America's youth is a powerful, but incomplete, narrative. For one, it overlooks how there was always a knowing commercial element to Brown's work, even if this wasn't the face he put on publicly. His *The Wet Set* (1960) was made as a clothing advertisement for Hobie MacGregor Sportswear, while *Slippery When Wet* was "backed and equipped by a flush Dale 'World's Largest Manufacturer'

Velzy, a surfboard manufacturer [whose products make an appearance in the film], produced with the intention of making 'a surf film that would promote Velzy's team riders.'"[14] By 1963, Brown had achieved sustained cross-over success after signing a "production agreement with The Clayton Organization to produce [a] proposed TV series about surfing around the world and one-hour surf special planned for fall showing . . . [and] named Clayton's sales division as representative for his library of action films."[15] This led to further opportunities for appearing on TV shows such as the "Hanging with Bruce" episode of *True Adventure*.

More than an emergent surprise hit, *Endless Summer* was the culmination of consumer trends that had thrived for the better part of a decade selling visions of frontier ambitions to segments of a baby boomer generation enjoying varying degrees of affluence and privilege, yet bored with the comfortable but unimaginative routine of mainland suburbia. The quest for the "endless" summer, adds Ormrod, "could

Figure 6.2. Prolific quasi-amateur filmmaker and avid surfer Bruce Brown (seen here in his most famous film, *Endless Summer*, while documenting a head gash he received while out on the waves) prided himself on making documentary films that not only rejected the campy, canned, and formulaic Hollywood surf films of the period (such as *Gidget* and *Gidget Goes Hawaiian*), but also captured the raw spontaneity, unexpected adventures, and even outright physical dangers of surfing, which was meant as an implied rejection of the safe, predictable experiences of other tourists in the age of mass travel and the prepackaged vacation.

not have been made by any other society or subcultural surfing group than American, specifically Californian, at this time."[16] Surfing thrived, writes Booth, "in a period of economic prosperity and political idealism, and Hollywood and aficionados captured it all on celluloid."[17] A strong manufacturing economy and collective workforce led to increased leisure time for some—the most immediate beneficiaries were the emergent demographic of teenagers with the most amount of available time and money to spend. In 1965, *Variety* estimated that US teens had over $11 billion dollars of disposable income annually[18]—an obscenely lucrative market that reached far beyond attendance at the local movie theater, stops at the local record store, or a night at the nearby diner.

Here the "frontier" of these amateur surf documentaries was at once ideological (the limitless possibilities of rebellious youth), technological (new possibilities for amateur filmmakers and nontheatrical exhibition), and consumerist (the economic freedom associated with the baby boomer demographic of the prosperous postwar period). Both the Hollywood beach movies and the "pure" surf independent films emerged from, and reinforced, these same historical conditions based on the consumer demands of the emergent "teenager" demographic. Many in this demographic not only had the disposable income necessary to spend on surf-themed movies, music, and magazines, but some of them also to a point had the luxury of time and money to *make* such movies, and take them on nontheatrical exhibition tours, in the first place. Without all these cultural and industrial contexts, Brown's quest for the "endless" summer would have remained only a youthful fantasy.

Rather than see these "pure" surf films as reactions against the Hollywood industry's appropriation of the beach experience, as the subculture saw itself, they are better seen as mutually determinative. A certain kind of indexical authenticity—capturing real moments of surfing at their most intense out on the ocean instead of following hokey teen love stories on the beach—was key to the surf documentary's product differentiation, something that the filmmakers vocally promoted. A 1963 *Variety* article discussed the new trend:

> [The] films follow a loose, pre-planned story line. . . . Asked why a sturdier story line is not incorporated into film for possibly greater mass appeal, [Dale] Cole contended that this would immediately alienate their hard core following. "One phony line, one little bit of padding and they'd hoot us out of the theatre.[19]

Brown also promoted such a contrarian mentality, retrospectively explaining why he failed to build on the popularity of his early surf movies to sustain a longer and more successful feature-length film career: "After the release of *The Endless Summer*, people in the movie business would tell me, if I wanted to be successful in the motion picture industry, I would have to move to Hollywood. I said I would rather be a milkman at the beach than live in Hollywood."[20] Yet Brown's surfer documentaries also suggested a lack of creative versatility—all featured surfers searching restlessly for new places to apply their sport, often over difficult and dangerous terrain, followed by endless montages of surf footage, and all accompanied by corny voiceovers and hip soundtrack music.

Featuring trendy jazz and rock 'n' roll scores and flippant narration, quasi-amateur surf documentaries promoted a kind of *hipster tourism*—anti-Hollywood in their lack of traditional narrative structure and heavy emphasis on actuality footage, and anti-tourist in their at times explicit contempt both for other (older, wealthier, physically unfit) tourists and for the usual, tired travel destinations and tourist traps. While opposed to the clichéd experiences that flooded Hollywood screens and boosted travel agencies, these documentaries were still very much tourist narratives depicting young white men traversing the globe, fulfilling a consumerist desire to discover new places and people. While Brown's films indulge the appeal of surfing on Waikiki, most of the documentaries focus more on the difficulty in finding other locations off the beaten path. In an enactment of both frontier ideologies and what Dean MacCannell has called tourism's back region "quest for authenticity,"[21] the movies had a particular fascination with finding surfing spots that they claimed had largely never been surfed before.

"Go Native in a Limited Way"

Brown began surfing near his home in Southern California in the early 1950s, and like many young enthusiasts quickly developed a fascination with the islands. While serving in the Navy, he was stationed at Pearl Harbor "and then picked duty that kept him on the island so he could surf."[22] His memories of Hawai'i are typically nostalgic—inflected heavily by mediated images of the islands. "The first night I went down to Waikiki," he recalled later, "I got a newspaper and slept on the beach. . . . I thought it was just amazing. I'd seen pictures of Hawai'i and one of Bud Browne's movies, but being there was something else."[23] Given that constructed exotic fantasy of the islands, it should be unsurprising that many surf movies situate Hawai'i as the most ideal surfing location. There are moments in *Endless Summer* where the young surfers are situated on one side of the globe, only to find themselves daydreaming about being back in O'ahu (part of this was Brown finding places to insert leftover island footage). Hawai'i daydreaming also appears in *Slippery When Wet*, when one surfer receives a letter from his Honolulu friend, inviting him to make the trip out—leading to a cringeworthy moment where the young man imagines himself laying by a grass hut, waited on hand and foot by hula girls. (Engle puts this moment in a different postwar context: "A young man empties a mailbox, an innocuous act that nevertheless once held a certain underlying drama. Here, though, it contains no draft notice but rather a collection of Hawaiian photos that play a remarkably similar role: essentially ordering post-adolescent American males to enlist in a newly organized expeditionary corps and head out overnight to a faraway Pacific archipelago."[24]) Brown's entire body of work often feels structured like a daydream—in ways consistent with Jane Desmond's argument about Hawai'i's "destination image"[25] (a fantasy constructed through media), or Ormrod's point that "tourists may anticipate the holiday or daydream about it using tourist literature."[26] Here the daydreaming device reinforced the mediated construction of Hawai'i as a mythical vision in the US and surfers' collective imaginations.

Implicitly evoking a colonial frame, surf films of the postwar period were travelogues following white, upper- and middle-class, young males as they try to conquer the beaches of the world in a new age of Western expansion. The mainland fascination with water sports such as canoeing and surfing, writes Desmond, "provided tourists with a commodified version of such cultural practices, one that allowed the visitors directly to purchase the experience of such things for themselves, to 'go native' in a limited way."[27] The subject of surfing calls forth a history that was—alongside hula and Hawaiian music in the prewar period—perhaps the most direct appropriation of local cultures by European outsiders. The fascination with Hawai'i surfing for American visitors promoted, as Desmond argues,

> a tone of celebratory primitivism—bronzed skin, near nudity, the nostalgia of a vanishing race, the authenticating link to the "islands of old," intimations of natural (native) physical prowess, the surfer at one with the forces of nature—a version of the "natural native in Nature" that is akin to the hula girl.[28]

Figure 6.3. A surfer's point-of-view shot of Waikiki and Diamond Head, most likely filmed by Brown himself, in *Endless Summer* (1964). While his and other documentary surf films of the period traveled across many points on the globe, Hawai'i is repeatedly situated as the ideal destination for the surfer—"truly the land of the endless summer," the director calls the islands in voiceover. Earlier, in *Barefoot Adventures* (1960), he noted that "the dream for most California surfers was to go to" Hawai'i, which is often situated in his films as an object of daydreaming, the ultimate place to go and escape real-world responsibilities.

This description suggests that surfing was as symptomatic of the conflicted mainland fascination with Hawai'i as any other aspects of the emerging tourist economy. Depictions of white surfers navigated this tension with ambivalence—acknowledging Native Hawaiians as the "original" surfers, but without addressing the narratives of conquest attached to that fact (both the colonialization of sovereign nations like Hawai'i, as well as the white conquest of the sport itself). The perceived innocence of the postwar baby boomer generation, those just looking to have "fun," enjoyed a kind of *naïve colonialism*—benefiting from (and at times perpetuating) such historical developments without necessarily being consciously aware of their ugly history.

Repeatedly, surfers traveling the globe, looking for ideal surfing conditions, were depicted as "civilizing influences."[29] This condescending attitude toward colonialized people in Brown's documentaries finds its most acute appearance not in representations of Hawai'i, but in *Endless Summer*'s South Africa section, where for him great surfing waves were "going to waste in Cape St. Francis." Here, although attempting an ironic tongue firmly in cheek, Brown repeatedly makes snarky and at times blatantly racist jokes about the white surfers' encounters with Africans. "Would they be speared by the natives?" is one particularly cringeworthy attempt at humor (the term "native," Ormrod points out, is "used incessantly by Brown"[30]). Even at the time such attitudes were anachronistic—a *Variety* review observed that Brown "delivers [the narration] in such a flippant, spirited manner that the audience finds itself laughing at some pretty dated material."[31] Some surfers seemed completely oblivious to the colonial origins of the sport—one complained, apparently without irony, that the inauthenticity and exploitation of the beach stories by Hollywood producers was similar to "treat[ing] surfers about as well as . . . the American Indian."[32] Booth notes the alternative scene of "pure" surf cinema emerged as a reaction against Hollywood exploitation of surfers, but without the surfers' awareness of their own exploitation of indigenous cultures.

Paintings by nineteenth-century European explorers show Hawaiians riding the waves at Waikiki with perfect symmetry. Around the same time period, the missionaries tried to effectively outlaw the practice of surfing. It was partly an attempt to Westernize the local population, but there was also a fear that surfing was some kind of pagan ritual that threatened their Christian values and the process of religious conversion (at one point in *Endless Summer*, Brown makes the comment that the African "natives" might see surfing as violating a sacred religious principle of some kind). Another reason the missionaries tried to ban surfing was the sexual tension that the locals on the beach were imagined to have presented to the modest (and repressed) Christian visitors unfamiliar with the explicit depiction of semi-nude bodies—the same kind of mildly transgressive sexuality that Hollywood and independent surf films exploited for box office success roughly a century later. As with the revival of hula after the overthrow of the sovereign government and annexation of Hawai'i in the late nineteenth century, the colonial presence on the islands became invested in promoting surfing again—trying to preserve that which they were also complicit in mostly destroying. But the reemergence of the water sport at the time was also primarily tied to the travel industry: "When the tourists started visiting Waikiki beach," writes Lofgren, "surfing was almost gone as a local tradition, and mainland Americans helped revitalize it."[33]

By the 1920s, beachboys emerged as the original Hawaiian tour guides within this new economy. In *Barefoot Adventures*, Brown remarked that the Hawaiian "beachboy was the closest you could get to a professional surfer" (an apt label for not only their skill set but also for how they were financially compensated for their work). Ironically, though, white male surfers are mostly the only ones included in his movies. Long before postwar baby boomer daydreaming, beachboys symbolized an escape from the stifling obligations of modern life. Desmond writes that they "facilitated not only the romantic fantasies of female visitors but also the transformation of males. . . . Beachboys represented a fantasized utopian vision, an antidote to the stress of jobs in a post-1929 decade."[34] It would perhaps be the fantasy of *Endless Summer* to indulge in this quest to excess, to explicitly articulate that latent desire to embrace life and all forms of pleasure, but the postindustrial escape from labor and everyday routines was already in place within the affluent tourism economy of the prewar era. A renewed embrace of surfing was not only a way for local business interests to promote the preservation of an "authentic" Hawaiian heritage, but also a way to further differentiate the islands' tourist economy from other exotic destinations, and to maximize the skill set of the local workforce. Writes Desmond, they "taught swimming and surfing [to visitors], and gave outrigger canoe rides; they took guests sightseeing, kept an eye on visitors' children, supplied *lomi lomi* (traditional Hawaiian-style) massages, handed out towels, set up beach chairs, applied suntan lotion, clowned around with jokes and skits, played music in the afternoons, and, out on the pier at night, occasionally even did a hula."[35]

The close physical contact between working Hawaiian beachboys and white tourists on the beaches raised the specter of not only colonial exploitation but also a transgressive sexuality unlike anything allowed back on the mainland (where crossing racial boundaries was generally taboo, and even carried the risk of death in many parts of the country). Some of the very earliest touristic accounts of the beachboy involved,

> first, the admiring, sometimes gushing, tone in which both male and female writers from the mainland describe the surfing Hawaiian male, and, second, the access to wealthy Caucasian females that beachboys had, at a time when potentially intimate interactions between white women and nonwhite men were still under strict censure, and when interracial marriage was still illegal in several states.[36]

"The liminal nature of the beach," notes Ormrod, "coupled with scanty beachwear and lack of adult supervision offered [numerous filmmakers of the postwar period] the opportunity for frolics and sexual innuendo in the sand dunes."[37] As John Urry notes in *The Tourist Gaze*: "In the postwar period it has been the sun, not the sea, that is presumed to produce health and sexual attractiveness. The ideal body had come to be viewed as one that is tanned."[38] Although racial difference would be increasingly whitewashed from the history of surfing as mainland surfers dominated the sport in the postwar period, surf movies of all kinds continued to exploit this permissive sexuality concerning (young) bodies on display.

The perception of surf as leisure, though, risked reinforcing the dangerous assumption of the beachboy as lazy, someone uninterested in hard work and only concerned with laying in the sun and playing in the water all day. *Endless Summer* implies as much in the trip to South Africa, where the local population is made to appear as though they had nothing else to do but wait around the beach until the two white surfers showed up. Brown claimed later:

> I could never figure out why golf, tennis, baseball, football or being a cheerleader was "useful" but surfing wasn't. Then the Hollywood beach movies came and that didn't help us out. They just confirmed what most people thought anyway—a bunch of surfers having food fights and drooling.[39]

As part of the narrative of 1960s teenagers on the boundary between childhood naïveté and adult obligations, Hollywood movies promoted this Depression-era idea of the beach as an escape from responsibility—*Gidget*, *Blue Hawaii* (1961), *Ride the Wild Surf* (1964), *Bikini Beach* (1964)—but always while showing that they were ultimately dedicated to a capitalist work ethic and willing to enter the workforce as necessary. Meanwhile, the "pure" surf films did not address those issues directly but did attempt to counter the idea that surfing was just a passive activity for beach bums by highlighting how it was technically a very sophisticated (and often dangerous) sport. Serious surfers didn't imagine themselves as a bunch of relatively well-off kids who had time and money on their hands, or as trying to avoid responsibility and maturity. Rather they saw themselves as being on a serious quest, and Brown's documentaries occasionally drew attention to the considerable expenses of traveling and to other material markers of class distinction, even while mostly eliding the privileged positions that enabled those journeys in the first place.

"I'm Sure I Had Some Disparaging Remarks"

As teenage generations are often apt to feel, the desire to rebel against their elders was a common and convenient theme in the baby boom marketplace. This is overtly reinforced in *Barefoot Adventures'* mocking attitude toward what the film saw as the other overweight and lazy middle-aged tourists that visited the islands. The film's existing voiceover was recorded in the 1990s by Brown, who claimed the original copy of his scripted remarks had been lost in the intervening decades. Early in the film, the older Brown acknowledges over a montage of O'ahu tourists, "I'm sure I had some disparaging remarks [about their appearance] to make about these tourists but I can't remember what they were. Now, thirty years later, I look just like them." However, perhaps attempting to capture the spirit of his original narration, Brown continues to chide older Waikiki tourists in the footage for wearing long pants and socks and sitting idly by the beach instead of taking risks in the water. Later, the narration then mocks several older women's lack of physical skills as they awkwardly attempt to learn hula dancing skills on a hotel patio.

Dating back to the 1950s, narratives of rebellion—in literature, music, and movies—fed this youthful desire to differentiate from previous generations. "The emergence of a mobile, rock 'n' roll–fired youth culture in the late '50s dovetailed perfectly with the subculture depicted in" Hollywood beach movies,[40] writes Kampton. Within this cultural milieu, adds Booth, "surfers became both subversives and outlaws."[41] Ormrod argues that by the end of the 1950s, "surfing, previously regarded as transgressive, was caught up in the clean teen phenomenon."[42] The surf movie genre presented a relative normalizing of those mildly transgressive impulses—it was ultimately less about cultural revolution or challenging deep-seated hegemonic norms and more about simply having a good time. Kampton adds:

> Like 1954's *The Wild One* and 1955's *Rebel Without a Cause*, *Gidget* exposed an underground society of youth living by its own rules. But the film *Gidget* was a relatively tame piece of kitsch. . . . These films, all set in California, form a kind of evolutionary trilogy.[43]

He argues that *Gidget*'s depiction of a surfing subculture laid the ideological foundation for the mainstream success of more rebellious, more "pure" surf films like *Endless Summer*. *Gidget* (and other "beach" movies like *Blue Hawaii*) crystallized a proven niche market for teenagers that independent (or more "authentic") filmmakers and musicians were less challenging than reaffirming through a modest amount of product differentiation. Despite positioning themselves to the contrary, independent

Figure 6.4. Part of these surf films' hipster tourism was their dismissive attitude toward the other tourists who visited places like Hawai'i, which is implied to not only be the product of ageism and class resentment, but also of the older visitors' perceived disinterest in taking any adventurous risks, or in going "off the beaten path" while on the islands (in his own old age, Brown later acknowledged the irony of his own disparaging remarks toward his elders). No doubt, Brown was probably particularly amused by the fellow barefoot amateur filmmaker seen here, whom he captured at Waikiki Beach while filming footage for *Barefoot Adventures* (1960).

surf films were as complicit in cultural and economic norms as *Gidget* had been (this was yet another reality elided in the "endlessly" deferred summer of baby boomer youth).

The popularity of surfing among American teenagers first found its way not into movie theaters but into record stores. In a review of 1963's *Surfin' 'Round the World* album, *Billboard* pointed out that "there are many surfing albums to choose from [presently] and it takes a special touch to get something new going."[44] In the late 1950s and early 1960s, as *Variety* reported, there had been a market for the surf movie, but it "has gone quietly about its business picking up good coin for its handful of practitioners in areas indigenous to the big wave cult, primarily the California coast line, Hawaii and Australia."[45] Only with the synergetic success of surf music did those films eventually expand beyond that specific niche. In the prewar period, surfing had been associated with forms of hula music, but with the youthful infusion of Southern California sensibilities, a new market of surf music emerged shaped heavily by the influences of jazz and rock 'n' roll. Brown's early documentaries featured the jazzy scores of Bud Shank, while *Endless Summer* switched to a more conventional surf rock style of The Sandals.

As with the Elvis films and other musicals of the period, the goal for producers was increased album sales as much as box office revenue. *Variety* noted in 1965 the degree to which teen movies were designed almost exclusively for their music sensibilities, and "paralleling the upbeat in the music biz, by and for teeners, is the onslaught of 17 musical films, either current or upcoming, whose sole purpose is to rock-rock, then roll, the kids into a state of free-spending ecstasy."[46] Relatively "raw" surf footage was a low-cost, profitable, investment for record companies looking to promote their music. Del Fi Records president Bob Keene purchased color footage of surfing in 1963 for the sole purpose of adding his company's own collection of surf music to the soundtrack and then releasing the film in an effective bit of cross-promotion. Then, according to *Billboard*, once the film left theaters, he sold 16-mm prints to disk jockeys to screen at "deejay hops"—local dance parties where DJs played music for the teen crowd.[47] What partly enabled the rise of the surfer documentary was how much low-budget surf footage, however truly pure or otherwise, were a perfect companion to this music marketplace.

By the 1960s, the perceived subculture of surfing was a thriving multimedia industry. A front-page article in *Variety* noted: "With interest kindled outside [California, Hawaii, Australia] by the surfing music phenomenon, a tremendous potential market expansion is to be expected. Dale Cole, general manager of Severson [Productions], which with Bruce Brown [Productions] all but monopolizes the field, discloses that deal has been made with the Joe Pasternak–Charles Walters–John Darrow production combine for all 35mm rights to films."[48] The plan was to compile existing footage that John Severson had shot on 16-mm into a relatively new feature-length film. Severson was a crucial part of a thriving industry of media convergence built on the popularity of surfing. Severson had met Brown in Hawai'i in 1960, when both were in the islands shooting their own respective surf movies.[49] Severson published the

First Annual Surf Photo Book as a printed companion piece to his 1960 movie *Surf Fever*, [where] many of the photos in its thirty-six horizontal pages were "frame grabs" from the 16mm film. . . . Titled *The Surfer*, the little book was a modest but exciting success—enough that Severson felt the market was ready for a quarterly. *The Surfer Quarterly* (later *Surfer Bi-Monthly* and later still, simply *Surfer*) created and defined the surf magazine and, in doing so, an industry and a good measure of the sport itself.[50]

The surfing magazine, reported *Variety*, boasted a circulation of 70,000.[51] This hugely lucrative industry somewhat casts skepticism on how "the exploitation of the sport dismayed many of the bona fide surfers," or how "it was in an effort to depict an authentic surf lifestyle that Bruce Brown claims he produced *The Endless Summer*."[52]

"A Splendid Combination of Facts, Imagination and Outstanding Photography"

An effort to "depict an authentic surf lifestyle" also speaks to the documentary genre's role in the popularity of these films (as does its occasional pseudo-ethnographic lens, given the genre's long intertwined history with neocolonial forms of observational, and at times intrusive and exploitative, exploration). The rhetoric of realism that this subculture strived for was inseparable from the raw indexicality this type of filmmaking privileged. Brown's films thrived on not only stunning location photography of exotic locations but also reels upon reels of impressive surf footage. *Endless Summer*'s crossover success says much about the emergence of what was then still an aesthetically and commercially forming media genre. Kampton promoted the idea that "Bruce Brown wasn't the kind of person to do that much planning anyway. He was more in the 'school of flow.' Even when they had no luck with the surf, something would happen. They'd meet someone; there'd be something to do. It was *cinéma vérité*."[53] These documentaries, in their own way, were as carefully planned through staging, scripting and editing as the latest Hollywood beach story. Although Hawai'i had been the focus of actuality footage since the earliest days of cinema, and often with government propaganda or commercial travelogue films (such as those produced by Cine-Pic Hawaii or the Hawaii Tourist Bureau), it was less often directly associated with the documentary genre per se. And in part this may have been because the boundaries of the genre were relatively less established than they'd be decades later. When it was released, *Endless Summer* was often referred to as a documentary. In 1966, *Variety* situated it as "a documentary [that] capitalizes on current teener craze,"[54] while Elston Brooks of the *Fort Worth Star-Telegram* asked rhetorically, "Who would have thought I would sit enthralled for 91 minutes by a documentary about surfing!"[55] Cleveland resident J. G. Prutton, meanwhile, wrote that the "splendid documentary with its marvelous scenery makes an ideal picture to see."[56]

More so than define the genre in and of itself, the use of the term "documentary" distinguished *Endless Summer* in the marketplace from Hollywood productions and low-budget independent beach stories, reinforcing the perception of its more authentic status. Ormrod argues that *Summer* "falls into the documentary mode, although . . . it does not represent a true picture of what happened."[57] In this context, the absence of "truth" can be defined by the fact that "they are not sober and objective narratives but, certainly in the early 1960s, are produced to be exhibited in front of a live audience. . . . The film is therefore meant to 'stoke' the audience."[58] As scholars such as Bill Nichols and others have long argued, however, documentaries are not necessarily intended to be objective depictions of reality.[59] While they take presumably authentic footage of places, people, and events, documentaries invariably rework that raw material to tell a story with a particular message about the world. In this regard, movie exhibitor Lois Baumoel's comment that *Endless Summer* was a "splendid combination of facts, imagination and outstanding photography"[60] (echoing John Grierson's famous definition: "the creative treatment of actuality") moves the film about as close to an existing definition of the documentary as any other contemporary account. Its "travelogue" structure fits one of Nichols's "models" for defining documentary categories. What ultimately undermines actuality-based surf films of the time as fully formed documentaries, however, might be the flippant commentary and blatant falsehoods (mostly played for laughs) that Brown's voiceovers offer instead of an honest and sober account of events (as well as the many clumsily staged comedic sequences). While Brown's films do not take an overt agenda, as we might usually associate with the "voice" of other documentaries (which attempts to persuade audiences about some issue in the world that must be addressed), they are hardly devoid of a strong point of view either—to be confused neither with objective journalistic accounts, nor with the straightforward sales pitch of travelogue commercials.

Keith Beattie has reworked Nichols's definition of documentaries to account for surf films by replacing a "discourse of sobriety" (the assumption that documentaries deal honestly and directly with the world) with what he terms a "discourse of delirium." This involves "a general lack of concern with a historical event and the eschewing of causality or motivation. The threat of an aesthetic 'pure delirium,' a 'flailing, wild hysteria' is, in a positive and non-derogatory sense, achieved in the aesthetic tensions"[61] between documentary representation and the excessive spectacle of surf footage. For Beattie, this pushes surf movies to the boundaries of the avant-garde in its playful attempt to "meld documentary and experimental stylistics and practices in an expressive and innovative non-fictional form."[62] He adds:

> The visual elements, together with the aural aspects, contribute to a discourse which in its documentation of events and actions, is based on sensory experience. In these ways, the "delirious" melding of avant-garde and documentary styles and practices of surf film and video is characterized by, to paraphrase Nichols' description of delirium, a heightened and frequently excessive visual and aural intensity brought to bear on the isolated action of surfing in order to reveal its secrets and meanings.[63]

The surf film's avant-garde elements for him are both formal and thematic, echoing the subculture's countercultural "emphasis on personal freedom, hedonism, and, in their shared distrust of industrial technology and its effects, various allusions to a lost pastoral ideal."[64] Beattie might be pushing the point too far. There was always an avant-garde tradition embedded in the documentary, but there was also a mildly experimental impulse in other early amateur filmmaking, as people played with the boundaries of the form as a part of the learning process in a way that commercial filmmakers avoided. But that kind of aesthetic trial and error was hardly a radical impulse intended to challenge political or cultural hegemonies. Moreover, a certain amount of stylistic experimentation was necessary to disrupt what was both the amateur surf film's greatest strength and glaring weakness—the inevitable monotony of endlessly repetitive sequences featuring shots of indistinguishable surfers riding similar looking tropical waves. Consider, for instance, *Variety*'s review of ABC's derivative TV program *Hit the Surf* (1967):

> The motive [of the show] is stronger to pitch the product [Bristol-Meyers] than to deliver a rewarding program. The sport of surfing figured to be surefire bait for a youthful audience, and with this cheap and indifferent presentation the sponsor made it clear that it was only exploiting a good thing. . . . As to the surfing footage, it was like most other familiar surfing footage. Riding the waves is beautiful and graceful, but it soon palls as a spectacle because it's repetitious. It calls for imaginative filming, which it doesn't get here.[65]

Similarly, *Surfari* (1967)—another *Endless Summer* clone—was criticized by one critic as "a group of home movies stretched out interminably to feature [length]."[66] Such criticisms were common of surf films that featured occasionally striking documentary-like footage, but which generally struggled for stylistic differentiation in a marketplace that saw surfing as another product to help sell still more products.

Rather than enact an avant-garde agenda, the indexicality of the surf movie largely legitimated the fascination with an experience already commodified. Most filmmakers like Severson, Brown, and others were fully complicit in a capitalist system that supported their work—despite the rhetorical performance of an oppositional status superficially regarded as countercultural, but which was as much as part of consumer culture as *Gidget*. The fantasy of an escape from responsibility and adulthood also implies a retreat from any kind of political voice that might otherwise find such oppositional agency in the films themselves. And, of course, part of the appeal of "pure" surf films like Brown's was their intentional aimlessness—the sense that they were first and foremost about having fun, about capturing the moment, and then working in the editing room (and auditorium) from there. After shooting footage, a rough cut was thrown together for an audience, where, "on the tour, Brown developed a script from which he distilled the best of the jokes and script elements before recording a permanent soundtrack."[67]

Nontheatrical Cinema

The last, and perhaps least acknowledged, context for the surf film's popularity was the postwar explosion—thanks to the emergence of amateur 16-mm projectors—of nontheatrical distribution, the screening of movies outside the cinema in unique settings such as universities, high schools, public libraries, civic auditoriums, and the like. Surfing footage found its most lucrative market ultimately on television, where older short subjects could be recycled and newer ones could be easily packaged and sold. The big money of network TV sustained the surfing subculture in many ways. "Surfing competition," *Variety* reported in 1966, "is beginning to get some realistic budgeting, thanks to TV deals."[68] More than the Hollywood beach stories, this market helped establish the lucrative value of "raw" surfing footage, one that didn't necessarily depend upon corny melodrama or surf rock soundtracks. Starting in 1963, ABC's *Wide World of Sports* filmed the Makaha International Surfing championship in Honolulu for several years, while also covering the expenses of "import[ing] top surfers from California, France, Peru and Australia."[69] Similarly, CBS started funding Hawai'i surf contests in 1965. Two years later, a documentary called *Always Another Wave* (its title a pretty transparent echo of Brown's "endless" summer), was put into syndication on television and featured Eddie Albert's voiceover narration, tracing "the history of surfing and [featuring] surfing sites around the world."[70]

But even before TV, as Robert C. Schmitt noted in his catalogue of Hawaiian-themed films, there was a long history of surf films and nontheatrical exhibition.[71] A 1942 *Variety* article made reference to a surf-heavy, ten-minute short-subject called *Playtime in Hawaii*, "one of the slickest black-and-white sports reels on aquatics," which featured "experts at Honolulu using surf boards and outrigger canoe for thrills."[72] Similarly, *Surf on the Wild Side* was a Hawaiian-filmed twenty-minute actuality short popular with audiences in the mid-1960s. Such movies were among the few Hawaii-themed ones as popular on the islands as on the mainland. "Surfing films invariably draw large audiences here" in Honolulu, reported *Variety* in 1966, "mostly teens, but generally have been unreeled in high school auditoriums and similar facilities."[73] By the end of the 1950s, Honolulu-based commercial filmmaker George Tahara had built a large collection of nontheatrical short subject films featuring the islands, which he distributed through his company, Cine-Pic Hawaii. In addition to loaning out films for itinerant screenings, he also leased out footage for use in commercials.[74] The most high-profile ones that Cine-Pic Hawaii promoted were tourism-oriented (*Discover Hawaii*, *Hawaiian Holiday*, etc.), and/or surfing films. One was called *Surfing in Hawaii*, which featured

> surfing by experts in the best surfing areas in Hawaii—showing techniques of surfing, tandem and trick surfing. This picture

has many high lights [sic] such as a dog that goes surfing, experts riding gigantic combers, and unusual shots of surfing taken with cameras strapped to the surfboards.[75]

Another one, *Riding the Big Surf*, was popular with NBC president Pat Weaver, who admitted to "giving it frequent playing to friends and associates."[76] (Weaver regularly sought surfing footage in the 1950s and 1960s for commercials and television programs, such as an early 1960s episode from James Michener's *Adventures in Paradise* called "The Big Surf."[77]) In Tahara's catalogue, the film was described as "spectacular surf board riding by experts on the largest and most dangerous surfs in Hawaii which build up to 25 ft. height during the month of November."[78]

Meanwhile, Severson Productions had established its own proven nontheatrical exhibition circuit for surf films, a steady lineup of venues for filmmakers to tour with their latest products. By the early 1960s, reported *Variety*, Severson

> produced [movies] pretty much on a one per year basis, each brought in for around $50,000. Featuring footage lensed in California, Mexico, Hawaii, Australia and occasionally South America, films are playdated on a concert basis with two day runs the norm. Most are screened with university or high school tie-in, with profitable exceptions like the bi-annual stands at the Santa Monica Civic Auditorium. . . . At $1.50 per head, gross is a potential $3,500 per night.[79]

A detailed nontheatrical exhibition circuit was in place for *Endless Summer* even before its success as a theatrical crossover two years later. In 1963, Severson had "plotted an eastern invasion with a swing through NY, Virginia, New Jersey and Maryland. . . . Playdates have been booked on the basis of the interest engeneered [sic] by the surfing music fad."[80] The film was originally released in 1964 to the usual venues, "with [Paul] Allen arranging the shows and coordinating publicity."[81] The film was not only accompanied by Brown's narration, but also included an intermission, despite the film's modest hour-and-a-half running time. Reportedly, "Brown requested the break so theatre patrons could discuss the surfing action and various styles displayed therein—evidently one of the rituals indulged in by surfers."[82]

As a result of success on the usual nontheatrical circuit, Brown made a more formal push to find a theatrical distributor: "Hoping a successful run in the US heartland would be convincing (if it worked), they booked a theatre in Wichita, Kansas,"[83] a place "without a [surf wave] within 1,500 miles. According to Brown, it outgrossed *My Fair Lady* during the second week, but the rigorous pilot shot still didn't impress the distribs."[84] From there, the film moved on to the Kips Bay Theater in New York City. Consistent with the underdog persona he carefully crafted, Brown was quoted in *Variety* at the time as "insisting he doesn't want to turn it over to a major distributor but this depends presumably on the offers he gets."[85] Despite the theatre's modest size and stature, though, the promotion was strong. The film's premiere in NYC was aided by the sponsorship of "the city's Special Events Commissioner John (Bud) Palmer, a sports enthusiast, who had seen some of Brown's previous surfing film footage."[86] *Endless Summer* played the Kips Bay for over sixteen weeks, "building each week via the surfing grapevine. Inquiries about the feature were received from as far away as Boston."[87] *Endless Summer* was acquired by Cinema V for theatrical rights, and was at the time credited for reviving the distributor's bleak financial prospects: "Lensed in 16m color (though [Cinema V president Donald] Rugoff defies anyone to discern it in 35mm blow-up) during Brown's two-year global hegira in search of the world's best surf, it carries what the sand and sun kiddies demand—authenticity and an approach to the material mirroring their own obsession."[88] (Many reviews at the time commented on the impressive amateur photography, despite being blown up to 35-mm from the original 16-mm.)

Once the film was picked up for distribution, the business savvy Brown continued an aggressive promotional push. In Florida, the state's Development Commission offered a global air trip contest to win, while Burdine's department stores had a "surf lingo" contest where soundtracks were given away as prizes.[89] *Boxoffice* reported then that the filmmaker "went on three days of personal appearances from Miami to Fort Lauderdale . . . and was interviewed at radio stations, television stations, department stores and by newspapers."[90] He also appeared in department stores that hosted surf fashion shows.[91] Meanwhile, playbills for the film were distributed in JC Penney department stores, Thom McAn shoe stores, and surfing shops.[92] In other, colder, parts of the country, the movie did well, playing to capacity crowds in New Jersey[93] and appearing for over thirty weeks at the Exeter Street Theatre in Boston:

> Viola Berlin, manager of the theatre, said that many students have come to see the film three or four times. Northeastern University has started a surfing club and many other colleges

in the area are following suit, providing a wonderful tie-up for Cape Cods which will show the film this summer. Due to the influence of the Brown film, surfing apparently will become a major sport in New England.[94]

Despite the film's appeal to a self-identified "rebellious" surfing subculture, *Endless Summer* was applauded for its family-friendly qualities at the time. It was a rare documentary to win the National Screen Council's "Blue Ribbon" Award for "the most outstanding release which was good entertainment for the whole family."[95] At least some of this could be traced back to the perceived documentary educational value (even if Brown's goofy irreverence might not be considered as such). Chairman of the Kansas City branch of the Missouri Council on Arts James Loutzenhiser praised how it "teaches, entertains, thrills and enthralls one simultaneously."[96] Dick Osgood of WXYZ Detroit felt the film "counteracts, in some measure, the snide sex of those 'beach party' movies,"[97] while Dearborn Press's James Limbacher lauded it as "remarkable in its almost child-like naïveté."[98] Harry Evans of *Family Circle* magazine added that "any individual under 30 is almost certain to share the current national interest in surfing. It ranks with ski jumping as a challenge in which there is a considerable possibility of danger."[99]

The More Innocent Time

With the film's success firmly established, imitators followed and the market was soon flooded with a type of travelogue documentary that was always already somewhat repetitive in nature. Shortly after the Makaha International Surfing championship ended in Honolulu, *Surfari* had a sneak preview at the New Royal Theatre, the same place where *Endless Summer* premiered on the islands a year earlier.[100] "It was inevitable," the *Variety* review observed, "that other pix would try to follow up [*Endless Summer*'s] surprise success. But 'Surfari' looks like it was put together . . . solely for this reason. It lacks wit, pace, beauty and excitement of the earlier pic, although it may generate some [box office] action on the strength of the similarity of subject matter."[101] As further commentary, the review noted, "if *Endless Summer* seemed at times almost a film poem on surfing, this new one is nothing but an extended travelog [*sic*]."[102] Only technical advances in cinematography seemed to keep the trend going. In 1968, the well-received *Golden Breed* was released, lauded by *Variety* as "a near-masterpiece of documentary filmmaking on the sport of surfing. . . . Dale Davis' color photography is extraordinary, often magnificent. . . . Much, probably the major portion, of the footage was filmed from shore with a 1,000m lens, which gives the appearance almost of a closeup as the surfers, at express-train speed, roar toward shore."[103] Then, in 1969, Cinerama released the widescreen *Follow Me*, another nonfictional travelogue, "with most of the [Severson] publishing firm's major magazines, such 'Surfing,' 'Teen,' 'Skin Diver' and 'Motor Trend,' involved in a major promotional push."[104] Around this time, United Artists added *Wet and Wild* to its lucrative *Pink Panther* comedic cartoon series—parody being perhaps the clearest sign of a trend's imminent exhaustion.

By the time *Endless Summer* was broadcast on TV on September 14th, 1969, as an ABC Sunday night movie (opposite NFL football and *Bonanza*),[105] the moment of the surf movie cycle—both as independent production and Hollywood spectacle—had already begun to pass. And yet the popularity of *Endless Summer* was only just beginning. Its longevity was in some ways assured precisely because that mythical summer season of the early 1960s, and the perceived moment of innocence being symbolized therein, had ended so definitively by the end of the decade. The desire of baby boomers to hold on to the imagined innocent and carefree attitudes of their youth in the face of personal challenges such as adulthood, and collective ones such as the profound political shifts of the 1960s, may ultimately best explain the enduring success of something like *Endless Summer*. That is to say, in the final analysis, the actual sport of surfing was most likely not the key factor in its generational significance:

> What was the film's special attraction? "I don't know," Bruce Brown admits. "I've run into so many people who saw *The Endless Summer*, particularly back East, and said it had some effect on them. But a lot of 'em, they didn't surf, and they never *did* surf. It's always been a mystery to me.[106]

The success is not entirely unknown for the various industrial, technological, cultural, and aesthetic reasons highlighted earlier. Like many Hawaiian-themed media, the surf films were both a beneficiary of, and a contributor to, distinctively timely historical contexts. Beyond the emergence of prolific amateur film production, nontheatrical cinema, surf rock, and increasing mainstream acceptance of the documentary genre, its appeal transcended being *only* about the luxurious indulgence of a white middle class resisting the responsibilities of adulthood.

And still there is that ambivalent frontier shot, as those surfers stare off into the horizon, of the bright red sun across the ocean—it is a sunrise, or a sunset? Is it a beginning, or an ending? By the 1970s, the idea of "endless" summers also represented a collective desire to hold on to an imagined state of innocence before the US' full immersion into the Vietnam War, a conflict that took the lives of many young people more or less the same age as the surfers in these documentaries. August, one of the surfers in *Endless Summer*, believed that the film "was a reminder to Americans of a more innocent time, providing them with a time out from Vietnam and the possibility to have fun for a while."[107] Perhaps too the primitive production values of Brown's film—which today looks and sounds like little more than a gloried home movie in the wake of more sophisticated and polished surfer films still to come (as though an artifact found in a relative's attic)—adds to this wistful appeal. While having little to do with pure surf cinema's initial success in the late 1950s and early 1960s, such nostalgia makes more sense looking back—the idealized yearning that the conflict in Vietnam induced for many Americans was not yet in effect when *Endless Summer* initially played in theaters in the mid-1960s. But this tragic angle remains one powerfully retrospective explanation for this deceptively simple film's enduring appeal in subsequent decades.

7

If You Can't Find It, Don't Write It

Genre and Competing Notions of Realism in *Hawaii Five-O* (1968)

> In the event we [*Hawaii Five-O* producers] don't know where [the location] is—we'll help you look. If you find it, great—tell us in the script where it's at and we'll go shoot it. In the unhappy event, you don't find it—change it. Chances are, in your hunt you will have spotted a location that will work as well or better. So it seems a good rule is—stay loose and let the location spark you.
>
> —*A Writer's Guide to Hawaii Five-O* (1967)

AMONG *HAWAII FIVE-O* (1968–1980) scriptwriter Sy Salkowitz's personal collection of notes regarding his contributions to the long-running hit crime show was a tourist's map with the city of Honolulu on one side, and the larger island of Oʻahu on the other.¹ Was the map a research guide, a souvenir, or both? *Hawaii Five-O* scriptwriters were often sent to Oʻahu for inspiration, since the show's producers prided themselves on shooting as much as possible on location in Hawaiʻi. Location, writes Sue

Turnbull, long "played a key role in the development and differentiation of the police procedural as a [television] sub-genre. Here the distinction is more likely to be between East Coast and West Coast crime, or be between the urban and the rural, with the occasional excursion into more 'exotic' locales."[2] *Hawaii Five-O*'s use of the islands was one of network television's most ambitious early examples of using location as a form of product differentiation. In 1998, David Poltrack, executive vice president of research at CBS, looked back with the observation that the show "was considered the ultimate travelogue. . . . The ascent of Hawaii as a major tourist location coincided with the strong years of that program. It really hit a chord."[3] In 1974, at the height of its popularity, Hawai'i's acting governor, George R. Ariyoshi, believed that "many people from other parts of our Nation derive a large part of their impressions about Hawaii from the program."[4] A 1975 *Good Housekeeping* article on the show's star, Jack Lord, noted that "the Hawaii Visitors Bureau unofficially credits Jack and his program with bringing in 25 percent of all first time tourists" since the show's debut seven years prior.[5] In total, *Hawaii Five-O* was believed to have generated over a billion dollars just for Hawai'i's economy over the span of its record-breaking run.[6]

Hawaii Five-O chronicled the adventures of a fictional state police unit, the "Five-O," that investigated a range of special crimes on the islands that—within the narrative logic of the show—went beyond the kinds of day-to-day criminal activity that otherwise occupied the Honolulu police force. "Guidebooks even today must remind tourists," writes Karen Rhodes, "that Hawaii does not, and never did, have a state police unit."[7] Led by Captain Steve McGarrett (Lord), the team was also comprised of Danny "Danno" Williams (James MacArthur), Chin Ho Kelly (Kam Fong Chun), and Kono Kalakaua (Gilbert Lani Kauhi). McGarrett was described by producers as "a cop, the best. He is involved. He is with it. He cares. . . . Perhaps his dominant characteristic is one of compression."[8] He was exemplar of a long TV genre tradition, according to Jonathan Nichols-Pethick, where "the figure of the cop [was] an interstitial figure, the product of a range of sometimes contradictory discourses: at once the figure of a distanced and paternal authority (one who cannot 'take it personally'), an involved social worker, and a holder of a special, 'mythical,' class-based knowledge about 'the way things are.' "[9] Other team members came and went across the show's record-breaking twelve-season run (thirteen, if the one season of the solo spin-off *McGarrett* is included). Although the show focused overwhelmingly on McGarrett and his partnership with second-in-command Williams, *Hawaii Five-O* was considered relatively

Figure 7.1. *Hawaii Five-O*'s (1968–1980) elite police unit (Jack Lord, right, and Steve MacArthur, left) investigates a murder that occurred in broad daylight at the Honolulu airport, presumably one of the "safest" places for tourists to pass through while visiting the islands. Many of the crimes investigated during the long-running television program focused on tourists and other travelers to the islands, which as the show writer's guide made clear were a higher priority for the Five-O police unit than most of the other day-to-day crimes that occurred in Hawai'i. The emphasis on "crime in paradise" stories, which *Hawaii Five-O* did so well, worked to inject an imagined sense of danger, adventure, and unpredictability into what was by the 1960s, both onscreen and in real life, an increasingly formulaic routine offered by the prepackaged Hawaiian vacation experience.

progressive at the time for its depiction of a multicultural police unit, and for its economically practical routine of casting local professional and nonprofessional actors in various roles.

Also among Salkowitz's collection was the official *Hawaii Five-O* writer's guide—the show bible that explained who the characters were, what kinds of plots should be written, and what the general tone and style of the show would be. As the fictional "Five-O" unit only handled certain criminal investigations, the guide had to make a point of distinguishing which ones were worthy of their particular attention. The first listed were the problems of a million and a half tourists with money to spend and desperate for a good time and to cope with the inevitable hordes of boosters, con men and assorted cutthroat opportunists that trail in the tourist's dollar-strewn wake. Tourism is the state's second largest industry. That makes it Five-O business.[10]

Later, the guide explicitly repeats that one of Five-O's few acceptable missions would be, in addition to murders of prominent civic leaders and politicians, anything "threatening the state's second largest industry, tourism—that is Five-O's business."[11] Following this touristic focus, the show's producers insisted to writers, "If you can't find [the setting], don't write [the scene]!" Part of this was financial necessity—shooting on existing locations was cheaper than building new ones, particularly when there were few sustained production facilities available on the islands. But there was also the visual appeal of real Hawaiian backdrops. Generally, the box office successes of increasingly location-based films such as *Hawaii* (1966) and *Blue Hawaii* (1961)—as well as relaxed labor standards (leading to producer Leonard Freeman's crack that the cop show was a "*flyaway* production" instead of the more common "runaway production" used to describe films and shows shot away from Los Angeles to decrease costs by avoiding stricter union requirements)—encouraged producers to begin seeing Hawai'i itself as a timely location to shoot films and television shows. "Hawaii, the 50th State," added the *LA Times* in 1965, "is the paradise that western migrants think they've reached when they reach Southern California. What [*sic*] more natural, then, that Hollywood's moviemakers should be utilizing its beauties for more and more pictures."[12]

As much as for its record-breaking run on CBS across parts of three decades, this travelogue quality represents what the show was most known for. "Something happens to an actor on location," Lord told the *LA Times* in 1970, "the smell of reality does something to a guy. I think it transmits itself to the screen—*the smell of reality*."[13] At the time of its debut in the late 1960s, *Hawaii Five-O* was one of only two weekly series shot on location (the other being the short-lived travel adventure *Then Came Bronson*).[14] A *Variety* review noted in 1971, with a hint of amusement, that "this successful formula law-and-order series has often, and probably rightly, been accused of having the locale as its star."[15] Similarly, the *LA Times* commented that this quality seemed to elevate *Hawaii Five-O*'s otherwise formulaic nature: if the show, wrote one critic, "spends much of its time chasing conventional crooks in conventional cops 'n' robbers tales, its setting in these incredibly beautiful islands makes it a thing apart."¹⁶ Both the emphasis on location shooting and Salkowitz's map, as well as the often traveler-focused plot lines, highlight the degree to which a touristic lens first and foremost framed the popular TV program's representations of the islands in ways both obvious and subtle.

Despite the attraction for producers, the islands lacked a permanent production infrastructure. "Hawaii doesn't have a film industry as long as Hollywood units only visit there to make films," actor-producer Richard Boone commented in 1968.¹⁷ *Hawaii Five-O* was part of a larger attempt at providing sustainable production facilities and trained professionals on the islands. Interiors for the show were recorded at the newly built Diamond Head Studios, while outdoor shooting was largely limited to the island of Oʻahu in particular for budget restrictions.¹⁸ The show appeared in the wake of *Kona Coast* (1968), which was made, Boone said, "to prove a film could be brought in on time and within budget in Hawaii."¹⁹ *Kona Coast* associate producer William Finnegan later replaced Bob Stambler as *Hawaii Five-O*'s Hawaiʻi-based producer.²⁰ Stambler left the show in 1971 to become vice president of Celebrities Ltd., which would "deal in all aspects of the entertainment business in Hawaii."²¹ The company was headed by Van Barker, who started out by promoting entertainment shows on the lucrative military circuit.²² When *Hawaii Five-O*'s run ended in 1980, the follow-up crime show *Magnum PI* (1980–1988) was pitched in part as an opportunity to take advantage of the same production resources based in Oʻahu.

During the increasingly politically reactionary time of the 1970s, the crime show genre gained considerable popularity, as critic John Culver wrote, because of the perceived need for some "for reassurance that today's lawlessness can be controlled."²³ *Hawaii Five-O* followed in a long line of procedural police shows on US network television, such as the original *Dragnet* (1951–1959), *The Naked City* (1958–1963), *77 Sunset Strip* (1958–1964), *The Untouchables* (1959–1963), and *The FBI* (1965–1974). Traditionally, writes Nichols-Pethick, "this formula provides moral reassurance and champions an inherently conservative social agenda by focusing on the essential wisdom and virtue of those who enforce the law. . . . Furthermore, the genre suffers a fundamental contradiction, in which its realist aesthetic (practical location shooting, handheld cameras, naturalistic lighting, etc.) is constantly undermined by the conventions of melodrama."²⁴ Originally a successful radio program, *Dragnet* is typically seen as the trail-blazing show in this regard, featuring Jack Webb as the straight-laced Joe Friday, who along with a series of partners investigated various wrongdoings based on real-life crimes that had reportedly occurred in Southern California. David Marc observes that "Jack Lord kept Webb's Manichaean tradition alive in *Hawaii Five-O*. . . . Though we see a share of sumptuous shots of Hawaiian beachscape, the day-to-day glamour of life in the Aloha State (which is harped on in [Roy] Huggins' *Hawaiian Eye*) is largely missing from the show."[25]

"In every sense," wrote the *Hawaii Five-O* writer's guide, "this series is striving for truth and the documentary look and feel."[26] "Realism" in the show thus was situated at the intersection of two genres that prided themselves on particular and seemingly contradictory notions of authenticity—the police drama and the travelogue. "Realism" involved both an early embrace of location shooting and the use of crime stories sometimes based on real-life incidents (*Hawaii Five-O* specifically was more interested in the former than the latter, though it did draw narrative inspiration from real-life events as well). To an extent, the genre show was hardly unique in this regard: "Style, of course, has been a central part of the police genre since at least as early as *Dragnet*," writes Nichols-Pethick, "in particular, the need for 'realism.'"[27] As John Fiske has noted, television "realism is not a matter of any fidelity to an empirical reality, but of the discursive conventions by which and for which a sense of reality is constructed."[28] It was defined, he wrote, by its adherence to larger cultural beliefs taken for granted as self-evident: "Realism involves a fidelity both to the physical, sensually perceived details of the external world, and to the values of the dominant ideology."[29] Even the show's creators weren't always clear on what actually defined a gritty police genre realism. Producer Stan Kallis rejected Salkowitz's story for "The Little Crime" because he wanted something "harder," but Salkowitz "could not, for the life of me, think of an idea that would fit what he wanted."[30] At the same time, *Hawaii Five-O*'s embrace of location shooting was at odds with how realism was usually portrayed in the cops and criminals genre. Instead of seedy warehouses, gritty back alleys, and other grimy urban spaces (though it did occasionally depict these as well), the show's travelogue-based realism was first and foremost a touristic one—the ways in which its visuals did and did not align with Hawai'i's mass-mediated image of tropical calm and natural splendor over the previous several decades. The tensions between these two competing forms of realism—the ugly violence of the police procedural and the virtual escapism of the travelogue—was perhaps never more acute during its initial broadcast run than in controversies around the television program's then-relatively daring representations of violence.

"Why Would Anyone Watch This Thing?"

Upon its debut in 1968, *Hawaii Five-O* was greeted with a range of critical audience reactions. *Backstage* treated the show's appearance with skepticism, noting that it "would appear to have overtones of other late and unlamented Hawaii detective type shows," though admitting to the show's star power in Lord.[31] Ironically, the location authenticity of Hawai'i was not considered an asset initially. One network executive was quoted as telling show producer Freeman that "people who have been to Hawaii have already seen the place. And those who have never been there obviously don't care. So why would anyone watch this thing?"[32] Yet, as much as some at CBS may have been skeptical of the islands' unique appeal to viewers, that didn't stop them from trying to sell it. While taking VIP broadcasters on a cruise tour of Pearl Harbor, CBS executive Mike Dann promoted the show as a "sure bet" and even claimed that the plan at the time was to run ninety-minute episodes, with a budget for the entire first season originally at $12,000,000.[33] Costs ran to $1,660 an hour to shoot on location,[34] and while they had a budget of $210,000 an episode, overruns went past $500,000 in the first season.[35] By the ninth season, the budget ballooned to $340,000 an episode.[36] The network hosted promotional events on location in Hawai'i for mainland journalists and advertisers to help sell the 1970 season—a tour that included visits to the sets and interviews with Lord.[37] In these latter instances, media promotion of the show became another Hawaiian tourist experience.

The network may have under-considered the travelogue appeal of *Hawaii Five-O* at first as the show undoubtedly offered its own vicarious, virtual touristic pleasures—especially for those who could not afford the trip themselves. The reality of financial constraints was humorously highlighted in 1973 by a Nielsen viewer as he described some of his nightly viewing habits: "There is also the fact that I watch television while paying bills. It eases the pain of checkwriting somewhat. Since this often occurs on Tuesday, it may explain my ambivalence toward *Hawaii 5-O*. It also suggests an advertiser is wasting his time trying to sell me anything on that show. I'm nearly always in bad sorts."[38] In contrast, one fan wrote the governor of Hawai'i to say that "Tuesday is the happiest day of the week for me because that is when I can watch and hear Mr. Lord, as well as view some of that beautiful Hawaiian scenery."[39] Another wrote him to say that she and her friends "love the Hawaii that we see [on the show].... My ex-husband was a Pearl Harbor survivor, [and] some day [sic] I hope to visit your beautiful island."⁴⁰ A writer for the *Oakland Post* suggested in 1974 that the show was, at the very least, a substitute for the vacation itself: "To get yourself ready for such a trip, you can watch *Hawaii 5-O* (smile) and just see yourself on the Seaflite enroute to have lunch at one of the other islands."⁴¹ Rhodes has written of "young mothers" (part of the show's key 18–34-year-old audience demographic) who "would have their children in bed and other chores completed by 10pm, ready to 'get away' to Hawaii for an hour!"⁴²

Rhodes's anecdote about parents putting their children to bed before settling in to watch *Hawaii Five-O* also speaks to the show's biggest controversy, one which rested right at the intersection of the police procedural genre and the travelogue aesthetic—the depiction of violence. Lord himself explicitly defended the violence as what gave the show its realism: "We live in a violent world. We are not filming a travelogue."⁴³ In some sense, the touristic assumptions for some mainlanders about what the "real" Hawai'i looked like as a modern-day paradise may have made the violence even more thrilling or jarring, depending on the audience. Lord, however, personally believed the opposite: "It's no more violent than other cop shows. Less, I think, because there's a suspension of disbelief about a violent act in the lush beauty of the islands."⁴⁴ One woman wrote to the Hawai'i governor to express her dismay. Despite admitting that she had never visited the islands herself, she observed that "this Hawaii TV programe [sic] 'Hawaii 5-O,' we see on TV is so full of violence, we wonder what has happened to your beautiful islands."⁴⁵ In response, the Governor's Office wrote that unfortunately crime is a reality of the world, even in Hawai'i, adding, "In the event that you decide to come, I would suggest you prepare yourself for the difficulties of cosmopolitan life as well as for the beauties and delights of Hawaii."⁴⁶ Meanwhile, another viewer who had been to Hawai'i and recalled nothing but "charm and peace," wrote the governor to "express [her] displeasure regarding a CBS television show that professes to show the real Hawaii. . . . For an hour every Wednesday, the lush green landscape of the islands is turned into a bloody pool of horror. . . . The production makes Honolulu look like New York at its worst."⁴⁷ The writer begged the governor to intervene in the show's production and "preserve one man's memories of a very beautiful land,"⁴⁸ to which the Governor's Office responded by suggesting, "Although we do have crime in Hawaii, viewers of *Hawaii Five-O* adopt the same frame of mind as, for instance, viewers of professional wrestling, or of a good many mystery shows with locations closer their homes [sic], in which they almost consciously enter a sort of dream world of escapism, often including the violence that does not affect the viewer."[49]

In her book on *Hawaii Five-O*, Rhodes suggests that part of the show's initial struggles with audience ratings—prior to its move to 10 p.m. in late 1968—was due to parents who liked the show, but "the original Thursday 8:00 p.m. time slot put them in the dilemma of wanting to watch *Hawaii Five-O* but not wanting their small children exposed to the show's violence and grittiness."[50] The show was also singled out by self-proclaimed media violence critic Leo Singer in 1974, whose company, Miracle White, pulled "nearly $3 million" in ad money from shows like *Hawaii Five-O* in favor of programs hosted by such personalities as Carol Burnett and Merv Griffin. "I approve of Westerns," he told the *Washington Post*, "and dramatic action type shows. But not violence for the sake of violence!"[51] One California viewer was so upset by a 1973 episode, "Tricks Are Not Treats" (about a war breaking out between rival prostitution operations in Honolulu), that he wrote the state's acting governor to implore him to do something: "Judging by the crime depicted in the program *Hawaii Five-O*, you are having a real problem in Hawaii.... [The episode] was one of the most gruesome shows I have ever witnessed on television and in my opinion has no business on television at all."[52]

The author insisted that such depictions might actually hurt the state's tourism: "I have visited [Hawaiʻi] at least ten times and have urged my friends to go there, but lately I have been wondering if it is a good idea for people to visit."[53] The Governor's Office, meanwhile, responded later by expressing sympathy that the state's image not be distorted, nor excessive media violence condoned, but that "under our free enterprise, this State Administration does not have the power to determine the type of programs offered by the electronics medium."[54] Lord himself noted that he and his wife were "concerned with violence more than most people because we are nonviolent by nature. But it's difficult to do a police format without mayhem."[55] Elsewhere, he added that the violence was no worse than what's shown on nightly news broadcasts.[56] Other fans of the show defended the depiction of violence: "I think *Hawaii Five-O* is doing our country a great service in causing people of the mainland beyond California to realize that there is a fiftieth state which not only is an exotic place to dream about and hope one day to visit but is a real LIVE state with all the problems facing the rest of the UNITED STATES today."[57] Upon receipt of the letter, the Governor's Office passed it on to the show's public relations office, adding, "I have received a number of letters through the recent years . . . expressing much the same type of avid enthusiasm for the program."[58]

"Hawaii Is the State That United Built"

The show's oft-repeated variations on a "trouble in paradise" narrative ironically was inseparable from tourism industry partners who both supported the genre show and doubled down on the lucrative appeal of those same touristic clichés, in spite of the genre representations of constant danger surrounding them. One such key figure was industrialist Henry J. Kaiser, who hoped to further his own economic interests in Hawai'i in part through the use of television. Kaiser made a fortune as a shipbuilder during WWII, and then turned his attention to tropical real estate in the postwar period. "Although Kaiser refused to become an officer of the partisan [Hawaii Statehood Commission]," wrote Christine Skwiot, "he opened his lobbying organizations to it and spoke to Congress, media, and tourists on Hawai'i as melting pot, statehood candidate, and bridge between the United States and Asia."[59] One of his major projects in the early post-statehood period was the "Hawaii Kai" land development on the eastern side of O'ahu. Integral to that effort was a larger promotion to television audiences of traveling to the islands. Kaiser pushed ABC to make *Hawaiian Eye*, a crime show modeled on the popular *77 Sunset Strip* (1958–1964) and set (but not shot) at his Hawaiian Village resort. Later, other influential films and television shows, such as *Blue Hawaii*, would also be shot on location at the Village.

Only after statehood did three television programs fully dedicated to stories on the islands debut (all filmed in Hollywood); in addition to *Hawaiian Eye*, viewers were also introduced to *Adventures in Paradise* (1959–1962) and *Follow the Sun* (1961–1962), all of which anticipated *Hawaii Five-O* in terms of being adventure and mystery-oriented narratives that often foregrounded the centrality of travel and tourism on the islands. The short-lived *Follow the Sun* featured the adventures of two magazine writers who became involved in local mysteries while in pursuit of touristic copy to write. Meanwhile, *Hawaiian Eye*, *Hawaii Five-O*'s most direct predecessor, often focused on the dangers posed to island visitors. In a 1959 memo, the NBC television network pitched to Kaiser and other interested parties some ideas for possible shows set in Hawai'i. The memo left open the possibility of any number of genres to work with, but stressed in any event, the essential element, the glamorous, breathtaking locale of our events . . . the chief element in this series is that it is from Hawaii. We can make up lots of stories, build unforgettable characters, create drama that will outlive us, but fundamentally, this series starts with Hawaii. Its bill, one might say, is paid by Hawaii.[60]

Among the main ideas for "typical storylines" were adaptations "with the island locale important as background to characters that we can use" and "locale shows" where—in a foreshadowing of *Hawaii Five-O*—"we can get writers to build stories around locations in the islands. These are somewhat manufactured, but not impossible for writers. We take Diamond Head and do a story based on that incredibly unforgettable profile. . . . The big hotels (with [Kaiser's own] Village [resort] getting an unforgiveable edge somehow), are backgrounds to so many kinds of stories—newlywed, swindle, adventure, espionage, etc."[61]

Aside from establishing some of the basic criteria for conveying Hawaiian adventure through television, the preceding NBC memo was also significant in so far as it established United Air Lines as another active participant in this collaboration between Kaiser's Hawaiian Village, TV networks, and other tourism-based businesses to sell the islands to mainland audiences. In 1959, United coordinated with both NBC and Kaiser to help promote the "Hawaiian Village Holidays" tourism campaign during broadcasts of the Kaiser-sponsored hit show *Maverick*[62] (1957–1962)—offering to cover $20,000 of the $50,000 required for the commercials.[63] The brand connection between this airline and the islands was so strong that one industry analyst observed in 1953 that "the Hawaiian service may be regarded as a stimulant to traffic throughout the [national] United system."[64] United began flights from San Francisco to Honolulu in May of 1947.[65] Flights from LA, meanwhile, began three years later. By 1951, the airline had already logged ten thousand flights between Hawai'i and California.[66] In 1960, United became the first to offer single-plane service from New York and Chicago to Honolulu.[67] As a partner with the Hawaii Visitors Bureau, the airline did more than offer trans-Pacific flights, producing everything from its own United-imprinted "aloha" shirts to its own Hawaiian tourism guidebooks. United Air Lines was not only a prominent sponsor on *Hawaii Five-O*,[68] but also promoted the show during its original run in the pages of *Mainliner*, its own in-flight magazine travelers would read across its empire of domestic destinations.[69] Additionally, the airline provided publicity photos of celebrities to various print press outlets as they flew to Hawai'i to shoot guest spots on the show.⁷⁰ (From 1964 to 1973, United also sponsored a vaguely Hawaiian-pastiche-influenced Enchanted Tiki Room, which was originally conceived as an audio-animatronic luau dinner show, at Disneyland in California.) While "generally [finding] visual media simply too expensive to justify" from an advertising standpoint, one tourism-oriented public relations expert noted in 1973 that United's sponsorship of *Hawaii Five-O* (along with the professional tennis event, the Hawaiian Open) was a rare hugely successful example of a situation "where a continuous association can be created between a product [airline] and a destination [Hawai'i]."⁷¹

Figure 7.2. United Air Lines not only shuttled travelers to and from the islands but also produced literature and prepackaged itineraries for visitors that covered all the usual tourist sites, and that echoed the narratives of many postwar films and TV shows.

The commercial aviation giant was less interested in promoting *Hawaii Five-O* itself than in reiterating the much broader idea that United and its fleet of brand-new jet aircraft was *the* ticket to paradise in the postwar, post-statehood, era. In 1948, United produced its own travelogue for nontheatrical exhibition, entitled *Highway to Hawaii*,[72] which was "awarded the commercial film industry's 'oscar' in the travel field" and was estimated to have "an audience of at least eight million during the useful life of the film."[73] The airline also sponsored Harry Owens's television program, *Harry Owens and His Royal Hawaiians* (1949–1958),[74] a 1959 NBC special broadcast on the islands entitled *Hawaii—Pacific Miracle*,[75] and then another twenty-eight-minute television special called *Holiday in Hawaii*.[76] Around the time of statehood, United helped promote the pro-statehood propaganda film *South Seas Adventure* (1959) and started its own travel advertising campaign called "Take the DC-8 [the newest commercial jet liner] to the 50th State."[77] In 1960, United flew "more than 60 TV personalities, columnists and newsmen" on a "whirlwind jet junket" to the islands.[78] The late US senator from Hawai'i Daniel K. Inouye was quoted as saying, "If I was a United publicist, I would take the position that Hawai'i is that state that United built. United played a key role in statehood. Today we look at United as our pioneer airline."[79] In 1958, United Air Lines president W. A. Patterson (who was born in Waipahu, Hawai'i) expressed a hope to Kaiser "of applying every effort to build up this vital segment of our market [Hawai'i]. Our people have been giving particular consideration to this problem in view of the approaching jet age when we will be operating Douglas DC-8 jetliners between California and Hawaii. . . . I am most appreciative of your deep and constructive interest in building Hawaiian tourist travel and you may count on United Airlines' continued support wherever possible."[80]

Notions of a "typical" Hawaiian tourist experience in the media largely coincided with United's own promotion. Hawai'i, wrote Rob Wilson, was "fetishized into United Airlines' sign of erotic longing."[81] The airline was integral to introducing "the technologies of space-time reduction, cheaper airfares, and packaged tours"[82] to the islands. The airline's 1962 brochure "Vacations to Hawaii!" articulated three different package options for a trip to the islands, ranging in length from seven to fifteen days. Each option offered a detailed itinerary for the traveler in anticipation of the trip. Though varying in detail and options, all emphasized many of the same points: a trip to Pearl Harbor, Nuuanu Pali Lookout, the Royal Mausoleum, a luau, shopping in the International market, and of course ample time on Waikiki Beach "with Diamond Head in the background."[83] In addition to such brochures, United also published their own tourist guidebook through Doubleday Press: *The New United Air Lines Guide to the Hawaiian Islands: ALOHA, HAWAII* (1967). Written by noted travel writer Horace Sutton, the 276-page book was sold for $1.95 and went beyond just planning individualized trips for the "single person," "Honeymooners," "Family," and those "with children," to also offer detailed accounts of the islands' history, culture, geography, and people. United saw the importance of selling an experience beyond the perceived dullness of the canned "tour package" experience, even as they were aggressive in pitching the details of those standardized six-night-, seven-day-type deals. "There is an infinite peace in the islands," Sutton wrote in the 1967 guide, ". . . anyone who has spent lazy days in Hawaii finds, on the first reacquaintance with life on the mainland, a hustling *unreality*."[84] Far from a crass listing out of various lodging and food options, noted tourist destinations, package tour options, and so forth (though the last hundred pages attends to such details), the writerly United Air Lines guide situates a trip to Hawai'i as part of a deeper engagement with a rich and exotic paradise with a history and culture all its own.

United understood the importance of utilizing media screens both big and small in order to solidify its associations with the Hawaiian tourist experience. As early as 1952's *Big Jim McClain*, fictional characters can be seen flying to Honolulu on United aircraft—in this first case, the Boeing 377 Stratocruiser, one of the first propeller-driven planes to routinely travel back and forth between the mainland and the islands. By the 1960s, United's first jet engine plane, the Douglas DC-8, served as product placement in many prominent Hawai'i tourist narratives of the time, such as *Blue Hawaii* and *Paradise Hawaiian Style* (1966), *Gidget Goes Hawaiian* (1961), *The Brady Bunch* (1972), and so forth. But none was more well known than its prominent placement in *Hawaii Five-O*'s iconic opening credit sequence. Known primarily for its surf rock theme song by veteran TV composer Morton Stevens, the sequence is also an impressive work of montage-style editing by 1960s US television standards. Using a fish-eye lens, the camera repeatedly gazes upon a United DC-8 as it sits by the airport jetway. Close-ups in particular fetishize the plane's modern-age jet engines to an excessive extreme. A low angle shot shows the plane takeoff from the runway and fly directly over the camera. While relatively brief, the several shots of the United plane are matched in duration in the credit sequence only by the several shots of Waikiki hotels earlier.

On the surface, this rhetoric of Hawaiian authenticity deployed by the *Five-O* producers, one based on the desire for immediacy, intensity, and danger, might seem opposed to the more laidback experience of a premodern paradise away from the stresses of the mainland that United was also promoting at the same time. Yet they both share an overtly mainland lens that depended upon the assumption of an "authentic" touristic experience to be achieved by the traveler—while United sought to promote it directly, *Hawaii Five-O*'s fictional crime unit each week on television sought to protect it from unsavory influences. Perhaps more significantly, this tension typified the nostalgic contradictions of post-WWII, post-statehood Hawai'i as in a period of rapid political and economic transition, yet balanced out by its contradictory image as still a calming, tranquil touristic space. *Hawaii Five-O*'s attention both to the specific exigencies of crime on the Hawaiian streets and more generally to the cultural and political challenges of a state in transition, coupled with its (often) implicit appeals to collective memories of military conflicts and more direct ones to Hawaiian history and heritage, straddled the divide that defined that historical moment. Combined, *Hawaii Five-O* and United Air Lines constituted a touristic dialectic of danger and safety, unreality and reality, unpredictability and predictability, necessary to maintaining the appeal of the mass travel, prepackaged Hawaiian vacation by the end of the 1960s.

Danger in the Touristic Back Regions

Despite the attention to location shooting in *Hawaii Five-O*, there was decidedly less commitment to issues actually affecting Hawai'i at the time. Crew and technicians were almost all from the mainland.[85] The producers encouraged new show writers to "tell it like it is. Hawaii is a very complex and deceptive socio-economic potpourri. It is imperative that the writer dig the local scene."[86] However, scriptwriters tended to spend little time while on vacation with the actual Honolulu police force or interviewing local news sources. As scripts were processed at Freeman's Hollywood office back across the Pacific, the show was criticized at times for storylines that didn't deal enough with local concerns. For example, one episode about the "hippie problem," wrote an *LA Times* critic in 1970, focused on an issue that was "much less evident [in Hawaii] than on the mainland."[87] Show scriptwriter Jerome Coopersmith was highly skeptical of the actual attention to locale-specific authenticity on the show. When he told Freeman that he wouldn't be able to visualize Hawai'i having never visited there, the producer was reported to have responded, "Just write it as if it was New York and we'll change the names of the streets."[88] In order to write to a specific tropical location, Coopersmith found "a solution. My wife Judy and I had been to Puerto Rico several times on vacations. It occurred to me that Puerto Rico was of a similar size and had a similar climate to Hawaii. From then on, I used Puerto Rico for my visualizations and no one ever knew the difference."[89] After three years writing for the show, he finally took a trip to Hawai'i, as many of the other screenwriters had: "The trip was a lovely vacation for Judy and me, but useless as far as ideas for the show were concerned. . . . I went back to getting my ideas from newspaper articles, my own imagination and my visions of Puerto Rico."[90] Still, at the height of its success, the show was hugely popular on the islands themselves, grabbing an 84 percent share of the audience in Hawai'i—the highest of any geographic location in the United States.[91]

Hawaii Five-O operated as travelogue both through the explicit narrative emphasis on stories involving tourists as they traveled to and from Hawai'i, and the more indirect framing of the islands' touristic locales as a way to satisfy a desire for those back on the mainland to see the actual state through the show's virtual tourism. An episode from *Hawaii Five-O*'s first season, "Strangers in Our Own Land," aptly demonstrates the film's subtle touristic lens. In the episode, a land commissioner is killed by a bomb in a taxicab, shortly after arriving at Honolulu International Airport. This storyline articulated a common theme in the show regarding tensions between Native Hawaiians' desire for sovereignty and land rights, and the emergent tourism industry on the islands. *Hawaii Five-O*, wrote Wilson, "localized (and even indigenized, as in the Hawaiian land struggle episodes) its plots, characters, and languages, drawing on a wide array of Asian and Pacific locals."[92] Stanley Orr has argued that "Strangers" utilizes standard "detective story conventions and allusions to modern drama toward a sophisticated critique of paternalist colonialism in Hawai'i."[93] Citing the contribution of the episode's American Samoan screenwriter John Kneubuhl, he adds that the episode "goes against the grain of crime and espionage conventions, not to mention anticommunist narratives about Hawai'i, to project an island community simmering with rage and insurgency in the wake of conquest."[94] The main villain in this episode is mad that his fellow Hawaiians have sold out to *haole* business interests and torn up the land for modern development, yet he himself is a nightclub owner who puts on a lucrative nightly hula show for the tourists. He becomes a powerful example of the cultural and economic ambivalence that some Hawaiians negotiated in the wake of statehood.

In the episode, the land commissioner's murderer is captured on 8-mm film by an amateur photographer on vacation in Hawai'i (in what evokes a very post-Zapruder moment). The opening shot of the home movie within the show—a shaking handheld vérité image of the airport control tower—is identical to the opening shot of the episode, so that when we finally watch the recovered footage later, we realize that the beginning shot was literally seen from a tourist's point of view. As the Five-O team watches the confiscated tourist film to find evidence, there is a lot of extra footage that's not particularly relevant to the investigation (or narrative)—shots of tourists, the airport's Japanese garden, hula girls with leis, the product placement of United jetliners. But the conceit here—beyond the self-evident reflexivity of a film within a film—allows the episode to not only foreground the touristic clichés of the islands, but also to excessively gaze about the diegetic space of the airport in a seemingly spontaneous, intimate, and random way. More so than the conventional crime plots, the appeal of *Hawaii Five-O* in a sense was how the show's travelogue aesthetic made it feel as though it literally existed within the real, day-to-day life of Hawai'i. Effectively, there is a brief moment of narrative rupture here where the random footage of the islands in the amateur home movie becomes just as, if not more, important as the actual crime being investigated. And yet the sense of danger that this sequence also highlights—the real threat of violence at something as seemingly routine and secure as an airport—adds an edginess to the sequence that both affirms and disrupts the potential of banality within the established conventions of the mass travel, prepackaged Hawaiian vacation. There is also, finally, something crucial about how this sequence self-theorizes the notion of knowledge in vision, how it authenticates the indexical power of actuality footage and location shooting. Just as the Five-O team is trying to see the real killer captured in the tourist's home movies, the footage of the airport captured—in all its random immediacy—conveys the idea to the television viewer that this is what Hawai'i really *looks* like (to see is to "know"), both within and in excess of the tourist lens.

This delicate balance of stripping away the overt glamour of Hawai'i's touristic experiences while also retaining an implied touristic framing of the islands was key to the show's appeal. Both the tourist-in-peril plots and the use of authentic locations gave the show an edge over both earlier Hawaiian-themed shows and other soundstage and backlot-bound crime shows. In a sense, the logistical move from shooting in the artificial confines of the studio soundstage to shooting out in the sunny, but unpredictable, actual streets of Hawai'i aptly visualizes a variation on the shift from (in Dean MacCannell's words) the "front region" to the "back region" of touristic spaces—a show set in the "real" Hawai'i instead of in only its most well-trodden travel clichés, focused on unsavory crimes instead of frivolous touristic indulgences. The *LA Times* located the show's authenticity specifically in "television [that goes] out of the studio and *in the real world*."⁹⁵ What makes *Hawaii Five-O* significant as a vehicle for

Figure 7.3. Even vital evidence from a crime scene in *Hawaii Five-O*—in this case, recovered 8-mm footage that might contain clues to solving a murder—manages to include product placement. Prominently featuring its new DC-8 jetliner in the iconic opening credits of the show ("Take the DC-8 to the 50th State," its marketing campaign declared), United Air Lines was a high-profile sponsor on *Five-O* and many other Hawai'i-themed radio and TV programs of the postwar period, not to mention a relentless advertiser in print media (see also its appearance in films like *Blue Hawaii*—figure I.8). Presided over by longtime, Honolulu-born CEO William Patterson (1899–1980), United aggressively sought to sell itself as the "official" airline of the newest state in the union, a title it would later relinquish to Hawaiian Airlines.

touristic anticipation (and recollection) was how it muddled the distinction between tourist and nontourist narratives in a way that *remystified* the idealized Hawaiian vacation by reframing the "back region" of island tourism as the place where criminal elements lurk just beneath the facades of paradise. In contrast, a film such as *Blue Hawaii*, which also featured a tourism-heavy storyline and stunning Panavision visuals, offered to mainland audiences a safely inoculated and self-contained, beautiful but bland, touristic space in both narrative and genre. In this respect, *Hawaii Five-O* sold itself as the antithesis to the lightweight island adventures of Elvis, Gidget, and the Brady Bunch.

The show's entire opening credit sequence reveals the its journey from the front region of established tourist attractions, framing the islands as an experience for visitors more so than locals by highlighting all the different iconography that defines Hawai'i as "Hawai'i" in the mainland imagination, to the back regions of the fiftieth state's hidden (criminal) spaces—symbolized by the exciting but ominous dangers of the night. After the slow-motion image of a large tidal wave, tracking aerial shots of Honolulu, Waikiki Beach, and iconic locations such as the Aloha Tower appear in rapid succession—evoking the visual effect of a jet traveler first arriving to the islands (while the tower evokes the earlier days of cruise ship travel and pre-WWII-era Hawai'i). The show cuts across several images of Waikiki Beach resorts before quickly tracking in with a sped-up helicopter shot of star Jack Lord as he stands atop the Ilikai Hotel. This particular resort was the exclusive location where the cast of *Paradise Hawaiian Style*, *Hawaii* (1965), *In Harm's Way* (1965), and others stayed during their respective productions, and which the *Washington Post* called in 1965 "the unofficial capital of moviedom in Honolulu."[96] Here, we see the show's main character literally adopting the point of view of a tourist, gazing across Waikiki and the Pacific Ocean. The sequence then employs a clunky match-on-action cut, jumping across the axis of action, as he turns around to face the camera. The awkward editing, however, allows Diamond Head to be subtly framed in the background behind his right shoulder. After quick shots consisting of tropical waters, a car racing down Kalakaua Ave., and veteran model Elizabeth Logue (one of the stars of *Hawaii*) running across a beach, the sequence features several images of the National Memorial Cemetery of the Pacific—a site of remembrance where thousands of US soldiers who died during WWI, WWII, the Korean War, and the Vietnam conflict are buried.

In this sequence, the show's overt touristic lens becomes grounded in a narrative of sacrifice that nationalistic rhetoric used to define the US militaristic presence in the Pacific (even as the cemetery itself also serves as yet another tourist attraction on display). The mournful acknowledgment merges seamlessly with the other parts of the credit sequence, highlighting the extent to which nostalgic narratives of militarism and tourism effortlessly converged in Hawai'i (similarly, the sequence of the cemetery, followed closely by the images of the cutting-edge United jetliner, reiterated how the twin pull of retrospective nostalgia and forward-looking technological progress coexisted in post-statehood Hawai'i). Thus far criticism of *Hawaii Five-O* has largely centered on its representation of the US military presence in the Pacific. Most harshly, in the wake of the September 11th terrorist attacks in 2001, Ed Rampell criticized *Hawaii Five-O* as a reactionary television show that sought to "glorif[y] the police, intelligence agencies and the Pentagon, at the very moment that millions of Americans and others around the world were rallying against these institutions" in the form of protests stemming from the Vietnam War, civil rights battles, and political assassinations that came to define the American counterculture movement.[97] Rampell focused the appeal of *Hawaii Five-O* on what he saw as its unconditional support for "Vietnam and Cold War efforts."[98] Along with *Hawaiian Eye* and *Magnum PI*, this cycle of Hawaiian-themed television shows, adds Peter Britos, acted as a complementary "paramilitary" cultural institution that "allows for an exploration of law and order issues in a controlled environment, with a predictable level of resolution."[99]

The television program during its production relied on its partnership with the military. *Hawaii Five-O* was a television series, added Rampell, "with a close collaborative relationship with the military, which does not lightly dispense such favors as location filming on military bases. A condition for Pentagon cooperation is the form of script approval, ensuring the Defense Department's depicted in a favorable light, one likely to bolster recruitment and burnish the Armed Services' image."[100] Some audiences at the time felt the show went too far in its cooperation with the Navy to the point of risking a reveal of military secrets.[101] The *Hawaii Five-O* writer's guide emphasized the military's considerable role: "Hawaii is our extended heartbeat into the Pacific. It is where we meet and touch two of the three billion persons on earth."[102] This echoes the long history of colonialist rhetoric that shaped the US' militaristic presence, and which performed "mutual work" alongside the tourism industry. Writes Vernadette Gonzalez: "American militarism is an obvious presence, but tourism—with its structuring ideas and practices of mobility and consumption—is *the* perfect partner to militarism's claims to security."[103] *Hawaii Five-O*'s ambivalent emphasis on a "law and order" approach to the conventions of the cop genre fit well with this rhetoric of "security." The Five-O unit kept tourists safe on a weekly basis just as the military claimed to do.

At the same time, for a show to have successfully reached a diverse television audience across thirteen seasons, it would have had to at least attempt to tap into conflicting ideologies simultaneously without alienating half of its massive audience. Culturally ambivalent episodes such as "Strangers in Our Own Land" express alignment with the larger claim of Native Hawaiian land rights through the symbolic character of Kono (offering at least some sympathy for the Hawaiian Sovereignty Movement of the 1960s and 1970s), even at the same time that another one of those independence advocates is revealed to be the primary villain (played by native New Yorker Simon Oakland). Meanwhile, another early episode, "Not That Different," explores the antiwar movement in ways that seek to unpack the protestors' generally peaceful ideology, even as it also ultimately affirms McGarrett's "thoughtful conservatism grounded in not only his duty to protect society, but in a genuine caring for the individuals who constitute it"[104] (this particular episode is ultimately more troubling for its undertones of homophobia). In "Once Upon a Time," McGarrett tells Kelly that he will be "giving a speech about law & order" to a local civic group. Kelly asks, "For or against?" All members of the Five-O unit enjoy a good laugh at the policeman's apparent joke, but using humor to avoid answering the original question suggests the show's careful ambivalence regarding controversial topics of the day (and in a sense allows its audience to see what it wants to see).

Tying back to the depiction of the National Memorial Cemetery of the Pacific in the opening credits, the ambivalent appeal of militarism in Hawai'i as depicted in *Hawaii Five-O* may not only reinforce pro-imperialist attitudes but also align with what in 1963 economist Paul Craig called the "veteran effect" of the postwar period: "Many veterans got their first contact with overseas areas (Hawaii included) during WWII. There was doubtless some tendency for them to want to return to these places in peacetimes."[105] While Craig was reflecting on the sudden explosion of travel to the islands in the late 1940s and 1950s, there's reason to assume that a continuing desire to "return" there (via television) may have been a factor as well—particularly as the Korean and Vietnam conflicts created a disturbing dynamic that sustained variations on this "veteran effect" for several more decades. At the same time, it's doubtful that these memories of war were purely nostalgic. Some *Hawaii Five-O* episodes dealt with the intensities of war with a bit more nuance, such as an episode from the first season called "King of the Hill," which explores not only the impact of Post-Traumatic Stress Disorder on soldiers returning from Vietnam, but also the corrosive role of racism among some in the military.

Moving further toward Hawai'i's touristic back region, the opening credit sequence then descends into night—the sunset reflects off the Pacific Ocean, the camera zooms in repeatedly through overlaps on the nighttime Honolulu skyline, and hula dancers perform for the male gaze of the tourist (we see only the shaking hips of the dancer while men watch in the background of the frame). Only at the very end of this sequence do we see any direct reference to the show's ostensibly primary genre status as a cop show. Williams is introduced to the audience while looking through a violently smashed out window; Kauhi (introduced by his stage name "Zulu") rushes toward the camera with shotgun in hand, plowing into an unnamed man obstructing his path. Chun is introduced as Kelly. These final moments establish the show's modestly diverse cast. More progressive than its reactionary military politics was its depiction of multiculturalism, a vision of racial relations different from some primetime television shows of the late 1960s, but consistent with many other films and shows of the time set in Hawai'i. *Hawaii Five-O* sat along other late 1960s crime-related programs, such as *The Mod Squad* (1968–1973) and *Mission: Impossible* (1966–1973), as featuring a relatively racially diverse team of individuals working together to solve various cases.

The writer's guide stressed how "our police stories must be special and indigenous to our seven island, multi-racial, multilingual Five-O state."[106] The casting of the show's key Five-O unit, while betraying traces of what Robert Stam and Louise Spence have called the condescending or "affectionate" racism of mainstream Hollywood media,[107] foregrounded the state's multicultural appeal. The character of Kono was described by producers as the "face of Hawaii. Two hundred sixty-five pounds of muscle in the shape of a walking telephone booth,"[108] while Kelly was described as "a burly, powerful Chinese with a grin that lights up the place. He is multilingual, wise as a Chinese proverb and a workhorse, which makes him a most effective cop."[109] In addition to the last chapter of Michener's *Hawaii* (1959), one of the suggested readings for *Hawaii Five-O* screenwriters was Lawrence Fuchs's *Hawaii Pono: A Social History* (1961)[110]—a book specifically about the islands' diverse racial history. The stable of local, often nonprofessional, actors employed for smaller bit parts on a weekly basis further reinforced this. While the show rarely directly addressed the question of racial difference in a way that more daring shows of the time did (such as *Mod Squad* or *Star Trek*), it always remained in the background. Still, the show was fairly criticized for its at times condescending racial lens of whiteness. In 1972, a writer for the *Oakland Post* observed: "When I see Jack Lord flaunting his non-Oriental superiority in *Hawaii 5-O*, I invariably wonder again if or when the entertainment media in general will recognize the glaring feasible need for genuine ethnic casting. It seems unlikely that in all Hawaii no Oriental can be found with sense enough to head their law and order faction."[111] The emphasis on foregrounding, if not openly celebrating, racial diversity in the show could be cynically read as in part a reflection of the islands' economic attempts at further diversifying its touristic appeal. "Hawaii must somehow be unique" for its tourism to survive, Craig wrote. "As a warm place in the sun, it has far too many competitors. Promotion must play up Hawaiiana and the racial-cultural appeal of Hawaii."[112] As this suggests, *Hawaii Five-O*'s depiction of the military and of island diversity originated in complex ways from a collective touristic vision of Hawai'i.

"The Importance of *Hawaii Five-O*"

In its later years, despite its success, the show consistently risked going off the air—mainly due to such issues as rising production costs, court battles between CBS and local residents over zoning, permits, and other production logistics, and to Lord's own ambivalence over continuing to play the same character. As early as 1974, for example, Acting Governor Ariyoshi claimed to have personally intervened to persuade Lord not to retire.[113] After the broadcasting of the show's tenth season, a 1977 editorial in the *Honolulu Star-Bulletin* entitled "The Importance of *Hawaii Five-O*" advocated for the show's return yet again, despite Lord's continual insistence that he wanted to complete other artistic projects in his life and to spend more time with his wife, Marie. The editorial admitted that many people on the islands "wince sometimes that it is the mixture of beauty with crime and violence that draws and holds those millions upon millions of viewers, but there is no denying that the *Five-O* show has brought more people to a fascination with Hawaii than even the strains of 'Sweet Leilani' or 'Aloha Oe.'"[114] Ultimately, the *Star-Bulletin* admitted its motivation had less to do with the quality of the show than its considerable impact both on Hawai'i's local economy and on its ability to lure national and international tourists. (In 1970, Lord had been named the "Hawaii Salesman of the Year" by the Sales and Marketing Executives in Hawaii [SME], an award presented "to the person who has done the best job of selling Hawaii throughout the world."[115])

Over its twelve-plus seasons, *Hawaii Five-O* ambivalently negotiated a vast series of discourses regarding competing and sometimes contradictory notions of realism that had come to define the mainland's understanding of Hawai'i as the lucrative era of post-statehood fascination gradually came to an end. *Hawaii Five-O*'s success was about more than its scenic beauty or (generally formulaic) police procedural storylines. Its epic narrative canvas, spanning over a decade, did not solidify the local tourist industry, align the Hawaiian image with the military, advocate in fresh ways for respecting Native Hawaiian history, or offer a radically new depiction of multiculturalism. Rather, more than any other one media text, it singularly reified on nightly network television so many of these preexisting and evolving questions regarding Hawai'i's identity already circulating in the mainland imagination by the 1970s. The show's touristic lens mediated in two senses of the word—both crafting a unique genre vision of Hawai'i for network television, and attempting to negotiate conflicting attitudes regarding the islands' relationship to the mainland. Television's deeper narrative format allowed the show to capture these contradictions of "paradise"—the US' complicated understandings and misunderstandings of the fiftieth state in ways reinforced by the islands' own negotiated position at the intersection of nostalgia and progress in the wake of war and statehood.

Conclusion

Hawai'i Bound

> Hawai'i called to the US mainland via music, image, hula skirt, and resort hotel, and American paradise-seekers came in droves like the Brady Bunch looking for some lost aboriginal treasure, some fun and sun in the surf, or just a good tan to boast about back in the suburbs.
>
> —Rob Wilson, *Reimagining the American Pacific*

In 1968, Hawai'i's governor Jack Burns wrote to Jack Valenti, the president of the then-titled Motion Picture Association of America (MPAA), asking for advice on a possible film festival to debut in Honolulu in 1970. The proposal was to encourage Hollywood's best talent—in front of, and behind, the camera—to travel to the islands in order to debut some of its most recent high-profile films at what would be promoted as the "official" United States Film Festival. In some respects, Burns's idea seemed inspired—merging the long and complex history of Hollywood's role in the construction of Hawai'i's mass-mediated touristic identity with its then more recent economic transition to actively encouraging various mainland businesses and companies to hold their yearly industry conventions on the islands themselves. (In the mid-1950s, the Hawaii Visitors Bureau had shifted its attention away from catering mostly to individual tourists, and focused increasingly on "convention and group movement" promotion.[1] This change was made more official by

1997, when the decades-old organization once again changed its name, this time to the "Hawaii Visitors and Convention Bureau.") What better way, Burns might have thought, to synergize those twin pillars of Hawai'i's mediated reputation—merging the glamour and spectacle of film with the steady stream of tourist travel—than to encourage Hollywood itself to tour the islands in order to show off and celebrate its latest cinematic achievements?

Yet given the number of film festivals already existing throughout various cities in the United States by then, as well as the fierce competition among them over exclusive access to the newest film titles both domestic and international, Valenti was understandably resistant in his response. "There will be very great obstacles facing an attempt to make any single U.S. film festival the official American film festival," he wrote candidly, adding that "no one could assure Hawaii, in spite of its many famous attractions, that the various elements involved in the American motion picture industry would cooperate with such a festival if it were held outside of Los Angeles."[2] Valenti instead suggested that Burns and others consider a more specialized topic, such as "the meeting of the East and the West"[3] (over a decade later, in 1981, the Hawaii International Film Festival, following a similar theme, debuted). The original idea's initial failure, however, was deeply symbolic. Valenti's belief that Hollywood would be generally resistant to cooperating with a festival that wasn't based in California—in spite of its own personal fondness for Hawai'i's touristic charms—highlighted just how little control the fiftieth state had over its representations in an industry it both benefited from, and was exploited by. Hollywood was willing to benefit financially from its own representations of Hawai'i but was more indifferent when it came to reciprocating that economic relationship. As the immense postwar, post-statehood popularity of Hawai'i in mainland film and television began to wane by the 1970s, Hollywood began to revert back to its own tired and generic touristic clichés about what it thought Hawai'i represented in the American imagination.

Following that logic, perhaps one of the best remembered—for better and for worse—Hawai'i-themed texts to emerge from Hollywood during this time was a three-episode arc of *The Brady Bunch* (1972) where Mike (Robert Reed), Carol (Florence Henderson), Alice (Ann B. Davis), and the rest of the clan headed to the islands for, appropriately, a *working vacation* (the architect Mike is only traveling because he needs to oversee the construction of his latest building project in Honolulu). The Hawai'i episodes remain one of the series' more iconic ones during its well-known five-year run, even shaping an important subplot in the parodic *A Very Brady Sequel* (1996). Today, the Brady family's adventures are the touchstone stereotype for the generic Hawaiian vacation enjoyed by white, middle-class American families in the second half of the twentieth century. In contrast to the high culture of Europe, writes Adria Imada, "Hawaii is a decidedly middlebrow, banal destination for outsiders. This was represented perhaps most emblematically by the quintessential American family, the Brady Bunch, exploring the islands during three television episodes."[4] The first one, "Hawaii Bound," focuses primarily on the family's trip across Oʻahu to see the usual staple of tourist destinations—making effective use of extensive location shooting for a show more often defined visually by its tacky 1970s studio mise-en-scène. The last two—"Pass the Tabu" and "The Tiki Caves"—focus on an absurd subplot wherein the Brady boys stumble upon a cursed tiki idol at the construction site and then proceed to find the ancient burial ground it

Figure C.1. The quintessential television family of the white baby boomer generation, the Brady Bunch, traveled to Hawaiʻi for a three-episode arc of the iconic series. The banal frivolities of their stereotypical Hawaiian vacation are momentarily disrupted by a somber trip to the USS Arizona Memorial at Pearl Harbor.

came from, only to be kidnapped by a mad archeologist (played with typically indulgent flair by Vincent Price) who is convinced they are attempting to steal his latest archeological find. The dramatic tension is minimal throughout, and everyone (Brady clan and Price's character) in the end celebrates the misunderstanding over a typical Hawaiian luau.

Imada aptly notes that the episodes embody the "middlebrow, banal" experience of the typical Hawaiian vacation. Whereas *Hawaii Five-O* situated such tired clichés as a backdrop to the police unit's more pressing criminal matters, *The Brady Bunch* seemed content to simply check them off the list of the usual visitor experiences associated with a preplanned, mass packaged Hawaiian itinerary. Certainly, the episodes reveal some self-awareness. When Bobby fails to recognize Diamond Head during their incoming approach (aboard a United 707 jetliner), Peter responds by saying, "That's Diamond Head, dumbhead." The lame humor at least reflects the recognition that Hawai'i's iconography and its attendant touristic conventions left little still to be discovered. But generally the episodes play the canned "Hawai'i experience" straight. Perhaps the most unique part of the episodes is the role of the hotel construction site itself. On the one hand, it fulfills several basic plot functions—explaining why Mike would have an excuse to travel to Hawai'i, why a supposedly long-buried tiki idol would suddenly emerge at the earth's surface, and how the Bradys are able to obtain a (free) tour guide, David (Patrick Adiarte), to show them the island sights, as David is a construction worker who is assigned by the company to escort the Bradys around.

David quietly continues the tradition of the beachboy as the original tour guide, a connection made more explicit later in the first episode when he lets Greg in on a local surfing contest he apparently just happens to run on Waikiki Beach in his spare leisure time. Beyond plot convenience, however, the construction site also serves as the only marker of Hawai'i's modernity, of its rapidly shifting post-statehood urban landscape, in a simplistic plot otherwise overrun at best by touristic clichés (leis at the airport, romantic dinners on Waikiki, surfing, hula lessons, luau shows) and at worst by primitivist stereotypes (Native Hawaiians easily given to ancient superstitions, undiscovered caves filled with artifacts still to be explored by Western travelers). As an apparently vengeful relic from Hawai'i's past, the cursed tiki idol found as a result of disturbing some sacred ground in order to build Mike's latest architectural design could be read as another variation on the kind of post-statehood liberal white guilt that began to emerge as more people began to confront the US' ugly colonial history in Hawai'i.

But that is probably giving *The Brady Bunch* too much credit—in the end, the show takes a generally playful attitude, as *Endless Summer* had in one scene a few years earlier, toward the notion of cursed tiki imagery. If anything, the idol evokes Jean Baudrillard's notion of the simulacrum, that "which has no relation to any reality whatsoever: it is its own pure simulacrum."[5] Despite the supposedly mythical powers of "tiki" statutes as represented in popular culture, writes Peter Britos, its representation paradoxically "usually comes to evoke the obsolescence of Native agency and superstition."[6] Ubiquitous throughout US popular culture in the 1950s and 1960s (most explicitly realized in the brief popularity of "tiki"-themed nightclubs), tiki imagery evoked the iconographies of South Pacific culture and history, but without much of any connection to specific traditions, places, or people. In the twentieth-century phenomenon he calls "Polynesian Pop," Sven Kirsten writes that "all Oceanic carvings became members of one happy family: the Tikis. These primitive effigies were the counteragents in the modern world of plastic and chrome: priapic moments to the primal urges that were otherwise suppressed under the ordered cleanliness of 50s suburbia."[7] (Given the tiki's postwar evocation of "sexual liberation" and "endless sensuality,"[8] its phallic presence in the thoroughly sanitized television world of the Bradys becomes doubly threatening.) An amalgamation of different mythical South Pacific deities, "tiki plays a fundamental role in the broad and multivalent Polynesian cosmogony," writes Francesco Adinolfi.

> For many Westerners, his name conjures up scenes of mystery and spirituality, evoking unexplored and deeply exotic worlds. In the 1950s and 1960s, wooden or stone symbols of this anthropomorphic being began to spring up in the United States. . . . The more common these statues became in gardens and living rooms of thousands of American homes, the less anyone stopped to consider their distinctive or contextual meanings.[9]

In this context, tiki signified a particular kind of exotic pastiche—an increasingly self-referential style constructed by a variety of media, merchandising, and leisure-based industries to evoke the conventions associated with historical myths of the South Seas, and Hawai'i in particular. Its function within *The Brady Bunch* was similar—the tiki as generalized diegetic symbol of ancient Hawaiian history (even as its presence admittedly also invites alternative readings that could, for example, situate the absurdity of a cursed tiki idol within the self-conscious and exaggerated comedic tone of the series as a whole).

Going a step further, the self-referential nature of the show's tiki artifact—as a simulacric symbol that refers only to itself and not to any specific history or culture—also signifies the ways in which these episodes of *The Brady Brunch* embodied in mundane fashion the pastiche contradictions of the archetypal Hawaiian vacation onscreen, which collectively emerged from the wide range of US television shows and movies during the postwar and post-statehood eras. When Greg goes out to surf midway through the first episode, the show's soundtrack plays an uncanny imitation of the iconic *Hawaii Five-O* score. Aside from implying that the Jack Lord police procedural was associated as much with tidal waves and surfers as with cops and criminals, the musical reference highlights the rather aimless nature of *The Brady Bunch*'s amusingly bland Hawaiian pastiche. The show is inextricably bound to a mediated version of "Hawai'i" that came before it.

While *Waikiki Wedding* had parodied the advertising clichés of the Hawaiian tourism industry over three decades earlier, *The Brady Bunch* emerges more as a blank parody with nothing left to satirize, but instead can only refer back to other such texts in a comedic hodgepodge of media clichés. *The Brady Bunch* awkwardly attempts to negotiate the tradition of lighthearted vacation narratives (*Gidget Goes Hawaiian*, *Blue Hawaii*) with the edgier fare of historical epics, surfer documentaries, and police crime shows. The curse of the tiki suggests the liberal guilt of *Hawaii* (1966), but without any pretense of historical knowledge or reflection. Mike's construction project hints at *Hawaii Five-O*'s sense of a modern state undergoing a process of economic and structural change, but without the awareness of the cultural and political contexts informing that transition (in contrast to "Strangers in Our Own Land"). The Bradys' travelogue vacation echoes the fun-in-the-sun frivolities of *Blue Hawaii*, but minus the Elvis film's awareness of the tourism industry's historical emergence as an outgrowth of the agricultural economy, or even its then novel use of the Technicolor location footage. Greg's fascination with being an elite surfer contains echoes of Bruce Brown's popular documentaries (even the excessive use of actuality footage within the show's otherwise taut narrative explicitly evokes the aesthetic of the amateur surf film), while at the same time, the humorous depiction of Alice attempting to learn the hula dance undercuts the derisive hipster attitude toward actual middle-class tourists that Brown expressed in *Barefoot Adventures* (1960).

But *The Brady Bunch*'s thoroughly mediated *unreality* comes to an explicit rupture during the show's somber visit to the USS Arizona

Memorial in Pearl Harbor. Whether the Bradys travel to the memorial to pay their respects to the sailors killed during the attack on December 7th, or because it's as much another "must-see" on the standard visitor itinerary, is left open. The mood turns quickly subdued; the laughs abruptly stop. Up until that moment, the show features one cheesy wisecrack after another as the family does the usual Oʻahu tourist circuit (attempts at irreverent humor that become grotesquely magnified by the canned laugh track accompanying them). But suddenly the Bradys find themselves in a solemn space of reverence, and the effect is jarring. Ever the architect, Mike explains the significance of the memorial's design as pointing to "ultimate victory" (a phrase used by its real-life architect, Alfred Preis). He then leads his family over to the dedication plaque, reading aloud to them (and the audience): "Dedicated to the eternal memory of our gallant shipmates in the USS *Arizona* who gave their lives in action 7 December 1941." The attraction itself demands this serious tone. As Vernadette Gonzalez writes, "Having been asked to behave solemnly and with respect, visitors spend their time on the memorial in a quiet and somber fashion."[10] In the following scene, as they cruise away back to shore, Carol remarks to her family, "Oh, I must say, Pearl Harbor sure is impressive, isn't it?" The impromptu tour guide David then pivots the story back to its cursed artifact subplot by telling the Bradys the story of a "shark queen god" (based loosely on the figure of Kaʻahupahau) who was said to reside in Pearl Harbor during ancient times and was angered by the decision to build a naval port there. Just as quickly as *The Brady Bunch* touches on a still painful subject (one further intensified by the unacknowledged present realities of the Vietnam War), it pivots back to its tacky tourists-in-exotic-peril narrative. The tonal awkwardness of the USS *Arizona* sequence speaks precisely to the tension between the "Hawaiian vacation" as a lighthearted tourist cliché by the 1970s and the still powerful, but fading, direct affective memory of WWII—which for all its horrors was nonetheless a paradoxically powerful component of the islands' (touristic) popularity with the mainland.

Despite the show's turn back to frivolous fun, the rupture remains. Befitting the contradictory touristic experience it seeks to represent (between a tropical escape from reality and reality's jarring wartime violence), the show feels emotionally obligated to engage with an intense affective moment that is wildly inconsistent in tone with the rest of the narrative. While *Big Jim McClain*'s (1952) anticommunist plot was no less ridiculous than the Bradys' quest to overcome cursed tiki artifacts, the latter's makeshift USS Arizona Memorial sequence was at least more tonally consistent with the rest of the propagandistic narrative. Even

Hawaii Five-O's references to military sacrifice fit effortlessly within the exigencies of its criminal investigations. Meanwhile, the imperialist past is also elided in *The Brady Bunch* through reverential acknowledgment of the King Kamehameha Statue and the Iolani Palace and a cheesy plot about cursed Hawaiian artifacts (even *The Hawaiians* at least attempted, however unsuccessfully, to confront and negotiate how Hawai'i went historically from sovereign monarch to US territory). In these episodes, characters speak the Hawaiian language, but only to set up the predictable punchline of the Bradys' difficulty in doing so as well. The inability to reconcile the frivolity of the Hawaiian vacation with the ugly histories coexisting therein become irreparably exposed in *The Brady Bunch*.

As Imada notes, this otherwise inconsequential three-episode arc on a popular 1970s family television show was emblematic of an era where the middle-class Hawaiian vacation—now little more than a class status symbol—had passed into banality in the age of mass tourism, seven-day itineraries, and industry conventions, but equally important was how so much of what defined that wartime and postwar era in terms of historical specificity were also beginning to fade. Pearl Harbor was becoming as much a tourist attraction as Waikiki Beach—that is, as much tourist attraction as its intended function as a war memorial—with only a fading collective historical trauma to ground it affectively in something beyond the predictable touristic routine (just as the violent history of Nu'uanu Pali as the site of King Kamehameha's gruesome military victory has little personal emotional connection today for the average tourist more interested in its stunning views). *The Brady Bunch* was both the beneficiary of Hawai'i's singular popularity on the mainland during the previous decades, and the harbinger of its imminent passing after decades of a "hard sell" that reduced the loosely demarcated prewar fantasy of a particular touristic experience, still marked by a certain space for irony, to a generic mass-produced commodity rigidly defined by standardized itineraries, obligations, and feelings.

Certainly, film and television representations of Hawai'i continued, and continue, to do complex ideological work—for example, *Hawaii Five-O*'s (1968) network follow-up, *Magnum PI* (1980), began to more directly mediate the personal and political legacies of the US' military intervention into Vietnam. More recently, there also remains the occasional attempt by high-profile studio films to continue negotiating the islands' complex culture and history (2011's *The Descendants*, 2015's *Aloha*)—problematic cinematic representations that, like the Michener adaptations several decades earlier, present still more questions than answers. There is room today for post-touristic games as one embarks on their own hypothetical Hawaiian vacation, virtual or otherwise. Mostly though, Hollywood itself seems to see the Hawai'i tourist experience these days as being as bland and predictable as it had been one hundred years earlier. Whereas the playfully reflexive 1930s Hollywood musicals maintained a humorous critical distance from the touristic myth of "Hawai'i" as romantic playground, *The Brady Bunch*'s blank parody suggested a distinction between mediated ideal and physical reality had dissolved in a particular age when Hawaiian vacations, both onscreen and off, had become so carefully scripted and mass-produced—a cliché that sometimes continues to define the islands within an often ahistorical touristic imagination to this day.

Notes

Introduction

1. "Hollywood Plans 5 Films in Hawaii," *New York Times*, July 8, 1960, 17.
2. Horace Sutton, "Aloha, Hollywood! It's Movietime in Hulaland These Days," *Washington Post*, August 29, 1965, G11.
3. Luciano Minerbi, "Hawai'i," in *Tourism in the Pacific: Issues and Cases*, ed. C. Michael Hall and Stephen J. Page (Detroit: International Thomson Business Press, 1996), 196.
4. "Before the Civil Aeronautics Board, Washington, D.C., in the Matter of the Pacific-Hawaii Renewal Case No. 8960, et al.," January 13, 1959, Series 1915, Box 5, Division of Aeronautics: Civil Aeronautics Board Case Records, 1946–1978, Wisconsin Center for Film and Theater Research, University of Wisconsin Archives, Madison, WI, 5.
5. "Before the Civil Aeronautics Board, Washington, D.C., in the Matter of the Pacific-Hawaii Renewal Case No. 8960, et al.," January 13, 1959, Series 1915, Box 5, Division of Aeronautics: Civil Aeronautics Board Case Records, 1946–1978, Wisconsin Center for Film and Theater Research, University of Wisconsin Archives, Madison, WI, 5.
6. *My emphasis*. Walt Christie, "Hawaiian Hospitality to Total Strangers Hits Islanders' Pocketbooks," *Variety*, January 6, 1960, 3.
7. H. Allen Smith, *Waikiki Beachnik* (Boston: Little, Brown, 1960), 4.
8. "General Information about Honolulu, Hawaii, U.S.A. and the Territory, Combined with Business Statistics" (Honolulu: Chamber of Commerce of Honolulu, 1939), 14.
9. *Hawaii U.S.A.* (Honolulu: Hawaii Tourist Bureau, 1942), n.p.
10. Delia Malia Caparoso Konzett, *Hollywood's Hawaii: Race, Nation, and War* (New Brunswick, NJ: Rutgers University Press, 2017), 5.
11. Jeffrey Geiger, *Facing the Pacific: Polynesia and the US Imperial Imagination* (Honolulu: University of Hawai'i Press, 2007), 2.

12. Paul G. Craig, *The Future Growth of Hawaiian Tourism and Its Impact on the State and the Neighbor Islands* (Honolulu: University of Hawai'i Economic Research Center, 1963), 11.

13. Craig, 69.

14. Craig, 1.

15. Beth Bailey and David Farber, *The First Strange Place: Race and Sex in World War II Hawaii* (Baltimore, MD: Johns Hopkins University Press, 1992), 56.

16. Haunani-Kay Trask, *From a Native Daughter: Colonialism and Sovereignty in Hawai'i* (Monroe, ME: Common Courage Press, 1993), 24.

17. Daniel Boorstin, *The Image, or What Happened to the American Dream* (New York: Atheneum, 1961), 116.

18. Hawaii Tourist Bureau, Report for July, 1936, July 1936, Box 33, Folder 29, MS Group 239—Theo H. Davies & Co. Collection, Bernice Pauahi Bishop Museum Archives, Honolulu, HI.

19. Konzett, 10.

20. Orvar Lofgren, *On Holiday: A History of Vacationing* (Berkeley: University of California Press, 1999), 216.

21. John Connell and Chris Gibson, "'No Passport Necessary': Music, Record Covers and Vicarious Tourism in Post-war Hawai'i," *Journal of Pacific History* 43.1 (June 2008): 57.

22. John Urry, *The Tourist Gaze: Leisure and Travel in Contemporary Societies* (London: Sage, 1990), 3.

23. Urry, 3.

24. Konzett, 11.

25. Jeffrey Ruoff, "The Filmic Fourth Dimension: Cinema as Audiovisual Vehicle," *Virtual Voyages: Cinema and Travel* (Durham, NC: Duke University Press, 2006), 1.

26. Paul Lyons, *American Pacificism: Oceania in the U.S. Imagination* (New York: Routledge, 2006), 151.

27. Konzett, 2, 3.

28. Konzett, 8.

29. Vernadette Vicuña Gonzalez, *Securing Paradise: Tourism and Militarism in Hawai'i and the Philippines* (Durham, NC: Duke University Press, 2013), 5.

30. Boorstin, 108–109.

31. Rob Wilson, *Reimagining the American Pacific: From South Pacific to Bamboo Ridge and Beyond* (Durham, NC: Duke University Press, 2000), 230.

32. Wilson, 11.

33. Joyce D. Hammond, "Photography, Tourism, and the Kodak Hula Show," *Visual Anthropology* 14.1 (March 2001): 3.

34. Jane Desmond, *Staging Tourism: Bodies on Display from Waikiki to Sea World* (Chicago: University of Chicago Press, 1999), 105.

35. Milly Singletary, *Hilo Hattie: A Legend in Our Time* (Honolulu: Mutual, 2006), 10.

36. Adria L. Imada, *Aloha America: Hula Circuits through the US Empire* (Durham, NC: Duke University Press, 2012), 11.

37. Wilson, 270.

38. Hammond, 4.

39. Cristina Bacchilega, *Legendary Hawai'i and the Politics of Place: Tradition, Translation, and Tourism* (Philadelphia: University of Pennsylvania Press, 2007), 18.

40. Bacchilega, 20.

41. George Lewis, "Beyond the Reef: Cultural Constructions of Hawaii in Mainland America, Australia and Japan," *Journal of Popular Culture* 30.2 (Fall 1996): 125.

42. "Hawaiian Follies," *Billboard*, January 29, 1938, 2.

43. Desmond, 109.

44. Imada, 157.

45. Dean MacCannell, *The Tourist: A New Theory of the Leisure Class* (Berkeley: University of California Press, 1999), 23.

46. *My emphasis.* "Greatest Travel Era Predicted by Tourist Official," *San Francisco Examiner*, September 16, 1932, 16.

47. Desmond, 128.

48. The Hawaii Visitors Bureau Program for Fiscal 1962–1963, October 2, 1962, Box 33, Folder 28, MS Group 239—Theo H. Davies & Co. Collection, Bernice Pauahi Bishop Museum Archives, Honolulu, HI.

49. Memorandum from the Attorney General to the Governor, January 12, 1959, GOV12 Folder 84, Gov. William F. Quinn Collection, Hawai'i State Archives, Honolulu, HI.

50. Report from the Citizens Advisory Committee on the Tourist Industry, February 11, 1959, GOV12 Folder 16, Gov. William F. Quinn Collection, Hawai'i State Archives, Honolulu, HI.

51. Uncle Sam's Paradise, April 1923, Box 11, Folder 2, MS Group 367—Everett Joseph Scharbach Collection, Bernice Pauahi Bishop Museum Archives, Honolulu, HI.

52. James Mak, "Creating 'Paradise of the Pacific': How Tourism Began in Hawaii," *UHERO Working Paper No. 2015-1*, Economic Research Organization at the University of Hawai'i, February 2015, 22.

53. Mak, 22.

54. Christine Skwiot, *The Purposes of Paradise: US Tourism in Cuba and Hawaii* (Philadelphia: University of Pennsylvania Press, 2010), 176–177.

55. Gordon Ghareeb and Martin Cox, *Hollywood to Honolulu: The Story of the Los Angeles Steamship Company* (Providence, RI: Steamship Historical Society of America, 2009), 10.

56. Mak, 48.

57. For more on the many Hollywood celebrities who cruised to and from Honolulu, see Ghareeb and Cox.

58. Ghareeb and Cox, 21, 36.

59. Ghareeb and Cox, 60.
60. Ghareeb and Cox, 243.
61. Ghareeb and Cox, 153.
62. Mak, 50–51.
63. Ghareeb and Cox, 157.
64. Mak, 43.
65. Smith, 12.
66. Desmond, 5.
67. DeSoto Brown, *Hawaii Recalls: Selling Romance to America—Nostalgic Images of the Hawaiian Islands, 1910–1950* (Honolulu: Editions, 1982), 86.
68. "Inside Stuff—Pictures," *Variety*, February 23, 1938, 27.
69. Hawaii Tourist Bureau Report for February, 1936, to the Chairman and Committee Members, February 1936, Box 33, Folder 29, MS Group 239—Theo H. Davies & Co. Collection, Bernice Pauahi Bishop Museum Archives, Honolulu, HI.
70. "Greatest Travel Era Predicted by Tourist Official," *San Francisco Examiner*, September 16, 1932, 16.
71. MacCannell, 36.
72. Trask, 180.
73. MacCannell, 92.
74. *My emphasis*. Geiger, 1.
75. Rona Tamiko Halualani, *In the Name of Hawaiians: Native Identities and Cultural Politics* (Minneapolis: University of Minnesota Press, 2002), 135.
76. MacCannell, 101.
77. Urry, 11.
78. Connell and Gibson, 51–75.
79. MacCannell, 24.
80. Louis Turner and John Ash, *The Golden Hordes: International Tourism and the Pleasure Periphery* (New York: St. Martin's Press, 1976), 12.
81. Robert Stam and Louise Spence, "Colonialism, Racism, and Representation," *Screen* 24.2 (1983): 3.
82. Bailey and Farber, 133.
83. Judy Rohrer, *Haoles in Hawaii: Race and Ethnicity in Hawaii* (Honolulu: University of Hawaiʻi Press, 2010), 2.
84. Rohrer, 4.
85. Rohrer, 2.
86. Christina Higgins and Gavin Furukawa, "Styling Hawaiʻi in *Haole*wood: White Protagonists on a Voyage of Self-Discovery," *Multilingua* 31 (2012): 179.
87. Wilson, 79, 80.
88. Barbara Kirshenblatt-Gimblett, *Destination Culture: Tourism, Museums, and Heritage* (Berkeley: University of California Press, 1998), 149.
89. *My emphasis*. Craig, 73.
90. Fredric Jameson, *Postmodernism, or the Cultural Logic of Late Capitalism* (Durham, NC: Duke University Press, 1992), 20.
91. Houston Wood, *Displacing Natives: The Rhetorical Production of Hawaiʻi* (Lanham, MD: Rowman & Littlefield, 1999), 93.

92. Nancy Martha West, *Kodak and the Lens of Nostalgia* (Charlottesville: University Press of Virginia, 2000), 17.
93. Wilson, 270.
94. Halualani, 135.
95. Urry, 111.
96. *My emphasis*. Norman Douglas and Ngaire Douglas, "Tourism in the Pacific: Historical Factors," in *Tourism in the Pacific: Issues and Cases*, ed. C. Michael Hall and Stephen J. Page (New York: International Thomson Business Press, 1996), 27–28.
97. Gonzalez, 117–18.
98. Gonzalez, 120.
99. Kirshenblatt-Gimblett, 150.
100. Robert C. Schmitt, *Hawaii in the Movies, 1898–1959* (Honolulu: University of Hawai'i, 1999), 19.
101. Geiger, 4, 5.
102. Schmitt, 1.

Chapter 1

1. Beth Bailey and David Farber, *The First Strange Place: Race and Sex in World War II Hawaii* (Baltimore, MD: Johns Hopkins University Press, 1992), 56–57.
2. George Lewis, "Beyond the Reef: Cultural Constructions of Hawaii in Mainland America, Australia and Japan," *Journal of Popular Culture* 30.2 (Fall 1996): 123.
3. "Harry Owens Back to Hawaii," *Variety*, August 14, 1940, 2.
4. Marion Squire, "Ray Kinney Credits F.D.R. and Bing for Hawaiian Music's Comeback," *Variety*, December 1, 1937, 47.
5. Harry Owens, *Sweet Leilani: The Story behind the Song* (Pacific Palisades, CA: Hula House, 1970), A.
6. Owens, 30.
7. "Harry Owens Back to Hawaii," *Variety*, August 14, 1940, 2.
8. As qtd. in Squire, 47.
9. "Kinney's 400 P.D. Tunes," *Variety*, December 25, 1940, 24.
10. "Harry Owens Back to Hawaii," *Variety*, August 14, 1940, 2.
11. Owens, 2.
12. "Harry Owens to Hawaii," *Variety*, May 1, 1934, 41.
13. Owens, 73.
14. DeSoto Brown, *Hawaii Recalls: Selling Romance to America—Nostalgic Images of the Hawaiian Islands, 1910–1950* (Honolulu: Editions, 1982), 131.
15. Nine-Month Report to Hawaii Visitors Bureau Members, 1953, GOV11 Folder 32, Gov. Samuel Wilder King Collection, Hawai'i State Archives, Honolulu, HI.
16. Squire, 47.

17. Robert C. Schmitt, *Hawaii in the Movies, 1898–1959* (Honolulu: University of Hawai'i, 1999), 13. For some of the more obscure and inaccessible titles, I have had to rely on Schmitt's plot summaries in place of primary viewing.
18. Lewis, 127.
19. Owens, b.
20. As qtd. in Bailey and Farber, 56.
21. Schmitt, 6.
22. Gordon Ghareeb and Martin Cox, *Hollywood to Honolulu: The Story of the Los Angeles Steamship Company* (Providence, RI: Steamship Historical Society of America, 2009), 70–71.
23. Schmitt, 3.
24. Schmitt, 6.
25. Jane Desmond, *Staging Tourism: Bodies on Display from Waikiki to Sea World* (Chicago: University of Chicago Press, 1999), 98.
26. Brown, 128.
27. Brown, 129.
28. Desmond, 109.
29. Brown, 8.
30. Gary Y. Okihiro, *Island World: A History of Hawai'i and the United States* (Berkeley: University of California Press, 2008), 64.
31. Schmitt, 4–5.
32. Delia Malia Caparoso Konzett, *Hollywood's Hawaii: Race, Nation, and War* (New Brunswick, NJ: Rutgers University Press, 2017), 3.
33. Schmitt, 37.
34. Lewis, 126
35. Brown, 124.
36. Owens, c.
37. Desmond, 110.
38. Desmond, 17.
39. "Chatter: Hollywood," *Variety*, May 19, 1937, 60.
40. Desmond, 11–12.
41. Poster tagline. Qtd. in Schmitt, 29.
42. *My emphasis.* Lloyd Pantages, "I Cover Hollywood," *San Francisco Examiner*, January 7, 1937, 12.
43. Robbin Coon, "Hollywood News and Gossip," *Post-Crescent* (Appleton, WI), February 1, 1937, 9.
44. "The Exhibitor Has His Say," *Boxoffice*, April 8, 1939, 34.
45. Adria L. Imada, *Aloha America: Hula Circuits through the US Empire* (Durham, NC: Duke University Press, 2012), 165.
46. Imada, 165.
47. Imada, 166.
48. Imada, 167–168.
49. Imada, 158–159.

50. Gavan Daws, *Shoal of Time: A History of the Hawaiian Islands* (Honolulu: University of Hawai'i Press, 1968), 390.

51. Jeffrey Geiger, *Facing the Pacific: Polynesia and the US Imperial Imagination* (Honolulu: University of Hawai'i Press, 2007), 16.

52. "Defer to Dixie: Alternate Versions of Film to Duck Prejudices," *Variety*, April 1, 1942, 5. The article speculated that two versions of the film would be made with light- and dark-skinned actresses.

53. Imada, 175.

54. As qtd. in Imada, 175–176.

55. Daws, 328.

56. David E. Stannard, *Honor Killing: How the Infamous "Massie Affair" Transformed Hawai'i* (New York: Penguin, 2005), 3.

57. Daws, 329.

58. "Coast Prints Quiet on Hawaii Attacks," *Variety*, January 5, 1932, 1.

59. Judy Rohrer, *Haoles in Hawaii: Race and Ethnicity in Hawaii* (Honolulu: University of Hawai'i Press, 2010), 63.

60. "Chatter—Honolulu," *Variety*, February 9, 1932, 39.

61. "Dodging Hawaii," *Variety*, January 12, 1932, 6.

62. Stannard, 276.

63. Schmitt, 37.

64. Stannard, 306.

65. Ghareeb and Cox, 165.

66. "*Black Camel* Being Filmed Here," *Honolulu Advertiser*, April 4, 1931, 1.

67. Ghareeb and Cox, 244.

68. Rohrer, 24.

69. Imada, 156.

70. Desmond, 98.

71. Daws, 312.

72. Fran Beauman, *The Pineapple: King of Fruits* (London: Chatto & Windus, 2005), 230.

73. Beauman, 230.

74. Daws, 332.

75. Desmond, 101.

76. Hawaii Tourist Bureau Minutes of Special Luncheon Meeting, May 7, 1934, Box 33, Folder 28, MS Group 239—Theo H. Davies & Co. Collection, Bernice Pauahi Bishop Museum Archives, Honolulu, HI.

77. Joseph Barber Jr., *Hawaii: Restless Rampart* (Indianapolis, IN: Bobbs-Merrill, 1941), 82.

78. Barber, 81.

79. H. Allen Smith, *Waikiki Beachnik* (Boston: Little, Brown, 1960), 30.

80. Christine Skwiot, *The Purposes of Paradise: US Tourism in Cuba and Hawaii* (Philadelphia: University of Pennsylvania Press, 2010), 142.

81. Barber, 83.

82. Barber, 84.

83. Brown, 8.

84. Hawaii Tourist Bureau Minutes of Special Luncheon Meeting, May 7, 1934, Box 33, Folder 28, MS Group 239—Theo H. Davies & Co. Collection, Bernice Pauahi Bishop Museum Archives, Honolulu, HI.

85. Annual Report of the Hawaii Tourist Bureau for 1931, GOV7 Folder 16, Gov. Lawrence M. Judd Collection, Hawai'i State Archives, Honolulu, HI.

86. Lawrence C. Lockley, "Trade Association as Advertisers," *Journal of Marketing* (1943): 190–191.

87. Annual Report of the Hawaii Tourist Bureau for 1931, GOV7 Folder 16, Gov. Lawrence M. Judd Collection, Hawai'i State Archives, Honolulu, HI.

88. Report of Executive Secretary, Hawaii Tourist Bureau, April 1934, Box 33, Folder 29, MS Group 239—Theo H. Davies & Co. Collection, Bernice Pauahi Bishop Museum Archives, Honolulu, HI.

89. Annual Report of Hawaii Tourist Bureau, December 31, 1936, Box 33, Folder 29, MS Group 239—Theo H. Davies & Co. Collection, Bernice Pauahi Bishop Museum Archives, Honolulu, HI.

90. Report of Executive Secretary, Hawaii Tourist Bureau, April 1934, Box 33, Folder 29, MS Group 239—Theo H. Davies & Co. Collection, Bernice Pauahi Bishop Museum Archives, Honolulu, HI.

91. Hawaii Tourist Bureau, Report for July, 1936, July 1936, Box 33, Folder 29, MS Group 239—Theo H. Davies & Co. Collection, Bernice Pauahi Bishop Museum Archives, Honolulu, HI.

92. Letter from George Armitage, Executive Secretary of HTB, to Gov. Poindexter, June 13, 1938, GOV8 Folder 27, Gov. Joseph Poindexter Collection, Hawai'i State Archives, Honolulu, HI.

93. Hawaii Tourist Bureau, Report for July, 1936, July 1936, Box 33, Folder 29, MS Group 239—Theo H. Davies & Co. Collection, Bernice Pauahi Bishop Museum Archives, Honolulu, HI.

94. Barber, 86.

95. Hawaii Tourist Bureau, Report for July, 1936, July 1936, Box 33, Folder 29, MS Group 239—Theo H. Davies & Co. Collection, Bernice Pauahi Bishop Museum Archives, Honolulu, HI.

96. Brown, 131.

97. Letter from Gov. Poindexter to George Armitage, Executive Secretary of HTB, August 26, 1936, GOV8 Folder 27, Gov. Joseph Poindexter Collection, Hawai'i State Archives, Honolulu, HI.

98. "Title Changes," *Variety*, October 20, 1937, 12.

99. "Philly Defies Lent," *Variety*, April 6, 1938, 8.

100. Schmitt, 43.

101. Letter from George Armitage, Executive Secretary of HTB, to Gov. Poindexter, June 13, 1938, GOV8 Folder 27, Gov. Joseph Poindexter Collection, Hawai'i State Archives, Honolulu, HI.

102. Report of Executive Secretary, Hawaii Tourist Bureau, April 1934, Box 33, Folder 29, MS Group 239—Theo H. Davies & Co. Collection, Bernice Pauahi Bishop Museum Archives, Honolulu, HI.

103. "Studio Notes," *Broadcasting*, July 15, 1937, 78.

104. Memo from Roy Frothingham to Roy C. Witmer, January 22, 1932, Box 10, Folder 44, National Broadcast Company Records, 1921–1976, Wisconsin Center for Film and Theater Research, University of Wisconsin Archives, Madison, WI, 1.

105. Memo from BNC to P. H. Beuter, January 16, 1931, Box 10, Folder 44, National Broadcast Company Records, 1921–1976, Wisconsin Center for Film and Theater Research, University of Wisconsin Archives, Madison, WI, 5.

106. Report of Executive Secretary Hawaii Tourist Bureau, December 1932, Box 33, Folder 28, MS Group 239—Theo H. Davies & Co. Collection, Bernice Pauahi Bishop Museum Archives, Honolulu, HI.

107. Hawaii Tourist Bureau Minutes of Special Luncheon Meeting, May 7, 1934, Box 33, Folder 28, MS Group 239—Theo H. Davies & Co. Collection, Bernice Pauahi Bishop Museum Archives, Honolulu, HI.

108. Barber, 86–87.

109. Hawaii Tourist Bureau Tentative Budget Fiscal Year, July 1, 1939–June 30, 1940, June 20, 1939, GOV8 Folder 27, Gov. Joseph Poindexter Collection, Hawai'i State Archives, Honolulu, HI.

110. *My emphasis*. *Hawaii U.S.A.* (Honolulu: Hawaii Tourist Bureau, 1942), n.p.

111. Geiger, 14–15.

112. Annual Report of Hawaii Tourist Bureau, 1931, GOV7, Folder 16, Gov. Lawrence M. Judd Collection, Hawai'i State Archives, Honolulu, HI.

113. Report for May 1935 to Committee Members, Hawaii Tourist Bureau, May 1935, Box 33, Folder 29, MS Group 239—Theo H. Davies & Co. Collection, Bernice Pauahi Bishop Museum Archives, Honolulu, HI.

114. Desmond, 111.

115. Report of Executive Secretary, Hawaii Tourist Bureau, on Mainland Trip September 1935 to January 16, 1936, January 31, 1936, Box 33, Folder 29, MS Group 239—Theo H. Davies & Co. Collection, Bernice Pauahi Bishop Museum Archives, Honolulu, HI. See also: Hawaii Tourist Bureau, Report for July, 1936, July 1936, Box 33, Folder 29, MS Group 239—Theo H. Davies & Co. Collection, Bernice Pauahi Bishop Museum Archives, Honolulu, HI.

116. Report of Executive Secretary, Hawaii Tourist Bureau, on Mainland Trip September 1935 to January 16, 1936, January 31, 1936, Box 33, Folder 29, MS Group 239—Theo H. Davies & Co. Collection, Bernice Pauahi Bishop Museum Archives, Honolulu, HI.

117. Annual Report of Hawaii Tourist Bureau, December 31, 1936, Box 33, Folder 29, MS Group 239—Theo H. Davies & Co. Collection, Bernice Pauahi Bishop Museum Archives, Honolulu, HI.

118. Annual Report of Hawaii Tourist Bureau, December 31, 1936, Box 33, Folder 29, MS Group 239—Theo H. Davies & Co. Collection, Bernice Pauahi Bishop Museum Archives, Honolulu, HI.

119. Annual Report of Hawaii Tourist Bureau, December 31, 1936, Box 33, Folder 29, MS Group 239—Theo H. Davies & Co. Collection, Bernice Pauahi Bishop Museum Archives, Honolulu, HI.

120. Letter from Gov. Poindexter to George Armitage, Executive Secretary of HTB, August 26, 1936, GOV8 Folder 27, Gov. Joseph Poindexter Collection, Hawai'i State Archives, Honolulu, HI.

121. Annual Report of Hawaii Tourist Bureau, 1931, GOV7, Folder 16, Gov. Lawrence M. Judd Collection, Hawai'i State Archives, Honolulu, HI.

122. Note from the Hawaii Tourist Bureau, 1934, GOV7, Folder 16, Gov. Lawrence M. Judd Collection, Hawai'i State Archives, Honolulu, HI.

123. Report for June, 1935 to Committee Members, Hawaii Tourist Bureau, June 1935, Box 33, Folder 29, MS Group 239—Theo H. Davies & Co. Collection, Bernice Pauahi Bishop Museum Archives, Honolulu, HI.

124. Annual Report of Hawaii Tourist Bureau, 1931, GOV7, Folder 16, Gov. Lawrence M. Judd Collection, Hawai'i State Archives, Honolulu, HI. See also: Report for May 1935 to Committee Members, Hawaii Tourist Bureau, May 1935, Box 33, Folder 29, MS Group 239—Theo H. Davies & Co. Collection, Bernice Pauahi Bishop Museum Archives, Honolulu, HI.

125. Hawaii Tourist Bureau Proposed Budget 1933–1934, circa 1933, GOV8 Folder 27, Gov. Joseph Poindexter Collection, Hawai'i State Archives, Honolulu, HI.

126. "Hawaii, Here We Come," *Variety*, November 18, 1941, 19.

127. Imada, 156.

128. Ghareeb and Cox, 244, documented the company's experiences shooting part of *Hawaiian Travelogues* (1930) aboard one of the LASSCO ships, the SS *City of Los Angeles*.

129. James Mak, "Creating 'Paradise of the Pacific': How Tourism Began in Hawaii," *UHERO Working Paper No. 2015-1*, Economic Research Organization at the University of Hawai'i, February 2015, 43.

130. Report of Executive Secretary, Hawaii Tourist Bureau, April 1934, Box 33, Folder 29, MS Group 239—Theo H. Davies & Co. Collection, Bernice Pauahi Bishop Museum Archives, Honolulu, HI.

131. Report of Executive Secretary, Hawaii Tourist Bureau, April 1934, Box 33, Folder 29, MS Group 239—Theo H. Davies & Co. Collection, Bernice Pauahi Bishop Museum Archives, Honolulu, HI.

132. Fifth General Report of Service, Hawaii Tourist Bureau, May 31, 1934, Box 33, Folder 29, MS Group 239—Theo H. Davies & Co. Collection, Bernice Pauahi Bishop Museum Archives, Honolulu, HI.

133. *Hawaii U.S.A.* (Honolulu: Hawaii Tourist Bureau, 1942), n.p.

134. Report for June, 1935 to Committee Members, Hawaii Tourist Bureau, June 1935, Box 33, Folder 29, MS Group 239—Theo H. Davies & Co. Collection, Bernice Pauahi Bishop Museum Archives, Honolulu, HI.

135. Letter from George Armitage, Executive Secretary of HTB, to Gov. Poindexter, June 13, 1938, GOV8 Folder 27, Gov. Joseph Poindexter Collection, Hawai'i State Archives, Honolulu, HI.

136. Hawaii Tourist Bureau 1948 Budget, circa 1948, Box 33, Folder 28, MS Group 239—Theo H. Davies & Co. Collection, Bernice Pauahi Bishop Museum Archives, Honolulu, HI.

137. 1958 Annual Report Hawaii Visitors Bureau, 1958, GOV12 Folder 84, Gov. William F. Quinn Collection, Hawai'i State Archives, Honolulu, HI.

138. Weekly Report of Activities Publicity Department Hawaii Tourist Bureau, August 20–25, 1950, Box 33, Folder 28, MS Group 239—Theo H. Davies & Co. Collection, Bernice Pauahi Bishop Museum Archives, Honolulu, HI.

139. 1958 Annual Report Hawaii Visitors Bureau, 1958, GOV12 Folder 84, Gov. William F. Quinn Collection, Hawai'i State Archives, Honolulu, HI.

140. Weekly Report of Activities Publicity Department Hawaii Tourist Bureau, August 20–25, 1950, Box 33, Folder 28, MS Group 239—Theo H. Davies & Co. Collection, Bernice Pauahi Bishop Museum Archives, Honolulu, HI.

141. Weekly Report of Activities Publicity Department Hawaii Tourist Bureau, September 5–9, 1950, Box 33, Folder 28, MS Group 239—Theo H. Davies & Co. Collection, Bernice Pauahi Bishop Museum Archives, Honolulu, HI.

142. Letter from Stewart Fern, Director of Public Relations, Hawaii Visitors Bureau, to Territorial Governor's Office, November 19, 1951, GOV10, Folder 9, Gov. Oren E. Long Collection, Hawai'i State Archives, Honolulu, HI.

143. "Television Pictures to Have Isle Setting," *Honolulu Star-Bulletin*, February 14, 1952, 28.

144. Letter from Stewart Fern, Director of Public Relations, Hawaii Visitors Bureau, to Territorial Governor's Office, August 22, 1952, GOV10, Folder 9, Gov. Oren E. Long Collection, Hawai'i State Archives, Honolulu, HI.

145. Letter from Stewart Fern, Director of Public Relations, Hawaii Visitors Bureau, to Territorial Governor's Office, August 22, 1952, GOV10, Folder 9, Gov. Oren E. Long Collection, Hawai'i State Archives, Honolulu, HI.

146. Report of Executive Director, Hawaii Visitors Bureau, December, 28, 1954, GOV11 Folder 32, Gov. Samuel Wilder King Collection, Hawai'i State Archives, Honolulu, HI.

147. "Several Hundred on S.S. Lurline," *Wilmington Daily Press Journal* (Wilmington, CA), January 7, 1938, 5.

148. 1958 Annual Report Hawaii Visitors Bureau, 1958, GOV12 Folder 84, Gov. William F. Quinn Collection, Hawai'i State Archives, Honolulu, HI.

149. Annual Report of Hawaii Tourist Bureau, 1931, GOV7, Folder 16, Gov. Lawrence M. Judd Collection, Hawai'i State Archives, Honolulu, HI.

150. Qtd. in "Charlie Chan Story May Be Filmed Here," *Honolulu Advertiser*, February 27, 1931, 2.

151. Ghareeb and Cox, 165.

152. Ghareeb and Cox, 165.

153. "Mrs. Weber to Film *Cane Fire* on Kauai," *Honolulu Advertiser*, August 24, 1933, 1. See also: "Shooting of *Cane Fire* Begins," *Honolulu Advertiser* (7 September 1933), 7.
154. Brown, 121.
155. Rick Altman, *The American Film Musical* (Bloomington: Indiana University Press, 1987), 200.
156. Altman, 251–252.
157. Altman, 252.
158. Dean MacCannell, *The Tourist: A New Theory of the Leisure Class* (Berkeley: University of California Press, 1999), 94.
159. Desmond, 111.
160. Owens, 79.
161. Schmitt, 2.
162. Brown, 126.
163. Bailey and Farber, 39.
164. "In Nearby Theatres," *Pottsville Republican* (Pottsville, PA), May 12, 1937, 6.
165. "Bing Crosby Is Due at Fox on Thursday," *San Francisco Examiner*, March 23, 1937, 22.
166. *My emphasis.* "Bing Crosby's Latest in 'Waikiki Wedding,'" *Culver Citizen* (Culver, IN), April 1937, 7.
167. "Theatre-Goers Will See Film 'Waikiki Wedding,'" *Bristol Daily Courier* (Bristol, PA), May 10, 1937, 1.
168. "Approaching Screen," *Baltimore Sun* (28 March 1937), 43.
169. Houston Wood, *Displacing Natives: The Rhetorical Production of Hawai'i* (Lanham, MD: Rowman & Littlefield, 1999), 117.
170. Frank Nugent, "The Screen," *New York Times*, Sep 29, 1939, 27.
171. "*Moonlight in Hawaii*," *Variety*, October 15, 1941, 8.
172. "The Exhibitor Has His Say," *Boxoffice*, April 8, 1939, 34.
173. "The Exhibitor Has His Say," *Boxoffice*, April 8, 1939, 34.
174. Edwin Schallert, "Bing Crosby's Next Film, '*Waikiki Wedding*,' Will Be Produced in Color," *Los Angeles Times*, August 4, 1936, 41.
175. "Locale for Gams," *Variety*, August 27, 1941, 5.
176. "*Song of the Islands*," *Variety*, February 4, 1942, 8.
177. Brown, 127.
178. "*Song of the Islands*," *Variety*, February 4, 1942, 8.
179. Bailey and Farber, 38.
180. Bailey and Farber, 39.
181. Lewis, 124.
182. "*Song of the Islands*," *New York Times*, March 12, 1942, n.p.

Chapter 2

1. Robert C. Schmitt, *Hawai'i in the Movies, 1898–1959* (Honolulu: University of Hawai'i, 1999), 5.

2. Beth Bailey and David Farber, *The First Strange Place: Race and Sex in World War II Hawaii* (Baltimore, MD: Johns Hopkins University Press, 1994), 15.

3. As qtd. in Kevin Thomas, "Dec. 7, 1941: It Happens Again in *Tora! Tora!*," *Los Angeles Times*, August 25, 1968, 14.

4. Orvar Lofgren, *On Holiday: A History of Vacationing* (Berkeley: University of California Press, 1999), 217.

5. Norman Douglas and Ngaire Douglas, "Tourism in the Pacific: Historical Factors," in *Tourism in the Pacific: Issues and Cases*, ed. C. Michael Hall and Stephen J. Page (New York: International Thomson Business Press, 1996), 27.

6. Robert Burgoyne, *The Hollywood Historical Film* (Hoboken, NJ: Blackwell, 2008), 2.

7. Lawrence Suid, "Pearl Harbor: More or Less," *Air Power History* 48.3 (Fall 2001): 38.

8. Robert Eberwein, *The Hollywood War Film* (Hoboken, NJ: Blackwell, 2009), 76.

9. Arthur F. McClure, "Hollywood at War: The American Motion Picture and World War II," *Journal of Popular Film* 1.2 (Spring 1972): 123.

10. Thomas M. Pryor, "MGM Plans Film on Pearl Harbor," *New York Times*, April 12, 1956, 27.

11. Eberwein, 29.

12. Pam Cook, *Screening the Past: Memory and Nostalgia in Cinema* (New York: Routledge, 2005), 11.

13. Vernadette Vicuña Gonzalez, *Securing Paradise: Tourism and Militarism in Hawai'i and the Philippines* (Durham, NC: Duke University Press, 2013), 119.

14. Mabel Thomas, "To the Shores of Waikiki," *Variety*, November 26, 1941, 2. The context was a crew in Honolulu to shoot footage for the war film *To the Shores of Tripoli*, which could not be shot in the Mediterranean region given the conflict in the European theater already underway. Somewhat amusingly, the trade paper then reported less than two weeks later that the crew had gone missing in the wake of the attack—only to reappear unharmed a week after that.

15. Mabel Thomas, "Variety Correspondent Pens Graphic Picture of Terror Striking Honolulu," *Variety*, January 9, 1942, 2, 52.

16. Gonzalez, 116.

17. Svetlana Boym, *The Future of Nostalgia* (New York: Basic Books, 2001), xiii.

18. Douglas and Douglas, 27–28.

19. Paul G. Craig, *The Future Growth of Hawaiian Tourism and Its Impact on the State and the Neighbor Islands* (Honolulu, HI: University of Hawai'i Economic Research Center, 1963), 69.

20. Mabel Thomas, "Three Months after Pearl Harbor," *Variety*, March 25, 1942, 55.

21. As qtd. in Peter Bogdanovich, *John Ford* (Berkeley: University of California Press, 1978), 136.

22. Ivan Spear, "*From Here to Eternity* a Truly Great Picture," *Boxoffice*, August 1, 1953, 20.

23. "*From Here to Eternity*," *Variety*, July 29, 1953, 6.

24. "From Here to Eternity Makes Record Hit," *Atlanta Daily World*, September 12, 1953, 6.

25. Bailey and Farber, 46.

26. "*From Here to Eternity* in Jersey City Disfavor," *New York Times*, October 25, 1953, 32.

27. George Stevens Jr., *Conversations with the Great Moviemakers of Hollywood's Golden Age* (New York: Alfred A. Knopf, 2006), 418.

28. Edwin Shallert, "*Here to Eternity* Blasts Viewers with Atomic Power," *Los Angeles Times*, October 1, 1953, B11.

29. Bailey and Farber, 24.

30. Shallert, B11.

31. Claudia Sternberg, "Real-Life References in Four Fred Zinnemann Films," *Film Criticism* 18/19.3/1 (Spring–Fall 1994): 112.

32. Shallert, B11.

33. "'From Here to Eternity," *New York Herald Tribune*, November 2, 1952, 1.

34. "*Stockade* Opens Tonight; Based on *Eternity* Section," *New York Herald Tribune*, February 4, 1954, 17.

35. "Navy Rejects *Eternity* Film but Army Is 'Stuck' with It," *Daily Boston Globe*, August 29, 1953, 1.

36. "*From Here to Eternity*," *Picturegoer*, November 14, 1953, 22.

37. DeSoto Brown, *Hawaii Recalls: Selling Romance to America—Nostalgic Images of the Hawaiian Islands, 1910–1950* (Honolulu: Editions, 1982), 110.

38. Linda B. Arthur, "The Aloha Shirt and Ethnicity in Hawai'i," *Textile: The Journal of Cloth and Culture* 4.1 (Spring 2006): 24.

39. *My emphasis*. Bailey and Farber, 125–126.

40. Sternberg, 114.

41. "Columbia Lines Up 'Here to Eternity,'" *New York Herald Tribune*, February 27, 1953, 10.

42. "Readers Voice Reactions to Some Recent Innovations and Current Feature," *New York Times*, September 27, 1953, 123.

43. Spear, 20.

44. "Mr. Shakespeare: Mr. Jones," *New York Daily News*, August 17, 1953, n.p.

45. "*Eternity* for Free James House and Miffs Columbia," *Variety*, March 24, 1954, 71.

46. "*Eternity* for Free James House and Miffs Columbia," *Variety*, March 24, 1954, 71.

47. "*Eternity* for Free James House and Miffs Columbia," *Variety*, March 24, 1954, 71.

48. Sven A. Kirsten, *The Book of Tiki: The Cult of Polynesian Pop in Fifties America* (Los Angeles: Taschen, 2000), 69–70.

49. Kirsten, 74.

50. Francesco Adinolfi, *Mondo Exotica: Sounds, Visions, Obsessions of the Cocktail Generation* (Durham, NC: Duke University Press, 2008), 4.

51. As qtd. in Peter Bart, "Hollywood Movies into a Cycle of Films about World War II," *New York Times*, October 5, 1964, 41.
52. "*In Harm's Way*," *New York Amsterdam News*, April 17, 1965, 21.
53. "*In Harm's Way*," *Monthly Film Bulletin*, January 1, 1965, 87.
54. Kenneth Tynan, "Preminger at Sea: Films," *Observer*, May 16, 1965, 25.
55. "Century's Hawaiian Theme for 'Harm's Way' Bally," *Boxoffice*, August 30, 1965, a2.
56. Elspeth Grant, "The Harm's Already Done," *Tatler and Bystander*, May 26, 1965, 444.
57. Bart, 41.
58. As qtd. in Bart, 41.
59. *My emphasis*. Vera Dika, *Recycled Culture in Contemporary Art and Film: The Uses of Nostalgia* (Cambridge, UK: Cambridge University Press, 2003), 80.
60. Christine Sprengler, *Screening Nostalgia: Populuxe Props and Technicolor Aesthetics in Contemporary American Film* (New York: Berghahn Books, 2009).
61. "Honolulu and Other Hawaiian Areas," *Boxoffice*, March 15, 1965, W-8.
62. Lawrence Suid, "Pearl Harbor: More or Less," *Air Power History* 48.3 (Fall 2001): 38.
63. Suid, 38.
64. Kevin Thomas, 14.
65. "Buying & Booking Guide: *Tora! Tora! Tora!*," *Independent Film Journal*, September 30, 1970, 1345.
66. Kay Bourne, "*Tora! Tora! Tora!* Has Angle," *Bay State Banner*, October 15, 1970, 11.
67. Suid, 38.
68. Vincent Canby, "Tora-ble, Tora-ble, Tora-ble," *New York Times*, October 4, 1970, 7.
69. "Tie-Ins and Advance Publicity Aid Engagement of *Tora! Tora! Tora!*," *Boxoffice*, June 28, 1971, a2.
70. "Showmandiser: Pearl Harbor Survivors Attend 'Tora!' Showing," *Boxoffice*, February 8, 1971, a1.
71. Gary Arnold, "Remember Pearl Harbor? Now It's a Movie," *Washington Post*, August 16, 1970, E3.
72. Christopher Anderson, *Hollywood TV: The Studio System in the Fifties* (Austin: University of Texas Press, 1994), 146.
73. Rick Altman, *The American Film Musical* (Bloomington: Indiana University Press, 1987), 251.
74. Progress Report: The USS Arizona Memorial at Pearl Harbor, January 28, 1959, COM30 Box 5, *This Is Your Life* Folder, The Pacific War Memorial Commission Collection, Hawai'i State Archives, Honolulu, HI.
75. Letter from Howard H. Ross to H. Tucker Gratz, December 3, 1958, COM30 Box 5, *This Is Your Life* Folder, The Pacific War Memorial Commission Collection, Hawai'i State Archives, Honolulu, HI.

Notes to Chapter 2

76. Progress Report: The USS Arizona Memorial at Pearl Harbor, January 28, 1959, COM30 Box 5, *This Is Your Life* Folder, The Pacific War Memorial Commission Collection, Hawai'i State Archives, Honolulu, HI.

77. Letter from Axel Gruenberg to H. Tucker Gratz, July 31, 1958, COM30 Box 5, The Pacific War Memorial Commission Collection, *This is Your Life* Folder, Hawai'i State Archives, Honolulu, HI. See also: Letter from Howard H. Ross to Joe Custer, March 23, 1961, COM30 Box 5, *This Is Your Life* Folder, The Pacific War Memorial Commission Collection, Hawai'i State Archives, Honolulu, HI.

78. Progress Report: The USS Arizona Memorial at Pearl Harbor, January 28, 1959, COM30 Box 5, *This Is Your Life* Folder, The Pacific War Memorial Commission Collection, Hawai'i State Archives, Honolulu, HI.

79. Letter from Howard H. Ross to H. Tucker Gratz, December 3, 1958, COM30 Box 5, *This Is Your Life* Folder, The Pacific War Memorial Commission Collection, Hawai'i State Archives, Honolulu, HI.

80. Progress Report: The USS Arizona Memorial at Pearl Harbor, January 28, 1959, COM30 Box 5, *This Is Your Life* Folder, The Pacific War Memorial Commission Collection, Hawai'i State Archives, Honolulu, HI.

81. Progress Report: The USS Arizona Memorial at Pearl Harbor, January 28, 1959, COM30 Box 5, *This Is Your Life* Folder, The Pacific War Memorial Commission Collection, Hawai'i State Archives, Honolulu, HI.

82. Progress Report: The USS Arizona Memorial at Pearl Harbor, January 28, 1959, COM30 Box 5, *This Is Your Life* Folder, The Pacific War Memorial Commission Collection, Hawai'i State Archives, Honolulu, HI.

83. Progress Report: The USS Arizona Memorial at Pearl Harbor, January 28, 1959, COM30 Box 5, *This Is Your Life* Folder, The Pacific War Memorial Commission Collection, Hawai'i State Archives, Honolulu, HI.

84. Letter from Howard H. Ross to H. Tucker Gratz, December 3, 1958, COM30 Box 5, *This Is Your Life* Folder, The Pacific War Memorial Commission Collection, Hawai'i State Archives, Honolulu, HI.

85. Letter from H. Tucker Gratz to Eddie Sherman, November 19, 1960, COM30 Box 5, *This Is Your Life* Folder, The Pacific War Memorial Commission Collection, Hawai'i State Archives, Honolulu, HI.

86. Letter from H. Tucker Gratz to Eddie Sherman, November 19, 1960, COM30 Box 5, *This Is Your Life* Folder, The Pacific War Memorial Commission Collection, Hawai'i State Archives, Honolulu, HI.

87. Letter from Howard H. Ross to Joe Custer, March 23, 1961, COM30 Box 5, *This Is Your Life* Folder, The Pacific War Memorial Commission Collection, Hawai'i State Archives, Honolulu, HI.

88. Sean Redmond, "Extraordinary Television Time Travel and the Wonderful End to the Working Day," *Thesis Eleven* 131.1 (2015): 54–64.

89. David Lowenthal, *The Past Is a Foreign Country* (Cambridge, UK: Cambridge University Press, 1985), 28.

90. Dika, 144, 145.

91. See: Bailey and Farber, "Hotel Street Sex," *The First Strange Place*, 95–132.
92. As qtd. in Kevin Thomas, 14.

Chapter 3

1. Gavan Daws, *Shoal of Time: A History of the Hawaiian Islands* (Honolulu: University of Hawai'i Press, 1968), 383.
2. Vernadette Vicuña Gonzalez, *Securing Paradise: Tourism and Militarism in Hawai'i and the Philippines* (Durham, NC: Duke University Press, 2013), 116.
3. Daws, 368.
4. Daws, 369.
5. *Hawaii—49th State* (television script), circa 1954, Box 542, Folder 1, National Broadcasting Company Records, 1921–1976, Wisconsin Center for Film and Theater Research, University of Wisconsin Archives, Madison, WI.
6. Roger Bell, *Last among Equals: Hawaiian Statehood and American Politics* (Honolulu: University of Hawai'i Press, 1984), 209–210.
7. Bell, 261–262.
8. Bell, 254.
9. I have previously developed the notion of a "post-racial whiteness" in earlier scholarship on media history. What I would add here are the ways in which it also reinforces a neoliberal mentality that seeks to erase the issue of class difference as well by conflating class prejudice with racial prejudices. See also: Jason Sperb, *Disney's Most Notorious Film: Race, Convergence, and the Hidden Histories of "Song of the South"* (Austin: University of Texas Press, 2012), and Jason Sperb, "*Islands* of Detroit: Affect, Nostalgia and Whiteness," *Culture, Theory and Critique* 49.2 (October 2008): 183–201.
10. Lori Pierce, "'The Whites Have Created Modern Honolulu': Ethnicity, Racial Stratification, and the Discourse of Aloha," in *Racial Thinking in the United States: Uncompleted Independence*, ed. Paul Spickard and G. Reginald Daniel (Notre Dame, IN: University of Notre Dame Press, 2004), 127.
11. Alan Marcus, "The Interracial Romance as Primal Drama: *Touch of Evil* and *Diamond Head*," *Film Studies* 11 (Winter 2007): 22.
12. "Film Review: *Diamond Head*," *Variety*, December 26, 1962, 6.
13. Marcus, 23.
14. Marcus, 18.
15. Judy Rohrer, *Haoles in Hawaii: Race and Ethnicity in Hawaii* (Honolulu: University of Hawai'i Press, 2010), 6.
16. Christine Skwiot, *The Purposes of Paradise: US Tourism in Cuba and Hawaii* (Philadelphia: University of Pennsylvania Press, 2010), 172.
17. Gonzalez, 35.
18. Bell, 253.
19. Bell, 253.

20. Skwiot, 184.
21. Skwiot, 187.
22. Max Lerner, "Hawaii Example," *New Pittsburgh Courier*, April 10, 1965, 9.
23. Daws, 391.
24. Bell, 293.
25. Skwiot, 177.
26. Skwiot, 177.
27. "More News about *This Is America*," September 8, 1947, COM18 Box 7, Hawaii Statehood Commission Collection, Hawai'i State Archives, Honolulu, HI.
28. Barsam, "'This Is America': Documentaries for Theatres, 1942–1951," *Cinema Journal* 12.2 (Spring 1973): 27.
29. The 49th State Exhibitors Sale Guide, 1947, COM18 Box 7, Hawaii Statehood Commission Collection, Hawai'i State Archives, Honolulu, HI.
30. "More News about *This Is America*," September 8, 1947, COM18 Box 7, Hawaii Statehood Commission Collection, Hawai'i State Archives, Honolulu, HI.
31. "More News about *This Is America*," September 8, 1947, COM18 Box 7, Hawaii Statehood Commission Collection, Hawai'i State Archives, Honolulu, HI.
32. The 49th State Exhibitors Sale Guide, 1947, COM18 Box 7, Hawaii Statehood Commission Collection, Hawai'i State Archives, Honolulu, HI.
33. Memorandum Regarding New York Trip January 15–16, 1947, COM18 Box 7, Hawaii Statehood Commission Collection, Hawai'i State Archives, Honolulu, HI.
34. Daws, 380.
35. Bell, 121.
36. Letter from Otto Janssen to the Office of the Secretary of the Interior, September 29, 1947, COM18 Box 7, Hawaii Statehood Commission Collection, Hawai'i State Archives, Honolulu, HI.
37. Remarks of Philip Reisman Jr., Supervisor of Production, RKO Pathé "This Is America" Series, October 7, 1947, COM18 Box 7, Hawaii Statehood Commission Collection, Hawai'i State Archives, Honolulu, HI.
38. Letter from Ralph Beck, Chairman, Advertising and Publicity Committee, Hawaii Visitors Bureau, to Arthur Manson, National Director of Advertising and Publicity, Stanley Warner Cinerama Corporation, November 13, 1958, GOV12 Folder 80, Gov. William F. Quinn Collection, Hawai'i State Archives, Honolulu, HI.
39. Hawaii Visitors Bureau Manual of Organization, 1958, GOV12 Folder 84, Gov. William F. Quinn Collection, Hawai'i State Archives, Honolulu, HI.
40. Letter from William Cogswell, Executive Secretary of the Hawaii Visitors Bureau to James Tabor, Vice President of Theo H. Davies & Co., Ltd., July 18, 1958, Box 33, Folder 28, MS Group 239—Theo H. Davies & Co. Collection, Bernice Pauahi Bishop Museum Archives, Honolulu, HI.
41. Minutes of Meeting of the Publicity and Promotion Sub-Committee, October 28, 1958, GOV12 Folder 80, Gov. William F. Quinn Collection, Hawai'i State Archives, Honolulu, HI.

42. Rough draft of letter from William F. Quinn, Territorial Governor, to Dwight Eisenhower, President of the United States, 1958, GOV12 Folder 80, Gov. William F. Quinn Collection, Hawai'i State Archives, Honolulu, HI.

43. Minutes of Meeting of the Publicity and Promotion Sub-Committee, October 28, 1958, GOV12 Folder 80, Gov. William F. Quinn Collection, Hawai'i State Archives, Honolulu, HI.

44. Letter from Arthur Manson, National Director of Advertising and Publicity, Stanley Warner Cinerama Corporation, to Ralph Beck, Chairman, Advertising and Publicity Committee, Hawaii Visitors Bureau, November 10, 1958, GOV12 Folder 80, Gov. William F. Quinn Collection, Hawai'i State Archives, Honolulu, HI.

45. Letter from Gardiner B. Jones, Administrative Assistant to Managing Director, Hawaii Visitors Bureau, to Arthur Manson, National Director of Advertising and Publicity, Stanley Warner Cinerama Corporation, November 6, 1958, GOV12 Folder 80, Gov. William F. Quinn Collection, Hawai'i State Archives, Honolulu, HI

46. Letter from William F. Quinn, Territorial Governor of Hawaii, to Robert Gray, Secretary of the Cabinet, December 4, 1958, GOV12 Folder 80, Gov. William F. Quinn Collection, Hawai'i State Archives, Honolulu, HI.

47. Letter from Robert Gray, Secretary of the Cabinet, to William F. Quinn, Territorial Governor of Hawaii, November 14, 1958, GOV12 Folder 80, Gov. William F. Quinn Collection, Hawai'i State Archives, Honolulu, HI.

48. Letter from Carl Dudley to Ralph Beck, November 25, 1958, GOV12 Folder 80, Gov. William F. Quinn Collection, Hawai'i State Archives, Honolulu, HI.

49. Adria L. Imada, *Aloha America: Hula Circuits through the US Empire* (Durham, NC: Duke University Press, 2012), 183.

50. Imada, 182.

51. Skwiot, 168.

52. Imada, 184.

53. Imada, 185.

54. Jane Desmond, *Staging Tourism: Bodies on Display from Waikiki to Sea World* (Chicago: University of Chicago Press, 1999).

55. "Luau in Front, Thanks to Infrared Heating," *Boxoffice*, March 11, 1963, a3.

56. "Travel Style Show at Preview Keys Fruitful Diamond Head Store Tie In," *Boxoffice*, March 11, 1963, a3.

57. "Heston No. 1 Jet-Age Star," *Los Angeles Times*, February 26, 1963, 24.

58. William Herbert, "Hollywood Report," *Boxoffice*, February 5, 1962, 16.

59. Theodore Taylor, "*Diamond Head* Emerges in Spite of Storms: Cold Shoulder," *New York Times*, April 29, 1962, 125.

60. "Pictures: Heston Resumes with Sam Bronston," *Variety*, May 2, 1962, 3.

61. Taylor, 125.

62. "Some of Industry's Ills Outlined by Jerry Bresler," *Boxoffice*, January 28, 1963, 8.
63. Taylor, 125.
64. "Pictures: Go for Diamond Head," *Variety*, October 10, 1962, 14.
65. "Pictures: Go for *Diamond Head*," *Variety*, October 10, 1962, 14.
66. "Feature Reviews: Diamond Head," *Boxoffice*, January 7, 1963, b11.
67. Marcus, 14.
68. Marcus, 26.
69. Marcus, 22.
70. Skwiot, 177.
71. "How to Give a Story a Bearable End," *Guardian*, July 8, 1963, 4.
72. Pierce, 126.
73. Mae Tinee, "Island Film Well Cast but 'Sudsy': *Diamond Head*," *Chicago Daily Tribune*, February 11, 1963, b10.
74. Marcus, 22.
75. "17 Theatres Book *Diamond Head*," *Atlanta Journal and Constitution*, April 14, 1963, 5D.
76. Marcus, 20.
77. Marjory Adams, "*Diamond Head* Big but Plot Is Sprawling," *Boston Globe*, February 8, 1963, 12.
78. Marjory Adams, "*Diamond Head* Big but Plot Is Sprawling," *Boston Globe*, February 8, 1963, 12.
79. "*Diamond Head*," *New York Times*, February 21, 1963, 5.
80. Mae Tinee, "Island Film Well Cast but 'Sudsy': *Diamond Head*," *Chicago Daily Tribune*, February 11, 1963, b10.
81. "Film Review: *Diamond Head*," *Variety*, December 26, 1962, 6.
82. "The Exhibitor Has His Say about Pictures," *Boxoffice*, July 22, 1963, a4.
83. "Film Firsts: Diamond Head," *New Pittsburgh Courier*, March 9, 1963, 8.
84. Mae Tinee, "Island Film Well Cast but 'Sudsy': *Diamond Head*," *Chicago Daily Tribune*, February 11, 1963, b10.
85. Marcus, 25.
86. Bell, 253.
87. As qtd. in Daws, 386.
88. Daws, 388.
89. Bell, 255.
90. Rohrer, 63.
91. Sidney Gulick, *Mixing the Races in Hawaii: A Study of the Coming Neo-Hawaiian Race* (Honolulu: Hawaiian Board Books Rooms, 1937), 1.
92. Gulick, 2.
93. Rohrer, 63.
94. Rohrer, 41.
95. "Film Review: *Diamond Head*," *Variety*, December 26, 1962, 6.

96. Marjory Adams, "*Diamond Head* Big but Plot Is Sprawling," *Boston Globe*, February 8, 1963, 12.

97. Philip Scheuer, "Dynasty in Hawaii Finds Going Rough: 'King' Heston Rides for Fall in Movie of *Diamond Head*," *Los Angeles Times*, February 15, 1963, D13.

98. "*Diamond Head*," *New York Times*, February 21, 1963, 5.

99. Rohrer, 5.

100. Rohrer, 7.

101. Bell, 259.

102. George Feinstein, "Hawaii Saga Has Eye on Hollywood," *Los Angeles Times*, June 26, 1960, B9.

103. Mary Ross, "A New State, a New Novel," *New York Herald Tribune*, July 3, 1960, D5.

104. George Feinstein, "Hawaii Saga Has Eye on Hollywood," *Los Angeles Times*, June 26, 1960, B9.

105. "Diamond Head Tells Story of Today's Hawaii," *Chicago Daily Defender*, March 5, 1963, 16.

106. George Feinstein, "Hawaii Saga Has Eye on Hollywood," *Los Angeles Times*, June 26, 1960, B9.

107. James Kelly, "Hawaiian Miscellany: *Diamond Head*. By Peter Gilman," *New York Times*, June 26, 1960, BR26.

108. "Pictures: Go for *Diamond Head*," *Variety*, October 10, 1962, 14.

109. Marcus, 23.

110. Marcus, 24.

111. Marcus, 23.

112. Bell, 260.

Chapter 4

1. Clayton Kilpatrick, "Hawaii's Entire Saga in Michener Novel," *Sun*, November 22, 1959, A9.

2. Judy Rohrer, *Haoles in Hawaiʻi* (Honolulu: University of Hawaiʻi Press, 2010), 11–12.

3. Haunani-Kay Trask, *From a Native Daughter: Colonialism and Sovereignty in Hawaiʻi* (Monroe, ME: Common Courage Press, 1993), 149.

4. James A. Michener, *Hawaii* (New York: Fawcett Crest, 1959), v.

5. Trask, 149.

6. Group Sales Manual, 1966, Box 4, Folder 10, U.S. Mss. 87AN; Disc 98A, Walter Mirisch Papers, Wisconsin Center for Film and Theater Research, University of Wisconsin Archives, Madison, WI, 2.

7. Christine Skwiot, *The Purposes of Paradise: US Tourism and Empire in Cuba and Hawaiʻi* (Philadelphia: University of Pennsylvania Press, 2010), 176.

8. Maurice Dolbier, "Hawaii's Non-Political Representative," *New York Herald Tribune*, December 6, 1959, E2.

9. "Best Read Best-Seller," 1966, Box 4, Folder 8, U.S. Mss. 87AN; Disc 98A, Walter Mirisch Papers, Wisconsin Center for Film and Theater Research, University of Wisconsin Archives, Madison, WI, 1.

10. "Important Information about *Hawaii*," 1966, Box 4, Folder 3, U.S. Mss. 87AN; Disc 98A, Walter Mirisch Papers, Wisconsin Center for Film and Theater Research, University of Wisconsin Archives, Madison, WI, 1.

11. Murray Schumach, "Hawaii á la Hollywood: Maze of Complications Keeps Michener Film from Cameras," *New York Times*, August 11, 1963, 95.

12. 1958 Annual Report Hawaii Visitors Bureau, 1958, GOV12 Folder 84, Gov. William F. Quinn Collection, Hawai'i State Archives, Honolulu, HI.

13. Rob Wilson, *Reimagining the American Pacific: From South Pacific to Bamboo Ridge and Beyond* (Durham, NC: Duke University Press, 2000), 165.

14. "Pictures: All-Time Box Office Champs," *Variety*, January 7, 1970, 25.

15. Rohrer, 63.

16. Jeffrey Geiger, *Facing the Pacific: Polynesia and the U.S. Imperial Imagination* (Honolulu: University of Hawai'i Press, 2007), 2.

17. Qtd. in Richard Lillard, "Panorama of Pineapple Paradise," *Los Angeles Times*, February 25, 1968, d44.

18. *My emphasis*. "Great Books Make Great Movies," 1966, Box 4, Folder 7, U.S. Mss. 87AN; Disc 98A, Walter Mirisch Papers, Wisconsin Center for Film and Theater Research, University of Wisconsin Archives, Madison, WI, 2.

19. Cristina Bacchilega, *Legendary Hawai'i and the Politics of Place: Tradition, Translation, and Tourism* (Philadelphia: University of Pennsylvania Press, 2007), 20.

20. Delia Malia Caparoso Konzett, *Hollywood's Hawaii: Race, Nation, and War* (New Brunswick, NJ: Rutgers University Press, 2017), 5.

21. Bacchilega, 1.

22. Bacchilega, 5.

23. Robert Stam and Louise Spence, "Colonialism, Racism, and Representation," *Screen* 24.2 (1983): 3.

24. Rohrer, 18.

25. Skwiot, 178.

26. Trask, 7.

27. Rohrer, 18.

28. Gavan Daws, *Shoal of Time: A History of the Hawaiian Islands* (Honolulu: University of Hawai'i Press, 1968), 65.

29. Samuel I. Bellman, "Michener Documents Hawaii Ethnic Praises," *Los Angeles Times*, January 24, 1960, E6.

30. Rona Tamiko Halualani, *In the Name of Hawaiians: Native Identities and Cultural Politics* (Minneapolis: University of Minnesota Press, 2002), 134.

31. Paul Lyons, *American Pacificism: Oceania in the U.S. Imagination* (New York: Routledge, 2006), 151.

32. Houston Wood, *Displacing Natives: The Rhetorical Production of Hawai'i* (Lanham, MD: Rowman & Littlefield, 1999), 48.
33. Stephen H. Sumida, "Reevaluating Mark Twain's Novel of Hawaii," *American Literature* 61.4 (December 1989): 587.
34. *A Writer's Guide to Hawaii Five-O*, 1967, Box 26, Folder 1, U.S. Mss. 130AN, Norman Katkov Papers, Wisconsin Center for Film and Theater Research, University of Wisconsin Archives, Madison, WI, 4.
35. Bacchilega, 9.
36. Bacchilega, 2.
37. James A. Michener, *Tales of the South Pacific* (New York: Curtis, 1946), 179–180.
38. Francesco Adinolfi, *Mondo Exotica: Sounds, Visions, Obsessions of the Cocktail Generation* (Durham, NC: Duke University Press, 2008), 6.
39. Adinolfi, 165.
40. Maurice Dolbier, "Hawaii's Non-Political Representative," *New York Herald Tribune*, December 6, 1959, E2.
41. "Michener Race Charge Disputed," *Atlanta Constitution*, April 9, 1961, 13.
42. Skwiot, 176.
43. James A. Michener, "Hawaii's Statehood Urged: Population Is Declared Politically Mature, Loyal to United States," *New York Times*, January 1, 1959, 30.
44. Wood, 90.
45. James A. Michener, "Hawaii's Statehood Urged: Population is Declared Politically Mature, Loyal to United States," *New York Times*, January 1, 1959, 30.
46. Maurice Dolbier, "Hawaii's Non-Political Representative," *New York Herald Tribune*, December 6, 1959, E2.
47. "Elmer Bernstein's Authentic Score for Film, *Hawaii*," 1966, Box 4, Folder 7, U.S. Mss. 87AN; Disc 98A, Walter Mirisch Papers, Wisconsin Center for Film and Theater Research, University of Wisconsin Archives, Madison, WI, 1.
48. Wood, 94.
49. Michener, *Hawaii*, 973.
50. Wood, 91.
51. John K. Hutchens, "*Hawaii*," *New York Herald Tribune*, November 20, 1959, 17.
52. Samuel I. Bellman, "Michener Documents Hawaii Ethnic Praises," *Los Angeles Times*, January 24, 1960, E6.
53. John K. Hutchens, "*Hawaii*," *New York Herald Tribune*, November 20, 1959, 17.
54. Samuel I. Bellman, "Michener Documents Hawaii Ethnic Praises," *Los Angeles Times*, January 24, 1960, E6.
55. John K. Hutchens, "*Hawaii*," *New York Herald Tribune*, November 20, 1959, 17.
56. John K. Hutchens, "*Hawaii*," *New York Herald Tribune*, November 20, 1959, 17.

57. Samuel I. Bellman, "Michener Documents Hawaii Ethnic Praises," *Los Angeles Times*, January 24, 1960, E6.

58. Murray Schumach, "Hawaii á la Hollywood: Maze of Complications Keeps Michener Film from Cameras," *New York Times*, August 11, 1963, 95.

59. Tom Wood, "Doing *Hawaii* on $14,000,000: That Was the Price Tag of the Film Based on James Michener's Massive Novel," *Los Angeles Times*, October 23, 1966, W28.

60. Murray Schumach, "Hawaii á la Hollywood: Maze of Complications Keeps Michener Film from Cameras," *New York Times*, August 11, 1963, 95.

61. Marjory Rutherford, "Michener 'Success Formula' Pays Off with *Hawaii*," *Atlanta Constitution*, November 22, 1959, 2E.

62. Tom Wood, "Doing Hawaii on $14,000,000: That Was the Price Tag of the Film Based on James Michener's Massive Novel," *Los Angeles Times*, October 23, 1966, W28.

63. Murray Schumach, "Hawaii á la Hollywood: Maze of Complications Keeps Michener Film from Cameras," *New York Times*, August 11, 1963, 95.

64. Tom Wood, "Doing Hawaii on $14,000,000: That Was the Price Tag of the Film Based on James Michener's Massive Novel," *Los Angeles Times*, October 23, 1966, W28.

65. Tom Wood, "Doing Hawaii on $14,000,000: That Was the Price Tag of the Film Based on James Michener's Massive Novel," *Los Angeles Times*, October 23, 1966, W28.

66. Peter Bart, "*Hawaii* Awash," *New York Times*, June 6, 1965, X11.

67. Murray Schumach, "Hawaii á la Hollywood: Maze of Complications Keeps Michener Film from Cameras," *New York Times*, August 11, 1963, 95.

68. Murray Schumach, "Hawaii á la Hollywood: Maze of Complications Keeps Michener Film from Cameras," *New York Times*, August 11, 1963, 95.

69. Murray Schumach, "Hawaii á la Hollywood: Maze of Complications Keeps Michener Film from Cameras," *New York Times*, August 11, 1963, 95.

70. Tom Wood, "Doing Hawaii on $14,000,000: That Was the Price Tag of the Film Based on James Michener's Massive Novel," *Los Angeles Times*, October 23, 1966, W28.

71. Tom Wood, "Doing Hawaii on $14,000,000: That Was the Price Tag of the Film Based on James Michener's Massive Novel," *Los Angeles Times*, October 23, 1966, W28.

72. Tom Wood, "Doing Hawaii on $14,000,000: That Was the Price Tag of the Film Based on James Michener's Massive Novel," *Los Angeles Times*, October 23, 1966, W28.

73. Memo from Dalton Trumbo to Walter Mirisch and Fred Zinnemann, January 31, 1963, Box 19, Folder 6, U.S. Mss. 87AN; Disc 98A, Walter Mirisch Papers, Wisconsin Center for Film and Theater Research, University of Wisconsin Archives, Madison, WI, 1.

74. Dalton Trumbo notes on *Hawaii* script summary, February 12, 1963, Box 19, Folder 6, U.S. Mss. 87AN; Disc 98A, Walter Mirisch Papers, Wiscon-

sin Center for Film and Theater Research, University of Wisconsin Archives, Madison, WI, 1.

75. Dalton Trumbo notes on *Hawaii* script summary, February 12, 1963, Box 19, Folder 6, U.S. Mss. 87AN; Disc 98A, Walter Mirisch Papers, Wisconsin Center for Film and Theater Research, University of Wisconsin Archives, Madison, WI, 1.

76. Dalton Trumbo notes on *Hawaii* script summary, February 12, 1963, Box 19, Folder 6, U.S. Mss. 87AN; Disc 98A, Walter Mirisch Papers, Wisconsin Center for Film and Theater Research, University of Wisconsin Archives, Madison, WI, 2.

77. Dalton Trumbo notes on *Hawaii* script summary, February 12, 1963, Box 19, Folder 6, U.S. Mss. 87AN; Disc 98A, Walter Mirisch Papers, Wisconsin Center for Film and Theater Research, University of Wisconsin Archives, Madison, WI, 3.

78. Philip K. Scheuer, "*Hawaii*'s Direction by George Roy Hill: O'Briens Talk Pirandello; Who Needs Public Domain?" *Los Angeles Times*, April 27, 1964, C19.

79. Tom Wood, "Doing Hawaii on $14,000,000: That Was the Price Tag of the Film Based on James Michener's Massive Novel," *Los Angeles Times*, October 23, 1966, W28.

80. Tom Wood, "Doing Hawaii on $14,000,000: That Was the Price Tag of the Film Based on James Michener's Massive Novel," *Los Angeles Times*, October 23, 1966, W28.

81. Andrew Horton, *The Films of George Roy Hill* (New York: Columbia University Press, 1984), 54.

82. Philip K. Scheuer, "*Hawaii*—Trouble with Paradise," *Los Angeles Times*, August 29, 1965, B1, B11.

83. Vincent Canby, "Screen: *Hawaii*, Big Long Film, Has Its Premiere," *New York Times*, October 11, 1966, 54.

84. Vincent Canby, "A Critical Time for Circuses: Critics, Circuses," *New York Times*, October 23, 1966, X13.

85. Vincent Canby, "A Critical Time for Circuses: Critics, Circuses," *New York Times*, October 23, 1966, X13.

86. Terry Clifford, "Acting and Scenery Help *Hawaii* thru Three Long Hours," *Chicago Tribune*, October 20, 1966, D1.

87. Tom Wood, "Doing Hawaii on $14,000,000: That Was the Price Tag of the Film Based on James Michener's Massive Novel," *Los Angeles Times*, October 23, 1966, W28.

88. "The Nose Knows," 1966, Box 4, Folder 8, U.S. Mss. 87AN; Disc 98A, Walter Mirisch Papers, Wisconsin Center for Film and Theater Research, University of Wisconsin Archives, Madison, WI, 1.

89. Tom Wood, "Doing Hawaii on $14,000,000: That Was the Price Tag of the Film Based on James Michener's Massive Novel," *Los Angeles Times*, October 23, 1966, W28.

90. Vincent Canby, "Screen: *Hawaii*, Big Long Film, Has Its Premiere," *New York Times*, October 11, 1966, 54.

91. "Souvenir Program," 1966, Box 4, Folder 8, U.S. Mss. 87AN; Disc 98A, Walter Mirisch Papers, Wisconsin Center for Film and Theater Research, University of Wisconsin Archives, Madison, WI, 2.

92. "Elmer Bernstein's Authentic Score for Film, *Hawaii*," 1966, Box 4, Folder 7, U.S. Mss. 87AN; Disc 98A, Walter Mirisch Papers, Wisconsin Center for Film and Theater Research, University of Wisconsin Archives, Madison, WI, 1.

93. "Elmer Bernstein's Authentic Score for Film, *Hawaii*," 1966, Box 4, Folder 7, U.S. Mss. 87AN; Disc 98A, Walter Mirisch Papers, Wisconsin Center for Film and Theater Research, University of Wisconsin Archives, Madison, WI, 2.

94. "Column Items," 1966, Box 4, Folder 8, U.S. Mss. 87AN; Disc 98A, Walter Mirisch Papers, Wisconsin Center for Film and Theater Research, University of Wisconsin Archives, Madison, WI, 2.

95. Horace Sutton, "Aloha, Hollywood! It's Movietime in Hulaland These Days: Of All Places," *Washington Post*, August 29, 1965, G11.

96. Philip K. Scheuer, "*Hawaii*—Trouble with Paradise," *Los Angeles Times*, August 29, 1965, B1.

97. Hedda Hopper, "Sunny Skies No Good for Hawaii," *Los Angeles Times*, March 17, 1965, D15.

98. Tom Wood, "Doing Hawaii on $14,000,000: That Was the Price Tag of the Film Based on James Michener's Massive Novel," *Los Angeles Times*, October 23, 1966, W28.

99. Tom Wood, "Doing Hawaii on $14,000,000: That Was the Price Tag of the Film Based on James Michener's Massive Novel," *Los Angeles Times*, October 23, 1966, W28.

100. Philip K. Scheuer, "*Hawaii*—Trouble with Paradise," *Los Angeles Times*, August 29, 1965, B1.

101. Peter Bart, "*Hawaii* Changes Directors Twice: Hill Is Replaced by Hiller, Then Takes Over Again," *New York Times*, August 4, 1965, 22.

102. Vernadette Vicuña Gonzalez, *Securing Paradise: Tourism and Militarism in Hawai'i and the Philippines* (Durham, NC: Duke University Press, 2013), 10.

103. John K. Hutchens, "*Hawaii*," *New York Herald Tribune*, November 20, 1959, 17.

104. Daws, 63.

105. Vincent Canby, "Screen: *Hawaii*, Big Long Film, Has Its Premiere," *New York Times*, October 11, 1966, 54.

106. Terry Clifford, "Acting and Scenery Help *Hawaii* thru Three Long Hours," *Chicago Tribune*, October 20, 1966, D1.

107. Peter Bart, "*Hawaii* Awash," *New York Times*, June 6, 1965, X11.

108. As qtd in Charlie Rice, "Julie Andrews: A Long Way in Ten Years," *Baltimore Sun*, September 5, 1965, M14.

109. Horton, 55.

110. Rohrer, 16.

111. Trask, 7.

112. Rohrer, 17.

113. Rohrer, 17.

114. Christine Higgins and Gavin Furukawa, "Styling Hawai'i in *Haole*wood: White Protagonists on a Voyage of Self-Discovery," *Multilingua* 31 (2012): 179.

115. Memo from Dalton Trumbo to Walter Mirisch and George Roy Hill, July 19, 1965, Box 19, Folder 4, U.S. Mss. 87AN; Disc 98A, Walter Mirisch Papers, Wisconsin Center for Film and Theater Research, University of Wisconsin Archives, Madison, WI, 3.

116. Bacchilega, 8.

117. Roger Bell, *Last among Equals: Hawaiian Statehood and American Politics* (Honolulu: University of Hawai'i Press, 1984), 12.

118. Bell, 21.

119. Bell, 24.

120. Marjory Adams, "Sequel to *Hawaii* Planned," *Boston Globe*, November 11, 1966, 44.

121. Marjory Adams, "Sequel to *Hawaii* Planned," *Boston Globe*, November 11, 1966, 44.

122. Sumida, 609.

123. Bell, 12.

124. Bell, 16.

125. Bell, 25.

126. Daws, 265.

127. Daws, 264.

128. Daws, 271.

129. Bell, 25.

130. Halualani, 134.

131. Trask, 17.

132. Trask, 20.

133. Skwiot, 39.

134. Bell, 36.

135. Trask, 10.

136. Bell, 27.

137. Peter Bart, "*Hawaii* Awash," *New York Times*, June 6, 1965, X11.

138. Peter Bart, "*Hawaii* Awash," *New York Times*, June 6, 1965, X11.

139. Peter Bart, "*Hawaii* Awash," *New York Times*, June 6, 1965, X11.

Chapter 5

1. Mark Feeney, "Elvis Movies," *American Spectator* (2001): 57.

2. Peter Guralnick, *Careless Love: The Unmaking of Elvis Presley* (Boston, MA: Back Bay, 2000), 147.

3. Paul Hooper, *Elusive Destiny: The Internationalist Movement in Modern Hawai'i* (Honolulu: University of Hawai'i Press, 1980), 22.

4. Letter from Tom Diskin, representative of Thomas A. Parker Management, to Tucker Gratz, Chairman, Pacific War Memorial Commission, January 8, 1962, COM30 Box 5, "USS Arizona Correspondence Fundraising. Presley Show.

Correspondence. 1960–1962, 1977" Folder, The Pacific War Memorial Commission Collection, Hawai'i State Archives, Honolulu, HI.

5. "Pictures: All-Time Box Office Champs," *Variety*, January 7, 1970, 27.
6. Feeney, 54.
7. "Change of Image Needed by Elvis, Critic Declares," *Boxoffice*, April 29, 1963, SE2.
8. Feeney, 54.
9. "Talent or Not, Elvis Has Fans," *Boston Globe*, August 3, 1965, 10.
10. Hedda Hopper, "Presley's Problem: If You Quit Rocking, Can You Still Keep Rolling? Elvis Thinks So," *Chicago Daily Tribune*, July 2, 1961, b8.
11. "Talent or Not, Elvis Has Fans," *Boston Globe*, August 3, 1965, 10.
12. "'Blue' Wins a Gold," *Disc*, January 6, 1962, 6.
13. "Elvis—Sensational Disc News," *Disc*, June 16, 1962, 1.
14. Guralnick, 123.
15. Feeney, 56.
16. "Pictures: Presley Stays Wallis," *Variety*, January 18, 1961, 7.
17. Jane Desmond, *Staging Tourism: Bodies on Display from Waikiki to Sea World* (Chicago: University of Chicago Press, 1999).
18. Rob Wilson, *Reimagining the American Pacific: From South Pacific to Bamboo Ridge and Beyond* (Durham, NC: Duke University Press, 2000), 168–169.
19. Diane Thomas, "Summer's Fun—and Comedies," *Atlanta Constitution*, June 13, 1966, 3A.
20. "The Exhibitor Has His Say," *Boxoffice*, April 30, 1962, 10.
21. "Hawaiian Production Dream Awaits Stages; A Boon in Dick Boone?" *Variety*, November 4, 1964, 5.
22. As qtd. in George Stevens Jr., *Conversations with the Great Moviemakers of Hollywood's Golden Age* (New York: Alfred A. Knopf, 2006), 596.
23. Guralnick, 123.
24. Rick Altman, *The American Film Musical* (Bloomington: Indiana University Press, 1987), 196.
25. John Connell and Chris Gibson, "'No Passport Necessary': Music, Record Covers and Vicarious Tourism in Post-war Hawai'i," *Journal of Pacific History* 43.1 (June 2008): 51.
26. Altman, 194.
27. Altman, 194, 196.
28. Richard Dyer, *Only Entertainment* (New York: Routledge, 1992).
29. Feeney, 58.
30. Dean MacCannell, *The Tourist: A New Theory of the Leisure Class* (Berkeley: University of California Press, 1999).
31. Houston Wood, *Displacing Natives: The Rhetorical Production of Hawai'i* (Lanham, MD: Rowman & Littlefield, 1999), 48.
32. Wood, 108.
33. Wood, 111.

34. Joy T. Taylor, "'You Can't Spend Your Whole Life on a Surfboard': Elvis Presley, Exotic Whiteness, and Native Performance in *Blue Hawaii* and *Girls! Girls! Girls!*," *Quarterly Review of Film and Video* 32.1 (2015): 21.

35. June Bundy, "Disk Industry Stands to Profit from High Musical Film Activity," *Billboard Music Week*, October 23, 1961, 3.

36. June Bundy, "Disk Industry Stands to Profit from High Musical Film Activity," *Billboard Music Week*, October 23, 1961, 3.

37. "Flick Execs Dig Deep into Disk Artist Ranks for Box Office Attractions; Tap Deejays, Too," *Billboard Music Week*, March 6, 1961, 3.

38. "Record Review: 'Kings,' Elvis' Soundtrackers, Cole's 'Story' Top Current LP Releases," *Variety*, October 4, 1961, 60.

39. Ren Grevatt, "Films Keep the Presley Legend Alive," *Melody Maker*, September 15, 1962, 21.

40. Guralnick, 123.

41. Albert Goldman, "Elvis? Ah, the Good Old Days!" *New York Times*, December 1, 1968, D21.

42. Letter from George Chaplin, Editor at the *Honolulu Advertiser*, to Tucker Gratz, Chairman of the Pacific War Memorial Commission, December 7, 1960, COM30 Box 5, "USS Arizona Correspondence Fundraising. Presley Show. Correspondence. 1960–1962, 1977" Folder, The Pacific War Memorial Commission Collection, Hawai'i State Archives, Honolulu, HI.

43. Letter to Rear Admiral E. A. Solomons, US Navy, February 9, 1961, COM30 Box 5, "USS Arizona Correspondence Fundraising. Presley Show. Correspondence. 1960–1962, 1977" Folder, The Pacific War Memorial Commission Collection, Hawai'i State Archives, Honolulu, HI.

44. Letter from Colonel Tom Parker to Joe James Custer, Pacific War Memorial Commission, February 27, 1961, COM30 Box 5, "USS Arizona Correspondence Fundraising. Presley Show. Correspondence. 1960–1962, 1977" Folder, The Pacific War Memorial Commission Collection, Hawai'i State Archives, Honolulu, HI.

45. Letter from Tom Diskin, representative of Thomas A. Parker Management, to Joe James Custer, Pacific War Memorial Commission, February 18, 1961, COM30 Box 5, "USS Arizona Correspondence Fundraising. Presley Show. Correspondence. 1960–1962, 1977" Folder, The Pacific War Memorial Commission Collection, Hawai'i State Archives, Honolulu, HI.

46. Letter from Lyndon B. Johnson, Vice President of the United States, to Tucker Gratz, Chairman of the Pacific War Memorial Commission, February 14, 1961, COM30 Box 5, "USS Arizona Correspondence Fundraising. Presley Show. Correspondence. 1960–1962, 1977" Folder, The Pacific War Memorial Commission Collection, Hawai'i State Archives, Honolulu, HI.

47. Guralnick, 93.

48. Letter from Colonel Tom Parker to Joe James Custer, Pacific War Memorial Commission, February 27, 1961, COM30 Box 5, "USS Arizona

Correspondence Fundraising. Presley Show. Correspondence. 1960–1962, 1977" Folder, The Pacific War Memorial Commission Collection, Hawai'i State Archives, Honolulu, HI.

49. Letter from Colonel Tom Parker to Joe James Custer, Pacific War Memorial Commission, February 27, 1961, COM30 Box 5, "USS Arizona Correspondence Fundraising. Presley Show. Correspondence. 1960–1962, 1977" Folder, The Pacific War Memorial Commission Collection, Hawai'i State Archives, Honolulu, HI.

50. Guralnick, 91–92.

51. Letter to the Editor, January 1961, COM30 Box 5, *Arizona* Folder, The Pacific War Memorial Commission Collection, Hawai'i State Archives, Honolulu, HI.

52. "Music: Elvis' Hawaiian Payoff," *Variety*, April 19, 1961, 57.

53. Letter from Tucker Gratz, Chairman of the Pacific War Memorial Commission, to Colonel Tom Parker, April 24, 1961, COM30 Box 5, "USS Arizona Correspondence Fundraising. Presley Show. Correspondence. 1960–1962, 1977" Folder, The Pacific War Memorial Commission Collection, Hawai'i State Archives, Honolulu, HI.

54. Jonah Ruddy, "Elvis 'Blue Hawaii' Album His Best Yet, Reports NME's," *New Musical Express*, October 20, 1961, 10.

55. Guralnick, 104.

56. Guralnick, 28.

57. Feeney, 55.

58. Allen Evans, "EPs," *New Musical Express*, March 19, 1965, 10.

59. Guralnick, 100.

60. Guralnick, 100.

61. Connell and Gibson, 58.

62. Wood, 108.

63. Guralnick, 104.

64. Julian Mitchell, "The Singer Not the Song," *London Magazine*, March 1962, 47.

65. Ed Sheehan, "Beachcombing: Way to See Hawaii—Hawaiian Style: Quiet Towns, Lost Beaches Await You," *Chicago Tribune*, April 17, 1966, H3.

66. MacCannell, 36.

67. Guralnick, 103.

68. "Fox Suspends Juliet Prowse," *New York Times*, March 15, 1961, 45.

69. Altman, 66.

70. "Teenage Hula Girls, Hawaiian Queens and Lei-Wearers Keep 'Hawaii' Hot," *Boxoffice*, February 12, 1962), 27.

71. "Teenage Hula Girls, Hawaiian Queens and Lei-Wearers Keep 'Hawaii' Hot," *Boxoffice*, February 12, 1962, 27.

72. "Teenage Hula Girls, Hawaiian Queens and Lei-Wearers Keep 'Hawaii' Hot," *Boxoffice*, February 12, 1962, 27.

73. "The Exhibitor Has His Say," *Boxoffice*, August 13, 1962, 10

74. "The Exhibitor Has His Say," *Boxoffice*, April 30, 1962, 10.
75. "The Exhibitor Has His Say," *Boxoffice*, July 16, 1962, 26.
76. "The Exhibitor Has His Say," *Boxoffice*, July 30, 1962, 10.
77. "The Exhibitor Has His Say," *Boxoffice*, August 13, 1962, 10.
78. "The Exhibitor Has His Say," *Boxoffice*, July 16, 1962, 26.
79. Guralnick, 103.
80. Guralnick, 123–124.
81. Derek Johnson, "Is Presley Making Too Many Films?" *New Musical Express*, April 6, 1962, 3.
82. "No Screams for Presley," *New Musical Express*, December 14, 1962, 10.
83. "*Girls, Girls, Girls,*" *Variety*, November 7, 1962, 6.
84. "Girls, Girls—and Elvis!," *New Musical Express*, January 18, 1963, 2.
85. "Allied Artists Shaking Things Up, Beginning with Elvis in Paradise," *Variety*, November 13, 1963, 29.
86. "AA Signs Elvis Presley for 'Isle of Paradise,'" *Boxoffice*, November 18, 1963, 9.
87. Tats Yoshiyama, "Honolulu and Other Hawaiian Areas," *Boxoffice*, April 13, 1964, W-8.
88. "Mex Authorities Nix 'Blue Hawaii,' Everyone Mum on the Reasons," *Variety*, November 7, 1962, 2, 17.
89. "Mex Authorities Nix 'Blue Hawaii,' Everyone Mum on the Reasons," *Variety*, November 7, 1962, 2, 17. According to Guralnick, there was no location shooting, however, due to security concerns (141).
90. Horace Sutton, "Aloha Hollywood! It's Movietime in Hulaland These Days: Of All Places," *Washington Post*, August 29, 1965, G11.
91. "Feature Reviews," *Boxoffice*, June 6, 1966, a12.
92. Guralnick, 207.
93. Guralnick, 211.
94. *My emphasis*. Guralnick, 208.
95. Guralnick, 208.
96. "'Paradise' Near," *Boston Globe*, June 5, 1966, A14.
97. Wayne Harada, "International News Reports: From the Music Capitals of the World—Honolulu," *Billboard*, May 31, 1969, 82.
98. Wood, 112.
99. Philip K. Scheuer, "Elvis Joins Picture Parade in Hawaii," *Los Angeles Times*, August 18, 1965, 9.
100. Wilson, 170.
101. "*Paradise, Hawaiian Style,*" *Variety*, June 8, 1966, 6.
102. Wood, 118.
103. "*Paradise, Hawaiian Style,*" *Variety*, June 8, 1966, 6.
104. "Elvis Presley's Latest Has a Point," *Washington Post*, July 15, 1966, A22.
105. Vernadette Vicuña Gonzalez, *Securing Paradise: Tourism and Militarism in Hawai'i and the Philippines* (Durham, NC: Duke University Press, 2013), 148.
106. Gonzalez, 149.

107. Wilson, 170.
108. Christine Skwiot, *The Purposes of Paradise: US Tourism and Empire in Cuba and Hawai'i* (Philadelphia: University of Pennsylvania Press, 2010), 185.
109. Tats Yoshiyama, "Honolulu and Other Hawaiian Areas," *Boxoffice*, August 2, 1965, W-7.
110. Horace Sutton, "Aloha Hollywood! It's Movietime in Hulaland These Days: Of All Places," *Washington Post*, August 29, 1965, G11.
111. Feeney, 59.
112. Feeney, 59.
113. "Elvis Presley's Latest Has a Point," *Washington Post*, July 15, 1966, A22.
114. Taylor, 23.
115. "*Paradise, Hawaiian Style*," *Monthly Film Bulletin*, January 1, 1966, 127.
116. "Presley Invades Hawaii," *New York Times*, June 16, 1966, 53.
117. "*Paradise, Hawaiian Style*," *Variety*, June 8, 1966, 6.
118. "Feature Reviews," *Boxoffice*, June 6, 1966, a11.
119. "*Healthy Film Business Bodes Well for Soundtrack Albums*," Billboard, January 28, 1967, 34.
120. "Blue Hawaii Push," *Billboard*, September 10, 1966, 10.
121. "The Presley Riddle," *Melody Maker*, June 23, 1973, 21.
122. Guralnick, 482.
123. "At Last—a REAL Elvis Film," *Melody Maker*, October 3, 1970, 9.
124. "The Presley Riddle," *Melody Maker*, June 23, 1973, 21.
125. "Elvis: Aloha from Hawaii," *Billboard*, April 14, 1973, 16.
126. Guralnick, 475.
127. "The Kalmus Corporation," *Variety*, May 2, 1973, 270.
128. "Elvis: Aloha from Hawaii," *Billboard*, April 14, 1973, 16.
129. "Elvis Everywhere in Sight and Sound," *Atlanta Constitution*, April 1, 1973, 23F.
130. "Elvis: Aloha from Hawaii," *Variety*, April 11, 1973, 52.
131. "Caught in the Act," *Melody Maker*, March 31, 1973, 35.
132. Guralnick, 103.
133. Tom Zito, "Elvis: Still Something Special," *Washington Post*, April 14, 1973, E7.
134. "*Blue Hawaii* Revisited," *Melody Maker*, February 17, 1973, 25.

Chapter 6

1. Drew Kampton, *Stoked: A History of Surf Culture* (Layton, UT: Gibbs Smith, 1997), 96.
2. Joan Ormrod, "*Endless Summer* (1964): Consuming Waves and Surfing the Frontier," *Film and History: An Interdisciplinary Journal of Film and Television Studies* 35.1 (2005): 40.

3. John Engle, "Manning Up on the North Shore: American Masculinity and the Early Surf Movies," *Bright Lights Film Journal* (June 18, 2018): https://brightlightsfilm.com/manning-up-on-the-north-shore-american-masculinity-and-the-early-surf-movies/.

4. Ormrod, 40.

5. Douglas Booth, "Surfing Films and Videos: Adolescent Fun, Alternative Lifestyle, Adventure Industry," *Journal of Sport History* 23.3 (Fall 1996): 313.

6. Engle, n.p.

7. Engle, n.p.

8. Booth, 313.

9. Kampton, 81–82.

10. *My emphasis.* Kampton, 84.

11. Booth, 317.

12. Engle, n.p.

13. Orvar Lofgren, *On Holiday: A History of Vacationing* (Berkeley: University of California Press, 1999), 219.

14. Kampton, 85.

15. "Fates & Fortunes: Programing," *Broadcasting*, September 2, 1963, 73.

16. Ormrod, 49.

17. Booth, 313.

18. "Teenagers, and Their Pocket Money, a Film Market unto Themselves," *Variety*, March 10, 1965, 4.

19. "It's 'Surfing' Film Now, Like Music," *Variety*, April 24, 1963, 76.

20. As qtd. in Kampton, 23.

21. Dean MacCannell, *The Tourist: A New Theory of the Leisure Class* (Berkeley: University of California Press, 1999).

22. Kampton, 96.

23. As qtd. in Kampton, 96.

24. Engle, n.p.

25. Jane Desmond, *Staging Tourism: Bodies on Display from Waikiki to Sea World* (Chicago: University of Chicago Press, 1999), 101.

26. Ormrod, 45.

27. Desmond, 126.

28. Desmond, 125.

29. Ormrod, 48.

30. Ormrod, 47.

31. "*Endless Summer*," *Variety*, June 22, 1966, 20.

32. As qtd. in Booth, 317.

33. Lofgren, 219.

34. Desmond, 128.

35. Desmond, 124.

36. Desmond, 122.

37. Ormrod, 41.

38. John Urry, *The Tourist Gaze: Leisure and Travel in Contemporary Societies* (London: Sage, 1990), 38.
39. As qtd. in Kampton, 23.
40. Kampton, 81.
41. Booth, 316.
42. Ormrod, 40.
43. Kampton, 81.
44. "Special Merit Picks," *Billboard*, August 17, 1963, 12.
45. "It's 'Surfing' Film Now, Like Music," *Variety*, April 24, 1963, 1.
46. "Teenagers, and Their Pocket Money, a Film Market unto Themselves," *Variety*, March 10, 1965, 4
47. "Surf Movie Offered for Deejay Hops," *Billboard*, June 29, 1963, 3.
48. "It's 'Surfing' Film Now, Like Music," *Variety*, April 24, 1963, 1.
49. Kampton, 85.
50. Kampton, 87.
51. "It's 'Surfing' Film Now, Like Music," *Variety*, April 24, 1963, 76.
52. Ormrod, 41.
53. Kampton, 96.
54. "Pictures: 'Surfer' a Sleeper in First Playoff," *Variety*, September 28, 1966, 3.
55. As qtd. in Velman West Sykes, "*The Endless Summer* (Cinema V) Wins Jan. Blue Ribbon Award," *Boxoffice*, February 13, 1967, 25.
56. As qtd. in "National Screen Council Comment," *Boxoffice*, February 20, 1967, b3.
57. Ormrod, 46–47.
58. Ormrod, 44.
59. Bill Nichols, *Introduction to Documentary*, 3rd ed. (Bloomington: Indiana University Press, 2017).
60. As qtd. in Sykes, 25.
61. Keith Beattie, "Sick, Filthy, and Delirious: Surf Film and Video and the Documentary Mode," *Continuum: Journal of Media and Cultural Studies* 15.3 (2001): 336.
62. Beattie, 333.
63. Beattie, 336.
64. Beattie, 334–335.
65. "*Hit the Surf*," *Variety*, July 26, 1967, 45.
66. "Surfari," *Variety*, July 19, 1967, 6.
67. Ormrod, 39.
68. "Television Reviews: ABC-TV Money Spurs Surfing in Honolulu," *Variety*, November 23, 1966, 42.
69. "Television Reviews: ABC-TV Money Spurs Surfing in Honolulu," *Variety*, November 23, 1966, 42.
70. "Radio-Television: Surfing Documentary," *Variety*, March 1, 1967, 31.

71. Robert C. Schmitt, *Hawai'i in the Movies, 1898–1959* (Honolulu: University of Hawai'i, 1999), 15.
72. "Resume of January Shorts," *Variety*, February 4, 1942, 8.
73. "Saturated in Surf," *Variety*, November 11, 1964, 24.
74. Memo from Sylvester Weaver to George Tahara, August 29, 1960, Box 14, Folder 11, 3M/33/V1-5, Pat Weaver Papers, Wisconsin Center for Film and Theater Research, University of Wisconsin Archives, Madison, WI.
75. *Cine-Pic Hawaii* Catalogue "Film Series . . . from Hawaii," circa 1960, Box 14, Folder 11, 3M/33/V1-5, Pat Weaver Papers, Wisconsin Center for Film and Theater Research, University of Wisconsin Archives, Madison, WI.
76. Memo from Sylvester Weaver to George Tahara, August 17, 1960, Box 14, Folder 11, 3M/33/V1-5, Pat Weaver Papers, Wisconsin Center for Film and Theater Research, University of Wisconsin Archives, Madison, WI.
77. Memo from Sylvester Weaver to George Tahara, August 17, 1960, Box 14, Folder 11, 3M/33/V1-5, Pat Weaver Papers, Wisconsin Center for Film and Theater Research, University of Wisconsin Archives, Madison, WI.
78. *Cine-Pic Hawaii* Catalogue "Film Series . . . from Hawaii," circa 1960, Box 14, Folder 11, 3M/33/V1-5, Pat Weaver Papers, Wisconsin Center for Film and Theater Research, University of Wisconsin Archives, Madison, WI.
79. "It's 'Surfing' Film Now, Like Music," *Variety*, April 24, 1963, 76.
80. "It's 'Surfing' Film Now, Like Music," *Variety*, April 24, 1963, 76.
81. Kampton, 96.
82. "Pictures: Rugoff Cinema V Shakes Moribund Tone, Comes Alive with New Zing," *Variety*, October 5, 1966, 5.
83. Kampton, 96.
84. "Pictures: Rugoff Cinema V Shakes Moribund Tone, Comes Alive with New Zing," *Variety*, October 5, 1966, 5.
85. "*Endless Summer*," *Variety*, June 22, 1966, 20.
86. "*Endless Summer*," *Variety*, June 22, 1966, 20.
87. "Pictures: Rugoff Cinema V Shakes Moribund Tone, Comes Alive with New Zing," *Variety*, October 5, 1966, 5.
88. "Pictures: Rugoff Cinema V Shakes Moribund Tone, Comes Alive with New Zing," *Variety*, October 5, 1966, 5.
89. "Showmandiser: 'Endless Summer' Producer Promotes Film with Florida Personal Appearances," *Boxoffice*, February 20, 1967, b1.
90. "Showmandiser: 'Endless Summer' Producer Promotes Film with Florida Personal Appearances," *Boxoffice*, February 20, 1967, b1.
91. "Showmandiser: 'Endless Summer' Producer Promotes Film with Florida Personal Appearances," *Boxoffice*, February 20, 1967, b1.
92. "Showmandiser: 'Endless Summer' Producer Promotes Film with Florida Personal Appearances," *Boxoffice*, February 20, 1967, b1.
93. "North Jersey," *Boxoffice*, July 10, 1967, E5.
94. "Boston," *Boxoffice*, May 15, 1967, NE-3.

95. Sykes, 25.

96. As qtd. in Sykes, 25.

97. As qtd. in "National Screen Council Comment," *Boxoffice*, February 20, 1967, b3.

98. As qtd. in Sykes, 25.

99. As qtd. in "National Screen Council Comment," *Boxoffice*, February 20, 1967, b3.

100. Tats Yoshiyama, "Honolulu and Other Hawaiian Areas," *Boxoffice*, February 13, 1967, W-7.

101. "Surfari," *Variety*, July 19, 1967, 6.

102. "Surfari," *Variety*, July 19, 1967, 6.

103. "*The Golden Breed*," *Variety*, November 13, 1968, 6, 26.

104. "New Surfing Pic," *Variety*, February 5, 1969, 4.

105. "Programing: New Crop Stirs Up Same Old Claims," *Broadcasting*, September 22, 1969, 50.

106. Kampton, 96.

107. As qtd. in Ormrod, 39.

Chapter 7

1. Honolulu and Oahu Detailed Street Map and Guide, 1966, Box 10, Folder 1, U.S. Mss. 141AN, Sy Salkowitz Papers, Wisconsin Center for Film and Theater Research, University of Wisconsin Archives, Madison, WI.

2. Sue Turnbull, *TV Crime Drama* (Edinburgh: Edinburgh University Press, 2014), 71.

3. As qtd. in Ed Rampell, "*Hawaii Five-O*: A Case Study in Haole-Wood Agitprop," *Television Quarterly* 33.1 (Spring 2002): 78.

4. Letter from Acting Governor George R. Ariyoshi to Mrs. Joseph LeBeau, August 14, 1974, GOV13 Folder 134, "*Hawaii Five-O*," Gov. Jack Burns Collection, Hawai'i State Archives, Honolulu, HI.

5. Marcia Borie, "The Jack Lord Nobody Knows," *Good Housekeeping*, October 1975, reprinted in *The Official Jack Lord Newsletter*, November–December 1975, The Jack Lord Collection, Hawaiian and Pacific Collection, University of Hawai'i at Manoa, Honolulu, HI.

6. Rampell, 78.

7. Karen Rhodes, *Booking Hawaii Five-O: An Episode Guide and Critical History of the 1968–1980 Television Detective Series* (Jefferson, NC: McFarland, 1997), 7.

8. *A Writer's Guide to Hawaii Five-O*, 1967, Box 26, Folder 1, U.S. Mss. 130AN, Norman Katkov Papers, Wisconsin Center for Film and Theater Research, University of Wisconsin Archives, Madison, WI, 1.

9. Jonathan Nichols-Pethick, *TV Cops: The Contemporary American Television Police Drama* (New York: Routledge, 2012), 13.

10. *A Writer's Guide to Hawaii Five-O*, 1967, Box 26, Folder 1, U.S. Mss. 130AN, Norman Katkov Papers, Wisconsin Center for Film and Theater Research, University of Wisconsin Archives, Madison, WI, 2–3.

11. *A Writer's Guide to Hawaii Five-O*, 1967, Box 26, Folder 1, U.S. Mss. 130AN, Norman Katkov Papers, Wisconsin Center for Film and Theater Research, University of Wisconsin Archives, Madison, WI, 8.

12. Philip K. Scheuer, "Elvis Joins Picture Parade in Hawaii," *Los Angeles Times*, August 18, 1965, 9.

13. *My emphasis*. Cecil Smith, "*Hawaii Five-O*: Crime Series in Lush Surroundings," *Los Angeles Times*, January 4, 1970, O2.

14. Cecil Smith, "*Hawaii Five-O*: Crime Series in Lush Surroundings," *Los Angeles Times*, January 4, 1970, O2.

15. "Television Reviews," *Variety*, September 22, 1971, 24.

16. Cecil Smith, "*Hawaii Five-O*: Crime Series in Lush Surroundings," *Los Angeles Times*, January 4, 1970, O2.

17. "Pictures: Dick Boone's Angles on Further Hawaiian Film and Studio," *Variety*, May 22, 1968, 20.

18. Cecil Smith, "*Hawaii Five-O*: Crime Series in Lush Surroundings," *Los Angeles Times*, January 4, 1970, O2.

19. "Pictures: Dick Boone's Angles on Further Hawaiian Film and Studio," *Variety*, May 22, 1968, 20.

20. "Finnegan Tapped for 'Hawaii,'" *Variety*, February 3, 1971, 50.

21. "Bob Stambler Ankles 'Hawaii Five-O' for New Enterprise on Island," *Variety*, February 3, 1971, 50.

22. "Bob Stambler Ankles 'Hawaii Five-O' for New Enterprise on Island," *Variety*, February 3, 1971, 50.

23. John Culver, "Television and the Police," *Policy Studies Journal* (Winter 1978): 504–505. Programs of this type routinely played up several falsehoods about actual police departments—namely, the overemphasis of criminal violence that in turn serves as a justification for police violence, and the "deceptively efficient" success of police in solving crime (504). Within a wide ideological spectrum of shows, from the strict enforcement of the laws to a slightly looser enforcement of order with wider discretion, *Hawaii Five-O* was situated according to Culver firmly within the *Dragnet* tradition of TV police as a "stabilizing force in a society running head-long into chaos," and who are uniformly "efficient, dedicated and above all professional" (504). Indeed, the *Hawaii Five-O* writer's guide emphasized that personal backstories on McGarrett would be "rare"—a trend that decreased as the seasons went on.

24. Nichols-Pethick, 2.

25. David Marc, *Demographic Vistas: Television in American Culture* (Philadelphia: University of Pennsylvania Press, 1984), 92.

26. *A Writer's Guide to Hawaii Five-O*, 1967, Box 26, Folder 1, U.S. Mss. 130AN, Norman Katkov Papers, Wisconsin Center for Film and Theater Research, University of Wisconsin Archives, Madison, WI, 4.

27. Nichols-Pethick, 33.
28. John Fiske, *Television Culture* (New York: Routledge, 1987), 21.
29. Fiske, 36.
30. Retrospective on *Hawaii Five-O* scenario, "The Little Crime," November 10, 1970, Box 10, Folder 3, U.S. Mss. 141AN, Sy Salkowitz Papers, Wisconsin Center for Film and Theater Research, University of Wisconsin Archives, Madison, WI.
31. David Loffert, "New Shows Set," *Backstage*, August 23, 1968, 18.
32. Jerome Coppersmith, "Book 'Em Danno! My Years Writing for *Hawaii Five-O*," *Mystery Scene* 84 (Spring 2004): 33.
33. "Mike Like 'Hawaii,'" *Variety*, January 17, 1968, 30.
34. Percy Shain, "*Hawaii Five-O* Star Won't Leave Island Location," *Boston Globe*, July 13, 1970, 30.
35. Percy Shain, "*Hawaii Five-O* Star Won't Leave Island Location," *Boston Globe*, July 13, 1970, 30.
36. Lawrence Laurent, "Jack Lord's Ninth Year of Hawaii Five-O," *Washington Post*, June 6, 1976, 249.
37. "Webs 'Sell' to Public Tees with CBS H'wood-Hawaii Star Trek for Press," *Variety*, June 24, 1970, 44.
38. James MacGregor, "Lightning Strikes a TV Critic," *Wall Street Journal*, January 30, 1973, 20.
39. Letter from Mrs. Joseph Le Beau to the Governor, August 7, 1974, GOV13 Folder 134, "*Hawaii Five-O*," Gov. Jack Burns Collection, Hawai'i State Archives, Honolulu, HI.
40. Letter from Mary Dobson to the Governor, August 12, 1974, GOV13 Folder 134, "*Hawaii Five-O*," Gov. Jack Burns Collection, Hawai'i State Archives, Honolulu, HI.
41. Barry Weekes, "Around the Town," *Oakland Post*, March 31, 1974, 5.
42. Rhodes, 9.
43. Marcia Borie, "The Jack Lord Nobody Knows," *Good Housekeeping*, October 1975, reprinted in *The Official Jack Lord Newsletter*, November–December 1975, The Jack Lord Collection, Hawaiian and Pacific Collection, University of Hawai'i at Manoa, Honolulu, HI.
44. Cecil Smith, "'Hawaii Five-O' Still Popular but Violence Will Be Reduced," *Morning Advocate*, May 5, 1975, reprinted in *The Official Jack Lord Newsletter*, 1976, The Jack Lord Collection, Hawaiian and Pacific Collection, University of Hawai'i at Manoa, Honolulu, HI.
45. Letter from Veronica Twiddle to the Governor's Office, March 9, 1973, GOV13 Folder 134, "*Hawaii Five-O*," Gov. Jack Burns Collection, Hawai'i State Archives, Honolulu, HI.
46. Letter from the Governor's Office to Veronica Twiddle, March 20, 1973, GOV13 Folder 134, "*Hawaii Five-O*," Gov. Jack Burns Collection, Hawai'i State Archives, Honolulu, HI.

47. Letter from Douglas R. Andrews to the Governor's Office, February 18, 1970, GOV13 Folder 134, "*Hawaii Five-O*," Gov. Jack Burns Collection, Hawai'i State Archives, Honolulu, HI.

48. Letter from Douglas R. Andrews to the Governor's Office, February 18, 1970, GOV13 Folder 134, "*Hawaii Five-O*," Gov. Jack Burns Collection, Hawai'i State Archives, Honolulu, HI.

49. Letter to Douglas R. Andrews from the Governor's Office, March 2, 1970, GOV13 Folder 134, "*Hawaii Five-O*," Gov. Jack Burns Collection, Hawai'i State Archives, Honolulu, HI.

50. Rhodes, 9.

51. Tom Shales, "One Man's Private War against Television Violence," *Washington Post*, March 12, 1974, B1.

52. Letter from Eric J. Wilson to the Governor, October 24, 1973, GOV13 Folder 134, "*Hawaii Five-O*," Gov. Jack Burns Collection, Hawai'i State Archives, Honolulu, HI.

53. Letter from Eric J. Wilson to the Governor, October 24, 1973, GOV13 Folder 134, "*Hawaii Five-O*," Gov. Jack Burns Collection, Hawai'i State Archives, Honolulu, HI.

54. Letter from Acting Governor George R. Ariyoshi to Eric J. Wilson, November 14, 1973, GOV13 Folder 134, "*Hawaii Five-O*," Gov. Jack Burns Collection, Hawai'i State Archives, Honolulu, HI.

55. "Jack Lord, 'Hawaii Five-O' Is Not as Violent as Nightly News," *National Enquirer* (1975), reprinted in *The Official Jack Lord Newsletter*, November–December 1975, The Jack Lord Collection, Hawaiian and Pacific Collection, University of Hawai'i at Manoa, Honolulu, HI.

56. Marcia Borie, "The Jack Lord Nobody Knows," *Good Housekeeping*, October 1975, reprinted in *The Official Jack Lord Newsletter*, November–December 1975, The Jack Lord Collection, Hawaiian and Pacific Collection, University of Hawai'i at Manoa, Honolulu, HI.

57. Letter from Margaret Kuppinger to the Governor's Office, December 9, 1971, GOV13 Folder 134, "*Hawaii Five-O*," Gov. Jack Burns Collection, Hawai'i State Archives, Honolulu, HI.

58. Letter from Governor's Office to Len Weissman, December 19, 1971, GOV13 Folder 134, "*Hawaii Five-O*," Gov. Jack Burns Collection, Hawai'i State Archives, Honolulu, HI.

59. Christine Skwiot, *The Purposes of Paradise: US Tourism and Empire in Cuba and Hawai'i* (Philadelphia: University of Pennsylvania Press, 2010), 177.

60. "Series of Half Hour Filmed or Taped Shows from Hawaii," February 6, 1959, Box 14, Folder 11, 3M/33/V1-5, Pat Weaver Papers, Wisconsin Center for Film and Theater Research, University of Wisconsin Archives, Madison, WI, 1.

61. "Series of Half Hour Filmed or Taped Shows from Hawaii," February 6, 1959, Box 14, Folder 11, 3M/33/V1-5, Pat Weaver Papers, Wisconsin Center for Film and Theater Research, University of Wisconsin Archives, Madison, WI, 3.

62. Memo from Sylvester Weaver to William G. Lipscomb, January 9, 1958, Box 14, Folder 11, Pat Weaver Papers, Wisconsin Center for Film and Theater Research, University of Wisconsin Archives, Madison, WI, 1.

63. Memo from Mort Werner to Sylvester Weaver, January 9, 1958, Box 14, Folder 11, Pat Weaver Papers, Wisconsin Center for Film and Theater Research, University of Wisconsin Archives, Madison, WI.

64. Selig Altschul, *United Air Lines: A Reappraisal* (Chicago: Corporation, 1953), 40.

65. Altschul, 39.

66. William Garvey and David Fisher, *The Age of Flight: A History of America's Pioneering Airline* (Greensboro, NC: Pace Communications, 2002), 157.

67. *Introducing United Air Lines* (Chicago: United Air Lines Education and Training Department, 1968), 9.

68. Tom Gardo, "Public Relations in Travel and Leisure—Impressions and Trends," *Public Relations Quarterly* (Fall 1973): 19.

69. Wayne Harada, "Show Biz," *Honolulu Advertiser*, February 12, 1970, 56.

70. "In 'Hawaii Five-O,' " *Honolulu Advertiser*, June 3, 1968, 34.

71. Gardo, 19.

72. "Non-Theatrical TV Film Round-Up," *Billboard*, December 13, 1952, 21,

73. Weekly Report of Activities Publicity Department Hawaii Tourist Bureau, August 20–25, 1950, Box 33, Folder 28, MS Group 239—Theo H. Davies & Co. Collection, Bernice Pauahi Bishop Museum Archives, Honolulu, HI.

74. "Film: Film Sales," *Broadcasting, Telecasting*, June 15, 1953, 36.

75. "Hawaii—Pacific Miracle," *Variety*, April 1, 1959, 48.

76. "Stations Select 50 Outstanding TV Films," *Variety*, July 8, 1959, 34.

77. Garvey and Fisher, 146.

78. "Jet Junket to Honolulu," *Variety*, March 2, 1960, 11.

79. As qtd. in Garvey and Fisher, 157.

80. Memo from W. A. Patterson to Henry J. Kaiser, July 9, 1958, Box 14, Folder 11, Pat Weaver Papers, Wisconsin Center for Film and Theater Research, University of Wisconsin Archives, Madison, WI, 1.

81. Rob Wilson, *Reimagining the American Pacific: From South Pacific to Bamboo Ridge and Beyond* (Durham, NC: Duke University Press, 2000), xv.

82. Wilson, xv.

83. *United Airlines 1962 Vacations to Hawaii Three Choice Mainliner Holidays*, author's collection.

84. Horace Sutton, *The New United Airlines Guide to the Hawaiian Islands: Aloha, Hawaii* (Garden City, NY: Doubleday, 1967), 3.

85. Cecil Smith, "*Hawaii Five-O*: Crime Series in Lush Surroundings," *Los Angeles Times*, January 4, 1970, O2.

86. *A Writer's Guide to Hawaii Five-O*, 1967, Box 26, Folder 1, U.S. Mss. 130AN, Norman Katkov Papers, Wisconsin Center for Film and Theater Research, University of Wisconsin Archives, Madison, WI.

87. Cecil Smith, "*Hawaii Five-O*: Crime Series in Lush Surroundings," *Los Angeles Times*, January 4, 1970, O2.

88. Coopersmith, 33.
89. Coopersmith, 34.
90. Coopersmith, 35.
91. Joan Crosby, "Lord to Wind Up *Hawaii 5-O*," *Atlanta Constitution*, April 15, 1972, 17T.
92. Wilson, x–xi.
93. Stanley Orr, "'Strangers in Our Own Land': John Kneubuhl, Modern Drama, and *Hawai'i Five-O*," *American Quarterly* 67.3 (2015): 920.
94. Orr, 921.
95. *My emphasis.* Cecil Smith, "*Hawaii Five-O*: Crime Series in Lush Surroundings," *Los Angeles Times*, January 4, 1970, O2.
96. Horace Sutton, "Aloha, Hollywood! It's Movietime in Hulaland These Days," *Washington Post*, August 29, 1965, G11.
97. Rampell, 77.
98. Rampell, 79.
99. Peter Britos, "Symbols, Myth & TV in Hawai'i. The First Cycle: An Overview," *Spectator* 23.1 (Spring 2003): 104.
100. Rampell, 81–82.
101. Some audiences of the time also felt that the show was too close to the military, though not in the way that Rampell intended. When *Hawaii Five-O* preempted local coverage of the California Democratic presidential primary in 1972, one person wrote to the *LA Times*: "What a great belly laugh! To be watching *Hawaii Five-O* when we expected to be watching the returns of the California primary! It seems the people have a right to know our nation's state and military secrets but not the results of its voting after the polls have closed, simply because the polls have not closed in San Francisco." As qtd. in "Letters to the Times: Some Postmortems on the June 6th Election," *Los Angeles Times*, June 11, 1972, G2.
102. *A Writer's Guide to Hawaii Five-O*, 1967, Box 26, Folder 1, U.S. Mss. 130AN, Norman Katkov Papers, Wisconsin Center for Film and Theater Research, University of Wisconsin Archives, Madison, WI, 3.
103. Vernadette Vicuña Gonzalez, *Securing Paradise: Tourism and Militarism in Hawai'i and the Philippines* (Durham, NC: Duke University Press, 2013), 4.
104. Rhodes, 50.
105. Paul Craig, *The Future Growth of Hawaiian Tourism and Its Impact on the State and the Neighbor Islands* (Honolulu: University of Hawai'i Economic Research Center, 1963), 8.
106. *A Writer's Guide to Hawaii Five-O*, 1967, Box 26, Folder 1, U.S. Mss. 130AN, Norman Katkov Papers, Wisconsin Center for Film and Theater Research, University of Wisconsin Archives, Madison, WI, 9.
107. Robert Stam and Louise Spence, "Colonialism, Racism, and Representation," *Screen* 24.2 (March 1983): 2–20.
108. *A Writer's Guide to Hawaii Five-O*, 1967, Box 26, Folder 1, U.S. Mss. 130AN, Norman Katkov Papers, Wisconsin Center for Film and Theater Research, University of Wisconsin Archives, Madison, WI, 1.

109. *A Writer's Guide to Hawaii Five-O*, 1967, Box 26, Folder 1, U.S. Mss. 130AN, Norman Katkov Papers, Wisconsin Center for Film and Theater Research, University of Wisconsin Archives, Madison, WI, 1.

110. *A Writer's Guide to Hawaii Five-O*, 1967, Box 26, Folder 1, U.S. Mss. 130AN, Norman Katkov Papers, Wisconsin Center for Film and Theater Research, University of Wisconsin Archives, Madison, WI, 4.

111. "Bill Smallwood," *Oakland Post*, April 6, 1972, n.p.

112. Craig, 71.

113. Letter from Acting Governor George R. Ariyoshi to Mary Dobson, August 20, 1974, GOV13 Folder 134, "*Hawaii Five-O*," Gov. Jack Burns Collection, Hawai'i State Archives, Honolulu, HI. See also: Letter from Acting Governor George R. Ariyoshi to Mrs. Joseph LeBeau, August 14, 1974, GOV13 Folder 134, "*Hawaii Five-O*," Gov. Jack Burns Collection, Hawai'i State Archives, Honolulu, HI.

114. "The Importance of *Hawaii Five-O*," *Honolulu Star-Bulletin*, December 20, 1977, reprinted in *The Official Jack Lord Newsletter*, 1978, The Jack Lord Collection, Hawaiian and Pacific Collection, University of Hawai'i at Manoa, Honolulu, HI.

115. "Jack Lord Named Salesman of the Year," *Honolulu Advertiser*, January 30, 1970, 35.

Conclusion

1. Letter from James Townsend, Managing Director of the Hawaii Visitors Bureau, to the Governor, December 12, 1958, GOV12 Folder 84, Gov. William F. Quinn Collection, Hawai'i State Archives, Honolulu, HI.

2. Letter from Jack Valenti to Governor Jack Burns, January 25, 1968, GOV13 Folder 44, "Film Festival 1970," Gov. Jack Burns Collection, Hawai'i State Archives, Honolulu, HI.

3. Letter from Jack Valenti to Governor Jack Burns, January 25, 1968, GOV13 Folder 44, "Film Festival 1970," Gov. Jack Burns Collection, Hawai'i State Archives, Honolulu, HI

4. Adria L. Imada, *Aloha America: Hula Circuits throughout the US Empire* (Durham, NC: Duke University Press, 2012), 7.

5. Jean Baudrillard, *Simulacra and Simulation*, trans. Sheila Faria Glaser (Ann Arbor: University of Michigan Press, 1994), 6.

6. Peter Britos, "Symbols, Myth & TV in Hawai'i. The First Cycle: An Overview," *Spectator* 23.1 (Spring 2003): 109.

7. Sven A. Kirsten, *The Book of Tiki: The Cult of Polynesian Pop in Fifties America* (Los Angeles: Taschen, 2000), 40, 42.

8. Francesco Adinolfi, *Mondo Exotica: Sounds, Visions, Obsessions of the Cocktail Generation*, ed. and trans. Karen Pinkus with Jason Vivrette (Durham, NC: Duke University Press, 2008), 2.

9. Adinolfi, 1–2.
10. Vernadette Vicuña Gonzalez, *Securing Paradise: Tourism and Militarism in Hawai'i and the Philippines* (Durham, NC: Duke University Press, 2013), 133.

Selected Bibliography

Adinolfi, Francesco. *Mondo Exotica: Sounds, Visions, Obsessions of the Cocktail Generation*. Edited and translated by Karen Pinkus with Jason Vivrette. Durham, NC: Duke University Press, 2008.
Bacchilega, Cristina. *Legendary Hawai'i and the Politics of Place: Tradition, Translation and Tourism*. Philadelphia: University of Pennsylvania Press, 2007.
Bailey, Beth, and David Farber. *The First Strange Place: Race and Sex in World War II Hawaii*. Baltimore, MD: Johns Hopkins University Press, 1992.
Barber, Joseph, Jr. *Hawaii: Restless Rampart*. Indianapolis, IN: Bobbs-Merrill, 1941.
Baudrillard, Jean. *America*. New York: Verso, 2010.
Beauman, Fran. *The Pineapple: King of Fruits*. London: Chatto & Windus, 2005.
Bell, Roger. *Last among Equals: Hawaiian Statehood and American Politics*. Honolulu: Hawai'i University Press, 1984.
Berg, Rick. "Losing Vietnam: Covering the War in an Age of Technology." In *From Hanoi to Hollywood: The Vietnam War in American Film*, edited by Linda Dittmar and Gene Michau, 41–68. New Brunswick, NJ: Rutgers University Press, 1990.
Boorstin, Daniel. *The Image, or What Happened to the American Dream*. New York: Atheneum, 1961.
Boym, Svetlana. *The Future of Nostalgia*. New York: Basic Books, 2001.
Briley, Ron. "John Wayne and *Big Jim McLain* (1952): The Duke's Cold War Legacy." *Film and History* 31.1 (2001): 28–33.
Britos, Peter. "Symbols, Myth & TV in Hawai'i. The First Cycle: An Overview." *Spectator* 23.1 (Spring 2003): 99–112.
Brown, DeSoto. *Hawaii Recalls: Selling Romance to America—Nostalgic Images of the Hawaiian Islands, 1910–1950*. Honolulu: Editions, 1982.
Castle, William. *Hawaii, Past and Present*. Charleston, SC: BiblioLife, 2010.
Ch'oe, Yong-ho, ed. *From the Land of Hibiscus: Koreans in Hawai'i, 1903–1950*. Honolulu: University of Hawai'i Press, 2006.
Daws, Gavan. *Shoal of Time: A History of the Hawaiian Islands*. Honolulu: University of Hawai'i Press, 1968.

De Grazia, Sebastian. *Of Time, Work and Leisure*. Garden City, NY: Doubleday Anchor, 1964.

Desmond, Jane. *Staging Tourism: Bodies on Display from Waikiki to Sea World*. Chicago: University of Chicago Press, 1999.

Dyer, Richard. *White: Essays on Race and Culture*. New York: Routledge, 1996.

Eco, Umberto. *Travels in Hyperreality*. New York: Harcourt, Brace, and Jovanovich, 1986.

Engle, John. "Manning Up on the North Shore: American Masculinity and the Early Surf Movies." *Bright Lights Film Journal* (June 18, 2018): https://brightlightsfilm.com/manning-up-on-the-north-shore-american-masculinity-and-the-early-surf-movies/.

Faucette, Brian. *Hawaii Five-O*. Detroit: Wayne State University Press, 2022.

Feeney, Mark. "Elvis Movies." *American Spectator* (2001): 53–60.

Geiger, Jeffrey. *Facing the Pacific: Polynesia and the US Imperial Imagination*. Honolulu: University of Hawai'i Press, 2007.

Ghareeb, Gordon, and Martin Cox. *Hollywood to Honolulu: The Story of the Los Angeles Steamship Company*. Providence, RI: Steamship Historical Society of America, 2009.

Gonzalez, Vernadette Vicuña. *Securing Paradise: Tourism and Militarism in Hawai'i and the Philippines*. Durham, NC: Duke University Press, 2013.

Goodrich, Joseph King. *The Coming Hawaii*. Charleston, SC: BiblioBazaar, 2009.

Gulick, Sidney. *Mixing the Races in Hawaii: A Study of the Coming Neo-Hawaiian Race*. Honolulu: Hawaiian Board Books Rooms, 1937.

Hall, C. Michael, and Stephen J. Page, eds. *Tourism in the Pacific: Issues and Cases*. New York: International Thomson Business Press, 1996.

Hammond, Joyce D. "Photography, Tourism, and the Kodak Hula Show." *Visual Anthropology* 14.1 (March 2001): 1–32.

Halualani, Rona Tamiko. *In the Name of Hawaiians: Native Identities and Cultural Politics*. Minneapolis: University of Minnesota Press, 2002.

Hereniko, Vilsoni. "Representations of Pacific Islanders in Film and Video." *Documentary Box* 14 (1999): 18–20.

Higgins, Christina, and Gavin Furukawa. "Styling Hawai'i in *Haole*wood: White Protagonists on a Voyage of Self-Discovery." *Multilingua* 31 (2012): 177–198.

Imada, Adria L. *Aloha America: Hula Circuits through the US Empire*. Durham, NC: Duke University Press, 2012.

Ireland, Brian. *The US Military in Hawai'i: Colonialism, Memory and Resistance*. New York: Palgrave MacMillan, 2010.

Iriye, Akira. *Pearl Harbor and the Coming of the Pacific War: A Brief History with Documents and Essays*. New York: Bedford/St. Martin's, 1999.

Kent, Noel. *Hawaii: Islands Under the Influence*. Honolulu: University of Hawaii Press, 1993.

Konzett, Delia Malia Caparoso. *Hollywood's Hawaii: Race, Nation, and War*. New Brunswick, NJ: Rutgers University Press, 2017.

Lofgren, Orvar. *On Holiday: A History of Vacationing*. Berkeley: University of California Press, 1999.

Lyons, Paul. *American Pacificism: Oceania in the U.S. Imagination.* New York: Routledge, 2006.
MacCannell, Dean. *The Tourist: A New Theory of the Leisure Class.* Berkeley: University of California Press, 1999.
Mak, James. "Creating 'Paradise of the Pacific': How Tourism Began in Hawaii." *UHERO Working Paper No. 2015-1.* Economic Research Organization at the University of Hawaii, February 2015.
Man, Glenn K. S. "Hollywood Images of the Pacific." *East-West Film Journal* 5.2 (1991): 16–30.
Marchetti, Gina. *Romance and the "Yellow Peril": Race, Sex and Discursive Strategies in Hollywood Fiction.* Berkeley: University of California Press, 1994.
Ng, Konrad Gar-Yeu. "Policing Cultural Traffic: Charlie Chan and Hawaiʻi Detective Fiction." *Cultural Values* 6.3 (2002): 309–316.
Okamura, Jonathan Y. *Ethnicity and Inequality in Hawaiʻi.* Philadelphia: Temple University Press, 2008.
Okihiro, Gary Y. *Island World: A History of Hawaiʻi and the United States.* Berkeley: University of California Press, 2008.
Ormrod, Joan. "*Endless Summer* (1964): Consuming Waves and Surfing the Frontier." *Film and History* 53.1 (2005): 39–51.
Orr, Stanley. "'Strangers in Our Own Land': John Kneubuhl, Modern Drama, and *Hawaiʻi Five-O.*" *American Quarterly* 67.3 (2015): 913–936.
Owens, Harry. *Sweet Leilani: The Story behind the Song.* Pacific Palisades, CA: Hula House, 1970.
Page, Stephen J., and C. Michael Hall. *Tourism in the Pacific: Issues and Cases.* London: International Thomson Business Press, 1996.
Pierce, Lori. "'The Whites Have Created Modern Honolulu': Ethnicity, Racial Stratification, and the Discourse of Aloha." In *Racial Thinking in the United States: Uncompleted Independence*, edited by Paul Spickard and G. Reginald Daniel, 124–154. Notre Dame, IN: University of Notre Dame Press, 2004.
Rampell, Ed. "*Hawaii Five-O*: A Case Study in Haole-Wood Agitprop." *Television Quarterly* 33.1 (Spring 2002): 76–82.
Reyes, Luis. *Made in Paradise: Hollywood's Films of Hawaiʻi and the South Seas.* Honolulu: Mutual, 1995.
Rohrer, Judy. *Haoles in Hawaii: Race and Ethnicity in Hawaii.* Honolulu: University of Hawaiʻi Press, 2010.
Said, Edward. *Orientalism.* New York: Vintage, 1979.
Satterfield, Archie. "Lights, Camera, Aloha! On Location in Hawaii." *Travel-Holiday* (August 1987): 37–41.
Schmitt, Robert C. *Hawaii in the Movies, 1898–1959.* Honolulu: University of Hawaiʻi, 1999.
Singletary, Milly. *Hilo Hattie: A Legend in Our Time.* Honolulu: Mutual, 2006.
Skwiot, Christine. *The Purposes of Paradise: US Tourism in Cuba and Hawaii.* Philadelphia: University of Pennsylvania Press, 2010.
Smith, H. Allen. *Waikiki Beachnik.* Boston: Little, Brown, 1960.

Sperb, Jason. *Disney's Most Notorious Film: Race: Convergence, and the Hidden Histories of "Song of the South."* Austin: University of Texas Press, 2012.

———. "*Islands* of Detroit: Affect, Nostalgia and Whiteness." *Culture, Theory and Critique* 49.2 (October 2008): 183–201.

Stam, Robert, and Louise Spence. "Colonialism, Racism, and Representation." *Screen* 24.2 (1983): 2–20.

Stephan, John J. *Hawaii Under the Rising Sun: Japan's Plans for Conquest.* Honolulu: University of Hawai'i Press, 1984.

Sutton, Horace. *The New United Airlines Guide to the Hawaiian Islands: Aloha, Hawaii.* Garden City, NY: Doubleday, 1967.

Stillman, Amy K. "Pacific-ing Asian Pacific American History." *Journal of Asian American Studies* 7.3 (2004): 241–270.

Takaki, Ronald T. *Pau Hana: Plantation Life and Labor in Hawaii, 1835–1920.* Honolulu: University of Hawai'i Press, 1983.

Taylor, Joy T. "'You Can't Spend Your Whole Life on a Surfboard': Elvis Presley, Exotic Whiteness, and Native Performance in *Blue Hawaii* and *Girls! Girls! Girls!*" *Quarterly Review of Film and Video* 32.1 (2015): 21–37.

Trask, Haunani-Kay. *From a Native Daughter: Colonialism and Sovereignty in Hawai'i.* Monroe, ME: Common Courage Press, 1993.

Turner, Louis, and John Ash. *The Golden Hordes: International Tourism and the Pleasure Periphery.* New York: St. Martin's Press, 1976.

Urry, John. *The Tourist Gaze 3.0.* London: Sage, 2011.

Veblen, Thorstein. *The Theory of the Leisure Class.* New York: Dover, 1994.

Venturi, Robert, Denise Scott Brown, and Steven Izenour. *Learning from Las Vegas: The Forgotten Symbolism of Architectural Form.* Cambridge, MA: MIT Press, 1972.

West, Nancy Martha. *Kodak and the Lens of Nostalgia.* Charlottesville: University of Virginia Press, 2000.

Whittaker, Elvi. *The Mainland Haole: The White Experience in Hawaii.* New York: Columbia University Press, 1986.

Wilson, Rob. *Reimagining the American Pacific: From South Pacific to Bamboo Ridge and Beyond.* Durham, NC: Duke University Press, 2000.

Wood, Houston. *Displacing Natives: The Rhetorical Production of Hawai'i.* Lanham, MD: Rowman & Littlefield, 1999.

Wu, Ellen D. *The Color of Success: Asian Americans and the Origins of the Model Minority.* Princeton, NJ: Princeton University Press, 2014.

Wu, Frank H. "Racism without Races: America's Future as Hawaii's Past." *Journal of American Ethnic History* 29.4 (2010): 113–117.

Index

77 Sunset Strip (1958 television program), 255

Abbott, Bud, 83–84
Adaptation (literary and other media), 100, 127, 145–149, 166–168
Adiarte, Patrick, 278
Adventures in Paradise (1959 television program), 163, 246, 260
Adler, Buddy, 100
"Affectionate Racism," 156, 175, 272
Alexander, Leila, 167
Aloha (2015 film), 282
Aloha Air Lines, 135
"Aloha Oe" (1878 song), 127, 134, 202
Aloha Oe (1915 film), 33, 44
Aloha from Hawaii (1973 television special), 190, 219–223
Always Another Wave (1967 documentary), 245
Amateur film production, 228–229, 231, 243–246
Andrews, Dana, 96, 107
Andrews, Julie, 154, 173
Ariyoshi, George, 252, 273
Armitage, George, 66, 69, 71
Arnaz, Desi, 117
Arness, James, 121

"Backstage" Musical Genre, 72–76, 78, 84, 200–201, 205–206, 222
"Bali Ha'i" (song), 161–163
Ball, Lucille, 117
Balsam, Martin, 118
Barefoot Adventures (1960 documentary), 35, 227, 235, 238–239, 280
Barker, Van, 255
Bay, Michael, 86, 94
"Bayonet Constitution," 181–183
"Beachboy," 48, 192, 195, 202–203, 206, 233–237, 278
Beamer, Louise, 48
Bendix, William, 117–118
Bernstein, Elmer, 170–171
"Big Five," 3, 29, 134–135, 148
Big Jim McClain (1952 film), 34, 121–123, 264, 282
Bikini Beach (1964 film), 237
Bird of Paradise (1912 play), 34, 38, 45–46, 127
Bird of Paradise (1932 film), 34, 45–48, 53–55, 73, 77, 127
Bird of Paradise (1951 remake), 34, 113, 127
The Black Camel (1931 film): and location shooting, 54–55, 71–72, 74; and sound technology, 72;

333

The Black Camel (continued)
  "hula girl" in, 48; narrative characteristics of, 43–44; post-WWII, 85; production history of, 54–55, 71–72; reflexivity in, 2–3, 34, 42–44, 60, 72, 74, 78; representation of surfing, 227
Blackman, Joan, 204
Bloch Arena, 113, 198
"Blue Hawaii" (song), 76, 127, 190–191, 195, 201
Blue Hawaii (1961 film): and nostalgia, 194–195, 200–201, 218; and representation of class, 195–196, 203, 206–207; and representations of race, 138, 195–196, 204–205; and representation of tourism, 192–194, 201–204, 206–207, 269, 280; and surfing, 237, 239; and United Air Lines, 35, 264; as "backstage" musical, 202–206, 223; as travelogue, 192–193, 254, 269; box office success, 190; comparison to other Elvis movies, 210, 213, 215, 217, 223; local promotion for, 207; production history, 114, 200–201; reception of, 208; reflection of post-statehood interest in Hawai'i, 4; soundtrack, 35, 190–191, 200
Bob & Ray (1951 television program), 2
Bogdanovich, Peter, 94
Boone, Richard, 255
Bouchet, Barbara, 107, 109
Bow, Clara, 48
Bowman, Sydney, 59–60
The Brady Bunch (1970s television program): and tiki culture, 278–280; and United Air Lines, 264; connection to WWII nostalgia, 34, 280–282; Hawai'i-themed episodes, 276–283; reflection of post-statehood interest in Hawai'i, 4; representation of colonialism, 282; representation of Native Hawaiians, 278–279, 282; representation of Pearl Harbor, 280–282; representation of tourism, 269, 278, 281–283
Breen, Bobby, 64
Bresler, Jerry, 137
"Broom Brigade," 122
Brown, Bruce, 35, 225–233, 235, 238–240, 242, 244, 246–249, 280
Buck Privates (1941 film), 83
Burnett, Carol, 259
Burns, Jack, 275–276

Capra, Frank, 93
Chakiris, George, 139, 144
Chaplin, Geraldine, 186
Charlie Chan Carries On (1931 film), 42
Charlie Chan in Honolulu (1938 film), 42, 78–79
Charlie Chan's Murder Cruise (1935 film), 42
Chen, Tina, 180
Chinese American representation in media, 157, 164–165, 167, 179–181, 186
Christie, Walt, 2–3
Chun, Kam Fong, 252, 272
Cine-Pic Hawaii, 241, 245–246
Cinerama, 134–136
Citizen Kane (1941 movie), 93
Civil Rights Movement (1960s era), 9, 27, 127–128, 141–142
Civil War (US), 142, 179, 185
Cleopatra (1963 film), 167
Cleveland, Grover, 183
Cocoanut Grove (1938 film), 79
Colbert, Robert, 116
"Cold War" (US-Russia) Context, 34, 88, 121–124, 131, 149, 164, 169, 270
Colonialism: and "affectionate racism," 156, 175; connection

to film and photography, 156; connection to nostalgia, 31, 90, 157–158; effect on push for statehood, 3; post-statehood negotiations with legacy of, 9, 28–29, 216, 278; rebellion and annexation, 176–186; representation in *The Endless Summer*, 234–235; representation in *Hawaii* (1966 film), 154–156, 158, 160, 171–176; representation in *The Hawaiians*, 176–186; role and history of New England missionaries, 154, 158–159, 171–177
Communism. *See* "Cold War (US-Russia) Context"
Constitutional Republic, Hawai'i (1893–1898), 183–185
Cook, James, 158, 173
Coopersmith, Jerome, 265–266
Corey, Wendell, 104
Costello, Lou, 83–84
Craig, Paul, 4
Crosby, Bing, 2, 38, 40, 60, 76–78, 195, 201–202, 220

Dann, Mike, 257
Darren, James, 116, 126, 137, 144
Day of Infamy (1957 novel), 88
Davenport, Harry, 97
Davis, Ann B., 276
December 7th (1943 film), 34, 87, 93–99, 116, 119
De Wilde, Brandon, 108
Del Rio, Dolores, 34, 45, 47
The Descendants (2011 film), 282
Diamond Head (1963 film): audience reception, 140; connection to Matson Navigation, 18, 20; differences from original novel, 145–149; labor controversy during production, 137; plot summary, 126–127; production notes, 137–138; reflection of post-statehood interest in Hawai'i, 4, 124, 147, 159; representation of interracial relationships, 128, 138–139; representation of labor and unions, 126, 145, 148–150; representation of "reverse racism," 143, 145, 178; representation of statehood era Hawai'i, 124, 128, 140–141, 145–146, 179
Diskin, Tom, 190
Disney, Walt, 197
Disneyland (California theme park), 213, 262
"Dixiecrats," 141–142
Documentary genre, 93–99, 110–111, 131–136, 219, 228–229, 231–232, 241–244
Dole, James, 16, 57
Dole, Sanford, 183
"Don the Beachcomber" (Donn Beach), 104–105, 134
Donovan's Reef (1963 film), 138
Douglas, Kirk, 107, 109
Dracula (1931 film), 71
Dragnet (1950s television program), 255–256
Dudley, Carl, 135
Dylan, Bob, 219

"Echo Tourism," 30
Edison production crews (early Hawai'i film actualities), 33, 227
Edwards, Ralph, 113–114
Edwards, Webley, 4, 63, 70
Eisenhower, Dwight, 135
Elvis (1968 documentary), 219
Elvis in Concert (1977 documentary), 219
Elvis on Tour (1972 documentary), 219
Elvis: That's the Way It Is (1970 documentary), 219
The Endless Summer (1964 film): and baby boomer demographics, 226, 230–231, 237–240, 249–250; and

The Endless Summer (continued)
consumer trends, 230–231, 239–241; and nontheatrical exhibition, 246; and nostalgia, 250; and tiki imagery, 279; and Vietnam, 250; as example of the documentary, 241–242; as tourist narrative, 232; colonialism in, 234–235; connection to "beachboys," 236–237; exhibition and reception, 247–248; promotional efforts, 247–248; reflection of post-statehood interest in Hawai'i, 4, 35; representation of Hawai'i in, 226–227, 232–233; similarity to other Brown surfer documentaries, 232; soundtrack, 232, 239–241; subsequent imitations, 248–249; summary, 225–226

Farrington, Joseph R., 133
The FBI (1965 television program), 255
Feet First (1930 film), 19–20, 34, 42–43
Film Festivals, 275–276
The Final Countdown (1980 film), 116
Finnegan, William, 255
Flaherty, Robert, 70
Flirtation Walk (1934 film), 72
Follow Me (1969 Cinerama film), 249
Follow the Sun (1961 television program), 260
Fonda, Henry, 107
Ford, John, 50, 93–96, 119
Fortescue, Grace, 51
From Here to Eternity (1953 film): adaptation of book, 100, 127; and censorship, 99–100, 127; and WWII nostalgia, 31, 34, 88, 91, 98; as pastiche, 100; comparisons to other Pearl Harbor-themed films and television shows, 103–106, 119; connection to Matson Navigation, 20; plans to shoot in color, 102; postwar popularity, 4, 98; representation of wartime Hawai'i, 98–103
From Here to Eternity (1951 novel), 88, 98, 100–101, 127
"Front" and "Back" Regions of Tourism, 22–23, 29, 48, 160, 204–206, 232, 268–269, 272
Fry, Dwight, 71
Fuqua, Samuel G., 113

Gable, Clark, 126
The George Burns and Gracie Allen Show (1950s television program), 112
Gidget (1959 film), 228, 237–239, 244
Gidget Goes Hawaiian (1961 film), 138, 228, 264, 269, 280
Gilman, Peter, 124, 146–147
Girls! Girls! Girls! (1962 film), 190, 192, 196, 208–210, 215
Godfrey, Arthur, 70
Golden Breed (1968 documentary), 248–249
Goldwyn, Samuel, 71
Gone with the Wind (1939 film), 126
Grable, Betty, 48, 79
Green, Guy, 137
The Grapes of Wrath (1939 movie), 93
Gratz, H. Tucker, 114–115, 198
Great Depression (1930s), 15, 19, 50, 56–59, 236–237
Griffin, Merv, 259
Gulick, Sydney, 143
Gumbo Ya-Ya (unrealized Elvis film project), 209

Hackman, Gene, 173
Hagman, Larry, 108
Hall, Juanita, 162
Hammerstein II, Oscar, 163
"*Haole*": and anti-statehood arguments, 124; and class, 126;

and labor movements, 53, 126; and pro-statehood arguments, 130, 143; and representations of colonialism, 179–186; and white privilege, 126, 128, 142–145; definitions, 26–27, 144
Harris, Richard, 173
Harry Owens and His Royal Hawaiians (1949 television program), 49, 70, 263
Hawaii (1959 novel), 10, 32, 36, 127, 147, 151–155, 159–160, 164–166, 172, 179, 272
Hawaii (1966 film): as literary adaptation, 127, 150, 153, 159, 164, 166; box office success, 35, 154, 186–187; location shooting, 109, 171, 254, 269; colonialism nostalgia in, 157; production history, 29, 153, 166–171, 186; reflection of post-statehood interest in Hawai'i, 4; representation of colonial history, 154–156, 158, 160, 171–176, 280; representation of "legendary Hawai'i," 161; representation of Native Hawaiians, 156–157, 160–161, 171–176; representation of religion, 154, 158–159, 171–176
Hawaii Calls (1935 radio program), 4, 38–41, 62–64, 127
Hawaii Calls (1938 film): as adaptation from radio, 127; as musical, 72, 79; connection to Matson Navigation, 20; critical reception, 78; differences from radio version, 64; narrative characteristics, 42–43; promotion controversy, 20
Hawaii Calls (1960s television program), 70, 127
Hawaii Five-O (1968 television program): as cop drama, 252, 255–256, 258, 271, 274, 280; broadcast records, 36, 254; casting, 170, 252–253, 272; controversies over its mature content, 258–260; effect on local tourism, 252, 273–274; Hawai'i-themed television predecessors, 260–261; location shooting for, 251–252, 254–256, 265–266, 274; nostalgia in, 269–270, 271–272; parallels to *Hell's Half Acre*, 105; production notes, 251–256, 265–266, 270, 272–273; reception by critics and audiences, 257–260, 271, 273; reflection of post-statehood interest in Hawai'i, 4, 274; reflexivity in, 267; representation of multiculturalism, 161, 272–274; representation of Native Hawaiians, 266–267, 271, 274; representation of the military, 269–272, 274, 281–282; representation of tourism, 255–258, 265–269, 272–274, 278, 280; tourism industry partnerships, 261–265
Hawaii International Film Festival, 276
Hawaii Pono: A Social History (1961 book), 152, 161, 272
Hawaii Press Bureau, 133
"Hawaii Sang Me to Sleep" (1939 song), 89
Hawaii Today (1948 promotional film), 70, 72
Hawaii Tourist Bureau: connection to Hollywood productions, 71–72, 106, 138, 154; early history of, 15–16, 59; media promotional efforts, 6, 40–41, 44, 59–72, 241; non-media promotional efforts, 60, 65; organizational focus on group tourism towards the end of the 20th Century, 275–276; print advertising, 61–62; promotion on cruise ships, 66, 69; promotional efforts after WWII (as "Hawaii Visitors Bureau"), 4, 70, 106, 154;

Hawaii Tourist Bureau *(continued)*
  response to Great Depression, 15;
  response to Massie trials, 53; role
  during WWII, 16, 70, 80; subject
  of satire, 2; support for statehood,
  131; theatrical exhibition of own
  films, 67, 69
Hawaii Visitors Bureau. *See* "Hawaii
  Tourist Bureau"
Hawaii Visitors and Convention
  Bureau. *See* "Hawaii Tourist
  Bureau"
Hawaii, USA (1939 promotional film),
  65–66
Hawaii, USA (1942 promotional
  booklet), 65, 69
Hawaii: A Literary Chronicle (1967
  essay collection), 161
Hawaii: The 49th State (1947
  promotional film), 131–134
Hawaii—49th State (1954 television
  program), 123
Hawaiian Airlines, 135, 170
Hawaiian Buckaroo (1938 film), 44
Hawaiian Eye (1959 television
  program), 260, 270
Hawaiian Holiday (1935 film), 44
Hawaiian Holiday (1951 promotional
  film), 70–71
Hawaiian Love (1913 film), 33, 45
Hawaiian Nights (1939 film), 34, 43,
  72, 78, 89
Hawaiian Sovereignty Movement, 271
Hawaiian Statehood Commission,
  129, 133–135
The Hawaiians (1970 film), 150,
  153–154, 156–159, 161, 164, 168,
  176–186, 282
Haworth, Jill, 108
Hearst, William Randolph, 52
Hell's Half Acre (1954 film), 34,
  104–105, 123
Henderson, Florence, 276
"Heritage" Tourism, 28–29, 32

Heston, Charlton, 126–128, 137, 140,
  168, 178–179
Hickman, Darryl, 118
Highway to Hawaii (1948 promotional
  film), 263
Hiller, Arthur, 171
Hill, George Roy, 168–171, 174, 176
"Hilo Hattie" (Clare Inter), 12, 76
"Hipster Tourism," 232
"Histouricism," 9–10, 159–160
Honolulu (1939 film): connection
  to Matson Navigation, 20, 74;
  narrative parallels to later films and
  television programs, 84, 112, 200–
  201; post-WWII, 85; production
  of, 71; reflexivity in, 3, 34, 42–44,
  62, 74–76; representation of hula
  in, 48–49
Honolulu (Waikiki) Aquarium, 69
Honolulu Nights (1939 film), 42, 44,
  48
Honolulu Chamber of Commerce,
  2, 15
House on Un-American Activities
  Committee (HUAC), 122
Houston, Walter, 93
Hula: and Kodak Film Company,
  11–12; and labor, 12, 14, 21–22,
  28–29, 49–50, 55–56; connection
  to agricultural economy, 13–14;
  connection to Native Hawaiian
  culture and history, 11–12, 49–50;
  hula tours on the mainland, 12–14,
  49; representations of, 47–48
"Hula Girl," 6, 11–14, 47–49, 79, 136,
  145, 202–203, 227
The Hurricane (1937 film), 50, 138

I Love Lucy (1950s television
  program), 112
In Harm's Way (1965 film), 31, 34, 88,
  105–110, 119, 269
In the Navy (1941 film), 44, 83–85,
  112, 200–201

Inouye, Daniel, 263
International Longshore and Warehouse Union (ILWU), 122
Iolani Palace, 23, 29, 160, 183, 282
The Island of Hawaii (1930), 66–68
The Island of Kauai (1930), 68
The Island of Maui (1930), 68
The Island of Oahu (1930), 68–69
Isle of Paradise (unrealized Elvis film project), 211
It's a Date (1940 film), 3, 34, 40, 42–44, 72, 79, 113
It's a Mad, Mad, Mad, Mad World (1963 film), 167

The Jack Benny Program (1950s television program), 112
Jack Paar Tonight Show (1960 television show), 114
Janssen, Otto, 133
Japanese American representation in media: in *December 7th*, 95–97; in *Hawaii* (1959 novel), 164–165, 167; in *The Hawaiians*, 157, 179–180
Johnson, Lyndon B., 198
Jones-Costigan Act (1934 US Congress bill), 59

Kahahawai, Joseph, 51
Kallis, Stan, 256
Kaiser, Henry, 260–261, 263
Kauhi, Gilbert Lani, 252, 272
Kearney, Carolyn, 118
Keene, Bob, 240
Keep 'Em Flying (1941 film), 83
Kennedy, Arthur, 108
Keyes, Evelyn, 105
King Kalākaua (1836–1891), 181–182
King Kamehameha (1782–1819), 282
King, Samuel Wilder, 38
Kinney, Ray, 38–40
Kneubuhl, John, 266
Kodak Hula Show, 11–13, 30, 160
Kona Coast (1968 film), 255

Krug, Julius Albert, 133

LaGarde, Jocelyne, 173
Lamour, Dorothy, 38, 50, 136
Law, John Phillip, 177
"Legendary Hawai'i" (representations of Native Hawaiian folklore), 13, 156, 161–162
Leigh, Suzanna, 189
Letters from Hawaii (1860s novel, published 1947), 160
Lilley, Joseph, 201
Logue, Elizabeth, 170, 269
Lord, Jack, 252, 254, 257–259, 269, 273–274
Los Angeles Steamship Company (LASSCO), 16, 19, 71
"Legendary Hawai'i," 13
Lugosi, Bela, 71

Ma and Pa Kettle at Waikiki (1955 film), 113
MacArthur, James, 252
MacMahon, Aline, 143
Magnum, PI (1980 television program), 255, 270, 282
Marno, Marc, 126
Massie, Thalia, 51
Massie, Thomas, 51
Massie criminal trials, 50–55, 59, 143
Matson Navigation Company: airline history, 20–21; and Kodak Hula Show, 11; control of island lodging, 19–20; connection to Hawaii Tourist Bureau, 16, 59–60, 66, 71; corporate history of, 18–21; influence on Hollywood, 18–20, 134; radio program, 20, 38; shipping history of, 18
Maverick (1957 television program), 261
McCarthy, Joe, 122
McCrea, Joel, 34, 45
McKinley Tariff (1890), 177

McLane, George, 133
Meredith, Burgess, 107–108
Michener, James, 10, 134, 147, 150–155, 159–166, 172, 179, 186, 246
Mimieux, Yvette, 126
Minerbi, Luciano, 2
Mirisch, Walter, 153, 171, 176
Mission: Impossible (1966 television program), 272
Mitchum, James, 109
Mitchum, Robert, 109
Moana Hotel, 19, 38, 60, 63
The Mod Squad (1968 television program), 272–273
The Moon is Blue (1953 film), 99
Moonlight in Hawaii (1941 film), 34, 42–44, 48, 72, 78
Motion Picture Association of America (MPAA), 275
Mount Tantalus, 206
"Multiculturalism" rhetoric: connection to statehood debates, 130, 137, 139–140, 144; effect on representations of colonial history, 27, 154–155; Hawai'i reputation for, 9, 25–28, 128–129, 142–145; historical representation of in *The Hawaiians*, 179–186; promotion in postwar literature, 161; relation to issues of class and labor, 27–28, 128–129, 139, 145–146, 149–150, 180, 195–196; representation of in Elvis films, 195–196, 215–216
Mutiny on the Bounty (1959 film), 167

The Naked City (1958 television program), 255
Native Hawaiian representation in media: and "legendary Hawai'i," 13, 156, 161–162; in *The Brady Bunch*, 278; in *Hawaii* (1959 novel), 164–165; in *Hawaii* (1966 movie), 156–157, 160–161, 171–176; in *Hawaii Five-O*, 266–267, 271; in *The Hawaiians*, 185–186; in "South Seas Romance" narratives, 3, 6, 33–34, 38, 42, 44–46, 50, 53–55, 78, 79. See also "Hula Girl" and "Beachboy"
Neal, Patricia, 107, 109
Nontheatrical Cinema, 229, 244–246
Nostalgia: affective nostalgia, 30–31; and "echo tourism," 30; and legacy of US military intervention, 9, 30–31, 34, 91, 198, 270–272; and preservation, 31–32; and technological changes, 101, 270; and time travel, 115–119; and touristic perceptions of Hawai'i, 22, 29–30, 92; connection to colonialism, 31, 157–158, 212; connection to December 7th attack, 85–93, 98–120, 270; connection to tourism, 31; film as nostalgic medium, 8, 30, 91–92, 107–108, 116; for pre-WWII Hawai'i, 80–81, 118–119, 201; for the tourism industry, 30–31; for war, 90–91; in *Blue Hawaii*, 195; television as nostalgic medium, 112–113, 218
Nuyen, Frances, 126

O'Connor, Caroll, 108
Oceanic Steamship Company, 16
Old Man and the Sea (1958 film), 71
One Way Passage (1932 film), 42
Owens, Harry, 38–41, 46–47, 63, 79, 263

Paar, Jack, 114–115
Pacific War Memorial Commission, 114–115, 190, 198
Pan-Am Airways, 21, 135
Pan-Pacific Bureau, 60, 62
Paradise Hawaiian Style (1966 film), 138, 187, 189–190, 192, 194–196, 210–218, 264, 269

Parker, ("Colonel") Tom, 190–191, 196–200, 211
Pastiche, 29, 79, 106–107, 155–156, 202, 279–280
Patterson, W.A., 263
Pearl Harbor (WWII): connection to *Hawaii Calls* broadcasts, 62–63; connection to tourism, 31, 92, 281; disavowal of, 30–31; effect on Hollywood, 34, 36, 79–80; nostalgia for, 30–31, 34, 38, 41, 80–81, 85–93, 98–120, 270–272, 280–282; promotion of *Hawaii Five-O*, 257; representations of, 42, 85–120; representations of military pre-WWII, 83–84, 92, 97, 100–101; USS Arizona Memorial, 92, 113–115, 121–122, 190, 197–200, 212, 219–220, 222, 280–282
Pearl Harbor (2001 film), 86, 94
Pickens, Slim, 108
Pineapple industry in Hawaii, 3, 13–16, 23, 43–44, 55–59, 64–65, 71, 135
Playtime in Hawaii (1941 short film), 245
Poindexter, Joseph, 64, 66
Polynesian Cultural Center, 23, 213–215
Poltrack, David, 252
Postindustrial Capitalism, 14–15, 21–25, 28, 42, 55–56, 78, 150
"Post-Tourism," 24–25, 74–76
Powell, Dick, 84
Powell, Eleanor, 48–49, 74–76
Pre-Code Hollywood, 34
Preminger, Otto, 99, 106
Preis, Alfred, 114, 281
Prentiss, Paula, 108
Presley, Elvis: and musical film genre, 194–196, 202–206; and representations of baby boomer generation, 189–190, 192, 194–195; and representation of inter-racial relationships, 138; and television, 220–223; box office success, 154, 186–187; comparison to other '60s films, 35, 109, 186–187; fanbase, 190–191, 201, 208; fundraising for USS Arizona Memorial, 114, 190, 197–200, 212, 219–220, 222; in *Blue Hawaii*, 200–208; in *Girls! Girls! Girls!*, 208–210; in *Paradise Hawaiian Style*, 212–218; movies compared to stage performances, 191, 219–223; narrative formulas, 193; personal interest in Hawai'i, 212; record sales, 218–219; similarities to "hula girl" stereotype, 202–203; soundtracks, 35, 190–191, 196–197, 200, 218–220; unrealized film projects, 211
Production Code, 107, 170
Prowse, Juliet, 205
"Pseudo-Events," 6, 11–12, 24–25

Queen Lili'uokalani (1838–1917), 181–186, 202
"Quest for Authenticity," 22–24, 232
Quinn, William F., 134–135

"Racial Harmony" rhetoric. See "Multiculturalism"
Racial Melodrama genre, 126–128, 136, 138–141
Raye, Martha, 76
RCA Records, 198
Reed, Robert, 276
Regan, Kenneth, 142
Remember Pearl Harbor (1942 propaganda film), 87
Reisman, Jr., Philip, 133
"Retaliation Films" (WWII), 87
The Revolt of Mamie Stover (1956 film), 34, 103
Ride the Wild Surf (1964 film), 237
Rodgers, Richard, 163
Ross, Shirley, 76

Royal Hawaiian Hotel, 19, 38–39, 42, 54–55, 60, 69, 72
Russell, Jane, 103

Salkowitz, Sy, 251–253, 255–256
Screen Actors Guild, 137
Selznick, David O., 45
September 11th (2001 terrorist attacks), 270
Serling, Rod, 117
Severson Productions, 240, 244, 246
The Shark God (1913 film), 33, 44–45
Sherman, Eddie, 115
Sinatra, Frank, 100
Slippery When Wet (1958 documentary), 35, 227–229, 233
Song of the Islands (1942 film), 43–44, 72, 79–81
South Pacific (1949 stage musical), 154, 161–162
South Pacific (1958 film), 71, 127, 134, 138, 154, 161–162
South Seas Adventure (1958 Cinerama film), 134–136, 263
"South Seas" clichés, 3, 6, 33–34, 38, 42, 44–46, 50, 53–55, 78, 79
Stambler, Bob, 255
Stanley Warner Theatres, 134–136
Star Trek (1966 television program), 273
Statehood: connection to anti-Asian attitudes in the US, 124, 129–130, 141–142, 163–164; connection to tourism promotion and rhetoric, 131, 150, 163; debates over, 123, 129–130; effect on islands' popularity, 1–2, 4, 159; Hollywood support for, 50, 131–136; mainland support for, 3; promotional efforts in support of, 129–136
Stevens, Morton, 264
Stevens, Naomi, 181
Such Sweet Thunder (1960 novel), 124, 127, 145–149
Surfari (1967 documentary), 244, 248

Surfing: and documentary genre, 228–229, 231–232, 241–244; and frontier mythology, 226, 232, 250; and Hawai'i, 226–227, 232–234, 245–246; as multimedia industry, 239–241; history of, 227–228, 232–236; trends in Hollywood, 238–241, 248–249; various representations in Hawai'i-themed media, 227–228, 245–246
Sutton, Horace, 265
"Sweet Leilani" (song), 38–41, 73–74
Sweet, Ozzie, 70

Tahara, George, 245
Tales of the South Pacific (1947 novel), 154, 161–163
Taradash, Daniel, 166–167
Taurog, Norman, 197, 208
This is Your Life (1950s television program), 113–115, 198
Thomas, Mabel, 89–90
Thurmond, Strom, 142
Thurston, Lorrin, 16, 131
Tickle Me (1965 film), 211
"The Time Element" (1959 television episode of *Westinghouse Desilu Playhouse*), 34, 116–119
"Time Travel" genre, 87, 115–119
The Time Tunnel (1966 television program), 34, 116–119
This is America (1940s documentary series), 131
"Tiki" culture, 100, 104–105, 162, 278–280
'Til We Meet Again (1940 film), 42
Toland, Greg, 93–96, 119
Tone, Franchot, 107
Tora! Tora! Tora! (1970 film), 84–86, 88, 110–112, 119–120
"Tourist Gaze," 7–8
Trade Winds (1939), 42
True Adventure (1960s television program), 226, 230
Trumbo, Dalton, 167, 174, 176

Tupou, Manu, 173
Twain, Mark, 160
The Twilight Zone (1960s television program), 116–117

Union (labor) activism, 20, 27–29, 52–53, 122–124, 126, 128–129, 137, 179–180, 254
United Air Lines: Hawai'i-related promotional efforts, 35, 260–265; own promotional media, 71, 263; partnership with James Michener, 163; postwar industry competition in Hawai'i, 21; product placement in Hawai'i-themed media, 35, 264, 267–268, 270, 278; statehood support, 135, 263
The Untouchables (1959 television program), 255
US Military in Hawai'i: importance to popularity of postwar media, 9; influence of tourism rhetoric during WWII, 80–81; personnel, 10; representation in *Blue Hawaii*, 202; representation in *Hawaii Five-O*, 269–272. See also "Pearl Harbor"
USS Arizona Memorial, 92, 113–115, 121–122, 190, 197–200, 212, 219–220, 222, 280–282

Valenti, Jack, 275–276
A Very Brady Sequel (1996 film), 277
Vidor, King, 34, 45, 50, 54
Vietnam War Context (US intervention), 112, 168–169, 250, 269–270, 272, 281–282
Virtual Tourism: and Kodak Hula Show, 11; and "work displays," 22; cultural and political implications of, 8; importance of music, 7; in Elvis movies, 192–193; in *Hawaii Five-O*, 257–258, 266–269
Von Sydow, Max, 172, 186

Waikiki Wedding (1937 film): Academy Award for, 40; affective nostalgia and, 30; narrative parallels to later film and television programs, 112, 201–202, 205, 217, 280; intended for Technicolor, 79; music in, 38, 72–74, 195; post-WWII, 85; reflexivity in, 3, 34, 42–44, 58, 60, 76–78; representation of hula in, 48; representations of labor in, 55–57; representation of surfing, 227; representation of whiteness ("haole"), 144
Waimea Falls Park, 23
The Wake of Red Witch (1949 film), 50
Wald, Jerry, 197
Wallis, Hal, 191, 193–194, 197, 200
Walters, Nancy, 201
War movie genre, 86–88
Wayne, John, 107–109, 121, 138
Weaver, Pat, 246
Webb, Jack, 255–256
Weber, Lois, 50, 72
Welles, Orson, 134
The Wet Suit (1960 documentary), 229
White Heat (1934 film), 44, 50, 72
Whiteness. *See* "Haole"
Why We Fight (1940s propaganda film series), 34, 93, 99
Wide World of Sports (1960s television program), 245
Williams, Elmo, 85
William Morris Agency, 198
Wilson, Tutasi, 50–51
Windjammer (1958 Cinerama film), 135–136
Wong, Linda, 214
"Work Displays," 21–23, 29, 55–57, 204
World War II. *See* "Pearl Harbor"

Yamamoto, Isoroku, 86
Young, Robert, 60, 74–76, 84

Zinnenman, Fred, 99, 166–168

THE SUNY SERIES

MURRAY POMERANCE | EDITOR

Also in the series

William Rothman, editor, *Cavell on Film*

J. David Slocum, editor, *Rebel Without a Cause*

Joe McElhaney, *The Death of Classical Cinema*

Kirsten Moana Thompson, *Apocalyptic Dread*

Frances Gateward, editor, *Seoul Searching*

Michael Atkinson, editor, *Exile Cinema*

Paul S. Moore, *Now Playing*

Robin L. Murray and Joseph K. Heumann, *Ecology and Popular Film*

William Rothman, editor, *Three Documentary Filmmakers*

Sean Griffin, editor, *Hetero*

Jean-Michel Frodon, editor, *Cinema and the Shoah*

Carolyn Jess-Cooke and Constantine Verevis, editors, *Second Takes*

Matthew Solomon, editor, *Fantastic Voyages of the Cinematic Imagination*

R. Barton Palmer and David Boyd, editors, *Hitchcock at the Source*

William Rothman, *Hitchcock: The Murderous Gaze, Second Edition*

Joanna Hearne, *Native Recognition*

Marc Raymond, *Hollywood's New Yorker*

Steven Rybin and Will Scheibel, editors, *Lonely Places, Dangerous Ground*

Claire Perkins and Constantine Verevis, editors, *B Is for Bad Cinema*

Dominic Lennard, *Bad Seeds and Holy Terrors*

Rosie Thomas, *Bombay before Bollywood*

Scott M. MacDonald, *Binghamton Babylon*

Sudhir Mahadevan, *A Very Old Machine*

David Greven, *Ghost Faces*

James S. Williams, *Encounters with Godard*

William H. Epstein and R. Barton Palmer, editors, *Invented Lives, Imagined Communities*

Lee Carruthers, *Doing Time*

Rebecca Meyers, William Rothman, and Charles Warren, editors, *Looking with Robert Gardner*

Belinda Smaill, *Regarding Life*

Douglas McFarland and Wesley King, editors, *John Huston as Adaptor*
R. Barton Palmer, Homer B. Pettey, and Steven M. Sanders, editors, *Hitchcock's Moral Gaze*
Nenad Jovanovic, *Brechtian Cinemas*
Will Scheibel, *American Stranger*
Amy Rust, *Passionate Detachments*
Steven Rybin, *Gestures of Love*
Seth Friedman, *Are You Watching Closely?*
Roger Rawlings, *Ripping England!*
Michael DeAngelis, *Rx Hollywood*
Ricardo E. Zulueta, *Queer Art Camp Superstar*
John Caruana and Mark Cauchi, editors, *Immanent Frames*
Nathan Holmes, *Welcome to Fear City*
Homer B. Pettey and R. Barton Palmer, editors, *Rule, Britannia!*
Milo Sweedler, *Rumble and Crash*
Ken Windrum, *From El Dorado to Lost Horizons*
Matthew Lau, *Sounds Like Helicopters*
Dominic Lennard, *Brute Force*
William Rothman, *Tuitions and Intuitions*
Michael Hammond, *The Great War in Hollywood Memory, 1918–1939*
Burke Hilsabeck, *The Slapstick Camera*
Niels Niessen, *Miraculous Realism*
Alex Clayton, *Funny How?*
Bill Krohn, *Letters from Hollywood*
Alexia Kannas, *Giallo!*
Homer B. Pettey, editor, *Mind Reeling*
Matthew Leggatt, editor, *Was It Yesterday?*
Merrill Schleier, editor, *Race and the Suburbs in American Film*
Neil Badmington, *Perpetual Movement*
George Toles, *Curtains of Light*
Erica Stein, *Seeing Symphonically*
Alexander Sergeant, *Encountering the Impossible*
Brendan Hennessey, *Luchino Visconti and the Alchemy of Adaptation*
William Rothman, *The Holiday in His Eye*

www.ingramcontent.com/pod-product-compliance
Lightning Source LLC
Chambersburg PA
CBHW051556230426
43668CB00013B/1875